D0432362

STANDS THERE A SCHOOL

Jane Frances Dove 1896

STANDS THERE A SCHOOL

Memories of
DAME FRANCES DOVE, D.B.E.

Founder of
Wycombe Abbey School

by
ELSIE BOWERMAN

Stands there a school in the midst of the Chilterns
Beech-covered hillsides encircle it round
Ivy and creepers entwine the old Abbey
Health and contentment within are found.

(SCHOOL SONG 1901)

Made and Printed in England by
THE DOLPHIN PRESS LTD
NEW ENGLAND HOUSE
NEW ENGLAND STREET
BRIGHTON 1
SUSSEX
ENGLAND

Published by WYCOMBE ABBEY SCHOOL SENIORS

CONTENTS

ILLUSTRATIONS

PREFACE

THIS BOOK is the simple chronicle of a woman whose character was direct and straightforward and whose life was governed by a remarkable singleness of purpose. It makes no attempt to deal with the complicated tangle of the educational theories of the present day. Dame Frances Dove did not expect for herself a niche in the hall of fame, but her quiet concentration on her self-appointed task nevertheless made history and created an atmosphere related to permanent values and enduring interests. The writer had the privilege of spending six years under her at Wycombe Abbey, and feels that her memory must be kept green so that future generations may realise the value of the heritage she bequeathed to them.

To the many others who share this view and who have helped me in my researches I am deeply grateful. I am much indebted to several members of the Dove family and particularly to the late Rev. J. Llewellyn Dove, M.A. for personal recollections and correspondence and to his son, Major General A. H. Dove, C.B.E., C.B.; to Canon Cartwright, Librarian of Peterborough Cathedral; to the Rev. S. A. Pilling, the former Vicar of Cowbit and to the Rev. Harold Moxon, the present incumbent of that parish; to Miss J. Macaulay, M.A., Head Mistress of St. Leonards School; to Miss A. W. Whitelaw, M.A. and Miss K. Walpole, M.A., former Head Mistresses of Wycombe Abbey School; to Miss P. A. Fisher, M.A., the present Head Mistress and to Miss W. B. Wilkins, Bursar of Wycombe Abbey School.

To the many friends who have encouraged me to attempt this book I apologise for the delay in its appearance and hope they will forgive its inadequacy.

ELSIE BOWERMAN

Cowbeech, Sussex   April 1965

I

The Dove Family

IN THE YEAR 1847 when Tennyson was writing '*The Princess*' and '*Jane Eyre*,' '*Wuthering Heights*' and '*Vanity Fair*' appeared, a young curate, John Thomas Dove was taking his nineteen year old bride for a tour abroad. After spending some time in Paris and St. Malo they finally reached Bordeaux where on 27th June their first child Jane Frances was born. This was a far cry from Lincolnshire, the county of their origin and from the Fenland squires who were their forbears, for John was the son of William Dove of Cawthorpe and the last representative of the family founded by John and Sarah Dove who went to Bourne about 1700.

The family may not always have been in Lincolnshire as it seems probable that they were related to the Thomas Dove who was Bishop of Peterborough in the reign of Queen Elizabeth I to whom he was a Chaplain. Gunton's history of the Church of Peterborough, published in 1686, states that 'one John Harrington saith he had known the Bishop to be greatly respected and favoured by Queen Elizabeth and no less liked and approved in the more learned judgment of King James. When the Queen first heard him she said she thought 'the Holy Ghost was decended again on this Dove'.' The only one of the Bishop's children of whom there is any record is the eldest son Sir William Dove, who lived in the Manor of Upton near Peterborough which had been purchased by his father. Here there is in the church an elaborate tomb showing Sir William recumbent between his two wives, Frances and Dorothy. On the side is the family crest showing doves with olive branches which Jane Frances was to incorporate in the crest of Wycombe Abbey School when she founded it in 1896. When the Bishop died Sir William caused a handsome tomb to be erected to his memory in Peterborough Cathedral but this was demolished by Cromwell's soldiers in 1643 and now the spot where it stood is marked simply by a stone in the pavement. Fuller in his church history remarks that

Bishop Dove, after living in a poor bishopric 'died in the reign of King Charles leaving a plentiful estate to shew that it is not the moisture of the place but the long lying of the stone which gathereth the great mosse therein.' There is however no record of his descendants which definitely links him with the Lincolnshire family though it is noticeable that the names Thomas and William occur frequently in its pedigree.

The wife of the Reverend John Thomas was Jane Ding, daughter of Thomas Lawrence of Dunsby. They were married at Burton-by-Lincoln. After the birth of Jane Frances and lingering for about a year in Spain the young family eventually found its way back to Spalding in the hope that John might obtain the living of Cowbit in the Fen Country, of which some of his relatives were the feoffees. But he was disappointed so he returned south to London and was for some years a curate at Christ Church, Marylebone. His Rector was the Rev. Llewellyn Davies whose sister Emily founded Girton College.

The Doves had ten children, six of whom survived, and some of them were born in London. It was here that Jane Frances began her education, being taught by her father in company with her two brothers Horace and Arthur, destined respectively for the army and the navy. A friendly family of Jews lived next door to their home in Harewood Place and this led to the addition of Hebrew and German to the schoolroom curriculum. Subsequently Jane Frances attended Queen's College, Harley Street for nearly three years. The College had been founded in 1848 on the initiative of Frederick Denison Maurice following a lecture given by him in the Hanover Rooms on the subject of down-trodden and ill-equipped governesses. It was intended to provide 'ladies' with the necessary knowledge to teach, particularly in colleges for working women. Queen's College eventually developed into the pioneer school for the higher education of girls, with the North London Collegiate School for Girls and Cheltenham College close on its heels. Various Councils of Education for Women were also set up during this period, while in due course came the foundation of Bedford College in London and Girton and Newnham Colleges at Cambridge. During the girlhood of Jane Frances the question of the higher education of girls was very much in the air and the association with the Davies family in London must have kept her *au fait* with at least some of the developments.

Her father's appointment to the living of Cowbit in Lincolnshire in 1862 caused a complete change in the circumstances of the family. From a London terrace they were transferred to a plain square vicarage beside a small village behind the Cowbit wash. This wash or dyke is about fifteen miles long and a mile broad. It acts as a bulwark against the river Welland and has kept the water within bounds since the time of the Romans. Cowbit village is one-sided, behind one of the retaining banks along whose top runs the main road to Spalding. It is three and a half miles from Spalding which in the Doves' time could only be reached by road. With modern developments of fruit, vegetable and bulb growing the village has expanded and prospered, but in the nineteenth century its resources were very limited. The Vicar was a 'squarson' and farmed about eighty acres of his own land. The family depended for its supplies on the village and local farmers. They were glad to augment their larder with eels from the ditches and, in the winter time, with wild fowl shot by local gunmen who operated from flat-bottomed gunning punts reached by climbing over the 'wash.' Anything from Spalding, the nearest town, had to be fetched by dog-cart, the shortest route being blocked by a toll-bar. The railway was four miles distant and did not come to the village until 1875.

The vicarage had no conveniences of any kind. The sole water supply was rain water collected in a resevoir (a large bricked underground tank) and pumped up into the house by hand. The villagers' water was obtained from pits dug into the wash. The vicarage staff consisted of a cook, housemaid and an odd man. A member of the family has described his mother's life during his childhood as literal slavery. In the winter the cold was bitter. East winds blew straight off the North Sea and on the frequently frozen fens there was plenty of skating. But life in the fen country seems to develop a hardy, self-reliant and enterprising strain in all who dwell there. For the past thousand years it has been one of the wealthiest agricultural areas in England. Constant struggles with floods and other natural disasters have bred a sturdy and resourceful race with a history as rich as that of any part of the country. From the time when Hereward the Wake made the final stand against the conquering Normans in the Isle of Ely to the recent years when the coast dwellers have fought the floods, the same indomitable spirit has prevailed.

The stranger to the Fen Country receives his first great surprise when he approaches the city of Lincoln. He has probably imagined it as a flat place settled in the midst of a vast expanse of flat country. Instead he finds a city set on a hill, with its magnificent cathedral dominating the surrounding landscape, rich in architectural beauty, impregnated with history and with a thriving commercial life throbbing with enterprise and energy. Set apart from the great north road the Fen Country is disentangled and separate from the main currents of life in England, and seems to have developed an independent existence of its own with individual and personal characteristics. It teems with history. Its inhabitants have deep roots in the past though keenly alive to the opportunities of the present. Writers of the seventeenth and eighteenth centuries dubbed the fenmen wild and lawless but this was not the case. The commoners resisted the 'adventurers' who threatened to destroy their mode of living in order to exploit the potential wealth of their land, but were meticulous in the observance of the laws and customs governing the safety and economy of their community which were maintained by the vigilance of dike-reeves and fen-reeves. The struggle about the draining of the fens was fierce and long. The transition brought great hardship to many and naturally the changes were resisted with violence. Now most of the fens is under the plough. The growing of bulbs, potatoes, sugar-beet and fruit has brought great prosperity, and the conditions prevailing in villages and vicarages in the nineteenth century are unknown.

Some of the oldest inhabitants of Cowbit, alive a few years ago, still remembered Mrs. Dove with gratitude and affection for her generosity and many kindnesses during the Spartan times which the vicarage family shared with the parishioners. Their recollections of the Vicar were less affectionate, though full of respect. He was evidently a somewhat forbidding person. At the time of his death in 1902 he was the oldest incumbent in Lincolnshire. Throughout his life he was very active in local affairs though he took no part in politics. The obituary notice in the local newspaper says that he was always most 'assiduous in his attendance at his public duties'. He was a member of the Spalding Board of Guardians and for many years its chairman, a governor of the Spalding Johnson Hospital, a magistrate and chairman of the South Holland Bench. His son, the Rev. Llewellyn Dove, a headmaster and subsequently himself the vicar of a parish, ruefully recalled sitting for hours in a dog-cart in icy cold in Spalding while his father attended meetings there. The members of the Committee were regaled with glasses of sherry but nothing was provided for the shivering small boy waiting outside.

The Reverend John, when he arrived at Cowbit, found the fabric of the church in a parlous state. He determined to put it in repair and set to work to accomplish this with insouciant faith in the unimportance of financial obstacles which his daughter was later to inherit and to emulate. By 1884 the restoration was completed and the church, which had been temporarily closed for the purpose, was triumphantly re-opened. In later years Jane Frances presented a Queen Anne silver chalice to the church to replace the original which her father had sold.

While living at home at Cowbit Jane Frances became extremely domesticated. She helped her mother with the household and was an excellent needlewoman. A photograph of the family exists in which all the clothes worn (including the boys' suits) were the products of her needle. She also taught her young brothers and sisters and did a great deal of parish work including playing the harmonium in church and training the choir. This last duty must have been something of a strain as music was not her strong point. The only social life available was at Spalding but even this was very limited.

After about two years of this existence Jane Frances demanded to be sent to school and her parents eventually decided that something must be done about her education, so she went to a boarding school at Chiswick. They had found this place through an advertisement and it proved to be everything that a school should not be. The fees were £80 a year and there were about twenty pupils. The girls slept in a long dormitory. Jane Frances had a bed to herself but many others were two in a bed. The tuition was correspondingly inadequate and Jane Frances was removed after only one year there. Her experience in this place confirmed her in the determination which she had already conceived to obtain for girls educational opportunities comparable to those of their brothers at public schools. As she herself has said, 'There arose the first vision of a St. Leonards and a Wycombe, dim perhaps in its outlines but quite decided in the fact that a school at least there should be at which lonely country girls could gain the same advantages of intellectual stimulus and the inspiration of noble ideals of life as their brothers did at their schools.'

i) The Dove Family at Cowbit (*circa*) 1870

Georgina	Horace	Edgar	Jane Ding	Arthur	Frances	Rev. John Thomas	Julian
					Ursula	Emily	

ii) Students at Hitchin 1871

Jane Frances Dove

II

Queen's, Hitchin, Girton

IN SPITE OF THE REMOTENESS of her country home Jane Frances Dove was from her youth involved in one of the main developments of her day and generation, the gradual transformation of the lives and status of women which came to be known as the women's movement. This owed its impetus through the nineteenth century chiefly to the activities of certain outstanding women, each of whom in her own way concentrated on some particular reform for which she felt inspired to work. These women were not all feminists in the modern sense of the word. In fact many of them were only too anxious to preserve what were then considered the conventional attributes of womanliness. But they were not to be diverted from the pursuit of their particular enthusiasms and thus they made a major contribution to the general emancipation of their sex, and broke through the limitations and restrictions which hemmed in the women of their time.

They were mostly drawn from comfortable middle-class homes and their families were amongst the progressive minority who were sufficiently enlightened to give them a modicum of effective education denied to most of their contemporaries. Several were happily married and had large families but nevertheless found time to work steadily and with unfailing courage and perseverance for the benefit of others less fortunate than themselves. In many cases they were stalwartly backed up by their husbands and other men who shared their views and who helped them to overcome almost insuperable barriers of prejudice and vested interests. They were also moved by the strivings of that social conscience which current wrongs and abuses had set going, while many were deeply religious and felt that Christian principles were at stake.

Amongst such women one immediately thinks of Josephine Butler and her campaign against vice which resulted in the passing of the Contagious Diseases Act, Elizabeth Garrett who achieved the entry of British women into the medical profession, great educationalists such as Emily Davies and Barbara Leigh Smith who also strove to improve the economic position of women. Florence Nightingale was in a sense the prototype of women of this type and period and her success gave a tremendous impetus to all that they stood for. In spite of her favoured social position and a home with all the advantages of wealth and culture, she had in early life experienced that sense of frustration and limitation of which most intelligent women of her time were aware. Queen Victoria could hardly be described as a feminist yet even her first act on becoming queen was to insist on the privilege of being alone, while throughout the century every middle-class girl of spirit was hampered by the fact that every moment was filled with some trivial occupation so that she never really had any time to herself. A series of pointless social duties and long hours wasted in drawing-room futilities dwarfed the spirits of all thoughtful young women, while their counterparts in less sheltered circumstances were so driven by economic necessity and long hours of work that they too had no opportunity for self-realisation. The strong sense of vocation which inspired Florence Nightingale enabled her to overcome the obstacles in her path but all the same she suffered many hours, even years of disappointment amounting at times almost to despair. 'O weary days and evenings that never seemed to end,' she wrote in her diary, but her continuous preparation and secret training of herself to discover the call she believed would come, enabled her to meet the unique opportunity when finally it arose. The national emergency which gave her the chance to realise her ambition, and the publicity which attended her work were of the greatest help to other women of her time, though she herself was inclined to be somewhat contemptuous of the superficiality and inefficiency of her average contemporaries in the richer classes. She felt that this was in a great measure due to the social conventions which enveloped them and that if only they could have independent pursuits and freedom to develop their latent abilities the necessary awakening would come.

It was obvious that ignorance was the main obstacle to women's progress and with her innate gift for going to the root of a matter, Jane Frances Dove decided very early in life that she would devote herself to the promotion of the higher education of girls. Not only was the need for this borne in upon her through her own personal experience and the inevitable comparison with her brothers, whose education was provided for as a matter of course, but through her father's association with the Rev. Llewellyn Davies, brother of Miss Emily Davies, she must have come in contact with the founder of Girton College, and heard of her determination to secure practical expression of her ideals for girls' education. In speaking of her childhood in London Jane Frances has said that she then 'knew many of the famous men who did so much to help girls', and during her brief period at Queen's College she must have met many young women who were later to play outstanding parts in the struggle for women's emancipation.

The programme at Queen's College was at first very modest, aiming only, as Maurice said, at 'teaching all branches of female knowledge'. What precisely was meant by this was left to the imagination, but any crumb of education was valuable to the women who, without any qualifications, were endeavouring to equip themselves to earn their living as teachers. The cautious promoters aimed to provide not 'what is dangerous but what is safe', and the students who flocked to the lectures were found to be lamentably ignorant even of the most elementary subjects such as grammar and arithmetic. A definite curriculum was, however, gradually evolved, a day school for younger girls was established, lectures were given in the evenings for older students, and a variety of classes were open to all.

A year after the foundation of Queen's College, Bedford College for Women, destined to be the first college for women in the University of London was established, while Miss Buss and Miss Beale, who were both amongst the early students at Harley Street, gave a lead to the secondary education of girls by the development of the North London Collegiate School for Girls and Cheltenham Ladies' College respectively.

As the acknowledged prophet of the struggle for the Higher Education of Girls, Miss Emily Davies concentrated on obtaining their admission to the Universities. Her methods were typical of the quiet yet purposeful manner in which some of the Victorian women pioneers pursued their aims. To begin with she worked to obtain the admission of girls to the Oxford and Cambridge Local Examinations. In this she was not supported by some of the most prominent Head Mistresses such as Miss Beale and Miss Hannah Piper, but nevertheless success crowned her efforts and in 1865 these examinations were officially thrown open to girls. Simultaneously Miss Davies set out to secure the inclusion of girls' education in the terms of referenceof the Schools Enquiry Commission set up by the Government in 1864 to inquire into the 'whole subject' of middle-class education. She organised an influential memorial to the Commission with the result that the needs of girls were included in their investigations, and an inquiry into the real state of things in girls' schools was made possible. Miss Beale and Miss Buss were induced to give evidence, though they faced the Commission with considerable trepidation.

The Secretary, Mr. Roby was most helpful and co-operative, and when the report came out in 1868 it emphasised the importance of the education of girls and their capacity for receiving instruction, and further went on to say, 'It cannot be denied that the picture brought before us of the state of middle-class female education is on the whole unfavourable . . . want of thoroughness and foundation; want of system; slovenliness and showy superficiality; inattention to rudiments; undue time given to accomplishments, and these not taught intelligently or in any scientific manner; want of organisation . . . a very small amount of professional skill, an inferior set of school books; a vast deal of dry uninteresting work; rules put into the memory with no explanation of their principles; no system of examination worthy of the name; a very false estimate of the relative value of several kinds of acquirement, a reference to effort rather than to solid worth, a tendency to fill rather than to strengthen the mind'. The publication of this report was a milestone in the history of girls' education and Miss Davies, through her persistence in this matter, laid a solid foundation for future developments.

She next turned her attention to the Universities themselves. She had already tried unsuccessfully to get London University to open its matriculation examination to women. All she had been offered was a special easier examination for 'females'. She rejected this with scorn as being contrary to the principle of equality, describing it as 'offering a serpent when we asked for a fish'. Having been disappointed in London she decided to try to found an independent college for women to be connected if possible for teaching and examination purposes with one of the major universities.

In 1867 while Jane Frances Dove was still a school-girl Miss Davies set to work, as she expressed it 'to bring the scheme down from the clouds' and to explore ways and means. She received considerable support for her ideas, especially from Head Mistresses in the newly formed London School Mistresses' Association, and collected a general committee and a small executive to try and raise funds, aiming at £30,000 as the requisite minimum to start with. She was careful to exclude from this committee anyone who might be considered an extremist of any kind, and to preserve this aura of respectability, even Barbara Leigh Smith (now Madame Bodichon), one of the most generous and active of supporters, was not invited to be a member because of her connection with the women's suffrage campaign.

The general public greeted the idea with derision and there was considerable opposition from quarters which might have been expected to help, such as Dr. Pusey and Miss Charlotte Yonge. Miss Davies continued nevertheless to pilot the ship tactfully through the shoals. Her innate conservatism in spite of her apparently revolutionary ideas about girls had led her to secure for her committee such highly respectable people as Lady Stanley of Alderley (wife of the Dean of Westminster) and two residents in Cambridge University, Mr. Sedley Taylor and Mr. Seeley. Mr. Tomkinson, chairman of the Sun Insurance Company, whose university connections and business capacity were invaluable, was also a staunch ally. Miss Davies had to continue to insist that her students should work for the Little-Go and Cambridge degree examinations in order that the future equality she planned should not be jeopardised. A difference of opinion on this matter was later to develop in the early days of both Girton and Newnham Colleges. Miss Davies' views finally prevailed at Girton where the students took the Tripos papers and followed the courses at the University exactly as set for the men. At Newnham both Professor Sedgwick and Miss Clough at first supported the idea of special examinations designed to suit the psychology and attainments of women and of the two great Head Mistresses, Miss Beale agreed with this view.

Other educationalists also believed that half a loaf was better than no bread. Miss Buss however backed Miss Davies, and shared her hopes that women should one day become full members of the University. Both schools of thought in the event made their contribution to the advancement of women's education and to the final outcome of the struggle.

There was also a serious division of opinion amongst the Girton Committee as to whether the college should be strictly interdenominational, or whether its religious services should be Church of England. On this matter too Miss Davies prevailed and the latter course was followed. In later years a chapel was built for the College and a scholarship to an organist student was awarded.

In 1869 Benslow House at Hitchin, twenty-six miles from Cambridge, was chosen as the first 'college' so that, for the reassurance of prospective parents, the experiment could be tried at a safe distance from 'brothers and friends' at the university. The women students were enrolled even before the premises had been secured, and included the Misses Woodhead, Cook and Lumsden, later to be immortalised in the College song, 'The Girton Pioneers', sung to the tune of 'The British Grenadiers'. Conditions at Benslow House were Spartan. One of the first entrants who wrote home describing her bedroom said 'our beds are to be as small as possible, we are not to be allowed dressing tables but a looking-glass large enough to see the tip of the nose is to be placed on the wall, the carpet is to be a small piece placed in the middle of the room, on the centre of which a student's table consisting of ten drawers is to be placed'. But the students were resolute young women, full of enthusiasm in their thirst for learning. They appreciated the opportunity for some solitude for study and soon added their own embellishments and comforts to the somewhat stark interior. The library with bay windows opening on to the lawn had a pleasant country house atmosphere. Games and music increased the social amenities and George Eliot (who had always taken an active interest in the enterprise) remarked when she visited the college, 'the beginning of Hitchin looks so happy and promising'.

To this place came Jane Frances Dove from her Lincolnshire home, as full of enthusiasm and hope as all the other young women there. By 1871 their number had risen to twelve, some of whom had to be housed in the gardener's cottage. They were mostly woefully ignorant of the subjects required. One had been brought up solely on '*Mrs. Markham*', '*Mangnall's Questions*' and '*The Child's Guide to Knowledge*', but they set to work with a will, with lecturers from Cambridge to instruct them. One of these, Mr. Seeley, the famous author of '*Ecce Homo*', so despised the Cambridge syllabus that he lectured on something quite different, while Mr. Hort, the incumbent of the Hitchin Church of St. Hyppolyt, discoursed to his students on the Acts, though the subject set for the Little-Go, for which they were supposed to be preparing, was St. Mark's Gospel. It was all a great strain, but the indomitable Miss Davies insisted that the students should conform completely with University regulations. Miss Lumsden, who had become in effect the 'senior student' and spokesman amongst the pioneer five remarked, 'There was a fine element in this, a total indifference to popularity ... but it was plain that we counted for nothing except as we furthered her plans.'

This strenuous atmosphere eventually resulted in a considerable amount of tension amongst all concerned. There were complaints about food and housekeeping, criticism of some points of discipline and the lack of any social life in such a restricted environment. These early students were girls, mostly in their twenties, with considerable independence and force of character, so relations with the somewhat rigid founder of the college became rather strained until a happier atmosphere was finally restored by the tactful intervention of Madame Bodichon. In 1873 they were all greatly cheered by the success of three of the five original students in passing the Tripos examination, Miss Cook and Miss Lumsden in Classics and Miss Woodhead in mathematics. A grace to admit women to these examinations had been rejected by the Council of the Cambridge Senate, but Miss Davies had managed to obtain copies of the Tripos questions and to persuade individual examiners to mark the girls' scripts in their private capacity. Consequently the candidates went to Cambridge, heavily chaperoned, and wrote their papers at the University Arms Hotel.

Jane Frances Dove arrived at the college towards the end of the Hitchin period, when plans for the permanent college at Girton were well under weigh though its teething troubles were still acute.

She did not obtain the scholarship to Hitchin for which she had tried in 1871, but she did well in the entrance examination and was first in mathematics. One of the examiners, the Rev. Llewellyn Davies wrote to her father that 'she did herself and you much credit. It was in her Latin especially that she failed as I believe she had been able to give very little time to this . . . it is a rarer thing to do mathematics well'. Frances herself received an encouraging letter from Miss Davies. Her success in mathematics was remarkable, as women students in those early days seem to have been particularly allergic to this branch of learning. In giving evidence before the Schools Inquiry Commission Miss Beale had recalled that in the entrance examinations for Cheltenham College the girls' ignorance of arithmetic was abysmal. The triumph of Philippa Fawcett in 1898, just over thirty years later, when she came out above the Senior Wrangler in the Cambridge Mathematical Tripos showed how much more this characteristic was due to lack of opportunity than to congenital incapacity.

The Hitchin establishment was incorporated under the name of Girton College in 1872 and the new building, just outside Cambridge, was first open to students in the Michaelmas term 1873. Jane Frances Dove always claimed to have been the first student to cross its threshold. The first part to be completed was a long rectangular wing now known as the Emily Davies Court. The buildings were of bright red brick and though the founder had wanted 'dignity in every way' it was many years before they mellowed at all, though they were gradually covered with a veil of green. They were surrounded by a large piece of land leaving room for later extensions and delightful grounds. In the early days these could only be visualised in the imagination, and the surrounding treeless fields were distinctly depressing.

The students were admitted before the buildings were nearly ready for them, and at first they had to endure much real hardship. They were not dismayed by the constant discomforts but these did not help to create a happy atmosphere for work, and there were many causes of friction between them and the authorities. There was also great difficulty in finding a suitable person to be Mistress of the College. There were no less than three Mistresses between 1869 and 1872 until finally Miss Davies felt obliged to take office herself. She was able to relinquish this post in 1875 when Miss Bernard, who was a great success, was appointed.

While Jane Frances Dove was in College there was a major dispute between Miss Davies, who wished to run the College entirely according to her own pre-conceived principles, and Miss Lumsden, one of the first students who had by this time become a college lecturer. At first there had been complete harmony between them but as Miss Lumsden emerged as a champion of the students in some of their protests there was a sharp disagreement. This became even more acrimonious when it was suggested that Miss Lumsden should be elected to the Executive Committee of the College. This proposal was finally withdrawn and Miss Lumsden resigned. She subsequently became the first Head Mistress of the newly founded St. Leonards School, St. Andrews, where Jane Frances Dove eventually became a member of her staff.

It may be assumed that Jane Frances supported Miss Lumsden in her struggle on behalf of the students, but there is no record of her participation in the dispute. She was hard at work equipping herself for the life's work she had planned for herself. She was one of the first two women to sit for the Natural Sciences Tripos at Cambridge, and in 1875 she secured the certificate of Girton College signed by Emily Davies, which was the equivalent of an ordinary Cambridge B.A. degree. In July of the same year she was appointed to the staff of Cheltenham College to teach physiology at a salary of £130 per annum. While she was there she arranged for her two sisters, Emily and Ursula to become pupils at another school in Cheltenham. Emily later qualified as a doctor and they both owed their education to their sister's efforts as they followed her to St. Leonards when she went there in 1882. The younger sister Ursula was the first St. Leonards girl to go to Girton.

III

St. Leonards School, St. Andrews

WHEN MISS LUMSDEN first arrived in St. Andrews to start the new school for girls which some local residents and members of the University Staff had decided to found, it was in a very embryonic state. She was fortunate that the people behind the venture were strongly in sympathy with the movement for the higher education of girls and had close links with Miss Constance Maynard and others of her fellow students at Girton. They were trying to establish a 'first class public school for girls', and were unanimous in resolving that Miss Lumsden, as she was so well-known in St. Andrews, was to be the Head Mistress, with other Girtonians on the staff.

The original plan was for a day school only but as requests for a residential school were received from such highly desirable parents as Sir Alexander Grant, principal of Edinburgh University, professors from other Scottish universities and others, it was decided to open a boarding house also and Miss Lumsden was put in charge of this as well as of the school. She immediately chose as her assistants Jane Frances Dove who like herself was on the staff of Cheltenham College, another close friend, Miss Constance Maynard who had taken the Moral Sciences Tripos at Cambridge in 1875, and Miss Georgina Kinnear.

The school was at first called the St. Andrews School for Girls. A company was formed to finance it and numbered amongst its first board of directors Professor and Mrs. Lewis Campbell, Miss Cook (daughter of the former principal of St. Mary's College, St. Andrews and a Girton pioneer), her sister Mrs. Rodger and Sir Robert Anstruther of Balcaskie. The first chairman was the Rev. John Tulloch, D.D., principal of St. Mary's College and known throughout Scotland for his championship of the Church of Scotland at the time of the disruption. The President was the Countess of Airlie (daughter of Lady Stanley of Alderley, one of the founders of Girton) and among the Vice-Presidents were Dean

Stanley, Lord Aberdeen and Bishop Wordsworth of St. Andrews. Miss Emily Davies gave much useful counsel.

The school made its modest beginning in two houses in Queen Street, St. Andrews on 22nd October, 1877 with forty-four girls, the company having been formed in the previous January. The staff had literally virgin soil to work on and it can easily be imagined how happy Jane Frances Dove must have felt to be associated with such an enterprise. Fresh from her own struggle to obtain the necessary education from the unavoidable restrictions of a country vicarage, from the Spartan atmosphere of Hitchin and Girton, and from the incredibly hard work to reach the standard of the Cambridge Tripos, to be let loose, as it were, to fulfil her dreams must have been an intoxicating experience.

St. Leonards, as the school came to be called when it was moved to the house and grounds of that name purchased in 1881, was one of the first in Scotland to be taught by well-trained women. The best schools had, up to the advent of Miss Lumsden, relied on masters. She insisted on the maintenance of the highest standards and though started as a day school, it attracted to it from a distance girls whose parents desired for them the best available education, and so became the first boarding school for girls on the lines of the public schools for boys. Some pioneers of girls' education such as Miss Beale had feared the effects of boarding school life on girls, but the establishment of separate houses with their care for the welfare of each individual girl expelled these doubts. Miss Lumsden agreed with the great headmaster Thring of Uppingham who had initiated the house system for boys when he said, 'Two opposite and most necessary principles are both secured by this system; the civilisation and gentler feelings of comparative home with all the hardy training of a great school.' She chose as her first house-mistresses women of outstanding personality of whom it has been said 'they found in their house not only a profession but a vocation . . . the house-mistress of those days also knew that she was taking part in a new movement and her work had the zest of adventure. The house system for boys meant restraint from too much liberty, for girls it meant escape from gentility into a new life with new opportunities. In the freedom of today such training has become a routine for all young people.'

In the early days of St. Leonards each house-mistress rented and furnished her own house and appointed the housekeeper who was in charge of the domestic economy and of the girls' health and played an important part in the life of the house. Later it was decided to relieve the house-mistress of this financial responsibility but the character of the houses continued as before. They provided that training in service and community life which was the most fundamental of Miss Lumsden's educational ideas. From the youngest girl to the eldest a sense of responsibility gradually developed, while complete trust in the integrity of each girl and the absence of rules created an atmosphere of freedom and confidence, which is still characteristic of St. Leonards and its subsequent sister schools, Wycombe Abbey and Benenden. The number of girls in each house, according to Miss Lumsden, should not exceed twenty-six but in later overcrowded days this can no longer be the maximum. Nevertheless interest in each individual girl is not allowed to be obscured and the older girls share with the house-mistress concern for the welfare and integration of younger members and new girls. Intense loyalty and devotion to the house is taken for granted by all concerned and is of course specially manifest in games. House-match days are times of breathless anxiety until the final whistle is blown and the unalterable result known, spreading gloom or joy in the hearts of the participants.

From the first house-mistresses were members of the teaching staff, and in lessons as well as in play girls came in contact with members of houses other than their own and participated in the enterprises of the whole school, whether in the sphere of school work, social occasions or community service. The academic standards set by the well-qualified staff were stimulated mainly by outside examinations; at first the Girton Entrance or London Matriculation, but later the Higher Certificate of the Oxford and Cambridge Joint Board as this was recognised as a qualification for entrance to universities and professions. In 1887 Kate Sorensen, a St. Leonards girl, was the first girl to pass in both Latin and Greek. In the same year the greatest academic triumph of the school was the placing of Agnata Ramsay, who had gone to Girton from St. Leonards with a classical scholarship, alone in the first division of the first class of the Cambridge Classical Tripos, while the highest men were in the second division. Punch celebrated this occasion with his famous cartoon of a girl entering a first-class railway carriage marked 'Ladies Only.'

But this is anticipating. After five years as Head Mistress, which she had used to establish the main principles on which the school was built, Miss Lumsden was obliged through ill-health to relinquish her post. Jane Frances Dove, her able coadjutor, was her obvious successor as she was so completely at one with her in ideas. She was appointed Head Mistress in 1882. It was just at this time that the opportunity occurred to purchase the buildings of the college of St. Leonards, partly ruins and partly of comparatively modern date, but all on the site of an ancient monastic foundation and redolent of history. The school had outgrown the Queen Street houses and the college property offered great possibilities which the new Head Mistress was quick to appreciate. The Council of the St. Andrews School for Girls accordingly took the plunge, bought the property, changed the name of the school, and Miss Dove, as we shall now call her, with the twenty-two girls in her house, took possession of St. Leonards house. The old college building was used as it stood and formed the nucleus of the school as it is today. As time went on, numbers increased, other houses and grounds in the neighbourhood were bought, new buildings were erected within the precincts and the school, within the sheltering wall of the priory, grew to its present dimensions.

The historic background to the new premises must have appealed greatly to Miss Dove, with her instinct for the appropriate and fitting. The town of St. Andrews itself is steeped in history, while the ancient buildings and ruins surrounding St. Leonards school, and indeed forming part of it, are reminiscent of the days when scholars of the Renaissance laboured there under the shadow of Erasmus. The school motto 'Ad Vitam' was taken from that of Prior Hepburn who carried out the expansion of the college, originally founded for poor clerks in 1512, and built the Priory wall still encircling the school. Here the girls could well be inspired to emulation of the scholars of old and to seize the opportunity of true education which had been denied to their mothers.

On the framework erected by Miss Lumsden, Miss Dove was able to build the great school which stands today. She has told the story herself in the St. Leonards Seniors Jubilee Book published in 1927, but she does not of course mention the great debt which the school owes to her. She once said, 'I can work but I cannot speak'. This is not strictly true as she could express herself very forcibly when need arose, but her unceasing labour and devotion to the school, coupled with her gift for organisation brought amazing results. In October 1883, when the school moved to St. Leonards, there were thirty-four house girls and thirty-six day girls. By 1888 the Council were deciding to limit numbers to two hundred, of whom one hundred and fifty were to be boarders, and were making plans for extensions to school buildings and houses and for a hall to hold five hundred. In 1894 a junior school was opened, named St. Katherines. This made more room at St. Leonards for girls over fourteen.

In the midst of this steady flow of prosperity and progress in October 1895 Miss Dove suddenly announced her resignation. In a letter to the Council she said, 'I take this step because I am possessed with the idea that the benefits which I believe to be conferred by this school should be more widely diffused, and that this may be done by founding one, or possibly, two or more sister schools . . . My own pleasure in organisation, coupled with the fact that St. Leonards, now thoroughly established, known and respected everywhere, with a strong band of loyal Seniors devoted to its interests, cannot suffer, makes me wish to try the new experiment myself . . .'

This was indeed a thunderclap, but to all who knew Miss Dove it did not come entirely as a surprise. Her courage and enterprise had no limit, while her vision and faith were deep and strong. It follows that when she saw a need she would immediately set to work to meet it. She had experienced the success of St. Leonards School, the first of its kind, and felt there must be such schools in England also and that she must create one of them. Her simplicity and directness are exemplified in this action, and her complete disregard of all obstacles is typical of the way she went through life.

Alone at first in her conception of the plan, she immediately set to work to find the ways and the means, and in the autumn of 1896, within two months of leaving St. Leonards, Wycombe Abbey School was opened.

Before she left Scotland however, she had characteristically marked out someone to succeed her. Throughout her career Miss Dove almost invariably showed a flair for finding able assistants. Though a dominant personality herself she managed to gather round her women of outstanding ability and character and left them free to use their gifts once she had decided that their quality was worthy of her confidence. In Miss Julia Grant, one of the first girls to go to school at St. Leonards and subsequently a member of the staff, Miss Dove proposed as her successor a name which was instantly accepted by the Council.

Miss Grant took up her duties in the autumn of 1896. No two people afforded a greater contrast than the new Head Mistress and her predecessor; yet they were very great friends and Miss Grant, supported by an influential and enthusiastic Council, carried on and developed the traditions of the school and made yet another great contribution to its life. The change of direction meant no slowing down or halting in its progress. With characteristic generosity Miss Dove, as her parting gift to the school, founded a Classical scholarship to be held by a St. Leonards Senior at Girton College.

iii) Wycombe Abbey

iv) Wing of the Dove Memorial Library with portrait of Dame Frances by Sir William Richmond

IV

The Founding of Wycombe Abbey School

THE LAST YEAR that Miss Dove spent in St. Andrews must
have been a very strenuous and exacting one, for she carried
on simultaneously her duties as Head Mistress of St. Leonards
with all that was involved in her impending departure and the
preliminary work for the proposed new school. She was greatly
encouraged by the active support of her many friends and admirers
in Scotland, and as she herself remarked, 'Never has any enterprise
. . . been blessed with so many well-wishers'.

In characteristic fashion she conceived the idea of founding the
new school with little anxiety as to where the money for financing
the scheme was to come from, but with unswerving confidence
that it would be available because the merits of the plan seemed so
obviously unassailable. She decided that the first thing to be done
was to form a company and to secure shareholders to provide the
necessary funds at a reasonable rate of interest. For all the business
arrangements she enlisted the help of her solicitor cousin, Francis
Larken, of Messrs. Toynbee, Larken & Co. of Lincoln. She could
not have made a happier choice as he proved a staunch ally and
worked untiringly to carry out her ideas. His valuable advice as
secretary of the Company was at the service of the Council of the
School for many long years, and he was eventually succeeded by
his son, Mr. Edmund Larken, who continued to act for the school
with equal devotion.

The Girls Education Company, as it was called, was duly registered on 28th February 1896. Following on this a Council and
officers had to be appointed and people found who were willing to
support the venture by taking up the thousand shares comprising
the first issue. During the six months after the registration Miss
Dove was in constant correspondence with her cousin, and the
applications for shares were anxiously counted from day to day.

33

Her St. Leonards friends rallied round her valiantly, sending out prospectuses to possible investors, to people known to be interested in education, and to potential parents.

Among the first members of the Council and signatories to the articles of association of the Company were the Dowager Countess of Airlie (daughter of Lady Stanley of Alderley, one of the founders of Girton College), Dr. H. Montague Butler, the Master of Trinity College Cambridge (who had married Miss Agnata Ramsay of Classical Tripos fame) and Professor and Mrs. Lewis Campbell. These were all drawn from St. Leonards circles, the Butlers being particularly close friends, but to them were added by degrees a number of most influential people in which medicine, law, religion, business capacity and social status were skilfully combined.

The first chairman of the Council was the Rev. Lewis Campbell, professor of Greek at St. Andrews University who, with his wife, had done so much for St. Leonards School. Some difficulty was experienced about the first President. Miss Dove had hoped that Adeline, Duchess of Bedford would fill this office but at the eleventh hour the noble lady became a prey to doubts as to the kind of religious teaching to be given in the school. She was under the mistaken impression that the Bishop of St. Andrews, a great friend of hers, was to be a member of the Council of Wycombe Abbey School, whereas in fact he had declined to undertake responsibilities so far away from his own diocese. When the Duchess heard this she became anxious about the religious complexion of the school. She need have had no fear on this score since Miss Dove herself was an ardent Anglican and had in fact been somewhat irked by the inter-denominational character of St. Leonards, due to its geographical position in Presbyterian Scotland. The girls there were allowed each Sunday to attend the church to which they belonged. It was decided by the govenors of Wycombe Abbey and stated in the first prospectus, that the school being situated in England, was to be a Church of England school. After a somewhat strained correspondence with Professor Lewis Campbell, the Duchess declined the invitation to become President of the Council, though she still averred her approval of the new school. The Master of Trinity College Cambridge, Dr. Montague Butler, most kindly stepped into the breach and so became the first President, and remained in that office until he was succeeded in 1901 by the Rev. H. M. Burge, later Bishop of Oxford.

By the time the first prospectus for parents was ready a governing body of eighteen, called the Council, had been appointed, including in its ranks six English ecclesiastics, one of them a Bishop. An impressive array of patrons had also been secured. This prospectus stated that religious instruction was to be given by the Head Mistress and that the girls were to attend the Parish Church of High Wycombe.

While carrying on a somewhat complicated correspondence to collect all these coadjutors Miss Dove was also, with the assistance of her father and Mr. Larken, searching for suitable premises for the new school. An enormous number of properties, both in the Midlands and in the South of England, were submitted for her consideration, as the owners of many large estates were at that time anxious to dispose of them since the era of estate duties had begun. Particulars from agents poured in by every post and all had to be investigated in case what Mr. Larken described as the 'el dorado' might be missed. In writing to his cousin at the outset of his search he reminded her that her wants included 'a site where there was the least rainfall, propinquity to a town, a large house, ample space for cricket and other sports, and a lake for swimming and other purposes'. After reducing the number of possible propositions to fifteen and spending most her Christmas and Easter holidays inspecting them, Miss Dove finally decided that Lord Carrington's house, Wycombe Abbey in Buckinghamshire, was the nearest to her imagined ideal, except that the price asked was much higher than had been envisaged. The place, however, seemed so desirable in every way that the Council appointed a negotiating Committee consisting of the Rev. H. M. Burge, Dean of University College Oxford, Mr. Arthur Butler, formerly a fellow of Trinity College Cambridge, and Mr. Larken to try and secure it.

After much bargaining and a vast correspondence between all concerned, Lord Carrington finally agreed to accept £20,000 for the Abbey and thirty acres of land surrounding it, though Mr. Larken considered this a fancy price. The contract was signed in May 1896 and the purchase completed in July of the same year. This did not leave much time to adapt the premises for school purposes by the autumn, so it was small wonder that when the first batch of girls arrived on Victoria's Day, 26th September, there was still much to be done. But Miss Dove had achieved her object and the school was duly opened on the appointed day. Moreover the delay in completion was a great help to the Company from a financial point of view, as there were still many shares to be taken up when the contract was signed and a mortgage had to be obtained for the balance of the purchase money and to pay for the initial alterations to the premises. The vital meeting of the Council, when the decision to purchase the property was finally decided upon, was on 24th April 1896. Miss Dove was on the same day formally appointed Head Mistress with Miss A. R. Burne, a Girtonian and her secretary at St. Leonards, as her assistant.

Wycombe Abbey certainly fulfilled most of the essential requirements Miss Dove had set before her when she began her search. It was about thirty-six miles from London in delightful surroundings in the Chiltern Hills, on the outskirts of what was then the charming old country town of High Wycombe. The Abbey dated from the period of the Georges but it had considerable history attached to it and was on the site of an earlier manor house. Lord Shelburne had lived there in the eighteenth century and amongst the distinguished guests who had visited the house were the younger Pitt, Benjamin Franklin, David Garrick and Dr. Johnson. Lord Shelburne employed the famous architect James Wyatt to transform the old Jacobean house into the present building with its Gothic aspect. The extensive grounds were filled with beautiful trees, and though the green swards destined for playing fields were all on a slope, there was actually a lake suitable for boating, though not for swimming, and an enormous ball room ideal for a school assembly hall.

At the top of the hill above the Abbey the grounds merged into the woods of Daws Hill, still in Lord Carrington's hands, while beyond the lawns facing the Abbey a beautiful avenue of lime trees melted into the distance. There was a feeling of spaciousness and repose about the whole place. In the early days of the school there were few buildings in sight from within the grounds and the red roofs of the town were dominated by the Parish Church, so large that there was ample room for the girls to worship there without unduly crowding the ordinary congregation.

Miss Dove planned to have four houses in the Abbey and to build on form rooms and other school buildings. Four other houses and the Hospice were to be erected on the hill rising to the south of the Abbey while the gymnasium, music rooms, workshop and other ancillary departments were to be in the stables and courtyard to the west of the house. But this could only be achieved by degrees and to begin with the Abbey housed the entire school and its activities. Money had to be found for the necessary alterations and for the new buildings, and during the first years of its existence the finances of the school were extremely precarious. Fortunately, Sir John Wolfe Barry, the famous engineer who had built the Tower Bridge, joined the Council during the first year and his business acumen and practical experience were invaluable. He literally saved the situation by securing for the Company a loan from the Rock Life Insurance Company on favourable terms, to replace the mortgage obtained for the purchase of the Abbey. This provided the necessary funds to cover the alterations to the Abbey and the building of the outside houses on the Marlow Hill. A house in the town was temporarily leased to serve as a sanatorium.

Mr. A. D. Caroë was appointed as architect for all this work which took some three years to complete. Electric light was installed throughout the buildings. This was considered a very modern idea in those days. Other urgent needs had to be met as time went on, such as the repair of dry rot in Big School, the building of extra form rooms and boot rooms and the Hospice. To cover these second mortgage debentures were issued.

The Lake also proved to be a mixed blessing and in 1899 Miss Dove reported to the Council that it had become so offensive that without waiting for their consent she had given the order for it to be cleaned out at a cost of £2,000, which she had advanced from her own pocket, awaiting reimbursement when the Company had money to spare for the purpose. The Council expressed great appreciation of her prompt action and generous help and made the necessary arrangements for her to be repaid as soon as possible. It may be pertinent to mention at this point that during those early days of the School the Head Mistress had more than once to await payment of her own salary, since the cash in the Bank was required for other purposes.

At a shareholders' meeting in 1898 Dr. Townsend, a parent, who was later to become the husband of Ursula Farwell, the first head of School, urged that the land between the Abbey and the High Street (now covered by municipal buildings) should be purchased. He was strongly supported by Mrs. Henry Fawcett. This was a most attractive piece of woodland, full in the spring of daffodils and bluebells, and would have been a great asset to the school and perhaps have protected it from the later inroads of the town. Unfortunately the Council did not think the finances were strong enough to meet this further outlay, though they secured Dyke Meadow on the north side of the lake. This had not been included in the original area purchased. It contained some fine cedar trees and a stretch of ground admirably suitable for use by the girls for their individual gardens.

As time went on the initial stringency steadily if gradually disappeared as all profits were ploughed back into the school, and a constant stream of applications was received from would-be parents. By December 1899 Miss Dove was able to announce that the school was full and numbered two hundred and ten girls. One of the reasons for this steady influx has been suggested by one of the earliest arrivals, the late Winifred Peck, daughter of Bishop Knox and author of many books including one called 'A Little Learning' which contains a vivid picture of Wycombe in its early days. She claims that Miss Dove had a sound educational business instinct which exactly met one of the needs of the time. It was the Victorian age of philanthropy, of social work and church work, and of the stirrings of the suffrage movement. The more serious society ladies were amongst the leaders and the effect of this enthusiasm amongst British matrons to improve the world was twofold. They began to feel that daughters well disposed of at boarding schools would leave their mothers ever freer for their activities, and that girls in a school like Wycombe would learn to carry on the torch and to devote their lives to public service even more whole-heartedly than their elders. From the girls' point of view, at the end of the first term, says Mrs. Peck, 'we went home for the holidays to boast of belonging to the most wonderful school in England.'

V

Early Days

IN THE EARLY DAYS a delightful country house atmosphere pervaded the school. This may in part have been due to the fact that when the first girls arrived the alterations to the house had scarcely begun, so everything was rather unconventional and informal. Miss Dove had brought with her four girls from her own house at St. Leonards who each became head of a house in the new school, for the Head Mistress built from the outset the framework of the structure which she envisaged for the future.

On the first day, 26th September 1896, there were only forty girls, the minimum of furniture and, as one of the girls expressed it 'no one knowing the way anywhere'. Parents arrived in the Abbey entrance hall to find house-mistresses busy sewing rings on to dormitory curtains and a general air of house-moving prevailing. There was no electric light and the girls were quickly set to work under the direction of the carpentry mistress to make wooden candlesticks which they carried with them everywhere, waving them about with gay disregard of fire risks. Lessons were given in any corner which was free from workmen though routine and regularity soon established themselves. In their free time the girls willingly helped in the practical work of getting straight.

The only railway service from London to High Wycombe at that time was from Paddington via Maidenhead, with a bottle-neck at Bourne End where the line became a single track. At this spot eagerly awaited stores and equipment very often stuck, and ingenuity was frequently sorely tried to make substitutes for urgently needed goods which had not arrived. Some of the gardeners who had been employed by Lord Carrington remained on at the Abbey and became the nucleus of the devoted staff which the school soon collected. Chief among these was the Gill family, a father and two sons who lived at one of the lodges and who could be seen tenderly cherishing the plants in the Palm House as the girls

rushed through on the way to the ball-room which had now become the school assembly hall and was known as Big School; or
sweeping up leaves and mowing grass as games were being played
on the well-kept lawns. Across the middle of the grounds was a
sunk fence which kept sundry cows or the lawn-mower pony from
straying on tc the playing fields, while above, beyond and beside
the Abbey were splendid trees, glorious at all seasons but particularly in spring and autumn with the vivid green and gold of the
beeches.

Inside the house there were soon a large number of maids who
assembled in rows for prayers in the evening attired in black dresses
and caps and aprons, and in the morning clattered (this time in print
dresses) into the dormitories with small cans of hot water which
were supposed to take the chill off the cold baths decreed as a fitting
opening to each school-day. These baths were small hip-tubs kept
under each bed, and had to be duly emptied by the same maids after
breakfast. They also made the beds, except on Sundays, and waited
at table for dinner. At supper and breakfast the girls took turns to
hand round the good plain food.

The furniture in the Abbey reflected Miss Dove's unerring taste.
She had a flair for choosing the appropriate and the congruous. The
china used was a special blue Rouen ware with large wide-open cups
and elegant shaped dishes; the dormitories, though furnished with
absolute necessaries only, had curtains of Liberty material with
Morris designs, while the rush-seated chairs in the house-studies
were simple but of good proportions. In the entrance hall tapestry
and antique furniture of a suitable size gave an immediate impression of dignity, while in her own drawing-room and study the
Head Mistress had some fine pieces of furniture and water colours
by good artists. In her zeal for an appropriate ambience she considered the terrace outside her drawing-room incomplete without
some peacocks to parade upon it. These caused some consternation
when they arrived, and then found their way into Big School and
perched high upon the rafters, screeching loudly when the girls
were trying to concentrate on prayers. Nevertheless, with this
appreciation of the elegant, Miss Dove combined a Spartan simplicity in her own way of life which everyone else was expected to
emulate.

She considered the health of the girls to be of the utmost importance and they received every care, but the daily cold bath was part of the régime in which she believed, and cold dormitories, music rooms and passages with a general hardiness were deemed to be almost a moral necessity. Hot baths, except for those under doctor's orders, were only available once a week. These principles applied as much to the mistresses in the Abbey as to the girls. Each house-tutor had a rather sparsely furnished and not very large sitting room and a very meagre bed-room. Her free time was very limited and most of her waking hours were occupied with the welfare and teaching of the girls. Fortunately these mistresses were young and enthusiastic and it never seemed to occur to them that this life of unselfish devotion was in any way unusual or unreasonable. In a remarkably short time everyone dropped into the niche which Miss Dove had designed for her and the pattern of the school crystallised. The first girls and staff inspired by the Head Mistress set the standards and traditions which have survived two world wars and established the school as it is today.

The alterations to the Abbey were quickly followed by the building of the four outside houses to the south on the slopes of the Marlow Hill. They were named after members of the Council as Campbell, Airlie, Butler and Barry respectively. The Abbey houses were called Pitt, Rubens, Clarence and Cloister. Pitt house study was in the rooms which had been occupied by William Pitt when he visited Wycombe in Lord Shelburne's day, Rubens was in the large room near the entrance hall where Lord Carrington's pictures, some by Rubens, were still hanging when the school took possession, and where the Dame Frances Dove Memorial Library now is; Clarence was upstairs on the first floor with a lovely view of the grounds towards the lime avenue, and is reputed to be named after a Duke of Clarence who had journeyed abroad with a member of the Carrington family; Cloister was behind the cloisters which linked the Palm House (at that time still full of exotic plants) and the Library.

VI

Staff and Curriculum

ISS DOVE was given by the Council complete control over the appointment of Staff and the internal arrangements of the new school, and from the outset her ideas were clear and definite. In the first prospectus it is interesting to notice that the subjects to be taught were Scripture Knowledge, Arithmetic, Literature, History, Latin or German, French, Physiography or Harmony, Gymnastics and Part Singing. The different branches of Mathematics and Natural Science, Greek and Italian were to be gradually added. The subjects selected were probably at first dependent on the members of the staff available to teach them, since the required specialists were still not easy to find.

Though a large number of applicants wrote asking for posts at Wycombe, their standards were not high enough for the type of education envisaged and the Head Mistress was looking for personalities as well as for academic qualifications. She brought with her from St. Leonards a nucleus consisting of Miss Burne who had been her secretary and whose indefatigable work in the office was to build a firm framework for the future organisation of the new school; Miss Scott and Miss Grierson, Girtonians with modern language qualifications who were in charge of Cloister and Pitt Houses. Other house-tutors were Miss Douglas who taught Divinity and was head of Rubens, and Miss Wallis, in charge of Clarence House, who had herself been the Head Mistress of a High School and who had taken Classics at Cambridge. To these were rapidly added other young and keen Girtonians; Miss Lang and Miss Daniel teaching Classics and German and destined to become house-tutors as soon as Miss Wallis and Miss Grierson moved out to Barry and Butler, their respective outside houses, and Miss Whitelaw who taught mathematics and was in later years to succeed Miss Dove as Head Mistress of the achool. The non-academic posts were also filled by outstanding women. Mary Hogarth, a sister of the explorer and a descendant of the artist of that name was in charge of the Art teaching and, in spite of her own great gifts, showed infinite patience with the struggles of even the youngest pupils.

Miss Agar, a trained gardener, was to inspire girls with enthusiasm for their own small plots as well as to be of the greatest help in the development of the grounds, while Miss Foulis, a delightful Scotswoman with a genius for woodwork rarely met with amongst women in those days, was to teach the carpentry and handwork with which the time-tables were to be varied. In charge of the music was Elizabeth Rhodes, a pupil of Clara Schumann, with her friend Edith Hoyle who set standards which the majority found it hard to reach. It is impossible to mention all the members of the staff in the first days of the school, but all were inspired by the enthusiasm and selflessness of their Head Mistress, and seemed to feel that they had embarked on a thrilling adventure.

Miss Whitelaw has written of those early days, 'In her day Miss Dove was far ahead of her time. She realised that many do not develop through the printed page and introduced hand-work into the time-table of every girl. This was a great innovation. Gardening, carpentry, Swedish drill all found a place, and organised games were very prominent. In the light of today's ideas there were defects. The paths of a new girl were closely ordered and her time overoccupied. Much individual attention was given to the girls by their house-mistresses, but in school the curriculum was not always suitable for their individual needs. The time-tables of the younger staff could scarcely be believed today. No domestic science was done. There was less musical education than at present and the singing was not comparable with what can be heard today. The standard of scholarship work, though occasionally high, was not reached by so many as it is now. But that was in the nineties and not in the twentieth century, and what was truly more important than any of these things was the sense of responsibility gradually instilled into each girl, by example, by living in an atmosphere of trust and freedom, of bodily and mental activity. Supervision by staff in dormitory or house-study was unknown.'

The informal character of the early days was intensified by the fact that lessons had to be given in any corner that was free from workmen. In corridors, boot-rooms, the minstrels' gallery, the school hall and other unconventional circumstances, the sound of teaching could be heard. There were few amenities but everyone was expected to give of her best, and gradually, as order emerged out of chaos with the will to work both of teachers and taught, a surprising amount of sound learning was achieved. For Miss Dove the welfare of the girls was the paramount consideration, and the staff were expected to sacrifice everything to this end. In comparison with modern standards their duties were very heavy, and they had little free time. The work was so arranged that the girls had very diversified time-tables. There were no long spells in class-rooms but lessons were interspersed with preparation, gardening, handicrafts and music, so that the staff could not count on consecutive periods of leisure but had to give lessons at all hours of the day. The half-holiday was on Thursday, to make a mid-week break for the girls, but this deprived the mistresses of Saturday afternoons and free week-ends. Their salaries were extremely low, though better than those received by governesses at the time. The Head Mistress herself received £300 a year, while the highest salaries of the teaching staff were £120 non-resident. The matron in the Abbey, who was responsible for the health of girls in four houses, received £50 a year (resident). She was the sister of a Bishop, much beloved by all who knew her, and played a great part in the life of the school, both by precept and example. Some members of the staff who had private means, voluntarily sacrificed part of their salaries to help the school in its early days of financial stringency.

The single-minded devotion of all these women doubtless helped to foster that disregard of material possessions which prevailed throughout the school. The girls knew little and cared less about the social position of their school-fellows, and none enquired whether their friends came from poor homes or rich. The giving of presents was discouraged, but if a special occasion called for one, subscriptions were limited to twopence each. Yet with all this simplicity of life, the beauty of the surroundings and the feeling that only the best was good enough, led to a very real scorn of the second-rate. A senior has written of her school memories, 'How can this record end . . . but on the note of gratitude not only for the loveliness of the place but for the people who inspired its common life.'

45

VII

The Seniors

NOT THE LEAST of Miss Dove's achievements was the founding of the Seniors, as the old girls associations of St. Leonards and Wycombe Abbey Schools are called. She hoped that these organisations would secure the continuation of the corporate life begun at school, and the consolidation in perpetuity of the ideals and principles which school life was designed to promote. They are divided into circles of about thirty contemporaries, each with its secretary responsible for keeping in touch with the members through correspondence and the collection of annual subscriptions. These subscriptions are not for any benefit to the members, but are for the support of any corporate piece of social work to which the association is committed. For when a Senior signs the Roll on leaving school, she pledges herself to 'foster that feeling of corporate unity acquired at school . . . by unity in a common work for the glory of God.' For many years for the Wycombe Seniors this has been the Union of Girls Schools for Social Service, but in the course of time other causes have also appealed to their generosity. A bursary fund to enable the daughters of Seniors to be educated at the school has been established and its capital fund is annually augmented by a contribution from the general fund of the association. At the time of writing there are sixteen Seniors' daughters in the school assisted by these bursaries, and since the foundation of the fund, no less than eighty-six girls have benefited from it. Those parents whose daughters have reached the school through this means are deeply appreciative, and on more than one occasion, when they have become better off after their daughters have left school, they have refunded the amount given to them as a token of their gratitude for timely help. Apart from these bursary girls there is always a large number of Seniors' daughters and granddaughters in the school. So the tradition is carried on. In one well-known family there are no less than twelve Seniors starting with a great-grandmother.

The Seniors are a self-governing body, with rules drawn up by the founder but modified as required from time to time at the annual general meetings which are held alternately at Wycombe and in London. An executive committee represents the various generations of the members who now number over two thousand. The circle secretaries, in conjunction with the general secretary and the honorary treasurer (who of necessity do most of the work) ensure the continuity and efficiency of the organisation. A President and Vice-Presidents complete the hierarchy which is a very active one. The vitality of the association is largely due to the foresight of Miss Dove, whose structure has stood the test of time and provides a firm bond of union between women in all parts of the world who have been at the school.

In 1948 the Seniors' Jubilee was celebrated and there was a stock-taking of the achievements of members since the foundation of the school. This brought to light a manifold variety of activities. The majority were married with families but had nevertheless found time for much public work, while the younger members were busy training themselves for the various trades and professions which had been thrown open to women after the two great wars. A register compiled during the second world war revealed that Wycombe Seniors were engaged in medicine, nursing, massage, hospital almoning, dentistry, pharmacy, and physical training. Some were artists, musicians and actresses. Others were architects, accountants, lawyers and journalists. Many were trained in domestic science or secretarial work. Some were teaching or had schools of their own, or were the wives of headmasters. A substantial number had undertaken voluntary public work; sixty-one were sitting on commissions, tribunals or panels. There were fifty Magistrates, six town Councillors (two of them Mayors) while others were engaged in various forms of local government work. This was a far cry from the days when Miss Dove had written: 'When I was a girl the chief idea of the mothers of that day appeared to be to give their daughters a superficial veneer of French, drawing and music, then dress them up and hawk them about until a husband was dazzled and caught. My whole soul revolted against this degradation of womanhood'. How this register would have rejoiced her heart. At the same time a wholesome fear of giving an account of her life to Miss Dove has

v) Dame Frances with her successor Miss A. W. Whitelaw

vi) School Cricket Team 1906

made many a Senior tremble when revisiting her old school. Though the Head Mistress considered home-making and the duties of a wife and mother should be pre-eminent, it was essential to be able to report some outside activities as well if full approval was to be secured.

Amongst Seniors who have reached special eminence in their chosen spheres, the school remembers with pride Mary Pickford, the first of their number to become a Member of Parliament and who had a most distinguished career, Margaret Hill (née Keynes) who was a pioneer in work for the aged and founded the Hill Homes at Highgate, a model and inspiration for subsequent work in this field, and Ethel Romanes, whose religious, social and educational work both in England and in India, was remarkable. Ethel Gabain was an artist whose pictures hang in many great galleries, and was President of the Society of Women Artists, while Ursula Farwell, the first head of school, was amongst the pioneers of work for cripples and for the education of young people in hospital.

Throughout its history the Seniors organisation has proved to be a great source of strength to the school. When it had to be re-started after the evacuation and unavoidable dispersal during the second world war many Seniors returned to help the staff in various capacities and assisted to achieve the re-opening in record time. In this most critical period the confidence of the Seniors in the future of the school was evidenced by the plans they made to provide it with a library as a Memorial to the Founder, as soon as circumstances would permit. In recent years, when a special fund has had to be raised for new buildings and for scholarships, the Seniors have contributed a large proportion of the necessary money. They are never appealed to in vain. After their first meeting in 1898 they were described as 'a band united in a common cause', and as time goes on this unity is in no way diminished.

VIII

Educational Ideas

So every spirit as it is most pure
And hath in it the more of heavenly light,
So it the fairer bodie doth procure
To habit in, and it more fairly dight
With cheerful grace and amiable sight.
For of the soule the bodie form doth take
For soule is forme and both the bodie make.
                                  SPENSER

ONE DOES NOT readily associate the tenets of Miss Dove
with Spenser's Hymn in Honour of Beauty, but with this
quotation from that poem she began an article on the
'*Cultivation of the Body*' which she contributed to a book on '*Work
and Play in Girls Schools*' published in 1898. Miss Beale of Cheltenham, who edited the book, wrote the section on '*Intellectual
Education*', while '*The Moral Side*' was dealt with by Miss Lucy
Soulsby of the Manor House School, Brondesbury. Miss Dove in
her article does not confine herself solely to physical culture but
outlines the general principles for the education of girls in which
she believed. She was well in advance of her time on the insistence
on the importance of the physical side, but she also wrote 'As the
object of school life, or rather life at school, is not merely teaching
but education, and as education means the gradual drawing out and
development of all the faculties of which the human being is
capable, we shall speak in this chapter not of the 'teacher' but of the
'mistress' as the person who in school life takes the place of authority
analogous to that of the parent in the home, and upon whom falls
the responsibility for the time being of seeing that a due balance is
maintained in the development of every faculty. The importance of
this harmonious development of the powers is manifest. We do
not desire girls to be brainless athletes any more than we wish they

51

should be delicate or stunted blue-stockings, and either of these exaggerated types is made doubly deplorable if, as sometimes happens, there is a deficiency of moral power. The most important conditions for health are first of all a wholesome environment; secondly, wholesome occupation for the mind; and thirdly, proper exercise for the body . . . The occupation of the mind will also come chiefly under the head of mental training, but here it may be desirable to notice that the mind must receive much of its training through the exercise of faculties other than intellectual. This truth is of course the foundation of the whole idea of recreation; re-creation consisting much more in change of thought and a difference in the objects on which the attention is fixed than in the particular form of exercise through which this object is attained.'

It is interesting to note that Miss Dove insisted on the importance of certain words as applied to her schools. She herself claimed that she was better at working than at talking, but her innate sense of the appropriate showed itself in the vocabulary she chose for the various aspects of school life. As she preferred the staff to be called 'mistresses' instead of teachers so she objected to the description of her schools as 'boarding' establishments, but wished them to be described as residential and to be distinguished from High Schools which she considered to be of a different character. From her St. Leonards tradition she derived the monastic word 'Hospice' instead of sanatorium for the building devoted to the care of the sick, and the school was divided into forms, not classes, with lessons given in 'form-rooms'. The leader of the school had to be called the Head of School, not the head girl, prefects were described as monitors, and past pupils were known as Seniors. Few of Miss Dove's writings survive, but when she did commit her thoughts to paper her style was characteristic. It was firm, decisive and clear, leaving no doubt as to her meaning and intentions.

In setting out to secure for girls the educational opportunities equal to those enjoyed by their brothers in the great public schools, Miss Dove did not believe that it was necessary slavishly to copy the masculine systems. Her practical mind realised that a *modus vivendi* must be built up to suit the special needs of girls, which differed radically from those of boys. But she realised that the greatest advantage the boys enjoyed at school was the opportunity for developing the corporate virtues. These it was essential the girls should acquire and school was the obvious place for them to do so. 'It must be pointed out' she said, 'patiently again and again where the girls' application of principles clashes with the interests of the majority. Thus the principles of corporate life are being imbibed every hour and minute of the day, though nowhere more completely than in the playground.' Thus she considered all aspects of recreation and hygiene of supreme importance. She was fortunate in being in charge of a residential school where she had opportunities denied to the heads of day-schools, for putting her theories into practice. She was consequently able to blaze a trail to be followed by all interested in the higher education of girls.

In her article on the Cultivation of the Body she deals first with games. She says that all kinds can be played by girls with the exception of football, and that in the playground 'large organised games such as cricket, hockey and lacrosse are the most useful'. Such games she claims develop the corporate virtues which she considers so essential. 'The woman who indulges family selfishness' she says 'is a bad citizen. To be a good citizen it is essential that she should have wide interests, a sense of discipline and organisation, *esprit de corps* and a power of corporate action'.

In order to provide the necessary facilities for games Miss Dove insists that every residential school should have several acres of grounds surrounding it, and the staff and girls in the school must so direct the games that every girl may have the opportunity to join in these organised games at least three or four times a week. She enumerates the qualities of each kind of game, lacrosse for its grace, hockey for the cheerful endurance required, and cricket for the development of gentleness and courtesy combined with strength and determination. She says that experience has shown that it is advisable to choose one game only for each term and to keep to it. Lacrosse is most suitable for the autumn, hockey for the spring and cricket for the summer. She includes tennis amongst the games which are desirable for small numbers, but are not so essential as team games for large numbers. She regrets that when it comes to bowling and throwing girls are at a disadvantage, because they are not, in their early years, allowed the same facilities as boys for physical activity. She has however no doubt that in this matter 'great strides will be made in the future, to the enormous gain not only physically but mentally and morally, both of women in particular and of the nation as a whole'.

In order to gain the maximum benefit from outdoor games and to avoid any ill effects, Miss Dove feels that gymnastic training for girls is essential. She advocates Swedish methods in order that the necessary muscular strength may be developed, yet over-exertion eliminated. Another reason for her belief in the Swedish system is that through it physical defects can be discovered and curative exercises presented. She speaks with compassion of the weak backs and anaemia due to ignorance, fashion and overwork so prevalent amongst Victorian girls, and urges that the growing child 'must have abundance of sleep, food, fresh air and exercise, and while living in cultivated surroundings and being encouraged in intellectual pursuits should not be expected to spend more than three or four hours a day in doing definite brain work. At the age of fourteen a healthy girl may be expected to begin to work as much as five hours a day'.

With these proposals Miss Dove outstripped the ideas of most of the educationalists of her day, but in spite of her great enthusiasm for physical education and development, perhaps due to the lack of these before her time, she constantly emphasises the need for a due sense of proportion. The physical training must be woven into the general pattern of girls' life at school. The limitation of the hours of purely intellectual work should also leave time for handwork, needlework, gardening and other pursuits. She specifically omits cooking, dressmaking, domestic economy, sick nursing and hygiene because she considers these subjects are best acquired by 'devoting six months or a year specially to this purpose when school life is over, as at school they do not admit of a sufficient amount of training in proportion to the time they consume'. She also has thought for the girls who do not shine in examinations, and says that they should be sent out from school 'healthy and vigorous, keenly alive to every opportunity that offers for self-improvement, earnest and self-restrained, with trained powers, ready to devote themsleves to the duties that offer'.

At the conclusion of her article Miss Dove gives much common-sense advice about environment, school premises, climate and food.

Many of the things she considers essential such as electric light were not yet available in most schools, though her ideas about heating (fire-places only for the houses) would be considered somewhat Spartan by present day standards.

Her final words concern the 'danger of over-stimulating the emotions'. 'Healthy bodily development is hindered or prevented if they are too early encouraged . . . The emotional nature' she says 'is over-stimulated by excessive time spent on music, especially if the music is of a certain kind. Much care is needed, more particularly if there is decided musical taste, to begin with composers who appeal least to the emotional nature, and not to specialise in music at all until a thorough intellectual groundwork has been laid in the general education. Latin, mathematics and vigorous games hold a far more important part in a general scheme of comprehensive education than is always apparent'. And yet she chose to include in the music staff of her own school two pupils of Frau Clara Schumann and, as art mistress, a descendant of Hogarth. She must always have the best. It is interesting to speculate as to what her views would have been of television and the radio as concomitants of education.

This article does not specially mention a policy which Miss Dove and also Miss Lumsden at St. Leonards considered of paramount importance, namely, the complete trust of girls in matters of discipline. The restriction and constant supervision which had previously been customary in girls schools were abolished, and the girls themselves were entrusted with the maintenance of order and good behaviour. Their response fully justified the confidence placed in them, and the free atmosphere in the schools resulted in a vital development of their powers and character. The system created a social conscience in the girls and a general respect for those in authority which was not due to rules and regulations. Miss Dove herself wrote, 'Make them trustworthy by trusting them, and straightforward by taking for granted they have nothing to hide'.

In her talks to girls at her schools Miss Dove never ceased to inculcate these ideas. At St. Leonards Speech Day in 1891 she said, 'Do not for one moment suppose that we can educate you. We do all we can to assist you but you must do the work for yourselves. Each of you by humble, continuous, earnest effort must be the architect of her own character. That is why you are taught Latin and Mathematics and you do gymnastics and play games . . . that you may be assisted in acquiring that command over yourselves that your powers in all directions may be led forth and educated is the reason why you are here at school; that you may be sent forth to your life's work, whatever it may be, fully equipped with as healthy a body, trained intellect and strengthened character as may be possible'.

On her last speech day at St. Leonards Miss Dove with customary humility, rejected the high praises given to her for the success of the school and, after generously acknowledging the work of the staff, she concluded, 'As for the girls, it is extraordinary what little trouble they have given. There never were such girls.'

IX

The Corporate Virtues

THE UNDERLYING PRINCIPLE of all Miss Dove's educational ideas was the preparation for a life of service and a sense of public duty. She thought that when girls had been denied the opportunities available to their brothers, this had restricted their ability to play their full part, both in the family and the nation. In 1907 she was asked to contribute a paper to a meeting of the Head Mistresses' Association on 'The Modern Girl'; so in order to test the effects of her methods she sent out circulars to all the Seniors of St. Leonards and Wycombe Abbey whose addresses could be found asking three questions. There were:

1. How have you spent the time since leaving school?
2. Do you feel that your life at school has been in any way a help to you?
3. Can you suggest any way in which school life could have been made more helpful?

She received a large number and a great variety of answers and the general impression that these made on her encouraged her to think that her educational theories were sound. The great majority of the writers lived at home, but from what they told her of their occupations they led very full and varied lives. About fifty per cent were married and several had large families.

In concluding her paper Miss Dove said, 'The great work our schools are doing is the raising of the whole moral tone of women's lives; honesty, fair-play and *esprit de corps* are taking the place of petty meanness and jealousy; if only every girl would go to school and stay there long enough to learn the corporate virtues, in two or three generations we should realise utopia. In the words of one of my correspondents, 'I feel that school has been a help in setting before girls high ideas of sincerity, public spirit, responsibility, thoroughness, honourableness, comradeship and friendship. I feel it teaches that the best part of one is something which lies above division of sex or society and makes one feel that only by being good in the widest sense can girls become good women. This is no doubt the ideal of all the noblest women but one does not find it to be always the ideal of schools or individuals and the modern schools . . . are the outcome of building on this foundation. One can hope that time and development will add to, enrich, tone and soften the outline without destroying the underlying idea'.

While still at school and as a preparation for their subsequent responsibilities, Miss Dove encouraged the girls to give practical support to social work at home and to missionary work abroad. For the former they were introduced to the United Girls Schools Mission, and for the latter they contributed to the Melanesian Mission in the South Seas. They were also brought to realise the importance of religious fervour without party spirit. The United Girls Schools Mission had been started in Camberwell, then one of the poorest parts of South London. It had its origin in the idea of Mrs. Bailey, wife of the then organising secretary of the South London Church Fund, who thought that girls at school should have a mission of their own, comparable to those supported by some of the boys' public schools. A committee was formed and included several prominent Head Mistresses with Miss Dove as one of the most active among them. Bishop Talbot, then Bishop of Southwark, gave the scheme his blessing and his support, while his wife, Mrs. E. S. Talbot became its first president. It appointed as its first missioner a Yorkshireman, The Rev. H. Veazey who wrote fifty years later, when he had become a Canon of Southwark Cathedral, 'The primary aim of the founders was of course that it should be part of the character education of the girls themselves; a mission to them while girls at school and by them afterwards'. The Bishop named St. Mark's, Camberwell as the first mission district and in this poor and crowded area, where children predominated, there was ample scope for girls at school to begin their work for others.

The problems of this part of London at that time cannot possibly be imagined by those born in the Welfare State. There was no house or vicarage for the Missioner and his wife to live in, no mission hall or buildings in which to work and hold services, clubs or Sunday schools. There were seven thousand adults and children living in three-storey tenements in the six and a half acres which formed the mission district, over one thousand to the area as against the then London average of eighty. There was acute poverty; no unemployment pay, old age pensions or maternity benefits; no provident collecting or jumble sales. There were no health services, not even a district nurse or a school clinic. Public-houses abounded and were the only places available for social and bodily refreshment or amusement. No one went to church, few said prayers. God either did not exist or did not care; nothing mattered, it was all the same in the end.

Miss Dove had no difficulty in arousing the interest and enthusiasm of the girls at Wycombe Abbey to help these dire conditions, and herself led the way by a generous gift of £300 which enabled the property for the first mission hall to be secured, and by a substantial loan for the Club premises so urgently required for the young people in the district. Every year in the summer term a party of several hundred men, women and children were invited to Wycombe for the day. As no motor charabancs were available in those days, the party was first shepherded across London by bus and then reached High Wycombe by train from Paddington. They proceeded from the station to the Abbey in a long crocodile and on arrival were regaled with buns and milk. After that they split up into various age groups, each of which was allotted to a party of girl hostesses. There was always a cricket match against the choir boys from St. Mark's; (the mission church) who naturally always had to win. In the Abbey grounds parties of children were punted up and down the lake, into which some of them invariably fell. These were hustled off to the cottage in the courtyard where a supply of dry clothes was in readiness for such eventualities. The Missioner himself, attired in flannels and a black straw-boater, enjoyed the day out with long games of tennis. Providence generally was kind and gave a fine day, so aged grannies and tired mums were able to sit about out of doors, while enthusiastic Wycombe juniors minded the babies and played with the toddlers. Large meals were served in tents, and at the end of the day, as the crocodile formed up again for the return trek to the station, each visitor as they went through the Abbey gates was presented with a bag of buns and sweets and a large bunch of flowers. All was amazingly orderly and disciplined and the guests were most appreciative. When they had gone the school exhaustedly relaxed but the girls generally felt it had been a wonderful day, and that they had glimpsed a new and hitherto unknown world. Many had acquired pen-friends to whom they had promised to write and whose birthdays they were not to be allowed to forget. Others who were about to leave school felt impelled to go to South London themselves to see what they could do to give some practical help. Thus the mission became a reality and not a mere pious undertaking.

In her choice of the Melanesian Mission for the foreign missionary work of the school, Miss Dove had also found an enterprise which would appeal to the imagination of the girls. The story of the martyrdom of Bishop Patterson in the early days of this mission, the romantic voyages of its ship, the 'Southern Cross', through the glamorous seas of the Pacific Islands, and the annual visits of the missionaries with interesting lantern slides, made the work seem vital and worth while.

These missions were closely linked with the religious life of the school. This was not felt to be in a water-tight compartment but was a background to all activities. The school motto, was chosen in 1898 by the Head Mistress after considering a number of suggestions sent in by the girls at her request. She evidently found none of them suitable, as 'In fide vade' the final choice, was the motto of her own family. It certainly exemplified the spirit of the place. From the day when its founder decided to leave St. Leonards and boldly to embark on establishing the new school, with little idea as to where the material means for it were to come from, the school progressed with a calm confidence and trust which can only have been based on spiritual values. Two of the girls wrote a school song beginning

> 'In Fide Vade, yea, such is our motto
> Deep is its meaning and wondrous its power,
> Binding us closely, each to the other
> In the glad things of life and in grief's darkest hour.'

The glad things certainly predominated at Wycombe but amid all the gaiety of youth and the enthusiasm for their many interests, the Head Mistress insisted on the unimportance of material things.

She held that education is 'the gradual and harmonious development of religious, moral and physical powers for each individual',
always in that order.

Miss Dove was not enthusiastic about the idea of a school chapel
but stressed the importance of close co-operation with the parish
church. High Wycombe is fortunate in having an exceptionally
large and beautiful church, so there was plenty of room for the
school to attend services on Sundays and Saints' days. The Vicar, the
Rev. E. D. Shaw, subsequently Bishop of Buckingham and Dean of
Christ Church Oxford, became a staunch friend of the school and
of the Head Mistress, and fully understood her ideals and her
practical way of realising them. He prepared all candidates for
confirmation, which in the early days of the school was celebrated
by the Bishop of Oxford.

On Sundays a number of girls made their Communion at the
eight o'clock service. The whole school attended mattins and most
of it evensong. At other times of the day short Sunday lessons were
given by house-mistresses to classes of various ages, and half an
hour was set aside for quiet reading. Saints' days were observed but
All Saints Day and Ascension Day were school holidays. In spite of
all the services there was plenty of time for relaxation on Sundays
which were generally enjoyed as days of freedom from the busy
school time-table. In the winter, walks had to be taken in the afternoon and the girls set out in parties of four, with the senior girl in
charge choosing various routes in the Buckinghamshire country-
side. There was no question of crocodiles or supervision by
mistresses, while in the summer term, instead of these walks, the
afternoon could be spent in the Abbey grounds, 'sitting out' or
climbing trees or on other quiet amusements. Sweets were also
available on Sundays and half holidays, and the custom was to share
them all, regardless of ownership, by handing round several boxes
issued by the housekeeper from a general store in which all sweets
were deposited when they arrived from home. Thus no one felt
deprived if their contribution was less ample than that of their
friends. By Sunday evening everyone felt the day had been in some
sense a preparation for the coming week. The thought was not
unduly oppressive, but these evenings were always a trifle nostalgic
for home, and when at prayers the hymn for 'our brethren neath the

western sky' was invariably chosen, slight melancholy prevailed. After prayers the older girls in each house had a monitors' meeting in the house-mistress' sitting room when the problems and projects of the house were discussed with considerable animation, and the girls given an opportunity to air their views as to future policy and plans.

X

Public Service

IN THE PARISH CHURCH of High Wycombe there is a
stained glass window, designed by Caroline Townsend, a
St. Leonards Senior, given by Jane Frances Dove and dedicated
on Ascension Day 1923 to the memory of 'The Ministry of Women
to their fellows through God'. This window contains portraits of
Florence Nightingale, Elizabeth Fry, Emily Davies and many other
famous women. Jane Frances Dove could well have found a place
amongst them herself for, in addition to her great work in her own
schools, she never ceased to make her contribution to the many
other causes which she considered of primary importance. First of
these came the Church. As she impressed upon the girls in her
schools that the Parish Church should be the focal point in every
community, that it should always have the priority in their obligations and everything connected with it be loyally supported, so she
herself was always ready to give generous help to the needs of the
moment, both in money and work.

When the school was founded, though High Wycombe was the
centre of the chair-making industry which had flourished for so
long amongst the beech-woods of Buckinghamshire, it was still a
quiet country town. But as time went on it became increasingly
industrial, with a corresponding growth of the population. There
was consequently a need for a new church and for more schools for
the local children, and Miss Dove of course felt that these must be
Church Schools. She was a prime mover in raising funds for the
building of St. John's Church in Desborough Road and of a new
Church of England School, Loakes Park. For these purposes she
cast her net far and wide, and never hesitated to meet urgent needs
out of her own pocket. At a later date she contributed generously
towards the cost of the creation of the Suffragan Bishopric in the
diocese of Oxford.

Miss Dove always took a keen and active interest in the wider current movements of the church, such as the Life and Liberty movement and the development of the church in South India. Her churchmanship was however always broad and tolerant (described by Lady Airlie, a member of her Council as 'moderate and sound') and was not linked to any particular section or party.

At St. Leonards, after her upbringing in an English vicarage, she was perhaps a little irked at the predominance of Presbyterianism in that interdenominational school, though this did not affect the happy relations with Scottish friends. When she came South she had no doubt that she wished the new school to be Church of England, and after various alarums and excursions amongst her supporters, carried her point and collected numerous clerics and four Bishops in her list of patrons, though this also included prominent members of the Scottish church and Professor Lewis Campbell as a Vice-President of the Council.

In addition to her interest in the social and missionary work of her school Miss Dove was personally very active in promoting schemes to meet the needs of the town of High Wycombe. In 1906 she inaugurated the Central Aid Society. This undertook welfare work of all kinds in the days before the various agencies for health and assistance, now taken for granted, had ever been thought of. Subsequent off-shoots were a branch of the Invalid Children's Society, the Workhouse Girls Aid Committee (Moral Welfare), the Children's Care Committee, an Infant Welfare Centre, a tuberculosis dispensary and many other enterprises. The first secretary of the Central Aid Society, Miss Read, on her retirement after thirty-two years successful work, acknowledged how great was her debt 'to the inspiration and support of Miss Dove, to whose energy and foresight so many developments were due'. Miss Dove was also a governor of the High Wycombe Royal Grammar School, of the Technical Institute and of the High Wycombe Grammar School for Girls. In 1905 she invited the teachers from all grades of schools in the town to a series of monthly 'conversations' at the Abbey to discuss informally the various aspects of education and to exchange views. She herself inauguarated the series with a paper on 'Character.'

Though a convinced supporter of the Suffrage movement Miss Dove never became involved in party politics, but she played a

vii) In Big School 1902

viii) 1962 (*reproduced by courtesy of the Associated Press Ltd*)

prominent part in municipal affairs. She was the first woman to be elected to the Town Council of High Wycombe and in 1908 was nominated to the Mayoralty. Before the actual election day she was hailed throughout the national press as the first woman mayor in England, so it was a bitter blow when finally she was defeated by only two votes, through the eleventh hour intrigues of a minority. There was great disappointment in the Borough, where she had headed the poll at the recent council election and where her nomination was popular. She herself remarked, 'I did not seek the honour, it was thrust upon me and some of those who thrust it upon me voted against me'. This fact must undoubtedly have caused her pain and chagrin but she showed no bitterness or resentment and continued her municipal work with undiminished energy and courage. After serving on the Council for several more years, in 1921 she presented the Mayor with a beautiful silver gavel as a memento of her association with the Borough, and wrote:

20th January, 1921

Dear Mr. Mayor,

I hope you will kindly accept on behalf of the Corporation this small gift of a silver gavel as a memento of the happy days I have spent among you. I should like to take this opportunity of expressing my great appreciation of the kindness and courtesy I experienced at the hand of every Mayor and every Chairman under whom I served, and especially from the Town Clerk, the Borough Surveyor and other officials of the Council.

I am Mr. Mayor, Yours faithfully

J. F. Dove

His Worship the Mayor of Chepping Wycombe

After her defeat at the mayoral election a writer in the '*Daily Mail*' of 25th October, 1908 paid tribute to her in the following words:

'Miss Dove is one of those women who have an air of quick influence and decision, who never need as the phrase goes to 'exert their authority' because they impress everybody without exertion as possessors of unusual strength of character. Her silvery hair surmounts a still young face, a face lit up by keen kindly eyes. She speaks with perfect self-command in public as well as in private, quietly, sincerely, modestly, yet with the distinction which comes of a well stored and widely interested mind. 'I need hardly tell you', she said, 'that I am in favour of women taking their part in public life. Men's work and women's work are to my mind complementary. The one is incomplete without the other. It is a pity that women have not yet, taken in the mass, realised their responsibilities more keenly. A great many do not take advantage, for instance, of the municipal vote. When they have 'found them-selves' and have got the parliamentary suffrage as well, they will I feel sure exercise a very wholesome influence on the course of events. There are many ways in which a woman can do good and useful work on a Town Council. I have served on the committees which have to do with health and the hospital and with the free library .The former especially offers scope for a woman's activity'. At the time of her death in 1942 no other woman had been elected to the High Wycombe Town Council, so she remained a solitary pioneer for a very long time.

When she resigned from her post as Head Mistress of Wycombe Abbey School, Miss Dove bought a house in the country at Little Kimble near Wendover, Buckinghamshire, where she planned to open a school for small children, using Montessori methods. This plan did not materialise but she continued her public work in High Wycombe and after a time returned to live in the town. She also became immersed in the work of the County Education Committee and in Diocesan affairs. In 1921 she was appointed a Justice of the Peace for the County. In order to facilitate transport to her many committee meetings she brought a motorcar which she learned to drive at the age of 72, causing her friends many anxious moments. Before this she had always ridden a tricycle. Her sister Ursula once described how she shivered in a taxi behind her as she pedalled from Paddington to Liverpool Street Station.

In 1928 she became a Dame Commander of the Order of the British Empire. She accepted this honour with the personal humility which was hers in spite of her dominant personality, but it gave her great satisfaction. She felt that it came direct from her sovereign and was a recognition by him of the importance of the work with which she was associated. By a strange coincidence Adeline, Duchess of Bedford, who had caused Miss Dove so much anxiety at the founding of the school, when she finally declined to be its first president, was the only other Dame Commander to be invested on the same day. She greeted Miss Dove with cordiality and said, amongst other things, 'you were always so kind'. Miss Dove firmly replied, 'I am sure I was never kind'. A recipient of the Royal Victorian Order at the same investiture was Sir Edward Elgar. In her account of the ceremony Dame Frances says, 'I felt quite overwhelmed . . . The chief impression left upon my mind was that all in the Palace from the highest to the lowest were imbued with a spirit of quiet dignity and willing service, surely an inspiring example for us all'.

XI

Legend and Legacy

THE PORTRAIT OF FRANCES DOVE, painted by Sir William Richmond in 1904, and now hanging in the Dove Memorial Library at Wycombe Abbey, gives the impression of a somewhat forbidding and aloof personality. With her white hair dressed high, her elegant lace fichu and silk dress, and her rather severe expression she appears essentially as the founder and the pioneer whose single-minded pursuit of her ideals brooked no opposition, and who carried all relentlessly before her. This side of her character is the source of much legend and many anecdotes. There is the story of the father of a St. Leonards girl who requested that she might be permitted to return to school a day late so that she might attend a function in the town of which he was Mayor. The telegraphed reply from the Head Mistress was 'Now or Never'. The father dared to answer 'Never' and this episode has passed into school history as typical of Miss Dove at that time. Another incident of a different kind was related by one of the earliest members of her music staff who was in charge of the orchestra at Wycombe. With some difficulty she persuaded Miss Dove to allow her to purchase some drums. The next concert at the school happened to be given by a string quartette. At the first interval the Head Mistress summoned the music mistress to her, and in her deep voice was heard to ask, 'And *where* are the drums? They were very expensive'. Many other similar stories were current about her, some true, others doubtless merely '*ben trovato*', yet all tinged with respect and a certain amount of amused and affectionate awe.

Her generosity was rare and unlimited but she did not brook abuse of it. When the United Girls Schools Mission was struggling into existence she unhesitatingly gave a donation of £300 to buy a much-needed Mission Hall, but when a higher price than originally stipulated had been paid without consulting her, she did not hesitate

69

to protest at her consent being taken for granted and went so far as to say, 'I do not consider that I am being fairly treated'. Her far-seeing and constructive mind made her impatient of any plans which she considered impracticable or lacking in foresight. In a printed letter to all members of the committee she said, 'I am very anxious about the new Settlement. From what I can hear Miss X is better at arousing enthusiasm than in making use of it'. She then gave a most lucid and practical outline of the principles on which the new enterprise should be based and of the allocation of the various duties of the staff. She was, as a rule, an excellent judge of character and did not spare the inefficient, but once she was con-vinced of the integrity and capacity of anyone in a responsible position, she gave them unquestioning loyalty and support. At times she may have seemed dictatorial but she said of herself, 'I am but an instrument especially designed and trained maybe, as indeed we all are for our particular work, but still only an instrument and therefore no credit is due to me'.

But there are other sides to the character of Miss Dove which are equally important. One who knew her well, both as pupil and friend, wrote of her after she had retired, 'If her commanding appearance struck awe into the timid, the discovery of the tender-ness and faithful friendship concealed beneath was all the more delightful. Her greatest gift is that sympathy with young people which she retains today as fresh as ever. Hard work, simplicity of life and a generous outlook, what finer ideal could be set before youth'. This tribute reveals the gentler side of her nature which was so firmly held in reserve. She deplored any lack of control of the emotions and so was misunderstood by many who had not dis-covered that intense love and devotion and the true humility which lay beneath the somewhat stern exterior. At her schools the artistic and the sensitive did not always find a congenial place. No time was allowed to 'stand and stare'. Every moment was fully occupied and though this was doubtless the most suitable and successful system for the average normal girl, there were a few exceptions with a musical or artistic bent, who disliked games and communal life and consequently did not always fit in. But sooner or later almost every-one discovered the kindness and consideration which any real trouble brought to light, and came to appreciate the aesthetic sense which found expression in gracious surroundings and appropriate accessories.

Not only was it deemed necessary to hold emotions firmly under control but there were tacit taboos which were accepted without question. In fact most girls were too busy to realise that they even existed. Sex was scarcely mentioned and though marriage was accepted as the probable goal of a girls' existence and the domestic virtues were fully appreciated, contemporary school affairs during school days filled most girls' minds. Social distinctions and home backgrounds were very rarely discussed. The austerity governing the life of the Head Mistress somehow came to be accepted as the normal for everyone in the school. After holidays there was perhaps a little innocent boasting of the joys of dances or of trips abroad, but it did not occur to anyone to calculate the wealth or influence of their friends' families or their social position or lack of it.

Another aspect, which some mothers deplored, was the lack of interest in clothes and personal appearance at Wycombe in its early days. The girls lived in dark blue gym suits most of the time, though they changed into dresses of their own choice for evenings and on Sundays. These gym suits were of the plainest and most unattractive variety and the underwear of the most massive kind; six high-necked long-sleeved woollen combinations, followed by white combinations of cotton material, headed the list of sartorial requirements supplied to every parent. Shoes worn for games were of the thickest black leather, with heavy rubber soles, and their appearance was in no way improved by the daily washing with which aged boot-men removed the mud of the playing fields. The only time when feminine charm had any chance was on Speech Days and for concerts when the girls all appeared in white dresses and presented a really attractive ensemble.

Amongst the first girls at Wycombe and at St. Leonards, Miss Dove was fortunate in finding some with outstanding family backgrounds who brought wide horizons into the schools and helped to create a civilised atmosphere. Her refusal to tolerate the second-rate, either in people or things, led her to secure the allegiance of staff and friends of sterling quality. Through them her ideals and principles percolated into every department of her work, both in the schools and outside. Though she was an undoubted autocrat she did not subdue the people she controlled, and the gifts and characteristics of both girls and mistresses were given every opportunity to develop. She was no musician yet she arranged for concerts to be given by Fanny Davies, Joachim, Charles Hallé and other great artists, and discovered musical examinations to test the girls' gifts. Her house-tutors and house-mistresses were personalities and were given a free hand to draw out the powers of the girls in their charge. Above all, a sense of responsibility was developed in everyone. This is probably the outstanding characteristic of the ethics of her schools. The smallest girl, from the day of her arrival, was made to feel that at some given moment it might fall on her to take charge of some situation in which the welfare or reputation of her fellows was involved, and though some may have fallen by the way, few failed to respond to the trust that was put in them. This feeling became so habitual that it was carried into life after school days were over, as the records of the Seniors show.

Fifteen years after the foundation of Wycombe Abbey School Miss Dove decided that the time had come for her to retire. She wished to hand over while all was still in top gear and when there was a worthy successor of her own choice available to take her place. This was to be Miss Whitelaw, a New Zealander who had been at Girton and who went straight from College to be one of the house-tutors in the Abbey. She had returned to New Zealand to be the Head Mistress of a school there, but when Miss Dove's resignation was tendered, the Council immediately recognised her as the obvious choice for Wycombe Abbey. She agreed to return there and her great gifts carried the school through some critical years, including those of the first great war, with flying colours. She resigned in 1925 while still at the height of her powers, and another outstanding head in the person of Miss Crosthwaite was discovered by Miss Dove and appointed by the Council. In her day the estate of Daws Hill, adjoining the Abbey grounds was put up for sale by Lord Lincolnshire (formerly Lord Carrington). The Council decided to purchase it so its two hundred and seventy acres, together with an Elizabethan house and garden, were added to the policies of the school. The new hospice on the Marlow Hill was also built under the auspices of Miss Crosthwaite, and she was responsible for the school during the evacuation period in the second great war and for its restoration when the premises were handed back by the government.

Miss Crosthwaite was followed by Miss Walpole who achieved the harmonious integration into the school of the Middlesex County Council girls, following the recommendation of the Fleming Report, and also the launching of the Jubilee Appeal for £250,000 to provide the new buildings required to bring the school within the scope of modern requirements and for an endowment fund for scholarships.

Miss Walpole was succeeded by the present Head Mistress, Miss Fisher who is carrying on with marked success and striving for many new developments. So Wycombe Abbey has been fortunate in the successors to its first Head Mistress as they have seemed immediately to become part of the school, and to make no break in the continuity of its traditions, though each contributing something to bring it up to date and to prevent it from becoming static. One can imagine the benevolent eye of the Founder surveying their work with genuine satisfaction, even if not always agreeing with some details which would have been unheard of in her day.

The sister school of Benenden was founded by three members of the staff of Wycombe Abbey after Dame Frances had left the school. She gave them all possible help and encouragement in the new venture though she was not actually a member of their Council. This development was fully consonant with her own ideas when she left St. Leonards, as she said, 'to found' one or possibly two more sister schools in England.

The security of Wycombe Abbey received a severe jolt in the second world war when the whole place was requisitioned and had to be evacuated at only sixteen days' notice to become the head-quarters of the U.S.A. Air Force in Britain. This was in the year 1942, and as High Wycombe had been considered a safe place, no thought had previously been given to alternative accommodation. In fact, at the beginning of the war St. Paul's Girls School, had been evacuated from London to Wycombe Abbey, but military require-ments had relentless precedence over educational ones. At that stage of the war, all large country houses and hotels had already been taken up, so the only possible course was to close the school, and to distribute the girls into other schools who most generously opened their doors to them.

By the devotion of the Head Mistress and her staff the library and other essentials were packed up in record time and preserved, but for four long years the premises were occupied by the U.S.A. Air Force and when they were finally returned, denuded of furniture and most necessities, the school had to be re-started from the foundations. Legal compensation was quite inadequate to cover the damage sustained, and a great financial setback was experienced due to the loss of annual revenue from fees. Nevertheless within a year of the return of the Head Mistress and a nucleus of pre-war staff, the school was almost back to normal. A few girls who had been there before the exodus also came back to help to restore the life of the school and before long, though the majority of the girls were new, the upheaval was almost forgotten, the traditions of Wycombe Abbey and all that it stood for were re-established and there appeared to have been no break in its continuity. If it could survive this severe test it was surely built on a rock.

The present generation of girls live in a new world, but the fundamentals of the school do not seem to have changed. The founder might be surprised or even shocked at some of their backgrounds and points of view but she, who was always receptive to new ideas and willing to listen to progressive suggestions, would doubtless sift the gold from the dross, and would be confident that those whom she trusted would not fail her. In the prosperous Edwardian days in which she built up the school, she would not have imagined that its existence could seriously be threatened by politicians. In this she may have been mistaken, but on the other hand, if all concerned can emulate her example and courage, her faith may be justified. Her attitude was always a positive one and her simple and direct methods left no place for the negative destructive point of view. Her answer to the agnostics, both in education and religion, would have been, 'whatsoever things are true, whatsoever things are honest, whatsoever things are just, whatsoever things are pure . . . think on these things'. She would have been convinced that this concentration on the best would inevitably bring its reward. She would have echoed the words of a present-day Bishop when he says, 'We must do what we can to assist the forces that are even now gathering to cleanse corruption from our public life. This we can do not merely by negative resistance but by positive endeavour to provide for others and for ourselves occupation for mind and body which is good and wholesome'. This Frances Dove tried to do and is a task which she has left her schools to carry on.

Though Wycombe Abbey and St. Leonards were founded to give to girls the educational advantages that their brothers enjoyed, they are not mere copies of boys' schools. They are essentially independent residential schools for girls, and have evolved and are still developing curricula best suited to meet the needs of girls. It is to be hoped that parents will be able to maintain the right to choose the kind of school they consider best for their daughters, and that the girls will retain their feminine outlook without in any way losing the benefits of the education which has been so recently won for them. If these schools were to be sacrificed on the altar of uniformity the loss to future generations would be incalculable. Above all they are the homes of 'religion and sound learning'. In her old age the Founder of Wycombe Abbey School wrote this prayer, 'For all my children, O my loving Father, I beseech thy loving mercy, that thou wouldst guard them and girdle them and draw them ever nearer to Thee and use them for Thy service, for Jesus sake our Lord – Amen'. May her prayer be granted.

Bibliography

Barley, M. W.; *Lincolnshire and the Fens*. B. T. Batsford Ltd. 1952.

Beale, Dorothea,; Dove, Jane Frances,; Soulsby, Lucy; *Work and Play in Girls Schools*. Longman's Green, 1898.

Davies, Emily; *The Higher Education of Women*, Alexander Strahan, 1866.

Grant, Julia; McCutcheon, Katharine,; Sanders, Ethel; *St. Leonards School 1877-1927*. Oxford University Press, 1927.

Kamm, Josephine; *How Different from Us*. The Bodley Head, 1950.

Megson, B.; Lindsay, J.; *Girton College 1869-1959, An Informal History*. W. Heffer and Sons, Cambridge

Strachay, Ray; *The Cause*. G. Bell and Sons, 1928

Woodham-Smith, Cecil; *Life of Florence Nightingale*. Constable 1950.

Young, G. M.; *Portrait of an Age*. Oxford University Press, 1952.

St. Leonards School Gazette.

Wycombe Abbey School Gazette.

Appendix I

PROSPECTUS TO POSSIBLE SHAREHOLDERS 1896

THE GIRLS EDUCATION COMPANY LIMITED
(registered under the Companies Acts 1862 and 1890)

CAPITAL £30,000

In 3,000 shares of £10 each.

£1 per share on application.

£2 per share or the balance at the option of the Shareholder on Allotment.

£2 per share in three months after Allotment.

The balance as and when required, but no call will be payable within two months after the last preceding call was payable.

BANKERS: Lloyds Bank Ltd., 54 St. James St., London.
SOLICITORS: Messrs. Toynbee, Larken & Toynbee, Solicitors, Lincoln.
SECRETARY: (pro tem) Francis C. Larken, Cantilupe Chantry, Lincoln.
TEMPORARY OFFICES: 6 & 7 Bank Street, Lincoln.

PROSPECTUS (for Shareholders)

This Company has been formed for the purpose of founding in England a School for the education of Girls upon the model of St. Leonards School at St. Andrews, Fife; and if successful of founding other schools upon the same model.

The proposed system of education aims at doing for girls, with suitable modifications, what the existing great Public Schools do for boys; and it in no way interferes or competes with the numerous High Schools for Girls which being essentially Day Schools are conducted on different lines and provide for different requirements.

The widely felt need for Schools such as the Company propose to found is proved by the remarkable success of St. Leonards School, where the nominations of pupils are far in excess of the possible number of vacancies.

St. Leonards School is limited in numbers to about 200 girls of 14 years of age and upwards, who are distributed in Boarding Houses within or in close proximity to the school. Each House is under the control of an assistant mistress and the number of girls in each house does not exceed 25. The education given is most thorough, embracing both Classical and Modern sides; in addition Music, Drawing, Dancing and Handwork. The curriculum of the studies is sufficiently elastic to allow any girl to take up any special subject after she has attained the necessary elementary proficiency. The teaching staff is unusually large and the

79

Forms are subdivided into very small sets; and time is carefully economized so as to ensure individual attention to each girl and to avoid over-pressure. This school is undenominational. The new one to be founded, being situated in England, will be a Church of England School.

Particular care is bestowed on the physical well-being of the girls. The hours of work are shorter than in most schools; no late evening work is ever allowed and out-door exercise, games and gymnastics are studiously encouraged. No one is allowed to compete for outside examinations until near the end of her school career.

To give an account of all the success achieved by past pupils of St. Leonards would be too lengthy but the following is an abstract of some of the important honours gained by them:

A First Class Historical Tripos, 1885. A First Class Classical Tripos, 1887. M.B. London in 1890 and again in 1891. A First Class Moral Sciences Tripos in 1894 and a First Class Classical Moderations. A First Class Moral Sciences Tripos in 1895. A gradually increasing number of Higher Certificates of the Oxford and Cambridge Joint Board has been taken for some years past as also a large number of Senior grade certificates in the Examination of the Associated Board of the Royal Academy of Music and the Royal College of Music. The success of the school is however much more truly shown by the mark which it stamps upon the lives and charcters of its girls.

The Report of the Oxford and Cambridge Joint Board of August 1895 contains the following paragraph: 'St. Leonards is a model of careful and thorough organisation, and the idea of education aimed at is eminently sound and healthy. The teaching is generally bright and interesting and much good work has been done in all subjects'.

The Company are exceptionally fortunate in having offered to them the services of Miss J. F. Dove, a certified student of Girton College, Cambridge 1874 who has been connected with St. Leonards for 19 years, during 14 of which she has been its Head Mistress and to whose administrative ability, energy and devotion its success has been chiefly due. Miss Dove has voluntarily resigned her post in order that she may further the principles of education with which she has been so long identified.

It is believed that a school conducted upon the lines above mentioned is sure to be eminently successful and that it will also yield a satisfactory return upon the capital invested. Pupils will be admitted upon the nomination of shareholders, the qualification for a nomination being the possession of five shares, or in certain cases of the Council of the School.

To provide the necessary education and to carry out the intentions of the promoters the fees, will as at St. Leonards, vary from £90 to £145 per annum inclusive.

It is proposed that the dividends to be paid shall be limited to five per cent, and that the surplus profits shall from time to time be devoted towards the repayment of the Capital of the Company, and that when all capital has been repaid an application shall be made for a Royal Charter.

An examination of the balance sheets of St. Leonards shows that while the expenditure upon the school to the present time has exceeded £80,000 the average profits for the last ten years over and above the dividend of six per cent have been very little short of £1,000 per annum, and this with the school only full during the latter half of the period.

From the number of applications already received and the greater accessibility of the proposed new school, it is confidently expected that if the accommodation can be quickly enough supplied the school will fill very rapidly, and will not only pay a dividend very shortly but will speedily amass a Sinking Fund.

The Company has been offered several very excellent properties, including houses standing in their own grounds in the most healthy and beautiful parts of England with natural advantages in respect of soil, water supply and drainage, good railway access and facilities for extension as required to which the Council are giving their careful attention.

It will be seen from the list of patrons printed above that the Company will start under the most influential auspices and has every prospect of a most satisfactory and useful career.

It is expected that the school will be in working order after the next Summer Vacation and several applications for admission have already been received.

Shares for a considerable amount have already been applied for and applications for the balance of the share capital are now invited or should be made upon the enclosed form, to be paid as follows:

£1 per share on application.

£2 per share or the balance at the option of the shareholder on allotment.

£2 per share in three months after allotment.

The balance as and when required but no call will be payable within two months after the last preceding call was payable.

The liability of the Shareholder is limited to the amount of the shares held by him.

Appendix II

LIST OF PATRONS

C The Right Hon. The Dowager Countess of Airlie, 4, Lowndes Sq., S.W.

H. J. Anstruther Esq., M.P., 6 Chester Street, London, S.W.

His Excellency The Hon. Thomas F. Bayard, Ambassador of the United States, 83 Eaton Sq. S.W.

F. C. J. Wolfe Barry Esq., C.B.

The Rev. G. C. Bell, Prebendary of Sarum, Master of Marlborough College

Miss Bishop, Principal of the Royal Holloway College, Egham

The Very Rev. A. K. H. Boyd, D.D., Minister of the First Charge, St. Andrews Parish Church, St. Andrews

Sir William H. Broadbent, Bart., M.D., F.R.C.P., 84 Brook St., Grosvenor Square, London, W.

The Rt. Hon. James Boyce, M.P., 54 Portland Place, London.

C The Rev. H. M. Burge, M.A., Fellow, Tutor and Dean of University College, Oxford

C The Very Rev. H. Montagu Butler, D.D., Master of Trinity College, Cambridge

C Mrs. H. Montagu Butler, Trinity Lodge, Cambridge

C Arthur J. Butler Esq., M.A., Formerly Fellow of Trinity College, Cambridge; Wood End, Weybridge

C Sir Guy Campbell Bart., Palace Gate Mansions, Palace Gate, Kensington, W.

C Lady Campbell, Palace Gate Mansions, Palace Gate, Kensington, W.

C The Rev. Professor Lewis Campbell, M.A., LL.D., Honorary Fellow of Balliol College, Oxford, and Chairman of the Council of St. Leonards School

C Mrs. Lewis Campbell, 35 Kensington Court Mansions, London W.

Edward Caird Esq., D.C.L., LL.D., Master of Balliol College, Oxford

Mrs. Boyd Carpenter, The Palace, Ripon

C The Rev. F. E. Carter, Tait Missioner, Canterbury

Henry Craik Esq., C.B., LL.D., Dover House, Whitehall, S.W.

James Cropper Esq., Ellergreen, Kendal

C The Rev. William Cunningham, D.D., Fellow and Lecturer of Trinity College, Cambridge. Hon. Fellow of Caius College and Vicar of Great St. Mary's

The Rev. C. Darnell, M.A., Cargilfield, Trinity, Edinburgh

Miss Emily Davies, Hon. Sec. of Girton College, Cambridge, 12 York Street, W.

The Rev. J. Llewellyn Davies, Chaplain in Ordinary to The Queen, The Vicarage, Kirkby Londsale

T. W. Dunn Esq., M.A., Head Master of Bath College

The Rev. W. Moore Ede, Hon. Canon of Durham; Huldean Lecturer 1895; The Rectory, Gateshead-on-Tyne

Mrs. Henry Fawcett, 2 Gower Street, London, W.C.

The Lady Helen Munro Ferguson, Raith, Kirkcaldy

J. Martineau Fletcher Esq., Barrister-at-Law, formerly Fellow of Caius College, Cambridge; 9 Stanhope St. W.

C Sir J. Walter Foster, M.D., D.C.L., M.P., 11 George St., Hanover Sq.

Mrs. Douglas Freshfield, 1 Airlie Gardens, Campden Hill, W.

Sir Ludovic Grant, Bart., Regius Professor of Public Law, University of Edinburgh

The Rev. C. E. Graves, Fellow and Tutor of St. John's College, Cambridge

The Very Rev. Robt. Gregory, D.D., Dean of St. Paul's, London

Miss Grove, The College Hall, Byng Place, W.C.

The Rev. W. A. Heard, M.A., Head Master of Fettes College, Edinburgh

Christopher Heath Esq., F.R.C.S., President, Royal College of Surgeons, 36 Cavendish Sq., W.

Sir George M. Humphrey, M.D., F.R.S., Grove Lodge, Cambridge

The Rev. H. A. James, D.D., Head Master of Rugby School

The Rev. W. Jones, Hon. Canon of Carlisle, Burnside Parsonage, Kendal

Sir Courtenay Ilbert, K.C.S.I., C.I.E., 67 Gloucester Place, Portman Sq., W.1.

Lady Ilbert, 67 Gloucester Place, Portman Sq., W.1.

Miss M. G. Kennedy, Hon. Secretary of Newnham College, Shenstone, Cambridge

Lieut. Col. Edgar Kensington, R.A., 5 St. Aubyn's, West Brighton

C Miss F. Kensington, Secretary and Bursar of Girton College, 89 Gloucester Terrace, Hyde Park, W.

Theodore Kensington Esq., M.A., Culver House, Winchester

William A. Knight Esq., LL.D., Professor of Moral Philosophy, University of St. Andrews

The Right Rev. The Lord Bishop of Lincoln

C. S. Loch, Esq., Secretary of the C.O.S., 40 Queen Anne's Gardens, Bedford Park

William Logan Esq., The Priory, St. Andrews

C The Hon. and Rev. Edward Lyttleton, Hon. Canon of St. Albans, Hertford. Master of Haileybury College

Mrs. Mactier, Kinnessburn, St. Andrews

Miss Maitland, Principal of Somerville College, Oxford

G. C. Martin Esq., Mus. Doc., Organist of St. Paul's Cathedral

C Mrs. Edward Micholls, 18 Airlie Gardens, Campden Hill, W.

J. W. Moir Esq., M.D., Medical Officer, St. Leonards School

Mrs. J. W. Moir, Chattan House, St. Andrews

T. T. Oliphant Esq., Queen Mary's, St. Andrews

Colonel G. E. O'Malley, C.R.A., Shorncliffe

The Rev. I. G. Owen, M.A., Rector of St. Andrews Church, St. Andrews

The Very Rev. Francis Paget, D.D., Dean of Christ Church, Oxford

Miss Penrose, Principal of Bedford College, London

The Right Hon. Lord Playfair of St. Andrews, 68 Onslow Gardens, South Kensington

W. S. Playfair Esq., M.D., LL.D., 31 George St., Hanover Sq., W.

The Rev. Bartholomew Price D.D., Master of Pembroke College, Oxford and Canon of Gloucester

Mrs. T. Purdie, 14 South St., St. Andrews

Sir James H. Ramsay, Bart., of Banff, Alyth

The Rev. J. H. Rawdon, Canon of Manchester, The Vicarage, Preston

The Rev. S. Harvey Reynolds, M.A., formerly Fellow and Tutor of Brasenose, Oxford

Mrs. Richmond Ritchie, The End House, Berkeley Place, Wimbledon

The Right Rev. The Lord Bishop of Ripon

Briton Riviere Esq., R.A., Flaxley, 82 Finchley Road, London, N.W.

The Right Rev. The Lord Bishop of Rochester

The Rev. Mathew Rodger, D.D., Minister of St. Leonards Parish, St. Andrews

Mrs. Rodger, Soyth Court, St. Andrews

Joseph Ruston Esq., Monks Manor, Lincoln

Lady Scott-Moncrieff, 11 Cheyne Walk, London, S.W.

The Rev. John H. Skrine, M.A., formerly Fellow of Merton College, Oxford; Warden of Trinity College; Glenalmond, Perthsire

Francis Storr Esq., B.A., Chief Master of Modern Subjects at Merchant Taylors' School, 40 Mecklenburgh Sq., W.C.

The Rev. John S. Thomas, M.A., The Bursar, Marlborough College

Lieut. Col. J. E. Thomson, 49 South Street, St. Andrews

Mrs. A. W. Verral ,5 Selwyn Gardens, Cambridge

C   Miss Wakefield, 28 Cork St. W.1

C   Miss J. H. Walker, M.D., Physician to the New Hospital for Women, 62 Gower St., W.C.

Miss Welch, Mistress of Girton College, Cambridge

The Rev. J. Stewart Wilson, D.D., New Abbey House, Dumfries

The Right Rev. The Lord Bishop of Winchester

Miss Wordsworth, Principal of Lady Margaret Hall, Oxford

C   denotes members of the Council

Appendix III

PROSPECTUS OF
WYCOMBE ABBEY SCHOOL
BUCKINGHAMSHIRE
Head Mistress: MISS DOVE
Address (until August)
c/o LLOYDS BANK LIMITED
54 St. James Street, London, S.W.

COUNCIL

President
The Very Reverend H. MONTAGU BUTLER, D.D.
Master of Trinity College, Cambridge

Vice-President
The Reverend LEWIS CAMPBELL
Emeritus Professor of Greek, St. Andrews University

Members
The Dowager Countess of Airlie
J. Wolfe Barry Esq., C.B., F.R.S.
H. M. Burge, Esq., M.A.
Mrs. Montagu Butler
Arthur J. Butler, Esq., M.A.
Lady Campbell
Mrs. Lewis Campbell
Rev. F. E. Carter
Rev. W. Cunningham, D.D.
Sir Walter Foster, M.D., D.C.L., M.P.
Miss F. Kensington
The Rev. Honourable E. Lyttelton
Mrs. Edward Micholls
The Right Rev. The Lord Bishop of Ripon
Miss Wakefield
Miss J. H. Walker, M.D.

Bankers
LLOYDS BANK LIMITED
54 St. James Street, London, S.W.

SOLICITORS
Messrs. TOYNBEE, LARKEN and TOYNBEE, Lincoln

TREASURER
Francis R. Larken, Cantilupe Chantry, Lincoln

TEMPORARY OFFICES
6 & 7, Bank Street, Lincoln

HEAD MISTRESS
Miss DOVE, Certificated Student of Girton College, Cambridge, 1874;
for fourteen years Head Mistress of St. Leonards School, St. Andrews, Fife

ASSISTANT MISTRESS
Miss A. R. BURNE, Certificated Student in Honours of
Girton College, Cambridge, 1884
Other Mistresses will shortly be appointed

PROSPECTUS

HIGH WYCOMBE is a pleasant town among the Chalk Downs and Beech Woods of Buckinghamshire, thirty miles from London on the Maidenhead and Oxford Branch of the Great Western Railway. Wycombe Abbey is on the outskirts of the town; it is a large and commodious building situated within its own beautiful grounds of thirty acres, and has been most favourably reported on, both as to position and arrangements, by Dr. W. H. Corfield, Professor of Hygiene in University College, London. The Abbey is large enough to accommodate the Head Mistress, and some of her Assistants, and about a hundred girls. For this purpose it will be divided into four Houses. Each House will be under a House mistress and will have its own sitting rooms and dormitories and tables in the Dining Hall, but all will be under the immediate superintendence of the Head Mistress.

A Gymnasium and Workshop will be among the first necessaries to be provided, and the buildings already include a Hall 120 feet long with a floor properly laid for dancing.

The grounds include a lake, an avenue of limes, other fine trees, an extensive tennis lawn and abundant space for cricket pitches, hockey grounds, and a golf course.

The School is intended to provide for girls an education which, while moderate in cost and especially adapted to their requirements, shall be as complete on all its sides as that given to boys at the great Public Schools.

The number of girls in the School is intended to be two hundred.

The subjects of instruction will be Scripture Knowledge, Arithmetic, Literature, History, Latin or German, French, Physiography or Harmony, Gymnastics, and Part Singing. The different branches of Mathematics and Natural Science, Greek or German, and Italian will be gradually added.

The hours of study will be strictly limited, and a good deal of valuable training will be given through the medium of handwork.

88

The girls will attend the Parish Church of High Wycombe, and religious instruction will be given by the Head Mistress.

The School will open on 23rd September. Applications for admission must be made to the Head Mistress, who will supply all information and the requisite forms. Preference will be given to those who wish to enter at the beginning of the School year in September.

Girls desiring to enter are expected to show by means of an examination, which may be conducted in their own homes, that they have an adequate knowledge of:

ENGLISH – Grammar and Elementary Analysis

LATIN – All the Declensions and the Active Voice of the Regular Verbs

FRENCH – Elementary Grammar, including Regular Verbs

ARITHMETIC – The Simple and Compound Rules, Factors and Vulgar Fractions. Also Political Geography and General Information. They must write a neat, clear hand, and be able to read distinctly and with expression, and to spell correctly. Special excellence in other subjects may under certain circumstances exempt from Latin.

The above Examination should easily be passed by girls of thirteen or fourteen, and will, to begin with, be used chiefly for the purposes of classification.

Girls are admitted on the Nomination of a Shareholder, with the sanction of the Council. A girl whose parent is unable to obtain a Shareholder's Nomination may be nominated by the Council, and pay an Entrance Fee of £10.

The School year is divided into three Terms of twelve weeks each, beginning about the last week in September, the middle of January, and the first week in May.

The Holidays consist of sixteen weeks in the year – usually four weeks at Christmas, three weeks in April, and about two months in Summer.

The School will be examined every July by the Oxford and Cambridge Schools Examination Board.

FEES PER TERM (payable in advance)

For Girls who enter under 15 years of age	£32
For Girls who enter over 15 years of age	£38

A small sum is charged for Concerts and School Entertainments.

EXTRA SUBJECTS. Fees per term

Piano	£2 2 0 to £4 4 0
Singing	£3 3 0
Violin	£3 3 0
Drawing	£2 2 0
Dancing by a Pupil of Mrs. Henry Wordsworth	£1 10 0

THE GIRLS' EDUCATION COMPANY, (Limited)
May 1896

Appendix IV

SPEECHES ON THE PRESENTATION OF THE PORTRAIT
BY SIR WILLIAM RICHMOND, NOVEMBER 1904

Dr. Burge . . . presenting the portrait said:
'It was no exaggeration to say that Miss Dove represented to them and to all those who were to come after all that they most admired and esteemed in that movement of modern chivalry' (the women's movement). 'Not only did she represent it but Miss Dove herself had inspired much of it with loftier and more refined thoughts which in after days would bear fruit beyond their calculations. However much they might honour Miss Dove for the place she filled in their public life in their own time, still more did they value her *personal friendship*. That personal friendship had been bestowed on many people without sparing herself, without thought of herself wherever and whenever she thought she could help in word or deed, by precept or by example'.

Miss Dove said:
'Dr. Burge, Members of the Council and Shareholders, Mistresses, Seniors and Girls of these Schools. How can I thank you for the beautiful picture you have given me of which I gratefully take possession to be handed down as a precious heirloom in this school. I can speak thus because I am able to stand outside and say much as Richard Baxter did when he had finished his thousand or so books, 'I am but a pen in the hand of God and what praise is due to a pen'. I am but an instrument specially designed and trained maybe, as indeed we all are for our particular work, but still only an instrument and therefore no credit is due to me. Well, with the picture hanging before you, you may like to know something of its subject. She was born before the end of the first half of the last century, just at the time when women's education was at its very lowest ebb. Her education began at home and was carried on chiefly alone with her brothers except for the visit of a Master twice a week who taught them Hebrew and German. At that time there was a Home for Governesses in Harley Street and Frederick Denison Maurice was a Professor at King's College. Professor Maurice became interested in the struggles of the governesses to obtain teaching for themselves, and as a result Queen's College was founded in 1848 on the model of King's College, and so the stone was set rolling which has resulted in the whole present system of Schools and Colleges for women and must culminate sooner or later in obtaining for them the rights of citizenship, the bestowal of the franchise. At Queen's College Miss Beale, who is still Principal of the Ladies' College, Cheltenham, and Miss Buss, the noble and beloved founder of the North London Collegiate School, received some of their early impetus. These two schools became the models upon which most of the present High Schools were founded. The subject of the picture was brought up

in London and knew, as a child, many of the now famous men who did so much to help girls. She was a student at Queen's College for nearly three years but at the age of fifteen went with her family into the country and was left entirely to her own devices, without any instruction, and little diversion other than watering the cabbages and looking forward to the return of the boys for the holidays. After about two years of this apparent waste of precious time, she demanded to be sent to school and received the answer, 'I do not know of a school fit to send a girl to' and then arose the first vision of a St. Leonards and a Wycombe – dim perhaps in its outlines, but quite decided in the fact that a school at least there should be at which lonely country girls could gain the same advantages of intellectual stimulus and the inspiration of noble ideals of life as the brothers did at their schools. As the result of her request, she went to one of the real old-fashioned boarding schools, which was distinctly better than nothing, and moreover helped the formation of the ideal by showing *everything that a school ought not to be*, and this accounts for the fact that her blood still boils whenever she hears of a girl being sent to school for one year 'to be finished'. On her return home her life became a very busy one, as she undertook the instruction of the younger members of the family all the morning (she was the eldest of ten) and made them clothes all the rest of the day; with the aid of a ruler, a pencil and a sewing machine even accomplishing coats and waistcoats; playing the harmonium in church, training the choir, teaching in the Sunday School, and parochial visiting done when it was too dark to see to stitch, with many another odd end filled up the years until one day her father returned from London full of all he had heard of the new College for Women, lately started, in October 1869 by Miss Emily Davies. 'The Mother of our Colleges to be'. The College papers arrived on Saturday night, her decision was soon made; her mother most nobly took over the stitching and teaching and on Monday morning she shut herself up to do what was possible alone almost unaided to prepare for the Entrance Examination. After sixteen weeks she went to stay with old friends, one of whom is now present, succeeded in passing the Entrance Examination and in due course, October 1871 entered the College. Only ten students had entered before her, and there she worked, enjoying to the full the grand new vistas it opened out. She knew no Greek, but plunged cheerfully headlong into Plato and there she might have been plunging still had not Miss Lumsden, one of the first students, who was at that time working for her own Tripos, taken her in hand and led her gently along until Part I of the Little-Go was safely passed First Class. Those were stirring times! She remembers the rejoicings at Hitchin as the earliest students passed first their Little-Go and then underwent the new and untried ordeal of a Tripos; never to be forgotten in College song as 'The Girton Pioneers'. She and two others were the first ladies ever privileged to attend a University Lecture, and she well remembers the quiet smile that passed over the face of the Professor as they entered and took their places quietly behind the undergraduates. From those same Professors and the undergraduates this was the beginning of much unvarying kindness. Then in October 1873 the College re-assembled in the new buildings at Girton. The subject of your picture, having only come from Lincolnshire, happened to be the very first to be set down among the empty cement barrels, the heaps of bricks and mortar and tiles and shavings and builder's rubbish generally that surrounded the new building. With much surprise she picked her way in and found that the first floor was just habitable, though there were neither windows nor doors on the ground floor and the workmen barricaded them in every night before they went home. The first day was spent in cleaning the College windows! After that, undaunted by such little incidents as cold dinners with potatoes cooked over the Classical (now the Combination) room fire, and with the joy of college life undimmed, she settled down to the trigonometry and mechanics that you girls do at school and finished the additional subjects with the carpenters hammering up the door-posts in the corridor outside. Nothing then stood in the way of her work in science and she finally took the Natural Sciences Tripos and earned the Ordinary Degree in December 1874. There had been no time to think what was to come after. She had said many times that in some way the beautiful College life should be justified but whatever was to come after it should not be teaching! That last term a new student from Cheltenham having ascertained that she was free, quietly wrote to Miss Beale to tell her that she had found exactly the right person she wanted. This led, though she was still a Questionist, to a kind offer from Miss Beale which was promptly accepted. In January she set off for Cheltenham, with a £10 note in her pocket, the last she had to demand from the family exchequer. The same kind friend had found her a lodging and then began the new and entrancing career for the Science Mistress. During the Easter holidays she persuaded her family to entrust her with the care of her former charges, two sisters and a brother, and carried them off with her to school at Cheltenham, and in 1877 became a member of Miss Lumsden's staff at the opening of what is now St. Leonards School, St. Andrews. In January 1879, having amassed the magnificent capital of £79 she opened the first assistant mistress's house and in 1882 was honoured by the Council by being asked to become Head Mistress. After fourteen years in that capacity she made a great venture of faith in leaving St. Andrews and setting forth in the hope of founding a school in England. Friends rallied round and you see the result. These all strove not that you girls should cease to lead the strenuous life, but that you should have the advantage of starting from a higher plane and that you and all the succeeding generations of St. Andrews and Wycombe girls may become more perfect instruments meet for the Master's use. That is what the picture means for you. For myself it is the symbol of all the gathered-up lore of my many hundreds of children, colleagues and friends whose devotion has made it possible to do whatever has been done; the Artist with consummate skill has made it represent what I still 'thro' time' hope to become, one who is gentle, calm, dignified and refined. I cannot be too thankful that the Committee arranged to put me into the hands of such a kindly and supreme master of his art as Sir William Richmond'.

Appendix V

June 1905. Speech Day at Wycombe Abbey.

'. . . . Sometimes it is not supposed by parents that we really care much what happens to the girls after they leave us. Let me assure you that we do care very much indeed. Every girl who has been here in this school, we feel the keenest interest in, and whatever happens to them in after life is a matter of the greatest interest to us; and one of the objects of our existence is that we may do what you will permit us to do to help forward the interests of the girls in every possible way. I do not think that any Senior has ever appealed to me without my doing what has lain in my power to render her assistance if she needed it. To see these young people growing up as youthful members of society is the keenest pleasure we have. Of course, the work of the Mistresses in a school like this which is very isolated in a way – I mean the Mistresses are cut off very much from their own families and friends and they have comparatively few interests outside their school work – constitutes a hard life. I do not say that it is too hard, and knowing that the parents appreciate the work that they endeavour to do for their children is the greatest assistance to them',

20th November, 1907. Extract from address on 'Religious Education in Secondary Schools', Ruri-Decanal Conference. W. A. Gazette, Vol. III No. 10. Feb. 1908.

'Now in what do the corporate virtues consist; what is their basis? Surely if we consult the laws of the Kingdom we shall find that they include all those principles by which our actions towards others are regulated and together with our duty towards God and to ourselves, make up the whole duty of man . . . Let us then always remember that religion is not so much a subject to be taught as a life to be lived'.

The Creation of a University System

The Creation of
a University System

Edited by
MICHAEL SHATTOCK

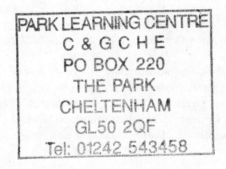
Blackwell Publishers Ltd

Copyright © Blackwell Publishers Ltd.

ISBN 0–631–20300–1

First published 1996

Blackwell Publishers
108 Cowley Road, Oxford, OX4 1JF, UK.

and
238 Main Street
Cambridge, MA. 02142, USA.

British Library Cataloguing in Publication Data

A catalogue record for this book is available from the British Library.

Library of Congress Cataloging in Publication Data

Cataloging in Publication data applied for.

Typeset by Cambrian Typesetters, Frimley, Surrey
Printed in Great Britain by Whitstable Litho, Kent.

Contents

Part Two: Robbins and After

Part Three: The Assertion of State Control

Preface

Michael Shattock

The first issue of the *Universities Quarterly* was published in November 1946. Its editor and founder was Ernest Simon, later Lord Simon of Wythenshawe, a Manchester industrialist who was Chairman of the Council of the University of Manchester from 1941 to 1957. From the beginning the *Quarterly* sought to identify itself with the important policy questions affecting universities, and the first issue contained welcoming articles from the Chancellor of the Exchequer, Hugh Dalton, reflecting the fact that the University Grants Committee (UGC) was formally answerable direct to the Treasury, and by his predecessor as Chancellor in the Coalition Government, Sir John Anderson. The launch capitalised on the sense of new opportunities opening up within the universities and society after the war years and the universities' contribution to creating them, and was so successful that the second issue carried an apology for printing only 2,000 copies owing to severe restrictions in the supply of paper, and a promise of a longer print run in future. The *Quarterly*'s first publisher was the Turnstile Press, of which Simon was chairman, which also published the *New Statesman*.

When he ceased to be editor Simon became chairman of the *Quarterly*'s editorial board only relinquishing that office in 1960. The *Quarterly*'s status was emphasised by the representative character of its editorial board with reserved seats for Oxford and Cambridge, London and the 'Modern Universities' and for universities in Scotland, Wales and Northern Ireland. Boris Ford, when he took over the editorship in 1956, rightly described the membership as 'formidable' (*New Universities Quarterly* 1986). Its combination of academic prestige (Blackett, Bragg, Bowra, Bonamy Dobrée and Tawney) and university leadership (Morris, Vice-Chancellor of Leeds, James – Southampton, Stopford – Manchester, Hetherington – Glasgow, Evans – Bangor, Fulton – Swansea (later Sussex) and Ashby – Belfast (later Cambridge)) meant that its influence on particular issues extended well beyond the pages of the *Quarterly*. Ford's immediate predecessor as editor, Charles Morris, later succeeded Simon as chairman of the board and served until 1967.

Boris Ford served as editor from 1956 to 1986, during which the
Quarterly changed its role and title from time to time. In 1968 it adopted a
subtitle 'Higher Education and Society', and in 1975 it became the *New
Universities Quarterly*, with a new subtitle, 'Culture, Education and
Society'. It dropped the *'New'* in 1982, reverting to its original title of the
Universities Quarterly but retaining the subtitle. During Ford's editorship
the journal hosted five Gulbenkian Discussions:

1960 New and Larger Universities,
1961 Intellectual Responsibilities and the Pattern of Higher Education,
1962 Research into Higher Education,
1963 Attention to Graduates,
1964 Changing Patterns of Study,

which were influential in the re-formation of higher education in the
Robbins era.

In 1986 Boris Ford stood down and I was invited by Blackwells, who by
this time had become the publisher, to succeed him. I was honoured to do
so and proposed a number of changes which have persisted over the last
decade. The name of the journal became the *Higher Education Quarterly*,
to indicate a formal broadening of its scope and recognise the growth in
importance to higher education of the polytechnics and the colleges of
higher education. The editorial arrangements were altered so that I
became General Editor and four people, Clive Booth, Lesley Wagner,
Gareth Williams and myself, became joint editors, each responsible for
one issue a year. Over this period Clive Booth and Lesley Wagner
relinquished their positions and were replaced by Peter Wright and
Malcolm Tight, but in accordance with past precedent Clive Booth has
become chairman of the editorial board. A further important change
occurred in 1986 when Blackwells agreed to the journal becoming the
responsibility of the Society for Research in Higher Education.

The changes of 1986 also brought with them a refocusing of the
Quarterly's remit. We put to one side the broader cultural and social
concerns of the *Universities Quarterly* in its latter years and took the journal
back to its initial concentration on the development of British higher
education policy. As such I believe we can justly claim to have made it the
primary journal in the field with a wide international as well as British
subscriber list. And the British list includes the main agencies for policy
formation, the Funding Councils, the Research Councils, government
departments and, of course, the policy community in higher education
itself.

The *Quarterly* is the oldest higher education journal in continuous publication. Throughout its 50-year life it has published important articles on policy issues, perhaps particularly on the issues of structure, size and resourcing of higher education. Its volumes are a treasure trove for historians of the development of higher education and for the policy-makers of the future. What this 50th anniversary volume seeks to do, through a selection of important and influential articles, is to trace the creation of a British higher education system from a small untidy post-war collection of university institutions containing no more than 51,600 students to the highly structured state-run higher education system of today with its 1.5 million students. If there is one conclusion to be drawn from this selection it is that neither Government nor the representative bodies of higher education themselves have given sufficient priority to policy analysis and in consequence we have failed, except haphazardly, to shape the future in any coherent way. The crisis that British higher education finds itself in today has been a long time in the making, but this selection of articles charts all too clearly the steps on that road and the inability of policy-makers to recognise them. There are lessons in that for the Dearing Committee and for the rest of us as we wrestle with the problems of higher education in the next century.

The Creation of the British University System

Michael Shattock

'There is no university "system" in Britain'

Fifty years ago, with the conclusion of the Second World War, the arrival of the 1945 Labour Government and the opening of the universities to demobilised ex-servicemen, a very different atmosphere prevailed from that of today. As the first article, by Simon, makes clear, the universities were facing an optimistic future; they were highly regarded by Government and their objectives seemed to match in every way the aspirations of the nation. A succession of government reports (Goodenough 1944, McNair 1944, Barlow 1946 and Clapham 1946) charted the course of development; the UGC was reformed and made into a more professional body to manage the university transformation required, and the universities, as described in 'A Historical Document: The Statement by the Committee of Vice-Chancellors and Principals' (CVCP) (pages 44 to 46), committed themselves to 'playing their own part in the co-operative planning of the whole university system', and perhaps even more important, 'to devise methods of working together to ensure the complete fulfilment of their common task'. This, as the editor noted, marked 'a new epoch' in planning the development of British universities.

But the Government too played its part in the funding of expansion. Relations between the Government and the universities were exceptionally good. The first issue of the *Quarterly* went so far as to congratulate the Chancellor of the Exchequer on his far-sighted policy (an act difficult to imagine in today's climate) and noted that the limits on expansion would not be finance, which was amply provided, but in universities' physical capacity; universities might even not be able to spend the funds they had been given for lack of the lecture rooms, laboratories and halls of residence that were required to accommodate the numbers involved (Simon 1946). Indeed, Simon went on to criticise Dalton mildly for 'accepting too readily the universities' own estimates that they cannot expand to more than

88,000 over the next ten years'. Two years later, when Dalton resigned as Chancellor, the editor recorded:

We have little hesitation in asserting that never has the government of any country given its universities such liberal grants and such complete freedom in essentials combined with the necessary degree of planning on a national scale. Our universities owe a deep debt of gratitude to Mr Dalton for the sympathy and courage he has shown in dealing with university affairs. (Simon 1948)

In the next issue the *Quarterly* carried a message from the new Chancellor, Stafford Cripps, to the effect that he had no intention of reining back on his predecessor's support:

The darkness of the economic outlook gives no ground for economy in the sphere of university grants . . . For it is on the advances that we make in scientific knowledge, and on the energy, initiative, directive capacity and courage of these young graduates that the economic future of the country will largely depend. (Cripps 1948)

Mutually supportive as relations between the universities and the Government were, the period up until the establishment of the Robbins Committee in 1961 did very little to identify what could be described as a universities' policy towards the nation's needs nor, for that matter, a government policy towards the universities. Simon's article 'The Universities and the Government' begins with the statement 'There is no university "system" in Britain' and, although the CVCP's statement 'A Note on University Policy and Finance in the Decennium 1946–56' (see pages 44 to 46) implied that the Committee had the power to co-ordinate a response to government policy, the Committee's powers to deliver a policy were limited (as they remain today). In fact, as Simon's article goes on to say what the nation had was '16 self-governing universities, each of which has developed in its own way'. While universities could come together through the medium of the CVCP to act in their mutual self-interest, they were not well placed to act in the national interest when it conflicted with their own. Fortunately the national and the universities' interests in this period showed a high degree of coincidence.

Even in the immediate post-war years, however, there were some divergencies of views. In recognition of the enhanced role that the universities were expected to play, and the anticipated consequential rise in cost to the Government, the UGC's terms of reference and constitution were reformed. Originally established as a body simply to distribute government resources to universities which derived most of their income from private sources in the form of fees and interest from endowments, the Committee was now given a planning role, and its terms of reference were added to by the words 'to assist, in consultation with the universities and other bodies concerned, the preparation and execution of such plans for the development of the universities as may from time to time be required in order to ensure that they are fully adequate to national needs'. The effect of this change was to put the UGC in the position of being 'a collective Minister' for the universities (Carswell 1985), since the responsible government department, the Treasury, did not profess to play any role itself in policy towards the universities. The membership and secretariat of the Committee was changed to strengthen its ability to carry out its new functions. However, a retiring member (she actually retired in 1948) who had served ever since 1919 when the UGC was founded, Margaret Fry, former Principal of Somerville College, Oxford, summed up university–state relations in a prescient article in the *Quarterly* in 1947. Although there might now be some disagreement over numbers 7 and 8, her series of axioms are as relevant in the late 1990s as clearly as they were in the late 1940s:

1. The provision of adequate teaching, study and research on a university level is essential to the well-being of a modern state;
2. The Government of each state has the responsibility of seeing that such provision is made (and that it is available to those who are qualified to make good use of it, some would add);
3. In Britain the cost of this provision has now far outstripped the total of endowments and of what students can pay, or local authorities or private benefactors be expected to give;
4. The state must therefore aid the universities, on an increasingly generous scale;
5. Public expenditure must, in the long-run, be subject to public control, i.e. to Parliament;
6. Universities should not be subjected to interference in the interests of any political party;
7. Public money should not be used to compete against itself;
8. Universities are the best judges of their own activities, whether as to subjects to be studied, standards to be maintained, staff to be appointed or research to be encouraged. They must therefore control the expenditure of their own funds;
9. Every necessary subject should be taught at some university, 'rare' subjects should not be wastefully duplicated.

Fry concluded her account of the UGC by admitting that its 'position can hardly be defended in strict logic' but hoping that it would prove sufficiently adaptable to 'juggle with the principles' which she had set out (Fry 1948).

The two most important divergencies of view between the universities and the Government were both centred on the creation of new university institutions. The Barlow Committee, in its call for a doubling of the existing output of graduates in science and technology, had also proposed that consideration should be given to the founding of at least one new university. The CVCP, however, in its otherwise strongly supportive 'Note on University Policy and Finance in the Decennium 1946–56', argued that:

If there were enough money, constructional material and equipment, and constructional manpower to spare for making a new university, in the national interest these had much better be spent in expanding the existing institutions properly.

This could be interpreted – and was by some – as reflecting the self-interests of a cartel, or as a sensible policy in the light of the pressures on the national resources. One consequence of the Barlow Committee's report was that a number of proposals began to be made to the UGC by aspiring communities for new foundations. At this stage the most notable was from Stoke which had strong support from Oxford and elsewhere, and considerable sympathy within the UGC, for its new ideas on inter-disciplinary teaching. The CVCP's criticism was scathing and in a 'Note on the Stoke Proposal' it condemned these ideas as seeming 'to provide not a new type of university institution but a new type of technical college' which 'could not be given even limited degree granting powers without serious   triment to the university system as a whole' (CVCP 1947 quoted in Mountford 1972). But the Stoke Proposal went ahead and the University College of North Staffordshire opened its doors to students in 1950. However, in the wider campaign for a new technological university based on the Barlow proposals the CVCP's line of argument was not successful in spite of a premature announcement in 1952 of the founding of a British MIT by the Lord President of the Council. In this case the funds set aside for an expansion of technological education were concentrated in a group of existing universities, a decision which has given the recipient institutions – Imperial College, Birmingham, Bristol, Cambridge, Leeds, Manchester, Sheffield and Glasgow Universities and the Royal College (later Strathclyde University) at Glasgow – a techno-logical strength which has persisted to this day.

One important step towards the creation of a university 'system' was the interest in the 1950s in the university admissions process. This arose partly from the statistical arguments for a further expansion of student numbers based on the explosion of post-war births and the increasing numbers staying on at school into the sixth form (the so-called 'bulge' and 'trend' debate), partly from an interest in questions surrounding social equity in entry to universities and partly from the self-evident inefficiencies in candidates submitting multiple applications to different universities. Kelsall's article (pages 57 to 60) introducing his 1957 *Report on an Enquiry into Applications for Admission to Universities*, which had been prepared for the CVCP, provided the basis for considering the organisational implications of the admissions process. (Kelsall himself was much more interested in the social implications of his research.) Although a centralised admissions system for universities did not begin operation until 1962, the Kelsall Report not only provided the agenda for the Home Universities Conference in 1957 but paved the way for a series of committees which finally brought the Universities Central Council on Admissions (UCCA) into being (Kay 1985). Perhaps the most important achievement was the incorporation of Oxford and Cambridge into the process, although it was on terms distinctly favourable to the two ancient universities.

The dominant role that Oxbridge played in the culture of British higher education in the 1950s and the extent to which it tended to impose a social stratification on university selection and an aristocratic value system on the development of particular disciplines is emphasised in Halsey's article 'British Universities and Intellectual Life' (pages 61 to 71). This value system gave high status to Oxbridge's primacy in liberal studies and in pure science, but condemned technological education and vocational studies more generally to the 'provincial' universities.

Perhaps because of this, the Barlow Committee's recommendations continued to cast a long shadow through the 1950s with the concern for a prolonged national investment in scientific and technological education at university level. The articles by Zuckerman who was later to become the Government's chief scientific adviser, and Bowden, who became Minister for Science in the first Wilson Government, are testimony to the strong public advocacy for a growth in science numbers. Zuckerman, who, at the time of writing, was Chairman of the Scientific Manpower Committee of the Advisory Council on Science Policy, the senior government scientific committee, addresses the growth of higher education almost entirely from the standpoint of scientific manpower and argues for a further doubling of numbers by the end of the 1960s (pages 72 to 79). The article applauds the 1956 White Paper on Technical Education which proposed wide-ranging reforms in what is now called further education (FE), including raising up to 20 colleges to university status with the title of College of Advanced Technology (CATs). (In practice only eight such colleges were created.) Locating advanced technological education in regional colleges of technology can be seen as a further example of Britain's educational value system; it also reflected the division of responsibility between the Ministry of Education and the UGC, with the Ministry responding quite separately from the UGC to pressure from the Parliamentary Scientific Committee and other bodies for a greater commitment to technological education (Shattock 1994).

Bowden's 'Too few academic eggs' (pages 80 to 94), written a year later, was a response to Simon's call in the *Quarterly* for a Commission on Higher Education (Simon 1958). But as Bowden makes clear, there was only modest support within the universities for such a Commission. At the Home Universities Conference of 1959 many universities were to offer resistance to an expansion of numbers of the scale that the Association of University Teachers (AUT) and many individual voices within universities were calling for. Bowden makes a powerful case in support of a Commission and for the argument that 'we have never faced the problems of technological research in universities', quoting both American and German experience to show how British universities were failing to match the progress of their competitors.

British higher education was not unaware of developments in America because relations between British and American universities – a legacy of scientific co-operation in the latter part of the war – had never been so close: but Britain chose to ignore those aspects of American university life which did not accord with its own culture. Shils's article 'Observations on the American University' (pages 95 to 106) concludes this portrait of the pre-Robbins period. While Britain was expanding higher education, at what it believed to be an appropriate rate, the American university scene was being transformed by a much more rapid growth which Trow was later to define as the entry to 'mass higher education' (Trow 1974). Shils painted the contrast between the 'buzzing, booming, confusion' of the typical American campus – 'this heterogeneity and dispersion' – with the 'determinate, well defined – perhaps too determinate and well defined' British university, with the 'uncongeniality [of its] environment to innovation'. In spite of its diversity he argued that American higher education could be said to have a 'unity' because it was influenced 'by the common traditions of American culture'. It was possible, he suggested, to talk about a 'university system because of an acceptance of universities having different functions' – the research universities, the undergraduate colleges, and so forth. He accepted that American universities had weaknesses, particularly in undergraduate teaching, and in the danger of an over-concentration on a research culture, but the picture he paints is of a freer, less tidy, more adaptable, and much less cautious university system. At the root of this difference lay the decentralised nature of the

American university system as compared to the UGC's centralised control of the universities in Britain.

Robbins and After

It was entirely appropriate that Simon, who retired from the Chairmanship of the *Quarterly*'s editorial board in 1960, should have moved the motion in the House of Lords which led to the establishment of the Robbins Committee, as he had campaigned energetically for a Royal Commission in the pages of the *Quarterly*. He moved the motion on 11 May 1960 but died in October, two months before the Government responded formally to announce the formation of the Committee. But in his last editorial he noted that 'the number of dons who care passionately for some reform of the universities, either administrative or academic, has proved to be disappointingly small' (Simon 1960). There was little enthusiasm for university expansion among the universities in 1959–60, and the UGC had proceeded of its own volition to establish the 'new' universities, beginning with Sussex, to meet the demand for places that was expected from the growing number of qualified 18-year-olds. In this respect the Robbins Report of 1963 represented a watershed for British higher education. But while the report was radical on the need for growth and greater social equity, it was conservative on the framework in which it would take place. It recommended that the majority of the expansion should be within a university system regarding 'a large university population within the total provision for higher education [as] something we conceive to be in the nation's interest' (Robbins para. 464). In addition it further sought to reinforce the university sector by recommending that the colleges of education should be transferred from LEAs and other bodies to the responsibility of the universities and should be funded by the proposed University Grants Commission.

It is difficult in 1996 to appreciate the sense of anticipation and excitement which the Robbins Report generated. Only a year before, the Chancellor had publicly rejected advice from the UGC for a faster rate of student number growth, an unpopular decision which certainly influenced the speed with which the Government, facing a General Election, accepted the main Robbins recommendations for expansion and for upgrading the CATs to university status. Indeed almost overnight the report had shaped a university 'system' with a plan for growth reaching for almost 20 years. Three immediate responses to Robbins are included in this section. 'First reactions to the Robbins Report' (pages 109 to 116), was written within days of the report's publication by Morris, who had succeeded Simon as

Chairman of the board. Morris had been a progressive Vice-Chancellor of Leeds and, at the point when the report was published, was about to retire from his post, having persuaded and bullied his university into a state of preparedness for rapid growth. Yet his reactions to the recommendations are as much about student needs in the new era as the more conventional concerns about finance and rates of growth and his call for a greater emphasis on teaching has a 1990s rather than a 1960s ring about it.

Looked at with the hindsight of over 30 years, the second contribution 'A Question of Size and Shape' (pages 117 to 132) by Martin Trow, then a young Associate Professor at Berkeley, goes to the heart of the problem that the Robbins structure posed. Trow rightly, as it turned out, suggests that Robbins had underestimated the likely demand for places but more importantly he asks whether the Robbins estimates represented a plan for places or a plan for 'a system of higher education which will be responsive to qualified demand'. He goes on to ask whether Robbins had not over-emphasised the need for scientists and technologists at the expense of the applied social sciences, skills which would be increasingly in demand in a complex industrial society. He asks whether the colleges of education ought not be accorded a role in this training rather than restricted to the narrow base of teacher training. But he broadens his critique when he suggests that 'the system of higher education recommended by Robbins will not, I think, substantially reduce the gross differences in educational opportunity and achievement among the social classes', a prediction which up to 1981 was certainly to be proved correct (Shattock 1981). He argues that British higher education needed a broader and more flexible base than just a university system, involving colleges 'more directly linked to the world of work' and he concludes by asking 'whether Britain in the second half of the twentieth century would not be better served by a system of higher education that is shaped like a pyramid rather than an inverted pyramid'.

The third contribution, 'The Academic Hierarchy – Appendix Three' by Halsey (pages 133 to 139), echoes this conclusion in considering Robbins's survey of university staff. He concludes that 'the quality of staff will fall temporarily in higher education as a whole and permanently in the re-defined universities' and he draws attention to the 'steep descent in average quality, within the university system from Oxbridge down through London and the redbricks to the CATs' in spite of academic staff being paid on national salary scales which might have been expected to produce a flattening of the structure. What the evidence pointed to, he suggests, was a hierarchy of institutions operating in a relatively fluid system where levelling factors such as equality of pay scales offered the prospect of competition only within a common framework. But he concludes, in a sentence which is only too accurately confirmed by the research and other league tables of the 1980s, that prevailing conditions were much more likely to produce 'a stable institutional hierarchy' which would be unlikely to see significant change. The conservative nature of the Robbins university system was confirmed by the publication in the same year of Clark Kerr's *The Uses of the University* reviewed by Morris in the *Quarterly* (pages 140 to 142). At a point when in Britain we were systematising a university structure in a common mould, Kerr was describing how a university can thrive and become internationally famous not simply by pursuing a tidy historically validated role but by being useful, by taking on broad social responsibilities and by diversifying its funding base through the pursuit of a range of activities which extended the concept of a university. Kerr, himself, was to suffer from the proximity of his university to the political process, but the pre-eminence of the University of California continued after his removal from its presidency.

The article by David Riesman, 'Notes on new universities: British and American' (pages 143 to 159), follows a similar theme but also provides a picture of British university life some three years after Robbins – the 'often disgruntled redbrick universities', the envy of Sussex then at the height of its *jeu d'esprit*, the sense of experiment and innovation he found at the 'new' universities but not elsewhere. But even the new foundations he compares unfavourably with the range and vitality of the satellite and experimental campuses being established out of major universities in America. He criticises the lack of variety in British universities, the difficulty they appeared to find in creating high quality alternatives to the traditional university model and the rigidities of quality in the British first degree compared to the greater unevenness in America where he nevertheless found the best quality undergraduate work more innovative and alive than what he had seen in Britain. Riesman may have succumbed a little to the graciousness of his hosts at Sussex but he visited 19 universities during his six-month stay and the contrast he found with the more vibrant, 'can do' style of expansionism in America is compelling evidence of the limitations of the more disciplined, more planned approach to expansion adopted in Britain in the 1960s.

The Robbins plan was, of course, dealt a severe blow by Crosland's Woolwich speech in 1965 which announced the creation of a polytechnic higher education sector. Robbins had recommended that ten or so of the regional colleges or the colleges of education might be upgraded to university status to take up the expansion sometime in the late 1970s, but in the student number forecasts the Report assigned them only 20,000 places, which implied that they would be of a modest size. Crosland proposed to go much further with the creation of up to 30 polytechnics immediately and the establishment of a genuinely alternative public sector of higher education. Robbins himself was wholly opposed to the implications of Crosland's speech:

If I had known that anything so reactionary and half baked as the binary line was going to be propounded, I certainly would have suggested adding a few paragraphs to the Report, dealing with this as it deserves. (Ford 1965)

Peter Venables, who had taken Aston from CAT to university status, is more measured in the article 'Dualism in Higher Education' (pages 160 to 172), and attributed the decision to create polytechnics more as being to prevent universities from taking over the better technical colleges to give themselves a stronger applied science base (as was proposed at Warwick) than to the stated aim to ensure that the nation needed a sector of higher education that was under 'social control'. He speculates that the Government might in the long run have been thinking of the emergence of 'state universities' in the public sector, a prediction which it could be argued was realised in the 1992 Act.

However, the creation of the polytechnics and the 'public sector' of higher education taken together with the Government's decision not to transfer the colleges of education to university responsibility, had important implications for the universities. First, the Government had created for itself an alternative vehicle to provide higher education, so that the universities did not benefit from the extent to which demand for places exceeded Robbins's estimates. Universities, therefore, remained small and were vulnerable when the financial difficulties of the 1980s emerged. Second, the polytechnics provided the mix of degree and non-degree work which the universities would have taken up had they sought to follow the kind of development route favoured by Trow and Riesman. This particularly affected the ex-CATs which, in order to concentrate on the first degree appropriate to the rest of the university sector, relinquished the non-degree higher education work that they had previously provided. Third, the creation of a new sector reinforced the stereotyping of universities which was implicit in the Robbins recommendation that such a high proportion of students should be taught in institutions which had a strong research mission.

All universities had, therefore, to be regarded as research active and funded accordingly, although it was obvious to the most casual observer, and confirmed by all the statistical indicators, that the degree of commitment to and success in research varied very widely. The result was that the hierarchy described by Halsey continued to be recognised informally, but there was no encouragement towards greater institutional differentiation as might have occurred under the pressure of student numbers, or if funding mechanisms had rewarded different institutional characteristics. Institutions themselves subscribed to a common rhetoric about research and its interrelation with teaching. Even the ex-CATs increasingly saw themselves as part of an elite sector, though their origins encouraged a more robustly 'useful' mission. Worst of all, the way the polytechnic sector was created, without consultation with the UGC or the universities, and, indeed, the explicit criticism of the universities in the Woolwich speech, gave some credence to the adverse reaction within the universities and the reluctance to recognise the polytechnics as equal partners in a higher education system, even after they had developed to maturity in the late 1970s and early 1980s. For two years between 1963 and 1965 Britain could have been said to have a university 'system' on the Robbins template, but after the Woolwich speech the 'system' was destroyed by the creation of a new tranche of higher education institutions which increasingly came to look like universities but which lacked the legal status, the funding structures and the public recognition which the universities enjoyed.

Nevertheless the immediate post-Robbins years were halcyon days for the universities from the point of view of finance and buildings. The civic universities which had been reluctant to expand before Robbins were now eager to do so and had the capacity to grow quickly. The 'new' universities with their greenfield campuses and their commitment to interdisciplinarity offered a challenge to the older universities while the new technological universities followed in their wake. The number of universities had doubled to 45 within a decade with the Open University coming into operation in 1970. But the tide started to turn when the wave of student revolt began to make headlines in the media. The failure of the Heath Government to rescue the economy or withstand the inflationary turmoil caused by the oil crisis led, inevitably, in 1974, to the breakdown of the quinquennial funding system, which had provided the bureaucratic backbone of university planning, and its replacement by annual grant allocations. The universities entered a period when, for the first time since Robbins, as student numbers continued to rise, unit costs began to fall. Already concern was being voiced in Parliament at rising university costs and the Public Accounts Committee began to question the cost-effectiveness of the building programme. But the universities and their leaders at the CVCP were slow to recognise the change in public mood and their vulnerability to the downturn in government finance. The transfer of the UGC to the new Department of Education and Science (DES) in 1964 meant that universities had increasingly to compete for priority against other parts of the education system, while the decision to allow the Comptroller and Auditor General access to university accounts gave the National Audit Office the capacity to comment on universities' management in a way that was impossible when they were under the Treasury. University attitudes, however, remained frozen in the euphoria of the Robbins period and at each turn of the screw university leaders believed that Government had only to be talked to at the right level for the position to be reversed.

A good example of this failure to understand the change that had taken place in political attitudes can be seen in Merrison's article 'The Education of Ministers of State' (pages 173 to 184). Merrison begins by quoting the way universities reacted to Shirley Williams's famous 'Thirteen Points' sent to the CVCP in much happier times at the end of the 1960s. The occasion for Merrison's article was the appointment of Lord Crowther Hunt to the post of Minister of State at the DES. Crowther Hunt was an Oxford politics don who had played a leading role in the Fulton Committee on the Civil Service. When first appointed he has recorded how he went to see Harold Wilson, the Prime Minister, to ask what the Government's policy was towards higher education, only to discover that one did not exist (Crowther Hunt 1983). He then proceeded to try to create one. For the CVCP this offered a unique opportunity: an academic had become the responsible Minister and was looking to create a policy; his chief political adviser was a professor, an economist from the University of London, Maurice Peston. They were part of the 'system' and, together with the CVCP and the UGC, they could have been helped to devise a workable plan. Instead, this article, written by a senior Vice-Chancellor soon to become Chairman of the CVCP, treats Crowther Hunt's ideas with what can only be described as 'hauteur'; it condemns the Woolwich speech as 'an appalling blunder', it describes Crowther Hunt's speeches as 'pretty thin stuff' without 'a single new thought' and it suggests that the proper place to debate the role of the universities was in the UGC and not in the Government. In a democracy there is nothing wrong in criticising Ministers and their ideas but Merrison's approach, exemplified by the title of the article, was written in the vein of an institutional head addressing a junior member of staff. He was not alone in his reactions. Peston responded in the next issue with an article entitled 'The Education of Vice-Chancellors' (Peston 1976). In fact even Crowther Hunt's civil servants, who were less than pleased at the way he attempted to define a policy without much reference to them, found themselves rallying to their Minister's defence. What Merrison's article suggested, however, was that the universities had lost touch with the political process. Mutual understanding between the DES and the universities was at a very low ebb when the 1979 election brought Mrs Thatcher to power.

The Assertion of State Control 1979 to 1996

The arrival of the Thatcher Government quickly exposed the extent such attitudes were misplaced. Within days of the new Government taking over, the universities lost about £100 million of recurrent grant over three years in the removal of that element which was attributable to the education of overseas students. This action, said to have been proposed by a relatively junior Treasury official to the incoming Secretary of State as a way of deflecting other cuts, set the tone for the next five years.

In spite of reassurances by the Secretary of State that there would then be a policy of level funding, it soon became apparent to the UGC that further cuts were on the way. The Chairman fought a battle within Whitehall to ensure that the UGC could undertake a planned restructuring of the university sector on the basis of a clear understanding of the financial position up to 1984–85 rather than deal with the uncertainties of year-by-year cuts (Shattock 1994). The recurrent grant letter of 1 July 1981 which conveyed the reductions in universities' income was therefore able to restore a longer time horizon than had been possible since the demise of the quinquennial planning system. But because of the depth and the selective nature of the cuts it also changed for ever the relationship between the UGC and the universities. Before, even in difficult times, the UGC, which still had a large majority of academics on its membership and was chaired by an ex-Vice-Chancellor, Edward Parkes, had been seen as a friend of the universities and, in Berdahl's phrase, as 'a benign agency' (Berdahl 1959). But the circumstances had now changed. In the past the UGC had allocated recurrent grant mostly on the basis of historic costs and in a situation where increased resources were available for increased student numbers. A fall in unit costs of about 10 per cent during the 1970s had been masked by rising numbers. For the first time, because the reduction in recurrent grant for the university sector as a whole was around 17 per cent over the three years 1981–82 to 1983–84, the UGC imposed a cut in student numbers. Since the Committee also detected what its Chairman described as genuine 'symptoms of malaise in the university system' it decided to allocate its reduced resources differentially and to penalise some universities more severely than others. The criteria used for these decisions provoked widespread discussion and criticism but one effect of the decisions was to recognise more accurately in funding terms some sort of hierarchy of universities. But to restructure in this way the UGC had to become less 'benign', and more 'dirigiste'. As Parkes told the CVCP in 1980:

> There is going to be in the future a somewhat greater degree of direct intervention by the UGC in the affairs of individual universities than has been customary or necessary in the past . . . I should add that the Committee is quite as staunch a defender of university autonomy as any of you are . . . .(UGC 1980)

This change in the balance of the relationship led the UGC to be seen increasingly, if unfairly, within universities as an arm of Government rather than as a body representative of the universities and put great strain on the credibility of its legendary 'buffer' status.

The article by Moore, 'University Financing 1979–86' (pages 187 to 201) describes the way the UGC approached its allocation of the 1981 cuts. Moore wrote from the vantage point of having been a member of the Committee and of the small sub-committee which determined the methodology and managed the process. The 1981 exercise was only partially performance-driven and some universities were assisted or disadvantaged by their subject mix. As Table 1 shows, the exercise nevertheless represented a considerable revaluation of the university sector. Many of the losers were ex-CATs but they included Keele, which had been dogged by the difficulties of post-war austerity in its early years, several of the 'new' universities and some older foundations like Aberdeen. Oxbridge, London (the London figure of 17 per cent disguised significant successes like Imperial College, the LSE and University College), and some of the civic universities were among the comparative winners as were some of the 'new' universities of the 1960s and two of the ex-CATS. The cuts league table did not, therefore, wholly reflect the hierarchy which Halsey described in 1963–64: there had been some changing of places, but the Robbins intention that the predominance of Oxbridge and London should be reduced over time had not been realised. Moore goes on to describe the 1986 allocation exercise, the first of the research selectivity exercises, which had the effect, like the later 1989 and 1992 exercises, of further differentiating university funding on the basis of research performance. The effect, over a decade, has been to establish an institutional hierarchy based on one aspect, albeit an important one, of university performance. Table 2 illustrates this by providing a ranking table based on the average of the aggregated scores for each academic unit assessed achieved by each university in 1989 and 1992. A sub-set of the

TABLE 1
The Student Number and Recurrent Grant Reductions announced on
1 July 1981

Universities ranked according to % loss of home students	Home and EEC students 1983–84 or			Grant £million		
	1979–80	1984–85	% change	1980–81	1983–84	approx. % change
Salford	3,940	2,750	−30	15.31	8.59	−44
Aston	4,670	3,640	−22	14.39	9.86	−31
Bradford	4,360	3,530	−19	14.45	9.64	−33
Stirling	2,470	2,020	−18	6.99	5.08	−27
Keele	2,680	2,230	−17	8.57	5.64	−34
Hull	5,070	4,200	−17	11.44	9.19	−20
Surrey	2,880	2,470	−14	11.81	8.78	−26
Heriot-Watt	2,430	2,120	−13	8.16	7.09	−13
Kent	3,430	3,180	−7	8.44	6.64	−21
St Andrews	3,110	2,880	−7	9.24	7.51	−19
Lancaster	4,210	3,920	−7	10.32	8.68	−16
Sussex	3,890	3,710	−5	11.67	9.21	−21
City	2,130	2,020	−5	10.31	8.24	−20
Reading	5,030	4,770	−5	15.00	12.66	−16
Aberdeen	5,140	4,940	−4	19.75	15.19	−23
Essex	2,240	2,150	−4	6.88	5.47	−20
Strathclyde	5,790	5,540	−4	17.90	14.69	−18
London	33,510	32,220	−4	200.00	165.03	−17
Bristol	6,650	6,390	−4	23.05	19.43	−16
Nottingham	6,380	6,150	−4	21.39	18.36	−14
Newcastle	6,880	6,600	−4	23.97	20.85	−13
Durham	4,530	4,360	−4	12.93	11.60	−10
Oxford	10,700	10,410	−3	34.00	29.74	−13
Glasgow	9,100	8,810	−3	33.08	29.56	−11
East Anglia	3,760	3,640	−3	11.25	10.28	−9
Leicester	4,340	4,200	−3	13.12	11.95	−9
Loughborough	4,670	4,550	−3	13.06	11.98	−8
Exeter	4,690	4,600	−2	12.21	9.69	−21
Manchester	9,930	9,710	−2	38.20	31.93	−16
Liverpool	7,060	6,910	−2	31.18	26.13	−16
Leeds	9,430	9,270	−2	33.93	28.72	−15
Cambridge	10,490	10,280	−2	32.27	28.91	−10
Warwick	4,600	4,550	−1	13.17	11.23	−15
Brunel	2,460	2,470	0	11.14	8.99	−19
Birmingham	7,750	7,770	0	30.81	25.69	−17
Univ. of Wales	17,330	16,130	0	57.20	47.67	−17
Dundee	2,490	2,480	0	12.64	10.53	−17
Sheffield	6,860	6,860	0	25.40	21.72	−14
Southampton	5,690	5,660	0	18.91	16.60	−12

TABLE 1 (*continued*)

Universities ranked according to % loss of home students	Home and EEC students 1983–84 or			Grant £million		approx.
	1979–80	1984–85	% change	1980–81	1983–84	% change
Edinburgh	8,830	8,840	0	33.81	30.20	−11
York	3,100	3,090	0	7.48	7.02	−6
Bath	3,190	3,260	+2	9.38	8.69	−7
UMIST	2,790	2,980	+7	15.94	11.08	−30
Manchester Bus. Schl.	120	170	+42	1.14	0.87	−24
London Bus. Schl.	170	290	+70	1.13	1.49	+11
Total GB	260,970	248,720	−4.7	971.85	808.07	−17

Source: Sizer, J. (1987) 'Institutional responses to financial reductions in the university sector – Final Report to the DES'. Table 2.

TABLE 2

The Results of the 1989 and 1992 Funding Council Research Assessment Exercises

1989			1992		
University	Units of assessment	Average score	University	Units of assessment	Average score
Cambridge	54	4.48	Cambridge	52	4.82
Oxford	46	4.41	Oxford	45	4.67
Imperial College	20	4.40	LSE	17	4.59
LSE	16	4.19	University College	43	4.49
University College	45	4.18	Warwick	26	4.37
Warwick	24	4.13	Imperial College	23	4.37
Essex	16	3.69	UMIST	20	4.09
UMIST	21	3.67	Edinburgh	56	4.07
Bristol	46	3.61	Lancaster	27	4.06
York	21	3.52	Sussex	30	4.03
Manchester	49	3.43	York	21	3.99
Sheffield	37	3.35	Birkbeck College	19	3.98
Southampton	41	3.27	Durham	32	3.96
Edinburgh	65	3.25	Manchester	52	3.95
Lancaster	29	3.24	Exeter	34	3.85
King's College	35	3.20	Birmingham	53	3.84

TABLE 2 (*continued*)

1989			1992		
University	Units of assess-ment	Average score	University	Units of assess-ment	Average score
East Anglia	26	3.15	Essex	17	3.84
Liverpool	49	3.14	East Anglia	30	3.82
Queen Mary College	25	3.12	St Andrews	25	3.80
Nottingham	48	3.10	Bath	23	3.80
Birkbeck	20	3.10	Southampton	38	3.79
Birmingham	47	3.09	Nottingham	47	3.75
Durham	37	3.08	Surrey	24	3.73
St Andrews	27	3.07	Leeds	56	3.66
Sussex	29	3.07	Bristol	45	3.64
Reading	41	3.02	Newcastle on Tyne	41	3.62
Newcastle	45	3.02	King's College	35	3.61
Surrey	22	3.00	Queen Mary College	29	3.59
Bath	21	2.95	Strathclyde	32	3.54
Exeter	35	2.94	Sheffield	39	3.52
Leeds	55	2.85	Royal Holloway	19	3.51
Glasgow	52	2.81	Liverpool	48	3.49
Leicester	33	2.79	Reading	40	3.48
Loughborough	25	2.76	Leicester	34	3.44
Aberdeen	39	2.72	UCW Cardiff	36	3.43
Kent	32	2.72	Open	22	3.43
Cardiff	40	2.68	Loughborough	23	3.39
Hull	36	2.67	Glasgow	55	3.36
Royal Holloway	21	2.67	Cranfield	6	3.36
Swansea	30	2.67	Heriot-Watt	19	3.25
Aberystwyth	27	2.59	UCW Aberystwyth	26	3.24
Aston	9	2.56	Stirling	23	3.22
Strathclyde	43	2.51	Swansea	32	3.20
Bradford	36	2.47	Kent	34	3.19
Bangor	22	2.45	Bangor	23	3.17
Dundee	23	2.43	City	19	3.17
Heriot-Watt	19	2.42	Goldsmiths'	22	3.15
Queen's Belfast	48	2.35	Bradford	21	3.15
Stirling	22	2.32	Aston	9	3.11
Brunel	21	2.19	Queen's, Belfast	49	3.07
City	17	2.18	Dundee	23	3.07
Salford	19	2.16	Brunel	20	3.05
St David's	11	2.09	Aberdeen	38	3.02
Ulster	22	2.09	Hull	35	2.98
Keele	29	2.00	Salford	17	2.94
Goldsmith's College	21	2.00	Ulster	24	2.91

TABLE 2 (*continued*)

1989			1992		
University	Units of assess-ment	Average score	University	Units of assess-ment	Average score
			Keele	30	2.86
			St David's	11	2.69
			Sheffield Hallam	17	2.36
			Kingston	11	2.33
			Oxford Brookes	22	2.28
			Plymouth	14	2.24
			South Bank	9	2.23
			Brighton	19	2.22
			Coventry	18	2.22
			Northumbria	22	2.21
			Middlesex	20	2.18
			West of England	18	2.12
			Westminster	21	2.09
			Manchester Met.	21	2.06

The following universities received an average score below 2:

North London	Staffordshire
Hertfordshire	Anglia
Greenwich	Liverpool John
Portsmouth	Moores
Guildhall	Nottingham Trent
Leeds	Thames Valley
Metropolitan	Glasgow
East London	Caledonian
Huddersfield	Humberside
Wolverhampton	Salford College
Robert Gordon	Central Lancashire
Sunderland	Abertay
Teesside	Paisley
Bournemouth	Napier
De Montfort	Glamorgan

Notes: The research assessment exercises scored each department/unit that a university submitted for assessment on a ranking of 5 to 1, each ranking being defined on a descending scale of excellence. The overall university ranking, which was derived from the unit of assessment rankings, represents the average ranking achieved in the research assessment exercise.

Sources: UFC Report on the 1989 Research Selectivity Exercise; UFC Circular 26/92

higher ranked universities has now sought to establish a separate identity as the Russell Group to further segment the university market.

The imposition of the 1981 cuts and the subsequent public debate, both in Parliament and elsewhere, raised important structural issues about higher education which took a decade to resolve. In 1982 the Government created the National Advisory Body for Public Sector Higher Education (NAB) to act as a parallel body to the UGC in co-ordinating the non-university sector of higher education. In the next year both bodies were invited by the Secretary of State, Sir Keith Joseph, to contribute public advice on the future of higher education. The UGC's response in September 1984, 'A Strategy for Higher Education into the 1990s' (UGC 1984), emphasised the research role of the university sector and the need for greater concentration of research into the most research intensive universities both on the grounds of getting better value for money and in order to raise Britain's research competitiveness. But the response also contained an opening chapter written jointly with NAB on 'Higher education and the needs of society', which emphasised the changes that had occurred since Robbins and that 'the focus of initial higher education must now be broader and the recent emphasis on continuing education must be maintained and accelerated'. The chapter went on to agree that 'there is a legitimate research role for major public sector institutions both to support and sustain teaching and as a contribution to the advancement and application of knowledge'. The Government's response in a Green Paper in 1985 did not support the UGC's argument for level funding and was described as 'a deeply disappointing document' by the Chairman of the CVCP and dismissed in the sentence 'clearly the Government has learned little or nothing from the consultations of the past two years' (Shock 1985). But these sentences in the UGC's strategy document represented a very important recognition of the growth in importance and standing of the polytechnics and of their place in a higher education system.

This theme is taken much further in Trow's 1987 article 'Academic Standards and Mass Higher Education' (pages 202 to 224) which, echoing parts of his 1963 article, contains a searching critique of the overriding consensus in Britain as to the future course of higher education. For Trow the differences between universities and polytechnics which seemed so large in Britain, seemed much smaller from a transatlantic perspective, and their common commitment to 'the British first degree on an academic gold standard' inhibited diversity and flexibility in the higher education system as a whole. He suggested that universities and polytechnics were discouraged from innovation by the fear that from the start they cannot hit a standard high enough to match what the system as a whole expects. But for the late 1990s the following might seem to be the core of the argument:

Perhaps the greatest constraint imposed by a national standard is on expansion. No country in the world could operate a system of mass higher education at the *per capita* cost levels of the British universities and polytechnics. These cost levels are not inappropriate for elite higher education – the higher education of full-time, highly selected and able students, taught at the most demanding levels of intellectual intensity and complexity . . . But genuine diversity would mean institutions operating at different levels of cost as well as of standard, and the possibility of lower cost higher education would allow academics and officials at least to think about the expansion of higher education.

It needs to be remembered that this was written in 1987 when polytechnic unit costs were high and before the great expansion of the early 1990s, but Trow goes on to offer the solution to the British dilemma of reconciling 'standards' with mass higher education by pointing to the parallels between colleges of further education and American community colleges and suggesting that the incorporation of these colleges, linked in America with degree-granting institutions, would offer access to higher education to a mass market. Most importantly, 'community colleges do not see themselves as failed degree-granting institutions'. Because they do not claim great academic distinction they do not see themselves as unsuccessful. Prophetically Trow concludes:

I submit that pressures for the expansion of post-secondary education are inherent in the development of modern societies. But the more this expansion is taken by the elite selective system, the more it tends to become a system of mass higher education, with less money *per capita*, less autonomy, more central intervention and control and lower standards. The only way a system of higher education marked by very high academic standards throughout can survive is if there stands alongside it – and related to it – a truly mass system of institutions marked by lower *per capita* costs and lower standards – one that accepts those democratising pressures, demands and functions, willingly.

The years between 1985 and 1992 represented the period of the greatest constitutional upheaval in the history of British higher education. The establishment of the Croham Committee, ostensibly to reform the UGC and resolve the public accountability issues raised by the Cardiff affair led inescapably, it can now be seen, to the replacement of the UGC by a new body, the Universities Funding Council (UFC) (Shattock 1994). The NAB experiment which tried to blend ministerial and local authority control of the public sector of higher education, having ceased to find favour in the DES, was also replaced in the 1988 Education Reform Act.

The Act removed public sector higher education from the control of the local education authorities and placed it under a new body, the Polytechnics and Colleges Funding Council (PCFC) which, like the UFC, was subject to direction on policy by the Secretary of State. In parallel, changes were taking place under the rationalising pressures of budget cuts in the organisation of civil science. At one level, the Government was anxious to achieve a better co-ordination of the work of the research councils and chose to reinforce the powers of the Advisory Board (ABRC). The ABRC's concern about the need to concentrate research into yet fewer institutions led it to publish a widely quoted Report 'A Strategy for the Science Base' (ABRC 1987) which proposed a systematic differentiation of universities into R (research), T (teaching) and X (mixed research and teaching) categories. This represented a startling – and some thought Trojan horse – incursion into UGC/NAB territory. At a second level the research council structure established by the Trend Committee (Trend Report 1963) was substantially reshaped. But even more fundamental was the re-organisation of Government in 1992 which swept away the ABRC, removed responsibility for research from the DES and located it in an Office of Science and Technology (OST) in the Cabinet Office with its own separate Minister. In 1995 OST was transferred to the Department of Trade and Industry. The implications of these changes and the later merger of the Department of Employment and the Department for Education can only be assessed in the longer term.

The *Quarterly* of this period carried a series of articles which examined these changes from many points of view. Particularly notable were 'Higher Education Planning' (Booth 1987), 'From Great Expectations to Bleak Houses' (Silver 1987), 'Le Röi est Mort; Vive le Quoi? Croham and the death of the UGC' (Moodie 1987), 'The Passing of the Education Reform Act' (Crequer 1989), 'Universities and the Public Purse' (Beloff 1988), 'The Merging of the PCFC and the UFC: Probable, Desirable or Inevitable' (Ball 1991), 'The White Paper and Academic Research' (Collins 1994), and 'University Autonomy: the 80s and after' (Eustace 1994), but three in particular provide an insight into the history of the period. The first, by Peter Swinnerton-Dyer, last chairman of the UGC and first chief executive of the UFC, entitled 'Policy on Higher Education and Research' (pages 225 to 239), reflects on the changes to the university sector between 1988 and 1991. As the chairman who drove the UGC down the research selectivity route it is interesting to note his comment, following Trow, that 'Institutions have a duty to teach courses appropriate to the students whom they actually have, rather than to those whom they wish they had . . . there are too many institutions both universities and polytechnics, which hope that the niche labelled "elite" will be big enough to accommodate them.'

The second article is by Christopher Price, one time adviser to Crosland, and first Vice-Chancellor of Leeds Metropolitan University, an ex-polytechnic, entitled 'Elegant and Democratic Values: How Will the New English Universities Gel?' (pages 240 to 247). This was written after the White Paper 'Higher Education: a New Framework' (1991) and just as the new legislation, The Further and Higher Education Act 1992, which gave the polytechnics university status, was being passed. It reviews the history of the binary line and argues that in the new system we need to identify more models than simply that of the research university. However, the article is also notable for the confidence with which the argument is made in contrast with the position that the ex-CATs took in the *Quarterly* some 30 years earlier when they achieved university status. Thus, at that time, Wyatt from Bradford wrote of the extent to which 'the CATs still resemble technical colleges more than universities' (Wyatt 1964), while Buchanan from Bath suggested that 'None of the potential Vice-Chancellors of the new universities could have guessed a decade ago what a fortunate twist of fate awaited them' (Buchanan 1966). Where these and other contributors appeared still to be aspiring to real university status in the 1960s, Price and other ex-polytechnic contributors in the 1990s take it for granted that they are not the humble tail end charlies in the new university system but the standard bearers of change.

The third article, 'Reflections on the British Government and Higher Education in the 1980s' (pages 248 to 259) by Richard Bird, the civil servant in charge of the higher and further education section of the DES in that period, describes with remarkable honesty how Government tackled higher education issues in this period and how policy was made largely reactively to pressures within Government, within higher education and, of course, within the political system. Bird denies the existence of a government strategy for higher education – the situation had not changed since Crowther Hunt's days – and accepts that there was no obvious clarity or consistency of theme. We remain too close to this period to reach a final judgment on it.

One of the successes of the period, however, was the improvement of the age participation rate for entry into higher education. From a figure which seemed to have stuck at around 15 per cent in the 1970s it rose to 31 per cent by 1995. However, the Government's rejection of planning and its reliance on frequently revised internal market mechanisms has left higher education in the financial crisis which the Dearing Committee has now been set up to solve. It is difficult not to conclude that if there was a guiding principle for policy over the period it lay in the constraints on government expenditure imposed by the Treasury. Viewed from this perspective the real break with the Robbins era occurred in 1974, when the oil crisis provoked a breakdown in the established machinery for funding universities. Thereafter the need to assert control over government expenditure, while it intensified after 1979, increased as the burden of the Government's public expenditure commitments rose. Higher education could not have expected to be exempt from this development. However, as Bird's article makes clear, neither ministers, DES civil servants nor the Treasury itself had any long-term strategy for dealing with the situation so far as higher education was concerned, so that policy was reactive to external political forces or to the Government's public expenditure round. Moreover, it was driven by bureaucratic considerations deriving primarily from dialogues within Whitehall rather than from a sense of educational priorities. The higher education community itself did not help the process by its unwillingness to confront the true nature of the problem and take positive steps to respond to it. The only pattern in the overarching structural changes that were enacted – the removal of the UGC and NAB, the later removal of the UFC and the PCFC, the removal of ABRC and so forth – lies in the increasing control which Government felt the need to assert over the higher education system and its related agencies for the funding of civil science. Policy was not so much driven by ideology or by an educational vision but by the demands of accountability and the need not to exceed public expenditure targets.

The final steps in the creation of a British university system were embodied in the 1991 White Paper 'Higher Education: A New Framework' and the subsequent 1992 Further and Higher Education Act. The editorial commenting on the White Paper (pages 260 to 262) welcomes the demise of the binary line and the incorporation of the polytechnics (and subsequently some other institutions) into the university system. For the first time since the Woolwich speech destroyed the Robbins consensus, Britain had a university system which incorporated all the major higher education institutions. But it also argues that the bureaucracy of co-ordinating four higher education funding bodies, the Higher Education Funding Councils for England, Scotland and Wales and the Department of Education for Northern Ireland, is likely to stifle the regional diversity which the new system ought to have offered institutions. It points to the layers of decision-making to be erected in Wales with a Funding Council operating above a federal University of Wales. But it also comments on the DES forecast of a 50 per cent expansion in student numbers that was expected to occur in the years up to 2000 with the age participation rate rising to 31 per cent. We now know that, driven by a market-led funding system, that growth was achieved by 1995 so that the Treasury was forced to bring expansion to a premature halt and the new Funding Councils, which were created to give institutions freedom to grow in the way they wished, were forced to impose penalties on institutions which accepted student numbers beyond those that they were contracted to take. What the editorial said was that

unless there is also to be a commitment to transfer significant additional funding into the DES from other departments, the dilemma that the Government will face will be a choice between cutting back on expansion or reducing the lower end of the higher education system to the kind of conditions which operate in similar institutions in many continental European countries and increasingly in America . . . there must be doubts whether the expansion proposed is affordable.

That prediction has proved to be correct in 1996–97.

Over 50 years Britain has moved from a position where it had 18 universities but no university system to one where it has 105 universities and a very clearly defined university system. But the system suffers from serious weaknesses and is inherently unstable. First, in spite of the decentralisation to four national funding agencies, the system is subject to almost Napoleonic central control and the funding agencies are so locked together bureaucratically that their range of individual initiative in areas that really matter is very narrow. The common imposition of research assessment and teaching quality exercises has had the effect of forcing the whole of British higher education into a centrally controlled common mould. The Government has honestly tried to create a more diversified system. The regionalising of the funding councils can be seen as a step in this direction but the dominance of the central machinery has tended to frustrate any real move towards regional diversity. The research assessment exercises, supported by the policy of greater concentration by the research councils, has done a great deal to recreate a natural hierarchy of institutions at least in research.

But the attempt to rely on a competitive internal market in a period of rapid growth in order to give universities greater freedom to create more individualised missions has not been successful. The dominance of the cultural impact of the research assessment exercise which has linked research status with better funding has, in a period of overall financial stringency, discouraged the emergence of alternative models. Even the introduction of modularisation and semesterisation which might have encouraged institutional differentiation has been so widely adopted and at such rapid and unthinking speed that it has become a new 'norm' which only a very few universities have stood aside from. Although teaching quality assessment has tried to encourage diversity by emphasising 'fitness for purpose', the overall impact has seemed to confirm the research-led hierarchy. There has been no effort to develop the American high quality non-research-intensive liberal arts colleges and, while franchising odd years of higher education programmes to further education colleges has created a further education/higher education interface, there has been no effort to shape an effective community college model. Further education itself remains centrally managed in each of the four areas; only in Wales, and for reasons of economy not philosophy, does further and higher education come under one funding agency.

But, most critically, the enormously rapid expansion of the early 1990s was allowed to take place primarily in the universities, whether created before or after 1992, so that the fears that Trow articulated in 1987 are fully realised. In 1995–96 we have 1.24 million students in universities, split evenly between pre-1992 and post-1992 universities, with only 260,000 in the rest of higher education. We have a large, seriously underfunded, centrally managed university system committed to a more or less common approach to academic standards and to the linkage of status to research prestige. And, for historical reasons, we have a hierarchy of institutions constructed on a basis which, while it stimulates competition, can also encourage a sense of failure in many institutions rather than success. The expansion of the early 1990s was allowed to proceed without careful thought as to its longer-term impact on higher education as a whole, and it is almot certainly too late to try to shift numbers out of the universities back into a community college system. But unless a greater understanding of the importance of institutional diversity and variety can be established, the last 50 years will be seen to have created a university system which will act as a straitjacket to prevent innovation and development in the next 50, except that which is stimulated by the central funding agencies. The survival of such a university system over the next 50 years in anything like its present form would be hard to predict.

References

Ball, Sir Christopher (1991), 'The merging of the PCFC and the UFC: Probable, Desirable or Inevitable', *Higher Education Quarterly*, Vol. 45, No. 2.

Barlow Report (1946), *Report of the Committee on Scientific Manpower*, Cmnd. 6824. London, HMSO.

Beloff, Lord (1988), 'Universities and the Public Purse', *Higher Education Quarterly*, Vol. 44, No. 1.

Berdahl, R. O. (1959), *British Universities and the State* (Berkeley, CA: University of California Press).

Booth, C. (1987), 'Higher education planning', *Higher Education Quarterly*, Vol. 41, No. 1.
Buchanan, R. A. (1966), 'The technological universities', *Universities Quarterly*, Vol. 21, No. 1.
Carswell, J. (1985), *Government and the Universities 1960–1980* (Cambridge: Cambridge University Press).
Clapham Report (1946), *Report of the Committee on Social and Economic Research* (London: HMSO, Cmnd. 6868).
Collins, P. (1994), 'The White Paper and Academic Research', *Higher Education Quarterly*, Vol. 28, No. 1.
Crequer, N. (1989), 'The passing of the Education Reform Act', *Higher Education Quarterly*, Vol. 43, No. 1.
Cripps, R. Stafford (1948), 'A message from the Chancellor of the Exchequer', *Universities Quarterly*, Vol. 2, No. 3.
Crowther Hunt, Lord (1983), 'Policy making and accountability in higher education', in Shattock, M. L. (ed.) *The Structure and Governance of Higher Education* (Guildford: SRHE).
CVCP (1946), A Note on University Policy and Finance in the Decennium 1946–56, July.
Eustace, R. B. (1994), 'University autonomy: the 80s and after', *Higher Education Quarterly*, Vol. 48, No. 3.
Ford, Boris and Robbins, Lord, 'Report on Robbins', Vol. 20, No. 1.
Fry, M. (1948), 'The University Grants Committee, an Experiment in Administration', *Universities Quarterly*, Vol. 2, No. 3.
Goodenough Report (1944), *Report of the Committee on Medical Education*, Ministry of Health and Department of Health for Scotland.
Kay, R. (1985), *UCCA Its Origins and Development 1950–1985* (Universities Central Council on Admissions).
Kelsall, R. K. (1957), *Report of an enquiry into applications for admission to universities.* Association of Universities of the British Commonwealth.
McNair Report (1944), *Report of the Committee on Teachers and Youth Leaders*, Ministry of Education.
Ministry of Education (1956), *Technical Education* (London: HMSO, Cmnd. 9703).
Moodie, G. (1987), 'Le Roi est Mort, Vive le Quoi? Croham and the death of the UGC', *Higher Education Quarterly*, Vol. 41, No. 4.
Mountford, J. (1972), *Keele An Historical Critique* (London: Routledge and Kegan Paul).
Peston, M. (1976), 'The Education of Vice-Chancellors', *Universities Quarterly*, Vol. 30, No. 2.
Robbins Report (1963), *Report of the Committee on Higher Education* (London: HMSO, Cmnd. 2154).
Shattock, M. L. (1981), 'Demography and social class: the fluctuating demand for higher education in Britain', *European Journal of Education*, Vol. 16, Nos 3–4.
Shattock, M. L. (1994), *The UGC and the Management of British Universities* (Open University Press).
Shock, M. (1985), 'The Government's Green Paper', *Universities Quarterly*, Vol. 30, No. 4.
Silver, H. (1987) 'From Great Expectations to bleak houses', *Higher Education Quarterly*, Vol. 41, No. 3.
Simon, Lord (1948), 'Editorial Notes – After Mr. Dalton', *Universities Quarterly*, Vol. 2, No. 2.
Simon, Lord (1958), 'University Commentary – A Royal Commission on the Universities?', *Universities Quarterly*, Vol. 13, No. 1.
Simon, Lord (1960), 'A Farewell Message', *Universities Quarterly*, Vol. 14, No. 2.
Trend Report (1963), *Report of a Committee of Enquiry into the Organisation of Civil Service*, (London: HMSO, Cmnd. 2171).
Trow, Martin (1974), 'Problems in the Transition from Elite to Mass Higher Education', OECD, *Policies for Higher Education*, from the General Report on the Conference on Further Structures of Post-Secondary Education (Paris: OECD).

UGC (1984), A Strategy for Higher Education into the 1990s: the UGC's advice to the Secretary of State (London: HMSO).

Wyatt, H. V. (1964), 'CATs and Robbins', *Universities Quarterly*, Vol. 19, No. 1.

Zuckerman Report (1952), Committee on Scientific Manpower, Office of the Lord President of the Council and Ministry of Labour and National Service.

PART I

'There Is No University "System" in Britain'

1. The Universities and the Government

Ernest Simon
Universities Quarterly Vol. 1 (1946–47), pp. 79–95.

Before World War II

There is no university 'system' in Britain. There are 16 self-governing universities, each of which has developed in its own way. Oxford and Cambridge, based on residential colleges, the federal universities of London and Wales, and the regional universities in the provincial cities, differing to some degree in England and Scotland. The independence and responsibility of the universities has always been regarded as essential not only by the universities themselves but by the public and the Government.

The active interest of the Government has been almost confined, except in war-time, to three lines of action:

(a) It has granted charters to the universities.

(b) From time to time it has appointed Royal Commissions to consider the problems of one or two individual universities. Some have been important. But in no case has the Government, as a result of the recommendations of a Royal Commission, taken action affecting the universities as a whole.

(c) The Government gave a grant of £1 million to the universities in 1919 and gradually increased it to £2.5 million in 1936. This grant is administered by a Treasury Committee – the UGC – which has consisted almost exclusively till recently of retired professors, who have had life-long experience of the existing government of universities and have been whole-hearted supporters of it. As a distinguished American has put it: 'The UGC has been a gentle but powerful influence for good . . . It has assisted what is good and quietly ignored all else. Its counsel and its funds have been almost equally acceptable' (Flexner 1940).

The individual universities are governed in academic matters by their teaching staffs; in the case of the modern universities by their professors. The activities of lay governing bodies have been almost confined to administrative matters of finance, buildings and equipment.

The results of this form of government have been that the universities have maintained high academic standards and by common consent have individually done in general a remarkably good job. But certain less desirable results have followed:

(a) The number of students has been smaller in relation to the population and the courses of study have been shorter than in any other comparable country.

(b) Nearly all the professors are academic specialists; most of them are not in close touch with the affairs of the outer world, though there has been a considerable improvement in this matter in the past 25 years, especially in departments like economics, science and medicine. It is widely thought that the members of university staffs ought to be more courageous than in the past in giving a lead to society on those matters on which they can speak with special competence.

(c) There has been no organised attempt to see that the universities as a whole produced the right number of graduates in the different fields, or that their research covered all desirable fields in reasonable proportions. There has been some redundancy and (what is much more serious) there have been gaps on a considerable scale.

The universities have been one of the few remaining examples of almost complete *laissez faire*.

1939–1946

A remarkable change began about three years ago; today the State is entering the field of university affairs with almost explosive force.

This is mainly due to the spectacular achievements of science during the war, which convinced the public and the Government of the potential importance of science in peacetime, of which they had not been fully aware. The Government spent money during the war on scientific research and development on a magnificent scale; even in this year of peace the Government is spending £28 million on aviation research and development alone – more than twice the total annual expenditure of all the universities. The Government and the public are both convinced today that good scientists are needed in greatly increased numbers and that they can be educated only at the universities. It is undoubtedly for this reason that the Government is already spending money on the universities on a quite new scale.

But the Government's interest is not confined to scientists; the following departments are actively concerned: the Ministry of Health (doctors), the Ministry of Education (teachers), the Lord President of the Council (scientists and social scientists), the Treasury (finance and general administration).

The Ministry of Health

The first government department to move was the Ministry of Health in appointing the Goodenough Committee to report on university medical schools. Its report recommended a revolution in clinical teaching and research, which has hitherto been carried out on a practically voluntary basis by leading consultants. It is recommended in future that the work shall be taken over mainly by full-time professors at salaries from £1,500 to £2,500 per annum.[1] The report also laid down what the size of the individual medical schools ought to be and what total numbers of medical graduates ought to be produced by the universities. It pointed out that to carry out the policy it recommended, the universities would need an additional grant up to £2.5 million per annum. The Chancellor of the Exchequer, Sir John Anderson, in his 1945 Budget, made an interim grant to the universities on the scale necessary to carry out the recommendations of the Committee in its earlier stages; and the UGC set up a special Medical Advisory Committee to administer the grant. This Committee instructed each medical school to report its proposals on the lines of the Goodenough Committee; schemes have been submitted in detail, discussed and approved by the UGC, and a considerable grant has been made to each university.

This whole procedure marks a revolution in the relations of the Government and the universities. Hitherto, with quite minor exceptions, the UGC has given an annual block grant to each university to spend as it wishes. Now for the first time this large additional grant is given for a specific purpose, subject to the approval of detailed proposals from each university as to how the money is to be spent. This is the first example of real planning and control of the universities by the Government. Some might call it interference.

The UGC has done the job with its usual tact; all the universities have accepted their conditions, though it is understood that in certain quarters there have been rather strong protests.

It may be added that the Ministry of Health in its new Health Services Bill is dealing with the whole question of the control, organisation and finance of the teaching hospitals and of their relations with the universities. Here again, it is clear that the Ministry of Health is likely to be involved closely in university affairs.

The Ministry of Education

The major responsibility of the Ministry of Education in relation to the universities is the education of the ablest boys and girls for entrance to the universities, without regard to the means of their parents. The Barlow report concludes that 'only about one in five of the ablest boys and girls actually reach the universities . . . There is clearly an ample reserve of intelligence in the country to allow both a doubling of the university numbers, and at the same time a raising of standards.'

This great task will certainly tend to bring the universities and the Ministry into close contact on the question of the kinds of school education best suited to prepare for different courses at the university, and the very difficult and vital question of university scholarship examinations, which at present tend to cause excessive specialisation in the higher forms of secondary schools.

The Minister has this year made a large grant to enable all winners of open university scholarships of £40 or over to go through the university without hardship.

The second field in which the Ministry is in close contact with the universities is the training of teachers. Nearly all teachers in training are subsidised by the Ministry. It is the Ministry alone which determines (on the recommendations of the examining body) who are to be recognised as qualified teachers.

In view of the great prospective increase in the demand for teachers after the war, the Minister of Education in 1942 appointed the McNair Committee to consider the whole question of the training of teachers and the part which the universities should play in it. The report pointed out that the universities in 1938 produced each year about 1,250 graduates for the teaching profession; the rest were trained in two-year training colleges under the Ministry. It estimated the annual need for teachers after the war at 15,000.

The universities are likely in the next few years to educate perhaps one-fifth of this number. The remaining 12,500 teachers needed each year will be educated at training colleges, and one vital question discussed by the Committee is the degree of responsibility which each university should have for the education of the teachers at training colleges in its region. All agreed that the universities should have some increased responsibility; but one-half of the Committee under Scheme A, wished to make this responsibility much greater than the other half, under Scheme B. There is still no agreement, and the Ministry proposes to approve different schemes in different universities. It seems likely that where the scheme adopted approximates to Scheme A the UGC will be responsible for finance; where it approximates to Scheme B the Ministry is likely to be closely concerned, and is likely to finance the proposed building on the university site for a regional educational centre. In short, it is clear that the Ministry will have more direct contact and more influence with the universities in the training of teachers than in the past.

A similar position may arise as regards technology. The number and size of institutions for higher technical education under the Ministry will certainly increase, and the problem of their relation with the technical departments of the universities will have to be settled between the universities and the Ministry.

The Ministry is in a planning mood. The present Minister, Miss Wilkinson, is the first Minister to be a graduate of one of the modern universities; she recently made the encouraging statement that she hoped and believed that the days of penury of the universities were over; and has already shown her active interest in the training of teachers and in the question of scholarships. It is clear that the relations of the Ministry with certain sections of university work will in future be much closer than in the past.

The Lord President of the Council

The Barlow Report. The Lord President of the Council (Mr Herbert Morrison) has the chief government responsibility for scientific research. At the end of 1945 he appointed a committee under the chairmanship of Sir Alan Barlow to consider the use and development of our scientific manpower and resources during the next ten years. In May 1946, the committee reported that the output of scientists from the universities ought to be doubled in ten years, and expressed the hope that there might be a similar increase in the humanities. Mr Morrison immediately announced that 'the Government are in general agreement with the conclusions of the Committee, which we recognise will involve a substantial liability on the Exchequer.' This is generally taken to mean that the target at which the universities are to aim is to double the output of students in ten years, without any lowering of standards, and greatly to expand the amount of research.

Success in carrying through this great plan of expansion involves a co-ordinated plan of action covering several different fields:

A national plan must be made by the UGC, in consultation with the universities, laying down a ten-year target for each existing and new university as to total numbers, and numbers in each faculty.

Entry: The ablest boys and girls must be suitably educated and enabled to study at a university, in the required numbers each year, without regard to the means of their parents.

At the universities: Staff and accommodation must be increased at the appropriate speed.

Finance: The necessary funds must be made available, mainly by the Chancellor of the Exchequer.

Careers: The demand for graduates of the different faculties, year by year, must be sufficient to absorb the increasing output.

The committee is to be warmly congratulated on this imaginative and courageous plan, and the Government on its ready acceptance of it. Immediately after the publication of the report, the UGC asked the individual universities to submit their proposals. Their response was remarkable. For instance, my own University of Manchester, which had been giving intensive consideration to the problems of post-war expansion for two years, submitted a plan to the UGC in July, rather more than doubling the total number of whole-time students in ten years (from about 2,400 to 5,000), and giving separate targets for each faculty. It is understood that other universities are tackling the matter with equal vigour.

The Clapham Report. Another important report was presented to the Lord President of the Council in July 1946, dealing with the much neglected question of the social sciences at the universities. It follows the precedent of the Goodenough Committee, in recommending that the Treasury should make a special grant to the universities for the social sciences, and that the University Grants Committee should set up a special sub-committee 'to survey systematically the range of work in this field undertaken by the several universities, and if gaps are revealed, as we believe they would be, to offer such stimulus as may be necessary to secure that they are effectively filled.' This means positive planning of university development by the UGC, and is the recommendation of a committee consisting of seven distinguished university teachers and one civil servant. Times are indeed changing fast!

The Treasury

The most conclusive evidence of the change of opinion as to the national importance of the universities is provided by the actions of the Chancellor of the Exchequer both of the Coalition and of the Labour Governments. The government grant to the universities had risen slowly from £1 million to just over £2 million per annum between 1920 and 1939. In 1945 Sir John Anderson almost trebled the annual grant, bringing it up to £5.5 million. This year, Mr Dalton has increased the total grant to over £9 million, and has for the first time included a substantial sum for capital expenditure. And statements by Mr Dalton, and the acceptance by the Government of the Barlow Report, make it clear that the Government intends to provide what financial aid is necessary to enable the universities to carry through the programme of doubling their numbers in ten years.

Assuming that costs settle down at 50 per cent above the 1938 level, expansion on this scale, and on the standards likely to be acceptable, may well involve a capital expenditure during the next ten years of £100 million, and an income in 1955 of perhaps £25 to £30 million.

Where is this money to come from?

The income from students' fees is about £2 million. There is wide agreement that fees ought to be reduced if possible; certainly not increased. So the maximum contribution from fees (when numbers have been doubled) should not exceed £4 million per annum.

The local authorities made for the year 1937/38 grants totalling approximately £566,000 to the universities. A substantial increase may reasonably be expected.

Gifts and endowments bring in about £1.5 million. In spite of all difficulties, recent gifts from industrialists and private benefactors have been on an encouraging scale; and it may be hoped that in view of the nationalisation of the hospitals, the universities may become the main recipients of benefactions, as they are in America. In that case, a large increase of capital gifts and some increase of income from these sources may be hoped for.

Such a development is of the first importance. The Government has shown, and is likely to show, moderation and wisdom in using its powers of finance to control the universities. But in the general interest it is most desirable that the other sources of income available to the universities should be on a scale comparable to the grants from the Government.

Even so, it seems quite clear that, if the Barlow plan is to be completed in ten years, the Exchequer will have to provide three-quarters of the capital needed (say £75 million) and three-quarters of the income of the expanded universities (say £20 million).

The Future

The University Grants Committee

The carrying out of the ten-year Barlow plan involves the setting up of suitable machinery both by the Government and the universities. The UGC has hitherto almost confined itself to the distribution of a block grant, and to friendly and useful advice. Much more positive action is now required.

The UGC is a Treasury committee. This is most unusual; normally such a committee would be responsible to some other department, with Treasury control in the background. Indeed, it has been suggested that the responsibility for the universities might be transferred to the Lord President of the Council or to the Minister of Education. But the present arrangement has worked well; it has the confidence of the universities; Sir John Anderson, a Fellow of the Royal Society, and Mr Dalton, a former university lecturer, have shown a keen interest in university affairs; and there seems to be general agreement that direct Treasury control of the UGC is the best arrangement.

Mr Dalton has already taken the first and most important step to adapt the UGC to the changed needs of today by giving it new terms of reference, in order that 'the Committee should play a more important and influential part than in the past'. For this purpose, the Committee is instructed 'to assist, in consultation with the universities and other bodies concerned, the preparation and execution of such plans for the development of the universities as may from time to time be required in order to ensure that they are fully adequate to national needs.'

The UGC will in future clearly be responsible

(a) for seeing that the right number of students are educated year by year for the country as a whole and in individual universities

(b) for creating new universities as required

(c) for ensuring that the right numbers are educated in the different faculties

(d) for preventing undue gaps and redundancies in the facilities available in the different fields

(e) generally speaking for seeing that the universities meet the requirements of the nation.

It is clear that these new terms of reference must be regarded as a deliberate decision by the Government that the UGC is to be a planning organ of the first importance; and it must be recognised that through its control of finance it will have very great power.

It is also given a new duty 'to collect, examine and make available information on matters relating to university education at home and abroad'. This is an important innovation. At present British universities are rarely fully informed, even as to what is being done in this country. Of what is being done abroad, most university people know very little. Further, the general public regards university education much as it did secondary education before 1902, as a remote sphere with which it has no concern. The UGC has hitherto done little to help in this respect; it is to be hoped that it will in future publish an informative annual report and special reports and memoranda on different problems of university policy.

To carry out its new duties successfully, the Committee needs two changes. Firstly, it has a secretariat quite inadequate even for its old duties. A much larger staff, of high quality, is essential. Secondly, the membership of the Committee requires broadening. It has hitherto consisted almost exclusively of professors or retired professors. The Committee is now to be responsible for ensuring that the universities 'are fully adequate to national needs'. The present Committee knows intimately the needs of the universities, but is not adequately in touch with national needs. It should be strengthened by adding persons with experience of the national needs in different fields such as public affairs, industry, education, and health services.

A Joint Universities Council

Since the UGC will in future be a powerful planning organ representing the Government, it is important that there should be a correspondingly influential organ representing the universities, which could put the universities' point of view to the Committee with authority. There are two possibilities: the present Committee of Vice-Chancellors, or a new Joint Universities Council.

The Committee of Vice-Chancellors is an informal body, which has grown gradually. It has been a meeting of busy administrators to discuss current affairs of mutual interest, and has been useful, and indeed indispensable, especially during the war, when the Government consulted it on many important matters. But it has no funds, and has never concerned itself with long-term policy. It has, so far as I know, never published any report of any kind.

If the Vice-Chancellors' Committee were formally recognised by the universities as their representative body, and were given funds for secretarial purposes it could probably be made into an efficient representative body. But it might be considered somewhat undemocratic. The Vice-Chancellors are officials appointed for life, and it is more usual for representatives on such a body to be elected by their constituents for a limited period.

There is, therefore, a case for the appointment by the universities of a new body, constituted perhaps rather on the lines of the Universities Conference held in September, which included four representatives from each university, a member of the governing body, the Vice-Chancellor, a professor, and a member of the junior staff. This might be called 'The Joint Universities Council'. Proposals to this effect have been made by the Association of University Teachers, and by others. Such a council should be useful in the following ways:

(a) to make representations to and negotiate with the UGC and other government departments; for this and other purposes an executive committee would be required, which would no doubt include Vice-Chancellors as well as representatives of other aspects of university life;

(b) to discuss matters of interest to the universities; to appoint committees to investigate problems; to publish reports;

(c) to hold an annual conference;

(d) to maintain contact with foreign universities and with UNESCO.

In order to do these tasks effectively, the Council would require a highly competent secretariat, and an income of not less than £10,000 a year for offices and staff.

Perhaps the best solution might be that the Vice-Chancellors' Committee should carry on their present functions with a stronger secretariat; and that a Joint Universities Council should be appointed to deal with larger matters of policy on the general lines here suggested.

The Freedom of the Universities

It we analyse the actions as regards universities which have been taken or announced by different government departments, they all appear to come under the following four headings:

1. Information, guidance, and advice:
(a) by the UGC on behalf of the Treasury;
(b) by other departments, such as the Ministries of Health, Education and Labour, and the Department of the Lord President of the Council. These departments act on the advice of their civil servants, reinforced by the reports of special committees, such as Goodenough and McNair. Before taking action, the Ministries always consult the universities freely; the committees on whose advice they act have all contained a strong element of university teachers and administrators.

2. An overall long-term plan as to the total number of graduates required from the different faculties, and the shares of the individual universities. The UGC is responsible for this; the Ministry of Education has the major responsibility for ensuring that the necessary number of boys and girls are suitably educated; the Ministry of Labour for trying to ensure that suitable jobs shall be available for all graduates.

3. Settling the relations of the universities with other institutions of higher learning, such as technical and teachers' training colleges. (Ministry of Education)

4. Finance:
(a) Direct grants from the Treasury through the UGC.
(b) Grants from other departments, such as Ministry of Education grants for scholarships, in connection with teachers' training, and perhaps Ministry of Health grants in connection with teaching hospitals.

There is, I believe, general agreement that the actions of the various departments of state, both under the Coalition and the Labour Governments, have shown a new appreciation of the services which the universities render to the nation and of their potential development, and a new willingness to do what lies in their power, financially and otherwise, to help to provide the conditions under which the universities can do their work most effectively. I believe that this new spirit of active helpfulness on the part of the Government is widely welcomed in the universities and that it may well mark the beginning of a new epoch in the history of British universities.

Is there any danger that all this government activity may develop so as to interfere with any of the essential freedoms of the universities?

I have never met anybody who does not believe that the real independence and full responsibility of the universities in their appropriate fields is of fundamental importance, and that any interference by the

Government would be disastrous. Academic matters such as appointments, standards and methods of teaching and research are left wholly to the individual university, and it is almost unthinkable that the Government should consider intervening, so long as all goes well. It is, I think, certainly true that none of the fields in which the Government has taken or is contemplating action have anything whatever to do with academic standards or methods. I am not aware of any protest, nor of any serious unrest at what might in the past have been regarded as the prospect of government control involving a risk of the undermining of university freedom and responsibility. But it would surely be a wise precaution for the universities to set up as strong and representative a body as possible to watch the actions of government departments and to put the university case clearly, effectively and authoritatively.

Conclusion

The most encouraging fact in the university world today is the discovery, announced in the Barlow Report, that only one in five of the ablest boys and girls now get a university education; and the most difficult task needed for the full achievement of the Barlow plan is undoubtedly to ensure that in ten years, instead of one-fifth, perhaps four-fifths of the ablest should go to a university. This would make it possible to double the size of universities, and at the same time, so far from lowering standards, to raise them to such an extent that the less able, who at present form half the students, would no longer be admitted.

Sir Cyril Norwood has pointed out persuasively (and somewhat pessimistically) in the *Times* that there are great difficulties in the very rapid expansion proposed in the Barlow Report, and has suggested that we should deal with the immediate problem of the large numbers of ex-servicemen, and then think again about the future. But can we afford to wait? The aim has been set high, and it will be quite impossible to achieve it if we adopt a 'wait and see' policy. Success depends on good planning and vigorous action *now*. And, fortunately, this is happening in a most encouraging and indeed remarkable way. At the time of writing less than five months have elapsed since the date of publication of the Barlow Report. In that time the Lord President has announced the acceptance by the Government of the report and of its financial implications; the Chancellor of the Exchequer has given the UGC the necessary authority to co-operate with the universities in the making and execution of the plan; the Minister of Education has shown her active sympathy, and taken important steps; the UGC has asked for proposals from every university;

the universities are hard at work – some of them have already actually sent in ten-year plans.

This is a fine response to a great and exhilarating plan. If all concerned continue for ten years to work at it steadily in the same co-operative spirit and with the same vigour and energy with which it has been begun, then surely they will succeed, and the nation will secure the greatly increased supply of able and highly educated men and women, which it so urgently needs.

Notes

[1] I know of no problem more difficult than the settling of a fair scale of salaries for professors. The conflict between the social and market value seems to be insoluble. Is it reasonable that professors of surgery should be paid twice as much as professors of philosophy?

2. A Historical Document: Statement by the Committee of Vice-Chancellors and Principals

Universities Quarterly Vol. 1 (1946–47), pp. 189–191.

The following statement has been received from Sir Hector Hetherington, chairman of the CVCP:

> *A Note on University Policy and Finance in the Decennium 1947–56* was prepared in July 1946 by the Committee of Vice-Chancellors and Principals, in order to present to the University Grants Committee the collective views of the Vice-Chancellors on certain important issues, both of policy and finance, which seemed to arise from the succession of official reports dealing with various aspects of university activity.
>
> The Committee of Vice-Chancellors and Principals, although constituted by formal acts of the governing bodies of the several universities, is a consultative body only; and no statement issuing from the committee without the prior approval of university governing bodies can be taken to express the views of these bodies, or to imply their assent. As is stated in the first paragraph of the note, that is the situation in the present instance. The note was prepared and approved by the Vice-Chancellors' Committee itself, and has not undergone scrutiny by any other body.
>
> As will be appreciated, it was written in a particular context, with reference to a particular set of documents, and primarily for the consideration of the University Grants Committee. But it seemed to the Vice-Chancellors that university governing bodies would be glad to be informed of the views at which the Vice-Chancellors had arrived after their study of the official reports. It was therefore agreed that copies of the note should be furnished to each university for distribution and use as might be thought fit. The note is not a private document. But the Vice-Chancellors desire that readers of the note should be aware of the limits, both of its authority and of the purpose for which it was prepared.

Part I deals with questions of administration; it includes much that is interesting and sometimes controversial. Part II deals with finance, and concludes that the proportion of university income to be found from government sources will be increased from roughly one-third to three-quarters in the next few years. Part III deals with the future relations of the Government and the universities. This is so important that we quote the following fairly full extracts:

> The universities entirely accept the view that the Government has not only the right, but the duty to satisfy itself that every field of study which in the national interest ought to be cultivated in Great Britain, is in fact being adequately cultivated in the university system and that the resources which are placed at the disposal of the universities are being used with full regard both to efficiency and to economy.
>
> In the view of the Vice-Chancellors, therefore, the universities may properly be expected not only individually to make proper use of the resources entrusted to them, but collectively to devise and execute policies calculated to serve the national interest. And in that task, both individually and collectively, they will be glad to have a greater measure of guidance from the Government than until quite recent days they have been accustomed to receive . . .
>
> From its foundation the committee has exercised a positive influence on the policy of every university . . . Probably in the last 20 years no university has undertaken any important development without full consultation with the committee and its officers: and the universities have always recognised that inevitably and rightly the committee has the duty of reflecting in its financial decisions, its judgment of the merits of their policies.
>
> Hence the Vice-Chancellors would be glad if the University Grants Committee were formally authorised and equipped to undertake surveys of all the main fields of university activity designed to secure that as a whole the universities are meeting the whole range of national need for higher teaching and research . . .
>
> The Vice-Chancellors would not exempt the universities themselves from the necessity of playing their own part in the co-operative planning of the whole university system. It falls to them, at least as much as to the Grants Committee, to devise methods of working together to ensure the complete fulfilment of their common task. There are matters which call for central discussion on the national scale. There are others which are best dealt with regionally. There is also the important and complex matter of relations with the Dominion universities, with the higher educational service of the Colonies and with the universities of the United States and of Europe . . . The Vice-Chancellors have recently appointed two committees drawn from experts in particular problems outside the membership of the commitee to report on matters of general consequence to the universities. Other similar studies will be undertaken as speedily as conditions allow. It is the hope of the Vice-Chancellors that in this way and in others, the universities will be able to co-operate with one another and with the University Grants Committee in the planning and development of a full range of university service.

Comment

This is clearly a document of outstanding importance. Together with the actions taken by the Chancellor of the Exchequer it inaugurates a new epoch of planning and of expansion in the universities of Britain.

The memorandum has now been circulated to the universities, and the universities have been asked to quadruple their grants to the Universities Bureau of the British Empire, a body which is, in practice, controlled by the Vice-Chancellors, and which finances the Committee of Vice-Chancellors and Principals. It is to be hoped that universities will agree, since the committee cannot work effectively without a strong secretariat. If the universities (after having received the memorandum) do make substantially increased grants to the bureau, this action would undoubtedly mean endorsement by the universities of the memorandum, and would also be implicitly a vote of confidence in the Committee of Vice-Chancellors and Principals as the official negotiating body on behalf of the universities. It is important that universities should realise that they are, in fact, taking this decisive step.

The Committee of Vice-Chancellors and Principals was constituted in 1919. In 1931 the universities authorised its continued existence as a body for discussion, but with no power to take action on behalf of the universities or to commit the universities. During the war years the Government did, in fact, consult the committee regularly about university affairs, and act on its advice.

During the past 12 months the committee has become much more active. Not only has it published the almost revolutionary memorandum which is the subject of this comment, but it has also appointed an important committee to enquire into the whole question of halls of residence for the modern universities, and the memorandum states that the Vice-Chancellors propose from time to time to appoint other similar committees of enquiry.

In view of the new powers and the greatly increased activity of the University Grants Committee it is clearly necessary that the universities should have a national negotiating body in which they have full confidence, and there can be no doubt that the universities are unanimous that the Committee of Vice-Chancellors and Principals must fulfil this function.

3. Student Numbers 1911 to 1971

Universities Quarterly Vol. 10 (1955–56), pp. 122–131.

The universities have rather suddenly become aware that the number of young persons fit for and wanting a university education is likely to increase on a considerable scale during the next ten years. This is due to two causes: first of all, the so-called 'bulge' in births immediately after the war, and secondly, the fact that the proportion of the age group reaching the sixth forms of the grammar schools has been increasing rapidly in the last few years and is likely to continue to do so. The object of this article is to suggest that action is urgently needed now in relation to two aspects of this matter: an immediate beginning should be made towards providing university buildings on a much larger scale than hitherto, and there should be a rapid increase in the number of students in science, but more especially in technology.

History of Student Numbers, 1911–1955

The history of student numbers at the universities of England and Wales in the last 50 years can teach us important lessons. The main facts are shown in Figure 1. In 1911 there were 20,000 students in the universities of England and Wales.[1] As a result of World War I the number was increased by 16,000 (or 75 per cent) in about two years. Then, the war stimulus having gone, the numbers remained roughly stable for the next 20 years.

In 1944 the Barlow Report demanded urgently that the numbers be increased by about 80 per cent within a decade. The Report pointed out that 'Only about 1 in 5 of the ablest boys and girls actually reach the universities . . . There is clearly an ample reserve of intelligence in the country to allow both a doubling of university numbers and a raising of standards.'

The demand of the Barlow Report to increase numbers by 80 per cent

FIGURE 1

Full-time University Students in England and Wales

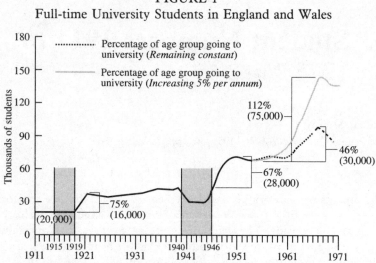

Sources: 1911 to 1954: University Grants Committee.
1955 to 1971: Based on estimates of the population aged 18, 19 and 20 made by Professor Lancelot Hogben on the basis of Life Table, 1950–52 prepared by D. W. Taylor.
Note: The UGC normally gives the academic year, e.g., 1910–11, which includes three months of 1910 and nine months of 1911. For the sake of simplicity in this article I propose to use the later year in each case, e.g., 1911.

was achieved not in a decade but in two years. To quote from the UGC Report published in 1948: 'The desired increase of numbers by about 80% within a decade can only be described as revolutionary . . . It has in fact been almost completed in two years.'

This very rapid increase ceased, though there was a further slow increase up to 1950 when the total number of students was 68,000, an increase of two-thirds on the 1939 figure. After 1950 the numbers slowly decreased. This trend was reversed in 1954, and there has been a welcome, though small, increase in the last two years.

The net result is that as compared with 1911 the number of students has been trebled; this increase took place almost entirely in two sudden bursts of two or three years, one after each war. They seem to have been due to four main causes:

(a)   The general change of opinion as to the importance of enabling a larger proportion of the population to enjoy university education.

(b) The realization of the urgent need for more scientists.

(c) The desire to meet the claims of the ex-servicemen to a university career who had missed their chance during the war.

(d) The financial generosity of the Government which greatly increased its revenue grants and began to make substantial grants for capital expenditure.

It was an astonishing and a most encouraging achievement. All the difficulties of providing teachers and buildings were somehow overcome by a great effort on the part of the universities, supported by generous grants from the Government, scholarships from the local authorities, and wise guidance by the UGC. It is generally agreed that this increase was achieved without any substantial lowering of standards.

The Bulge

The increase in births during the first few years after the war known as 'the bulge' has passed through the elementary schools and is now entering the secondary schools. It will reach the universities about 1960, and the peak year will be 1967. The increases in the figures of university numbers due to the bulge alone (not allowing for an increasing proportion staying on to the sixth form) are shown in the left-hand column of Table 1, reaching a maximum of 39 per cent above the 1954 figure between 1965 and 1969.

Much more difficult to assess is the probable increase in the proportion of the age group which is likely to reach the sixth form. This has increased by 5 per cent per annum between 1951–55 when the total age group remained virtually unchanged. It is thought that this rate of increase may continue and the right-hand column in Table 1 has been calculated on this assumption. It will be seen that if the 5 per cent increase does continue, the number who might wish for entry to the university would be more than doubled by 1967. How long it will in fact continue is a matter which will depend on the demand for graduates, and on action by the Ministry of Education, local authorities, schools and parents. No confident estimate can be made.

It seems, however, clear that if we are to give all sixth-form leavers the same opportunity of a university course as they now have, the entry in 1965 will have to be somewhere between 40 per cent and 100 per cent above the present level. Sir James Mountford, in his address to the Court of Liverpool University in November 1955, stated: 'I have formed the

TABLE 1
Full-Time University Students, England and Wales

	Percentage of age group going to university remaining constant		Percentage of age group to university increasing 5% per annum	
	Average number per year	Percentage increase on 1954	Average number per year	Percentage increase on 1954
1954	66,600	–	66,600	–
1955–59	69,500	4	70,300	6
1960–64	75,200	13	90,900	36
1965–69	92,400	39	134,000	101
1970–73	82,400	24	138,000	107

Source: Based on estimates of population aged 18, 19, 20 submitted by Professor Lancelot Hogben on basis of Life Table 1950–52 prepared by D. W. Taylor.

opinion that if we can accommodate them and if funds are provided to send them to us, the total number in the universities by 1964 is likely to be 50 per cent in excess of our present number.' This would mean that the number of students in England and Wales would increase to 100,000.[2]

Fortunately, it is not necessary to plan so far ahead. Only one thing is immediately urgent in this matter of total numbers: to begin at once to erect the necessary buildings. To quote again from Sir James Mountford's speech:

The one thing in which we have been starved has been the provision of buildings in which to carry on our work. In this matter our experience during the last ten years has been one of continuous disappointment and frustration; and within the foreseeable future, unless drastic action is taken now, the situation for the universities will become unmanageable and from a national point of view quite disastrous.

Technology

There is one field where rapid expansion is by universal agreement of first-rate and urgent importance: the field of technology. During the latter war years and the post-war decade, in spite of considerable pressure from certain quarters and the appointment of a number of committees, deplorably little has been done in Britain to expand technological

TABLE 2
Degrees and Diplomas awarded in Pure Science and Technology

	1948	1954	Increase 1954 on 1948
Pure Science	4,426	5,599	26.5%
Technology	3,031	3,359	10.8%

Source: UGC Reports for 1947–48 and 1953–54.

education at university level. After 1945 the number of scientists was rapidly doubled, as recommended in the Barlow Report. After 1948 expansion was much slower. Table 2 shows the degrees and diplomas awarded in Great Britain in pure science and technology respectively in 1948 and 1954.

The rate of increase in pure scientists over the period was 4 per cent per annum; the increase in technologists only 1¾ per cent per annum.

The urgency of this matter is illustrated in Figure 2 showing the number of graduates per year over the last 20 years or so in all scientific fields in the United States, the USSR and Great Britain. Great Britain is today producing about one-fifth of the number produced by the USA and one-eighth of the number produced by Russia. What this means is that both Russia and the USA produce about twice as many graduates in science and technology each year per thousand of the population as we do.[3]

There is nothing wrong with our scientists. A Nobel prize winner in physics has recently written: 'The Science Departments of our universities are better and more vigorous than they have ever been in the history of this country: they are good by any standard and compare well with those of any other country to-day.'[4] What is wrong in this country is that there are far too few engineers to develop our scientists' ideas as fast and as well as is done in some other countries. It requires engineers in considerable numbers to turn the results of scientific research into articles of practical value, and it is notorious that the Americans, thanks to their wealth of engineers, frequently develop and successfully put on the world market the results of the research of British scientists: penicillin is only one of the many outstanding examples.

As shown in Figure 2, the rate of increase of the output of graduates in science and technology in the Soviet Union in the last five years has been more than 10 per cent per annum. There can be little doubt that the Soviet

FIGURE 2

Graduates per Year in all Scientific Fields. United States, Soviet Union and Great Britain

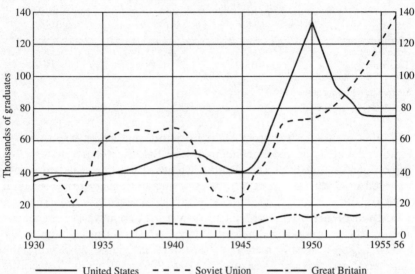

——— United States　　- - - - Soviet Union　　—·— Great Britain

Source: *New York Times*, 7 November 1954. 'A Comparison of the Output of Technicians in the USA and USSR.' The figures for Great Britain are taken from UGC reports.
The figures for all three countries include medical degrees.
Note: The figures for Great Britain exclude Higher National Certificates and National Diplomas. In 1954 just over 7,000 were awarded, and if these were included the figure for 1954 would be 50 per cent higher.
We know that there are many technical colleges in Russia which do not grant degrees. The number of students is unknown.

Union is making an effort to develop their education and particularly their scientific and technological education at the highest level, at a speed not previously attempted by any great nation in history. What is frightening is that as is well known a large proportion of their scientists and engineers are devoting their work to preparations for war. To quote Mr Lewis Strauss, Chairman of the US Atomic Energy Commission (*Manchester Guardian*, 22 November 1955): 'The Russian tests indicate an exceedingly intensive effort by the Soviet Government to develop their nuclear weapons potential.' And evidence, which is now overwhelming, has been rapidly accumulating in the last year or two that the quality of Soviet top scientists is excellent. Their achievements in the design of aircraft, of hydrogen bombs, of the radio telescope and in many other fields are as good as anything in the world.

A leading Professor of Physics writes: 'Soviet engineering of nuclear reactors is at a surprisingly high level; their research seems to cover all that we are doing, but in addition very much more.' To show the extent to which the Soviets are devoting their energies to high-level research, he tells the following story: 'Ernest Lawrence (the man who developed the cyclotron) met his opposite number, Professor Wechsler, who is in charge of the Russian nuclear machine programme. They are just now finishing an enormous machine which will remain unsurpassed for at least three to five years in the West. It contains 36,000 tons of steel and the total cost must be in the region of £15–£20 million! Lawrence asked Wechsler where he got the funds from for these machines. "I do not know what you mean." "I mean from where did you get the money?" Wechsler replied, "I do not understand; we decided that this was the machine we wanted and so we built it." ' To quote Sir Solly Zuckerman, Deputy Chairman of the Government Advisory Council: 'Everyone who has studied the Russian educational system has been impressed by its emphasis on science and engineering, by the high standards and equally high degree of specialization, and by the speed of its growth' (*Times Educational Supplement* 30 December 1955).

Another country which sets us an example is Switzerland. Its Zurich Technical University has just celebrated its centenary. The population of Switzerland is under 5 million: about equal to the population of the area served by Manchester University. But Zurich, which is one of the highest grade universities of technology in the world, has at present 2,700 whole-time degree students, which is more than our three largest institutions – Imperial College, Glasgow and Manchester – added together. Largely as a result of the work of the Zurich Technical University, Switzerland, with no coal, no iron, no home market, and no seaport, but with three times as many fully qualified engineers as Britain in proportion to its population, has built up an engineering industry of a considerable size and of a quality equal to anything in the world.

The number of graduate engineers produced in the United States, the Soviet Union and Great Britain in 1950 and 1954 is shown in Table 3.

In view of all these facts, it is perhaps not surprising, but it is profoundly disquieting, that the 50 British productivity teams which have visited the United States report with monotonous regularity that the output per man in that country is about double what it is in Britain. Can anybody doubt that a major factor in that difference is our shortage of qualified engineers compared with the USA?

No wonder that all progressive British engineering firms know the desperate shortage of graduates in technology and science at the present

TABLE 3
Graduate Engineers in 1950 and 1954

	1950	1954
USA	50,000	20,000
Soviet Union	28,000	54,000
Great Britain	3,600	3,400

Sources: For the USA and USSR, article in *New York Times*, 7 November 1954. For the UK, UGC reports – figures relate to academic years 1949–50 and 1953–54 and are for degrees and university diplomas in technology.

time. This is undoubtedly beginning seriously to hamper both home production and our very important engineering exports. Mr Butler has expressed his hope and indeed his confidence that we may double our standard of living in the next generation, but we are in increasingly keen competition with Germany, the United States and other industrial countries, and unless we are as well provided as they are with first-rate engineers our industries and our exports will inevitably suffer. Our standard of living depends on exports, and exports depend to a very large extent on a first-rate engineering industry which must be fully comparable in quality and quantity with the leading industrial countries of the world. Otherwise we shall certainly not achieve Mr Butler's ideal of doubling our standard of living in 25 years. All engineering firms are finding grave difficulties in recruiting good young engineers. My own moderate-sized firms are spending thousands a year in advertising for suitable graduates and we are failing to get more than about half our needs. What is much more serious is that even the Atomic Energy Authority, which has very high priority, states in its first report: '. . . the difficulty of recruiting and retaining sufficient skilled scientists, engineers and craftsmen has been acute throughout the ten years of the project, and shows no signs of becoming easier . . . our demand is not at present being met.'

The Government has recently – at long last – instructed the UGC to take energetic steps to increase the number of students in technology. Substantial grants are being made to Imperial College, and to the Technical Colleges in Glasgow and Manchester, and on a somewhat smaller scale to other universities.

This is a welcome beginning, but it is only a beginning, and there can be no doubt that we shall have to go much further and much faster if we are going to hold our own in the very competitive engineering markets of the world.

At what rate should we increase our output of technologists? Russia, which has still a relatively low standard of living, has as a matter of high policy been devoting a much greater proportion of her national income to technical and scientific education than we have. She has succeeded during the last five years in increasing the number of graduates in all scientific fields by over 10 per cent per annum; we have been content with 4 per cent for scientists and less than 2 per cent for technologists. The Russians, starting with a higher proportion of technological graduates, have increased their output more than five times as fast as we. Surely we cannot be content with so miserable a rate of increase? Should we not insist on increasing our output of graduates both in science and in technology at least as fast as the Russians?

Conclusion

This article has been almost entirely confined to the two questions: what total number of university students and what number of students of technology should we aim at? I have not considered the question of the demand for graduates in science and technology for teaching, for industry and elsewhere, nor the many difficult questions as to how the desirable increases in numbers are to be achieved. In view of the history of the demand for graduates in recent years and the small proportion of graduates in our population, we can surely take this demand for granted. The proposals I have made are simple: firstly, the rate of building for universities must at once be increased so as to provide reasonable accommodation for an increase of 50 per cent in the total number of students by 1965; secondly, we must take much more energetic action immediately so as to secure an increase of 10 per cent each year in the output of graduates of technology.

Table 4 compares this demand for an increase in the total size of the universities with what was achieved after the two world wars.

TABLE 4
Increases in Total Size of the Universities

	Increased percentage of full-time students	Time taken to achieve the increase
After World War I	75	2 years
After World War II	64	2–3 years
1955–65	50	10 years

Clearly the task before us today is relatively easy: a smaller proportionate increase, and four times as long in which to achieve it.

As regards the increase in technology, the difficulties can certainly be no greater than those which have been successfully overcome by the Soviet Union during the last five years.

The universities of Britain have done an outstanding job during the last ten years. This has been achieved as a result of much devoted work by university staffs and by Vice-Chancellors, aided by generous grants from the Treasury and scholarships from the local authorities, and wisely guided by the UGC. The schools, parents and industry have also played their part. Given real determination on the part of all concerned, the twin tasks of increasing the total university numbers by 50 per cent in ten years and of increasing the graduates in technology 10 per cent annually should offer no serious difficulties.

Notes

[1] Scotland is omitted because some essential figures are not available.

[2] It must be remembered that England has probably less university students per thousand of the population than any other industrial country. The figure is double in Scotland, treble in Australia and Canada, four times as great in Russia, and nine times as great in the United States. To take one point only: in Scotland all teachers in secondary schools are university graduates. If we adopted the same policy here it would increase the annual demand for graduates by about 2,500.

[3] The position is perhaps not quite so black for Britain as shown by these figures. Our graduates may well be on the average of a higher quality than the Americans; and we may produce more non-graduate technicians of good quality than America. Accurate comparisons with the USA are impossible; still more impossible with Russia.

[4] P. M. S. Blackett, 'The Education of the Scientist in the University of Today' *Universities Quarterly*, May 1950.

4. University Admissions: Report of an Enquiry

R. K. Kelsall

Universities Quarterly Vol. 11 (1956–57), pp. 331–34.

The *Report on an Enquiry into Applications for Admission to Universities*, prepared for the Committee of Vice-Chancellors and Principals (Kelsall 1957) provides essential factual information that was previously lacking on a very wide variety of university matters. It shows how many applications for admission to full-time first degree and diploma courses in the session 1955–56 were made to universities and colleges in Great Britain and Northern Ireland (other than Oxford, Cambridge and Aberdeen) after May 1954, and how many *applicants* were involved.

Its greatest significance for me, however, lay in the additional information it made available for the study of the career open to talents. The group of investigations first reported on in *Social Mobility in Britain* (1954) had given a more precise indication than before of the limited extent to which, in the half-century before the 1944 Education Act, talented children of parents low in the social scale were obtaining entry to high status occupations. My own study of one such occupation, *Higher Civil Servants in Britain* (1955), had shown the comparatively modest degree to which it was recruited from the working class. Of those above the rank of assistant secretary in 1950, for example, only 17 per cent were the children of manual workers; and amongst the new entrants to the administrative class by the open competitions of 1949–52 the corresponding proportion was 19 per cent. In the population at large, on the other hand, over 70 per cent of the occupied male population was engaged in manual work. And several investigations had recently made it clear that considerably more than half of the country's children in the highest-scoring group for measured intelligence came from working-class families. Finally, *Early Leaving* (1954) and Jean Floud's *Social Class and Educational Opportunity* (1957) had provided evidence that, in England's maintained grammar schools, the proportion of working-class children at the point of entry was roughly in accordance with what the relative size of the social strata in the general population would lead one to expect; but that those leaving these schools with a reasonable academic record showed a very different social-origin distribution.

In what respects does the present report add to our knowledge in this field? It provides detailed information regarding the proportions in which 'home' entrants to different faculties and different universities and groups of universities in 1955–56 came from the various social classes. The variations in these proportions as between the sexes, the faculties and the university groups are sometimes quite considerable, though they are not altogether unexpected. By themselves these variations do not, of course, prove that there has been either sex or social discrimination in student selection; for we do not know the social origin or the educational qualifications of the whole universe of candidates from which those entering a particular department or faculty of a particular university were chosen. One thing is, however, quite clear from the figures published in the report. Taking 'home' applicants only, the social-origin pattern of all those who entered British Universities (other than Oxford, Cambridge and Aberdeen) in 1955–56 for full-time degree and diploma courses, did not differ very much from that of all those who applied for entry but were not in fact admitted. Social discrimination at the point of university entry, therefore, cannot be the explanation of the low proportion of working-class children amongst the 1955–56 entrants as a whole.

This low proportion is clearly due, in the main, to the failure of those of humble social origin to apply for admission in sufficiently large numbers. This failure, in its turn, is mainly due to lack of paper qualifications, though not aspiring to university education must also be a factor of some importance. The sequence of events can be shown in a particularly striking form by concentrating our attention in the first instance on boys at maintained grammar schools in England. In the Central Advisory Council's Report, *Early Leaving*, it was shown, on the basis of a sample investigation, that some 66 per cent of the top selection group in the 1946 intake to such schools came from working-class families. It was also shown that, by Easter 1953, only 47 per cent of the boys in the group with the kind of qualifications needed for university entry were in that social category. The study of applications for university admission in 1955–56 now shows that, of the admitted men with English addresses who had been educated at maintained grammar schools, only 36 per cent had manual-working fathers. It also shows that, when those educated at direct-grant and independent schools are added to those from maintained grammar schools, the proportion of those of this social origin falls to 26 per cent.

TABLE 1

Social Origin of the 'Home' Students Admitted with Permanent Addresses in England who Attended Maintained Grammar Schools and Whose Fathers' Occupations Are Known

Compared with that of (1) the highest maintained grammar school selection group, and (2) those with the best maintained grammar school academic record in the *Early Leaving* Report.

(This table is reproduced from page 10 of the Report.)

Father's occupation	Males				Females			
	Early Leaving Report Maintained grammar school selection group 1 %	Maintained grammar school academic record category A %	All universities admitted with addresses in England who attended maintained grammar schools %	All universities admitted with addresses in England (irrespective of type of secondary school attended) %	*Early Leaving* Report Maintained grammar school selection group 1 %	Maintained grammar school academic record category A %	All universities admitted with addresses in England who attended maintained grammar schools %	All universities admitted with addresses in England (irrespective of type of secondary school attended) %
Professional, managerial and clerical	33.5	52.6	63.5	74.0	36.1	62.1	74.5	81.4
Skilled manual	45.3	38.8	30.3	21.7	43.9	32.8	21.9	16.1
Semi-skilled manual	16.3	7.1	4.9	3.4	14.6	3.7	2.8	1.9
Unskilled manual	4.9	1.6	1.3	0.9	5.4	1.4	0.8	0.6

The report also adds considerably to our knowledge of another aspect of the problem of the career open to talents, the closely related question of self-recruitment in the professions. Remarkably little information has hitherto been available showing the extent to which particular professions are recruited from the children of fathers engaged in those professions. In one chapter of *Social Mobility in Britain* an attempt was made to assemble such material as could be found, and to arrive at certain tentative conclusions regarding four professions. Now that we have data on the occupations of the fathers of those entering faculties of medicine in 1955–56 it is possible to provide a much clearer and more reliable picture of self-recruitment in the medical profession.

5. British Universities and Intellectual Life

A. H. Halsey
Universities Quarterly Vol. 12 (1957–58), pp. 141–52.

It is one feature of industrial society that the universities have never held a more central place in the structure of intellectual life than they do today. As the Vice-Chancellor of the University of Southampton has recently pointed out, 'it was London and not Christ Church which was midwife to Locke's *Essay concerning Human Understanding*. Oxford and Cambridge could hardly claim the Royal Society as their child and Newton found London more congenial than Cambridge . . . But all this was changed as the 19th century drew on; increasingly the great names in science, philosophy and history were university names (James 1956). Today the universities lead, if they do not monopolise, all branches of science and the arts except perhaps for the fine arts and poetry.

Yet superficial acquaintance with the great volume of recent discussion of liberal studies in the modern world quickly conveys an impression of pessimism, amounting almost to despair, on the part of the humanists. It is as if they accepted a general notion of historical development which postulates two extreme types of society, the aristocratic/feudal and the industrial/technological and which conceives of intellectual life as geared by irremovable chains to the technological base of society in its movement from the former to the latter. But leaving aside the simple minded monocausal nature of this notion, I would suggest that liberal studies are by no means necessarily in decline.

Of course, the crude historical theory underlying current pessimism has within it some truth concerning the intellectual balance of contemporary universities. It is true that the humanities are wedded historically to an aristocratic tradition. Their expression in the institutions of formal education originated in the vocational needs of aristocracy and its religious and secular administrations. Accordingly, as vested interests in the universities, the humanities remain most strong in the European universities of ancient foundation and least confident, most defensive, in American communities founded on modern industrialism. On the other hand technology has, in the universities, all the characteristics of the parvenu; a brash confidence in a successful future based on the conspicuous achievements of modern applied science and on financial support from the new industrial sources of patronage as well as from governments concerned with national defence and increased standards of material life; but also frustration, irritation and feelings of inferiority towards the entrenched and apparently obstructive power of the older disciplines.

Present conditions in the British universities are of special interest in this connection since Britain has seniority in age both in its membership of Western civilization and in its industrialism. Moreover it has, in the post-war period, been passing through a period of relatively rapid social change in which educational reconstruction has held an honoured, or at least a much publicised place. These changes, and especially the changes in relations between social classes, offer a challenge to the universities which will test their adaptive capacities to the utmost limit and which involves the place of the liberal arts within them.

The extent to which humanistic traditions pervade British as contrasted with American university life was impressed upon me during a year at the Centre for the Advanced Study of the Behavioral Sciences in California, where I was naturally led to reflect on the position of the social sciences in the two countries.

Two differences seemed to me to be most noticeable. First, the American social scientists are sufficiently numerous to form large and specialised occupational groups. There are, for example, some 2,000 teachers of sociology in American universities whereas the comparable figure for the United Kingdom is no more than 40. And yet, though it is the case in Britain that sociologists as such are scarcely recognised, sociological writing under other names holds an honourable place as part of an ancient tradition of humanistic writing. Second, the academic gods are different. In the United States natural science holds almost monotheistic sway over the social scientist whereas in Britain there is a polytheistic worship of diverse deities such as history, Karl Marx, positivism and the institution of the Royal Commission, and especially the humanistic aspect of each.

The training, research interests and writing of social scientists in the two countries are consonant with these differences. In American universities, the disciplines within the social sciences are more specialised and isolated one from another. Thus it is difficult in Britain to acquire a degree in sociology and yet remain innocent of economics, anthropology, philosophy and politics. The word interdisciplinary is characteristically American and the problem which it denotes is scarcely recognised in England.

On the side of research interests, the Americans seem to be much more anxious than the British about their scientific status. Social science in post-war Britain is still largely focused on problems of social policy. In the United States, by contrast, policy problems are usually subordinate to the search for rigorous scientific methods – albeit too often and too cheerfully applied to the more trivial aspects of social life. Professor R. K. Merton once aptly described American work on the sociology of knowledge by ascribing to it the motto, 'We don't know that what we say is particularly significant, but it is at least true.' Moreover, where there is reaction among American social scientists against what I would call the school of frantic empiricism, it often takes the form of a no less controversial, because too ambitious, theorising. The more humanistic, less scientific English sociologist would be less inclined to equate truth with precision or significance with theory.

Again it follows from the differences in numbers that the American social scientists are able to write for each other, whereas when the English sociologist takes pen to paper he has before him a wider and more heterogeneous audience – an audience of 'intellectual laymen' which is not nearly so apparent on the American scene. This partly accounts for the very obvious differences in terminology and the flavour of the language used by social scientists in the two countries. It also explains the howls of exasperation so frequently emitted by the review columns of that part of the British press which reviews American sociological books on behalf of the 'intelligent layman'.

Thus a glance at this small sector of intellectual life immediately reveals contrasts which reflect fundamental differences in the educational philosophy and institutions of these two countries. But now let us turn to look more closely at the British universities.

The British system of university education is highly selective in the sense that only between 3 and 4 per cent of the population passes through it, and also in the sense that the distribution of opportunity of entering a university is very unequally distributed between the various social classes. In fact England has probably less university students per thousand of the population than any other industrial country. The figure is double in Scotland but treble in Australia and Canada, four times as great in Russia and nine times as great in the United States (Simon 1956). In England, Scotland and Wales with a population of 50 million, there are now 21 universities, an independent university college and two colleges of technology of university rank attended by some 89,000 full-time students. Apart from the mammoth University of London with its 19,403 full-time students and the Universities of Oxford and Cambridge with 7,740 and 8,295 respectively, each of these institutions has less than 5,000 students and 13 of them have less than 3,000 (UGC 1957). Accordingly the British undergraduate remains a member of a tiny privileged minority attending a university in which it is still possible to have personal contact with a significant proportion of his fellows.

The ancient universities of Oxford and Cambridge have always occupied a special and dominating position in the structure of British university life. Both in their self-image and in the public mind they are clearly differentiated from all other institutions of higher learning. So enormous is their prestige that, to take two trivial examples, members of the one can still refer unambiguously to the other as 'the other place' and the *Times* or the *Manchester Guardian* can entitle a sports column 'The University Football Match' with the confident assumption that the reader will know that the game is not soccer but rugby football and the universities Oxford and Cambridge. Professor Shils, in his brilliant essay on the British intellectuals, is only too accurate when he writes that 'if a young man talking to an educated stranger refers to his university studies, he is asked "Oxford or Cambridge?". And if he says Aberystwyth or Nottingham, there is disappointment on the one side and embarrassment on the other' (Shils 1955).

The generalisation concerning historical development which I mentioned earlier might lead us to expect a quite different situation. The ancient universities are of feudal origin. They were well established before the development of the natural sciences made possible the present-day demand for highly trained technologists and they reached something like their present size and structure before the demand for equality of educational opportunity became sufficiently powerful to be taken seriously. Yet the ancient universities are far from being in process of eclipse by institutions more closely and directly linked to the dominant trends of economic and social life in Britain. On the contrary, it is possible to argue against the view that the Redbrick university is 'the university of the future' that Oxbridge has never had a firmer grasp onto its position at the apex of British educational and intellectual life. Indeed, Shils has described the successful post-war resurgence of the aristocratic-gentry culture on the basis of what he calls 'the London-Oxford-Cambridge axis' and its 'restoration to pre-eminence among the guiding stars of the intellectuals' after nearly a century of retreat and, paradoxically in a period when political and economic ascendancy has clearly been passing to those classes of society which were formerly excluded from participation in its way of life.

What is the explanation of Oxbridge pre-eminence? What are the consequences, for the aims and characteristics of the modern universities and for the place of the liberal arts within them?

The ancient universities have been the champions of two related causes, one social and the other educational. Socially they have been the preserves of aristocracy and, more recently, the assimilating institutions for young entrants to the country's political, business and professional elites. Educationally they have stood for a broad humanism against a narrow professionalism, for 'education' as opposed to 'training', Oxford more so than Cambridge, which was always more scientific and protestant. They are, of course, also scholarly institutions devoted to the advancement and preservation of knowledge. But undergraduate life in the colleges has traditionally maintained a nice balance between the intellectuals and the 'hearties'. The education of a gentleman involves attention to character and physique as well as to brains and if the claims of scholarship might not have been fully met by supply from within the ranks of the well-to-do classes then standards have been maintained and concessions at the same time made to popular demand by the provision of a proportion of competitive scholarship places for undergraduates. At the same time, a qualified support of intellectualism has fitted easily into the temper of widespread attitudes among the British – a respect for the grasp of matter-of-fact realities and a distrust of ideological cleverness or passion.

In the long history of the ancient universities the greatest challenge to their pre-eminence came with the beginnings of industrialism and the educational aspirations of Dissent. Subsequently during the last century and a half the educational needs of an increasingly technological age and the demands of educational opportunity for the plebs have resulted in the establishment of the modern universities first in London and later in the great provincial centres of modern industry and commerce, notably Manchester, Birmingham, Leeds and Liverpool. From the outset these universities have been devoted more to science than to the arts, more to the training of the specialist than the cultivation of the 'educated man' (even in the arts their main product has been school teachers), more to research at the frontiers of knowledge than to the preservation and transmission of accumulated scholarship. Their standards of scholarship are seldom equalled and probably not excelled either in Oxbridge or in the world. Yet their challenge to the social dominance of the ancient foundations has so far been completely without success. The reasons for this will take us into the peculiarities of the history of English class structure.

The modern universities of 19th- and 20th-century foundation are associated with bourgeois rather than aristocratic-gentry culture – the culture of the non-conformist provincial business classes. Shils describes how, in the 19th century, 'living to itself, puritanical, pharisaical, proud and excessively sensitive to the slights and denials of the traditional society, the bourgeoisie of the big provincial towns, partly from local patriotism, partly from resentment, partly from love of learning created . . . a genuine civilization – earnest searching and profound' – and with the modern universities as its chief monument. This culture, he adds, 'has now been routed': 'The aristocratic gentry culture has come back into the saddle, and with little to dispute its dominion.'

Perhaps the most outstanding characteristic of the English class structure historically has been the remarkable absorptive capacity, the judicious and un-Marxist Fabianism of the upper classes. The culture of the gentry and of higher officialdom never quite lost control of the rising provincial centres. If the successful northern businessmen were themselves excluded from entry into 'the establishment', their sons could cross the social barrier by southward movement through the public schools and Oxford by movement of religious adherence from Chapel to Church and by occupational movement from trade to profession or from a northern works to a London central office. To take but one of innumerable examples, I recently had occasion to explore the family biography of a leading firm of steel manufacturers: the first generation in the early 19th century – a northern non-conformist artisan nail maker; the second generation – a successful steel master who received a technical education at Owens College (later Manchester University); the third generation – public school and Church of England and including a knight, a barrister, a Conservative MP and the Chairman of the now large public steel corporation.

In discussing the present state of university education in the under-developed territories of the British Commonwealth, Mr Balogh has argued that education ought to be in closest harmony with the technical and administrative requirements of the country and goes on to criticise the influence of Oxbridge and 'the desperately ill-fitting educational precepts of the Whig bureau-aristocracy of the last century' (Balogh 1955). Whatever assessment we make of the value of its present influences, it is certain that the adaption of Oxford and Cambridge to rising demands in the 19th century for administrators both at home and abroad and for entrants to the liberal profession was markedly successful at the time and has been a powerful factor in their continued prestige. In alliance with a public-school system expanding on the model of Dr Arnold's Rugby, they were able to take the rising elements of the middle classes into their orbit and to educate them with minimal modification to traditional ideas concerning the upbringing of a gentleman.

The firm possession thus gained of the avenues of entry to the most prestigeful occupations has never been lost. The success of Britain as an imperial power in the 19th century and especially the quiet and incorruptible efficiency of its high-ranking civil servants and colonial administrators commanded universal esteem and at the same time a powerful validation of its educational institutions and the high value placed within them on classical studies and the liberal arts. In consequence, the humanities have been able to fight with more success in Britain than in America against the inroads of the social sciences (often referred to as the quasi-scientific studies) into the education of would-be entrants to the modern administrative professions. The education of Mr W. H. Whyte's 'Organisation Man' (Whyte 1956) is different in England. The English businessman will not look for a training in psychology or industrial sociology in his managerial recruits but rather for the vaguely defined qualities of the Oxbridge man. Another example is to be found in the journalistic professions. Mr Dwight Macdonald has recently eulogised the essentially amateur tradition of writing in the British press in contrast with America. Oxbridge and the liberal arts lie behind this difference. In fact wherever the qualities required for a profession are not unambiguously capable of formulation in terms of natural science or its applications, the superiority of an Oxbridge type of education for entry is as yet scarcely challenged.

Just as the aristocratic-gentry culture was never quite routed from the industrial provinces, so Oxbridge had a secure foothold in the modern universities from their inception. Especially in the early stages of their development the staff of the civic universities was heavily recruited by migration from the Oxford and Cambridge colleges. And with the migrants came the Oxbridge ideals. There was no alternative idea of a university which was not at least partially informed by traditional notions. Certainly the modern universities set out to foster the natural sciences and in large urban centres residential collegiate life was impracticable. But even the greatest exponent of the scientific university for an industrial civilisation, T. H. Huxley, could assert (before the Cowper Commission in 1892) that 'the primary business of the universities is with pure knowledge and pure art – independent of all application to practice; with progress in culture, not with increase in wealth' (Bibby 1956).

Of course, in the social conflicts of the inter-war period, traditional institutions came under heavy attack and the London School of Economics enjoyed its great days as a centre of intellectual radicalism. But again as Shils points out, the widespread alienation of intellectuals from established society did more damage to bourgeois than to aristocratic gentry culture. English radicalism of the left had always some aristocratic colouring and reintegration in the war and post-war years has only served to strengthen the hold on intellectual life of the London-Oxford-Cambridge axis.

The traditions of the ancient universities have bequeathed to the British universities two distinctive characteristics. First and foremost they provide basically for a training of élites, the trade union leader being the only notable exception, and secondly the humanities and pure sciences are more highly valued in them than the technologies and the fine arts. These two characteristics in turn give rise to two urgent current problems – a problem of assimilation of new aspirants to university education and a problem of developing technological studies within the existing framework of university organisation. The universities adapted successfully to the modest educational expansion of the 19th and 20th centuries. They learnt to live with the scientist and to mould new generations of undergraduates from more diverse social origin. They must now face the problem of preserving their traditional ideals while incorporating an expansion of technological studies and while assimilating vastly increased numbers from all classes of society.

Between the two World Wars there were about 35,000 students in the universities of England and Wales and even this low figure represented an expansion of 75 per cent over the 20,000 in attendance before the 1914–18 War. The student body was overwhelmingly upper and middle class. It included only a minute proportion of young people of working-class origin who had managed to win their way by scholarships through the grammar schools – a highly selected and intellectually able minority capable of easy assimilation into what were dominantly middle-class institutions. In 1944 the Barlow Report, echoing the widespread demand for educational reform generated during the Second World War, demanded an 80 per cent expansion of university places and stated that 'only about 1 in 5 of the ablest boys and girls actually reach the universities . . . There is clearly an ample reserve of intelligence in the country to allow both a doubling of university numbers and a raising of standards'. In the event the demands of the Barlow Report were easily met. By 1950 the number of students was 68,000 and within the next ten years a further expansion to at least 100,000 is expected.

These increases and expectations of further increases are, of course, partly a reflection of the main efforts of post-war reconstruction which was directed at the secondary schools under the terms of the great Education Act of 1944. A recent study of English Education (Floud, Halsey and Martin 1956) has shown that the Act has resulted in a major advance towards equality of opportunity in education. Expansion in grammar school provision and the substitution of competitive entry for fee-paying in state grammar schools has opened new opportunities for the mass of the population. In effect, the grammar schools, and therefore the highway to the universities, have been opened to large numbers of children from the homes of manual workers who have themselves received only the doubtful benefits of the older system of elementary education. At the same time many of these parents have revolutionised their attitudes towards education. The age to which they are willing to keep their children at school has increased dramatically in the post-war period with the result that each year an increasing proportion of children enters the grammar school sixth forms which prepare entrants for the universities.

Of course we must not exaggerate the extent to which the revolution has already gone. There remains a severe class-linked process of selection operating from the bottom to the top of the British educational system. Its severity may be judged by the fact that though the unskilled labouring class contributes each year about 12 per cent of the nation's births it accounts for only 5.6 per cent of grammar school entrants, only 1.5 per cent of those entering the sixth forms (Central Advisory Council for England 1954) and only 0.9 per cent of the boys (0.6 per cent of the girls) going on to the universities (Kelsall 1957).

Nevertheless, as the universities expand and as the full effect on the schools of the 1944 Education Act emerges, the proportion of working-class undergraduates may be expected to grow. Such a development can only be applauded. But there can be no doubt that it sets a pedagogical problem, especially perhaps for the teacher of the liberal arts. The problem in essence is one of bridging a cultural gap which is often not recognised for what it is. It is a problem with which the grammar schools have struggled painfully in the post-war years. The following expression of it by a grammar school headmaster is typical:

> The grammar school now includes among its pupils a much higher proportion of children from poor homes. Some of these children come from homes which are barely literate and where a book is an unusual phenomenon . . . Others have very low standards of cleanliness and appearance, some seem to have had very little training in social behaviour; even table manners may leave much to be desired. Children like these have very little to give to the social or cultural

life of the school; the school itself has to provide much which, before the war, would have been regarded as the normal contribution of the home. (Davies 1950)

It is hardly surprising that the master in the grammar school common room is perplexed by the paradox of post-war children who are able but ineducable. It is all too easy for him to dismiss them as uncultured louts. It is far less easy to communicate his own learning to the children of a population with the barest and most recently acquired literacy and that largely through a popular press of impressive vulgarity. For the English university don the problem is virtually a new one and he now finds himself 'having to provide much which before the war would have been regarded as the normal contribution of the *school*'.

The difficulties are exacerbated by the fact that Oxbridge has, for the most part, sloughed them off onto the modern universities. In a recent article on Cambridge, Mr D. Mack Smith claims that 'the social basis of the community has also quite changed . . . the gilded youth have retreated, the have-a-good-timers with their champagne breakfasts and parties at Newmarket are swamped and the university again fulfils its old function of promoting an osmotic assimilation between the classes' (Mack Smith 1956). This is Victorian thinking at latest. Mr Mack Smith's classes clearly do not include that three-quarters of the population which follow manual occupations *and which contributed only 9 per cent of the men admitted to his university in 1955–56*. The comparable figure for the University of Wales was 40, for the English provincial universities 31 and for London 21.

We are thus faced with a paradoxical situation. Current developments in the schools and expansion in the universities bid fair to amount to a revolutionary democratisation of opportunities for university education. Yet, given the background of dominance by the London-Oxford-Cambridge axis, there is grave danger that this revolution will leave the British universities more socially stratified than ever before.

Similarly with the problem of developing technological studies, it may be true as Mr Mack Smith suggests that 'During the last 20 years the older universities have both of them moved towards Redbrick, a direction symbolised by unexciting and efficient laboratory architecture.' Yet the main burden of technological expansion is being borne elsewhere, at Imperial College London, at Glasgow, Manchester, Birmingham and Leeds. The urgency of the need to expand is undisputed: both Russia and the USA produce about twice as many graduates in science and technology per thousand of the population as we do. But those who care for the liberal arts may be forgiven their anxiety in face of the fact that the solution of the problem is for the most part to be thrust onto those universities which are least firmly attached to the humanistic traditions of the ancient universities. The fact that the two problems are related makes the task doubly difficult. It is no accident that the technologies take in proportionately more young people of working class origin than any of the other faculties. If the proportion for arts is also high this is because of the function of arts faculties in the modern universities as professional schools for would-be grammar school teachers.

In consequence, the position of the arts don in a modern English university is beset with difficulty. He will often have a sense of failure through the very fact of being there rather than in an Oxbridge college. And an anxious hovering on the outside of the literary elite will not be conducive to the solution of the very real problems facing him in a university increasingly devoted to technological studies. He may easily yield to discouragement in the face of a student body which he sees as uncultured in its background and materialistically vocational in its aspirations: and of colleagues in the senior common room who talk cheerfully in north-country tones of the technicalities of turbo-jets and electronic computing machines. Yet he must learn to live with and communicate with both if the great traditions of scholarship which he represents are to survive into the technological age.

References

Balogh, T. (1955), 'Oxbridge Rampant', *Universities Quarterly*, Vol. 9, no. 3.

Bibby, C. (1956), 'T. H. Huxley's Idea of a University', *Universities Quarterly*, Vol. 10, no. 4.

Central Advisory Council for Education (England) (1954), *Early Leaving*, HMSO.

Davies, H. (1950), 'The Social Effects of the 1944 Act on the Grammar School', *The Bulletin of Education*, No. 23, November, p. 5.

Floud, J. E., Halsey, A. H. and Martin, F. M. (1956), *Social Class and Educational Opportunity*.

James, D. G. (1956), 'University Commentary', *Universities Quarterly*, Vol. 10, no. 2, pp. 117, 118.

Kelsall, R. K. (1957), *Applications for Admission to Universities*. Report on an enquiry commissioned by the Committee of Vice-Chancellors and Principals of the Universities of the United Kingdom, p. 10, Table F.

Mack Smith, D. (1956), 'The Changing University. A Report on Cambridge Today', *Encounter*, May, p. 54.

Shils, E.A. (1955), 'The Intellectuals. I. Great Britain', *Encounter*, April.

University Grants Committee Report on *University Development 1952–1956*, Cmnd. 79, HMSO, March 1957.

Whyte, W. H., Jr. (1956), *The Organization Man*, (N.Y.) chapters 6–10.

Lord Simon of Wythenshawe (1956), 'Student Numbers', *Universities Quarterly*, Vol. 10, no. 2.

6. The Growth of Higher Education

Solly Zuckerman

Universities Quarterly Vol. 12 (1958), pp. 241–48.

The post-war drive to increase the numbers of professionally trained scientists and engineers is now in its third phase. The prominent feature of the first was the university expansion programme which followed the recommendation of the Barlow Committee, published in 1946, that the output of graduates in the basic and engineering sciences should be doubled as soon as possible. This goal was reached in only four years, and the success achieved by the UGC and the universities was made all the more remarkable by the fact that there was no lowering of academic standards, in spite of considerable difficulties over accommodation and staff in the immediate post-war years.

The second phase was triggered by the warning, given in 1952 by the Scientific Manpower Committee of the Advisory Council on Scientific Policy, that the shortage of practically all kinds of trained scientists and engineers was likely to persist, and by the recommendation that every effort should, therefore, be made to go on increasing the supply of chemists, physicists and engineers. At that time total student numbers were, if anything, beginning to fall. This recommendation was the forerunner of additional plans, announced by the Government in 1953, to strengthen the engineering and scientific departments of a number of universities, and in particular, for the expansion of the Imperial College of Science and Technology. In this phase of the campaign may also be included the Government's proposals of February 1956 for the development of the technical colleges of the country, including the up-grading of a number of institutions into colleges of advanced technology.

The third and most recent phase of the campaign relates to the long-term estimates of demand for scientific manpower published jointly, in October of 1956, by the Ministry of Labour and National Service and the Scientific Manpower Committee of the Advisory Council on Scientific Policy, and endorsed by the Government later in the same year. The figures for demand were based on a census of the numbers of scientists and engineers in the country (with the known omission of those engaged in agriculture, and a few numerically unimportant occupations). The calculations assumed that there is a definite, even if as yet imprecise, relationship between the rate of increase of industrial production on the one hand, and the numbers of scientists and engineers employed in industry, on the other. In order to provide for the minimum of professional scientific manpower which it was calculated would be necessary to sustain an average increase of industrial output of 4 per cent per annum, and which at the same time would be sufficient to cater for minimum anticipated requirements in sectors of public employment, the Committee recommended that the annual output of professional scientists and engineers, which was then estimated at slightly more than 10,000, should at the least be doubled by the end of the 1960s. They also recommended that the output of engineers should increase at a much faster rate than that of graduates in the basic sciences.

The magnitude of this target can be seen only against the background of the achievements of the past ten years. In 1939 the universities turned out about 3,000 graduates in the basic and engineering sciences, including a certain number in specialised subjects such as textile science and glass technology. The corresponding figure for the first post-war crop of undergraduates (1947–48) was about 5,600. Four years later (1951–52) the number had risen to a post-war peak of nearly 7,000. It then fell to about 6,400 in 1953–54, and was still only about 6,100, plus about 400 in the special technologies, in 1955–56.

If one adds to the 1955–56 figure of about 6,100 first degrees and equivalent university diplomas in the basic and engineering sciences an estimated 5,600 men and women who did not go to a university, but who, after advanced courses in technical colleges, obtained external university degrees or gained qualifications in the professional institutions equivalent to first degrees, the total of professionally qualified scientists and engineers turned out in 1956 was nearly 12,000, as compared with a corresponding figure of about 11,000 for the year before. The figure for 1957 is not yet available, but is almost certainly higher. If we assume it is only 12,500, the annual output of professionally-trained scientists and engineers will have to increase by some 7,500 over the course of the next ten years if the target set by the Scientific Manpower Committee is to be met.

The way this task is likely to be divided between the universities and the technical colleges cannot be specified in detail. If the technical colleges succeed in increasing the output of their advanced courses, as proposed in the Government White Paper of 1956 on Technical Education, it would be possible to look to them for an annual output by the mid-1960s of about 9,500 professionally-qualified scientists and engineers, including 1,000 who will be taking external university degrees. By 1970, the figure could reasonably be expected to have risen to 10,500. To allow for this output the annual input into advanced courses in technical colleges by 1967–68 would have to be about 23,000. Those of the 23,000 who do not achieve a standard of qualification in the basic or engineering sciences equivalent to that of a university degree should end up as highly qualified technicians. Allowing for those who drop out on the way, one can assume that more than one-third would fall into this latter class.

This programme has got off to a very good start, and the numbers of young men and women who are taking full-time advanced courses in the technical colleges is already rising in accordance with expectation. Many of them are preparing for the examinations of graduate or associate membership of the professional engineering institutions, and nearly 1,400 are attending courses leading to the Dip. Tech. diploma of honours degree standard, which was established only two years ago.

If the technical colleges succeed in their task, the university output of graduates in the sciences, exclusive of external degrees, would have to rise to about 11,000 by the end of the 1960s – says 4,500 a year more than in 1955–56 – if the Scientific Manpower Committee's estimate is to be met, and if places are also to be available for some 1,500 special technologists who were not included in the Committee's forecasts. We already know that the figure is bound to increase sharply over the next few years. This encouraging conclusion follows from the fact that since 1953 the numbers of students who have been taking up the basic and engineering sciences in British universities have been increasing by about 10 per cent a year. Entries for the current academic year are, in fact, nearly 50 per cent higher than they were five years ago – 10,800 as compared with 7,300. The immediate omens are, therefore, very good.

At the end of February, the Government announced a £60 million building programme for the universities for the period 1960–1963 which, on top of the £12 million a year in 1958 and 1959, should permit of an increase in the university population from its present level of about 95,000 to about 124,000 by the mid-1960s, with the possibility of a further 10 per cent rise in the second half of the decade. In the statement of 20 February, 1958, in which he outlined these proposals, the Chancellor of the Exchequer went further, and suggested that 'the increase beyond 124,000 foreseen for the late 1960s may well prove to be permanent'.

If, as is to be hoped, this increase is achieved, it should be enough to permit the universities to do their part in the present doubling programme of professional scientists and engineers. But an analysis of the statistics published annually by the UGC shows that there is little margin to spare.

For every first science degree or diploma that is granted annually, there are between four and five undergraduate and postgraduate students in the science and engineering departments of the universities. Calculating on the basis of 4.5, it follows that the university population of scientists and engineers would have to rise to about 50,000 – about 20,000 more than in 1955–56 – if the number of first degrees and diplomas awarded to students from science and technology departments is to rise from the level of about 6,500 in 1955–56 to one of 11,000 by 1970. This, however, is less than the increase in the population of the university science departments which is envisaged by the present phase of expansion. The Government has always stated the hope that about two-thirds of the increase in university places should be filled by scientists and engineers. If this hope were realised, the increase would not be 20,000, but about 25,000, equivalent to an annual output of some 12,000 professionally trained scientists and engineers. On present plans this would leave some 70,000 places for students of other faculties. We may assume that there would be little or no increase in the 20,000 students who now fill the medical, dental, agricultural and veterinary departments (the Willink Committee, in fact, has suggested that a 10 per cent decrease in medical students is desirable during the next ten years). That would leave 50,000 places for the humanities, as compared with about 37,000 in 1955–56, or a cumulative increase averaging little more than 3 per cent a year as compared with one of 6.25 per cent for the basic and engineering sciences.

It is useful to consider what these figures (which apply to England, Scotland and Wales as a whole) mean in relation to the size of the sixth-form population of the country, which also has to provide for the teachers' training colleges – the third main pathway to a higher education. Once again, it is convenient to refer to the figures for 1955–56, the reference year for the current phase of expansion, to see what is involved numerically.

In that year 24,000 new undergraduates entered the universities. New entrants to advanced courses in technical colleges numbered 16,000, and of these about 3,000 were the products of the sixth form. Teachers' training colleges took in about 13,600 – making a total of nearly 54,000 new recruits to full-time higher education for the year. Of these we can safely assume that at least 4,000 were students from overseas, leaving about 50,000 who had been educated in British schools. This represents only about 8 per cent of the total 17-year-old group of 651,000 for 1955–56. If we exclude the 13,000 or so of the technical college students who were not sixth-formers, the new recruits to higher education for the year represented about 60 per cent of all 17-year-olds who were still at school in that year (61,000).

Now a university population of about 124,000 at the end of the 1960s implies an annual entry of about 35,000, all of whom, excluding some 2,500 students from overseas, will, of course, have completed the sixth form at school. If the 10 per cent increase above 124,000 to which the Chancellor referred in his recent statement is achieved, the annual entry would be 38,000, including some 3,000 students from overseas. It is not unreasonable to suppose that about half the technical college entry for the same period, which is not likely to be less than 23,000, will also be sixth-formers (as compared with 3,000 out of some 16,000 today). Assuming a three-year course in the teachers' training colleges, and no significant increase in their numbers or size, the new entry into these colleges in 1967–68 could be projected at about 10,500 – all of whom will also be sixth-formers. When the necessary allowances are made for overseas students, we may estimate that some 53,000 to 56,000 of the total intake of 64,000 to 67,000 into academic education in 1967–68 will be the products of the sixth forms, as compared with about 37,000 in 1955–56.

For some years now the 17-year-old population still at school has been increasing at an average rate of slightly more than 5 per cent a year. As already observed in 1955–56 it numbered 61,000 out of a total age-group of 651,000 (i.e. about 9.4 per cent). The figures for January 1957, were 63,300 out of 645,000, that is to say, nearly 10 per cent. Since the post-war rise in the birth-rate was at its peak in 1947, the 17-year-old age-group will be at its maximum in 1964–65, when it is expected to reach the level of 930,000. It then falls and reaches a minimum of about 730,000 in the period 1968–69, after which there will be a gradual increase, the limits of which cannot be estimated, since the number of births is at the present moment again rising each year. If the trend to later leaving continues at the present rate, the sixth-form population will be about 110,000 in 1967–68, and will constitute about 15 per cent of its age group. The estimates set out in the preceding paragraph suggest that some 53,000 to 56,000 of them (i.e. about 50 per cent) could be expected to continue their full-time education after they have left school.

Since the corresponding percentage today is about 60 per cent, it would seem at first glance that the schools will be able to feed the three streams of higher education in the sizes at which they are projected ten years ahead. Indeed, since it is unlikely that the universities will expand quickly enough, the figures actually suggest that ten years hence many boys and girls will fail to achieve the university education to which they will undoubtedly be looking forward – with, of course, the corollary that the quality of new entrants to the universities will tend to rise all the time. Simple arithmetic shows that, whereas some 3.5 per cent of each age group now achieves a university education, the proportion cannot on present plans exceed about 4.4 per cent during the 1960s, and that at the peak of the 'bulge' it will be much the same as it is today. Including advanced courses in technical colleges and teachers' training colleges in the category of 'academic' education, the figure will be about 7 per cent in 1965–66, rising to 9 per cent in 1968–69, as compared with 8 per cent in 1955–56.

If it were not for the fact that the technical colleges will also be transforming and expanding over the same period, the improbability that the universities can grow at a rate faster than that of the population could well become a source of frustration in the less able sections of the growing sixth-form population. To some extent this is almost inevitable, even though the sixth forms, quite apart from feeding the universities, colleges of technology and teachers' training colleges, will also have to contribute to the far more numerous and growing categories of sub-professional and non-university scientists and engineers, if the work of the fully-professional classes is to be properly supported. Indeed, frustration is already in evidence in a sporadic way, and its numerical basis is apparent in the *Report on an Enquiry into Applications for Admission to Universities* which was commissioned by the Committee of Vice-Chancellors and Principals. However many qualifications this report makes, the conclusion is clear that at the moment only about 60 per cent of those who are now applying for admission to a university find a place in the first year of their application. A little more than a third of those who fail are likely to find themselves in 'some institution of university rank' within a year, while a significant proportion of the remainder seem to abandon any efforts to continue their higher education as full-time students, whether in a teachers' training college, technical college or university. Such individuals could presumably contribute only to the 'tail' of the university entry.

Nevertheless, the fact that there are sixth-formers who are already becoming frustrated because of their failure to get into a university provides one reason why some authorities fear that the sixth-form population may not continue to grow at its present rate, regardless of the fact that a longer school education is a prize worth striving after even if it does not lead a boy or girl to a university. Another is the doubt that adequate staff and facilities will not be found to cater for the larger numbers of sixth-formers who are 'swinging' from the arts to the sciences.

The main pressure at pre-university levels is not going to affect the better-off independent and direct-grant grammar schools, which are hardly likely to grow very much over the next ten years, but the maintained schools. These have got to bear the brunt of the growth in the age groups and of the trend to 'later leaving', as well as the task of providing recruits for the universities, technical colleges and teachers' training colleges. About 36,500 of the 61,000 17-year-old boys and girls in schools in Great Britain in 1955–56 were in these schools. If the figures for 17-year-olds at school rises to, say, the level of 110,000 by the end of the 1960s, the sixth-form population in the maintained schools will presumably have to rise to the level of nearly 80,000. Such a rate of growth would be a formidable task at any time. It is much more so in the light of the difficulties which the schools are now experiencing in modernising, in enlarging laboratories and classrooms, and, in particular, in finding well-qualified teachers. There are few schools in the country which do not now find that the staff which they are able to recruit for the teaching of science and mathematics is declining in quality. There is little else one could expect in view of the more attractive opportunities that industry is able to offer.

But in spite of all these difficulties, past performance indicates that we can well afford to take an optimistic view of the prospect that the sixth forms will continue to grow at a rate sufficient to provide for the scientific and engineering recruits of tomorrow. It would, of course, be unrealistic to suppose that the correlated expansion of sixth-form and higher education will not continue to throw up difficult academic and physical, as well as social, problems over the next ten years. The schools have their special difficulties to overcome. So have the technical colleges and the universities. Keeping in step with each other, and adjusting curricula to meet new situations, will not be easy, especially when one bears in mind the very rapid rate of change that is implied by the figures that have been set out in this paper. To keep what is involved in perspective, it is well to remember that to increase the annual university entry by at least 8,000 students over the next ten years, which is what the present estimates entail, is equivalent to nearly a third of the total annual intake of all our universities today. Furthermore, so far as targets are concerned, the assumption that the universities can expand sufficiently to turn out 11,000 or even 12,000 professional scientists a year leaves little margin to meet any serious failure on the part of the technical colleges in their efforts to raise their annual output of professional scientists and engineers from a level of some 6,000 today to one of over 10,000 by the end of the 1960s.

The programme in front of the schools, technical colleges and universities is thus undoubtedly a tight one. But no problem which they may have to face is going to prove insuperable, provided they are liberally encouraged in their efforts to obtain staff and to put up new buildings. The goal towards which they are all striving is a realistic one. If as a result of their joint efforts we succeed in doubling the annual output of professionally trained scientific manpower over the next decade, at the same time as we train an adequate number of supporting technical staff, we shall on present reckoning be producing enough scientists and engineers to assure the healthy growth of the national economy and of our national institutions. And that, in effect, was the end with which the Scientific Manpower Committee was concerned when it produced its estimates at the close of 1956.

7. Too Few Academic Eggs

Vivian Bowden

Universities Quarterly Vol. 14 (1959–60), pp. 7–23.

It is desirable that a little external pressure should be brought to bear upon the universities. It would not do to trust either the universities or the colleges with the entire management of the reforms, for I believe that they are not the exception to the rule, which has been found to exist elsewhere, that hardly any Corporation is capable of entirely reforming itself without external pressure.

(Archbishop Tait)

Efficiency is a ruthless word, and it may seem to be cruel to do away with a very picturesque if out-of-date system; but if the interests of national education demand it, it will have to be done.

(A. I. Tilliard)

It is very clear from the reactions to Lord Simon's proposal for a Royal Commission on Universities (in an article in the *Universities Quarterly* 1958, second issue) that members of university staffs, or at least those who feel inclined to write for *Universities Quarterly*, are fairly well content with things as they are, and would regard the investigations of a Royal Commission into any of the affairs with which they are concerned with very great disfavour. I do not believe, however, that their antagonism to an enquiry is remotely comparable to the indignation with which the Royal Commissions were received a hundred years ago in Oxford and Cambridge. Nevertheless, it was these Commissions which began the conversion of our antiquated medieval universities into the great institutions we know today; the universities owe a great debt to Royal Commissions.

Universities form a fairly small and compact society; they realise that the work they are doing is good and they are very well aware of the prestige which they enjoy among the public at large. It is only too easy to assume that all is well and to feel that any enquiry would do nothing to help, and might waste the time of very busy men, but no institution should expect to be the sole judge of its own cause, and many of the questions which Lord Simon propounded seem to me to demand an answer. I see no method by which they can be properly answered unless they are studied by a Royal Commission which could investigate both the organisation of the universities themselves and the framework within which they are working. I believe that never since Dr Pusey so eloquently defended 'the sacerdotal functions of a celibate professoriat' has the need for such an enquiry been as great as it is today.

An enquiry into the size of our universities is long overdue. Lord Simon referred to this subject, but none of the essays which his article provoked seem to me to consider it seriously. The English university world has always been a very small one. At the time of the American War of Independence there were nine universities in the States; we then had two in England. During the last hundred years universities have been founded in large numbers throughout the whole world. Fifty years ago Ramsay Muir pointed out that we then had fewer universities in this country in proportion to our population than any other civilised country in Europe with the solitary exception of Turkey. How are we doing today? Lord Simon showed that the proportion of the population of this country in full-time attendance at a university is much smaller than it is in most other countries.

It is quite extraordinary that after 50 years, although we are still doing better than the Turks, we are still almost at the bottom of the table. A new technical university for 15,000 students is to be built in Ankara – it should be open in five or six years' time; Turkey is stirring at last – it may not be at the bottom of the list much longer. Poland is a small country which suffered very much from the war, most of its industry was ruined and it has been oppressed by political problems ever since the end of hostilities, during which it lost many of the ablest of its people. Nevertheless, out of a population of 27.5 million, about 140,000 are now at universities. A population not much more than half as large as ours supports a university population 50 per cent greater than ours. New Zealand and Canada have proportionally far more students than we have – WHY?

Australia already educates three times as many of its young people as we do, but Professor Matheson has just been appointed to be the first Vice-Chancellor of a new university in Melbourne; he hopes that a small staff will begin to teach in 1961 and that by 1970 he will have at least 12,000 students. No one can foresee how to solve in a decade all the multifarious and formidable problems to be expected in creating a university nearly as big as Oxford and Cambridge put together, but the Australian authorities are prepared to face them as they arise. If the new university is unable to accept the enormous number of students who will seek admission in twelve years' time, there will be a crisis in the educational world of Australia.

How are we to compare our universities with America's? About 40 per cent of English children survive in school to the age of 16. About 11 per cent go to sixth forms and 6 per cent go to university. In the United States almost all children stay at school until they are 18 years old and 35 per cent went to universities last year. Our university population is about 100,000 – theirs about 3,000,000; ours has doubled since 1930 and so has theirs; ours is likely to rise to 150,000 during the next ten years and theirs to 7 million.

There are about 1,840 universities and colleges in America; some have a few dozen students, others as many as 40,000. Some are almost unknown, others are world famous. Perhaps a hundred of them can be described as universities in the sense that we use the word in England. There has always been a great difference between the best and the worst of American universities. I believe that the best of theirs are very much like the best of ours. As for some of the others – well, perhaps their standards are comparable to those which our own ancient universities were prepared to accept from undergraduates 50 or even 20 years ago when many young men who went there in search of a liberal education were not very concerned about pure scholarship. Unfortunately many Englishmen who have seen some of the less distinguished American universities have blandly asserted that our own standards are so much better that we need not be worried by our much smaller numbers. This argument simply will not do any longer. The Americans try to give to their elite as good an opportunity as we give to ours, but in addition they try to give a much better opportunity than we do to a much larger proportion of their population. We have found in Manchester that the quality of our students improves as their numbers increase. In 1870 Mark Pattison complained that the universities could not find any more educable students (there were then less than 5,000 undergraduates in England). He would be a bold man who made such a statement today. An American child is three times as likely to go to a university as an English child is to go into a sixth form. In a few years time our youngsters will be competing with Americans for the markets of the world. Surely we could do more to help them.

In some American universities 40 or 50 per cent of the students fail and leave after the first year. English universities are much more careful to restrict admission to students who have a reasonable chance of surviving the course, and regard a large failure rate as evidence of inefficiency and waste. Americans believe much more strongly in the value of a year in a university, even to a man who cannot stay the pace and never gets a degree. Like many other American institutions their universities may be relatively extravagant and inefficient, but they are extremely effective and productive.

We seem to be suffering from a national neurosis which makes us accept our relative penury without being conscious of it; we seem to believe that if we are doing better than we were then no more should be expected of us, and we never seem to compare our institutions with their counterparts abroad. We have just ceased to make steam locomotives, but we shall be using them for years to come; the Dutch put their last steamer in a museum last year. Our telephone service is expanding more slowly than that of any other country from which data is available; almost every country in Europe has built more new hospitals than we have since the war; our cities still retain scars from bomb damage and our national productivity is rising appallingly slowly. An average English workman produces less than half as much as an American. It is possible that the American educational system has helped to improve the productivity of American industry? Next October we hope to complete a hundred miles of modern road from nowhere to nowhere in particular, and we seem to be quite unaware of the fact that almost all other countries did much more years ago, that many American States open ten times as much new highway every year, and that we are spending less on new roads (per capita) than any other important European country. We shall spend about £80 million on new roads next year; this is far more than we have ever spent before, and the authorities seem to be very proud of themselves, but Western Germany will probably spend six times as much as we do. Why can they afford to be so much more enterprising than we are? We are told to admire the new London airport, and many of us have come to believe that it is something to be proud of. Few Englishmen realise that in fact it does not handle as many aircraft as the airport at Little Rock, Arkansas, that transatlantic passengers still use old wooden huts which would suit the bus station in a small provincial town, and that London ranks about 80th among domestic and international airports of the world.

The world of science and technology has been doubled in size once every 15 years or so ever since Newton's time. This means that three-quarters of the scientists and technologists who have ever lived are alive and practising today. Other countries seem to be accepting the implications of this astonishing fact. Are we?

The English universities contributed nothing to the industrial revolution and in 1902 Reynold remarked that 'excepting only the private boarding schools which we know as Public Schools, there is no Department of English education in which such conspicuous success has been achieved as in the technical evening classes'. These classes have always played and will continue to play a vital part in English education, but surely by now we must admit that modern technology demands university courses, and cannot be taught properly to part-time evening students.

English universities accepted engineering slowly and reluctantly. Almost all other countries which have determined to industrialise themselves as fast as possible have established large specialised institutions of university rank devoted exclusively to the education of scientists and technologists. Why can't we have one in England? The idea was rejected by the Government a few years ago because whatever the merits of such an institution might be it was impracticable to establish one at the time. Since then the Germans have created a technical university in Aachen which is about as big as Oxford or Cambridge and is full of adequately staffed and well equipped buildings. Why should we have to believe that such a development is impossible here? Admirable though the Imperial College, Manchester 'Tech.', Glasgow 'Tech.', our university engineering departments and our new colleges of advanced technology may be, none of them is big enough by Continental standards. It may well be that a technological institution could become too big to be efficient – this is arguable, and no one is prepared to say at what point efficiency begins to decline; but, and this is the point, most authorities in other countries are convinced that there is a minimum size below which no such institution can be really efficient, and this minimum size is very big. The original plan for Aachen was based on the assumption that a technological university needs at least 100 professors (Charlottenburg has 127, and about 9,000 students) if all branches of technology are to be represented in the one institution, so that each department can draw on adequate resources and influence and be influenced by most of modern science and technology. Manchester University has about 6,500 students and 88 professors – so that the number of students per professor is about the same in Charlottenburg or Aachen as it is here, but only half the professors in Manchester are scientists or technologists.

All countries are expanding their universities; we may be expanding ours at a rate which startles us, but is it enough? Are we content to accept this position of relative inferiority to the greater part of the civilised world, or do we not believe in the idea of large scale university education? Perhaps we fear that if all the clever boys went to college there would be no one left to employ the graduates.

After making all reasonable allowances for variations in standard for our part-time students, and for the different functions which are discharged by universities in different countries, it does seem to me that there is a need for a fundamental enquiry into the nature of a university world which is relatively so much smaller than that of any other big country which pretends to be civilised.

For many years our universities have been able to rely on magnificent teaching in our secondary and grammar schools. We have all become aware of the national shortage of science masters; the appalling inadequacy of the laboratory accommodation in our schools has been shown up by the questionnaire recently organised by the Science Masters' Association. Only 8 per cent of the grammar and direct grant schools and 20 per cent of the independent schools have laboratories of adequate standard. Only 44 per cent of schools had labs which reach the minimum standard of the Ministry of Education, and this standard is much lower than that which was advocated by the organisers of the Industrial Fund.

If our universities are obliged to take over any significant part of the syllabus which we not entrust to the schools; if for this or any other reason we are obliged to follow the example of the rest of the world and extend our university courses from three years to four, then indeed we should face disaster. Should the Commissioners study this question too?

We spend nearly £600 million a year on education in this country; perhaps a third as much as we spend on defence. The Russians spend as much or more on education as they do on defence, and their defence vote is very much bigger than ours. The Americans spend about $14 billion a year, and are proposing to double it. The President's Scientific Advisory Committee recommends that in future all college students who do not major in science should devote 15 per cent of their time studying science. It is more than 50 years since Joseph Chamberlain remarked 'University competition between states is as potent as competition in building battleships' and Mr Churchill has recently told us that 'The future of the world is to the highly educated races, who alone can handle the scientific apparatus which is necessary for pre-eminence in peace or survival in war.' Far be it from me to suggest that the scale of university development should be decided for this reason; one may be forgiven for mentioning it in the hope that it might appeal to some of the people who are responsible for determining national policy.

When the Government is fully persuaded of the importance of any major development it nearly always seems to be able to make the necessary funds available. For example the egg subsidy cost £47.6 million last year, we are to fire 30 or 40 Blue Streak missiles which will cost between £500,000 and £1 million each, during the forthcoming Woomera trials. On the other hand the UGC spent altogether £37,387,000 on English universities (£28,253,000 recurrent expenditure and £9,134,000 non-recurrent grant), and the Department of Scientific and Industrial Research (DSIR) had £9,450,000 in 1958. An extra £80 million is to be spent on technical education during the next five years. Our problem seems to reduce to this. Can we persuade the Treasury that our universities are as important to the community as the egg subsidy? – that the DSIR is worth as much as the experimental trials of one type of missile or even better, that education is, let us say, half as important as defence? If we could do this the whole scale of our university development and (dare we say it?) the whole future of the community might be transformed. Surely there must be some way of conveying such a message to the authorities.

	£
Total UGC expenditure 1956/7	37,387,000
DSIR grant, 1958 (including £920,000 given by DSIR to help university research)	9,450,000
Egg subsidy	47,600,000
Advertising campaign run by the Egg Marketing Board (to get rid of the eggs)	800,000
Cereal subsidy	52,300,000
Fatstock subsidy	85,700,000
Total cost of agricultural support	289,400,000
National Health Service (treating diseases)	557,000,000
Medical Research Council (finding out how to treat diseases)	3,130,000
Tobacco	979,000,000
Alcoholic beverages	940,000,000
Advertising	350,000,000

I wonder how the Treasury decided on the relative importance of the various items on this table; in particular it would be most interesting to know how it was decided that we ought to spent five times as much on subsidising chicken feed as we did on the Department of Scientific and Industrial Research.

It is very probable that the West, and this country in particular, has more to fear in the long run from Russian industry and Russian competition in the markets of the world than it has from Russian arms. It is certain that the uncommittted nations will be swayed in their allegiance by the speed at which the Western and Eastern blocks can help backward countries to industrialise themselves and raise their standard of living. Scientists and technologists are the missionaries of the modern age. The days when a man might qualify himself to govern the Empire by studying

Greek and Latin verse are over. Few countries want us to administer them, but many want us to help to educate their young people so that they can mechanise their industries. Other civilisations often prefer their own philosophy, their own art, their own literature, and even their own religion to anything we may have to offer them – but, be this as it may, they all admire and envy our science and even more they envy our technology; most of all they envy the more efficient technology of the United States. In 1878 Huxley wrote:

> We are entering now upon the most serious struggle for existence to which that country was ever committed. The latter years of the century promise to see us in an industrial war of far more serious import than the military wars of its opening years. . . . The situation is grave.

How little we have learnt in 80 years! If we lose our hold on the minds and on the markets of the world our civilisation may go before long with a whimper and not with a bang.

Research in Technological Institutions

We have come to accept without question the importance of research in our universities, particularly in the science faculties, but we are apt to forget that for many centuries the universities believed that their only functions were to conserve and transmit the accumulated wisdom of the ages; they resisted any suggestion that they had a duty to try and extend the bounds of human understanding. The Royal Commissions of the 1850s were quite unconcerned with research. Mark Pattison spent most of the 1870s in an unsuccessful attempt to pursuade his contemporaries that research is as important as teaching. He complained that 'We have known no higher level of knowledge than so much as is required for teaching.' In 1909 the Chancellor of Oxford University (Lord Curzon) remarked:

> It is only too true that the amount of original work as yet turned out from Oxford is inconsiderable. . . . It is impossible for it to emulate a university like Harvard which has more than 350 post-graduate students in Arts.

Other English universities were much more enlightened than Oxford in those days and, of course, the changes which have taken place in the last half century are quite astonishing. Nevertheless it is as well to remember that the universities' preoccupation with research has been developed within the lifetime of many of us, and that it is therefore not surprising that the special problems of technological research in universities have not yet been solved in this country.

If technological research is to be effective, it must often be even more expensive than modern physics. If the universities are to attract the best men in the country, they must provide them – somehow or other – with the best equipment in the country. Any university which attempts to do technological research on a shoestring is bound sooner or later to become an intellectual backwater. The Americans have understood this much more clearly than we have. A series of historical accidents forced them to change completely their whole system of financing scientific and techno-logical research and development, and nowaways they do it much better than we do.

Radar was developed in England in two or three government laborat-ories. When the Tizard mission launched the Americans on their development programme it was not entrusted to government research establishments such as Camp Evans and Wright Field, but to a special new laboratory attached to and administered by MIT. I believe that this was the first of the great American research programmes to be administered by a university. The Radiation Laboratory was very much like the Tele-communications Research Establishment in this country, and its organisa-tion was inspired by ours, but TRE was run by the Ministry of Aircraft Production; the Radiation Lab. was attached to MIT and made use of all the facilities of that great institution; in particular the pre-war experience of the Department of Industrial Co-operation which had administered MIT's programme of sponsored research was vitally important.

The Radiation Laboratory was so successful that after the war the American Government decided to entrust the universities with most of its large-scale research and development in the fields of radar and atomic energy; for example the great secret laboratory at Los Alamos was handed over to the University of California, and Argonne to the University of Chicago. Nowadays the Atomic Energy Commission does no research itself, but contracts it all out to universities and one or two large industrial firms.

The Radiation Laboratory died at the end of the war, but from it other laboratories have been created, some of which are still administered by MIT. In particular, the plans for the Radar Reporting Chain for the defence of the North American Continent were studied in MIT. The Lincoln Laboratories have been responsible for the design and develop-ment of the whole of the necessary equipment. Large though the Lincoln Laboratories are, they are still administered by MIT.

The techniques of inertial navigation which were used by the Nautilus under the Polar icecap were developed in the Aeronautics Division at MIT. The propellants which are used in American rockets were studied in the California Institute of Technology, which is responsible for the administration of the great telescopes at Mount Wilson and Mount Palomar.

Immense research programmes in high energy nuclear physics have been undertaken on behalf of the Government by the Universities of Stanford, California and Harvard. The enormous research station at Brookhaven, which is in some ways comparable to Harwell, is organised and run by a consortium of universities.

The total academic budget of MIT, including salaries, maintenance of buildings, etc., was about $19 million last year. This is a large sum, but not unreasonable by our standards for an undergraduate population of about 3,600 and nearly 3,000 postgraduate students. But, and this is my point, the institution spent about $60 million last year on research work of various kinds – the Aeronautics Division alone spent $13 million. However one converts dollars to pounds, it is clear that MIT must spend more than the £12 million or so which all the English universities put together spent on their research programmes last year. Nevertheless, the MIT expects to double its graduate school during the next decade. In 1958 American universities spent about $550 million on sponsored research; the Federal Government provided about three-quarters of this sum (perhaps one-tenth of the total spent on research in America that year).

During the last ten years the Americans have entrusted their universities, and particularly their technological universities, with many more government research programmes, greatly to the benefit of everyone concerned. In this country the efficiency of our government laboratories made this policy unnecessary, but it has led in my opinion to a lack of contact between research and teaching which is greatly to the detriment of the country as a whole. I know that in saying this I am speaking only for a minority of the academic engineers of this country, many of whom feel, and are prepared to maintain with heat, that any change in the structure of the present university system is to be deplored and that the preoccupation of the Americans with large-scale development is made possible only at the expense of what in this country is regarded as their proper function. Suffice it to say that it is the considered opinion of many Americans whose judgment I trust, that despite all the difficulties and complication of their immense research programme, American universities have grown and profited tremendously from it, and that out of their difficulties has come their present strength.

There is much in the American system which we need not envy. One must be impressed by the enterprise and imagination which American universities have shown in studying themselves, their organisation and their programmes and making fundamental changes wherever they seemed to be needed. They have been far more critical of themselves than we have ever been, though they have never been prodded by a Royal Commission. Committees of Enquiry have completely reorganised faculties and departments and whole universities.

Enormous research schools can change and dominate a university; to many an Englishman this is sufficient justification for condemning them out of hand. American universities have learnt to accept them and so their undergraduates, research students and staff are at all times aware of the enormous importance and excitement of fundamental research which is conducted on a large scale with a sense of urgency and with the best apparatus which money can buy. Most Americans think that it is absurd that federal funds can be made available to support the universities only on the pretext that they are being used to defend the continent. This means that every graduate school in the States is formally dependent on the defence vote. In practice the system has been so devised that any university of repute can get support for almost any research project in which it is interested regardless of its nature. The 'defence of the continental United States' is an umbrella which shelters the most astonishing mixture of research and development (both pure and applied). Cumbersome though the system may appear, it has worked remarkably well in practice for three reasons. Very large resources are available; the Government has appointed university scientists as administrators, and they and their colleagues have been most understanding and enlightened, and thirdly (and in the opinion of some Americans most important of all) the very untidiness of the organisation has meant that there are half a dozen independent sources of funds. Americans would view with dismay a proposal that all research grants should be administered through a single organisation like the DSIR in this country. Lord Adrian has drawn attention to the danger of entrusting too much power to this monolithic (but administratively tidy) organisation.

I am sure that the Americans' instinctive mistrust of monopolies makes them wiser than we are.

On the continent of Europe a completely different organisation produces an intimate association between research, teaching and industry, an association which is vital to the success of each and all of them. Senior members of staff of the universities are often members of staff of research stations such as the Max Planck Institutes, and are almost invariably consulted by the big firms; the staff of the research stations and senior industrialists are often professors or 'extraordinary' professors in a local university; for example Herr von Laue is Director of the Max Planck Institute for Physical Chemistry, and Professor Extraordinary in the University of Charlottenburg. Senior men from the research departments of big firms such as Siemens in Berlin are on the staff of the same university. There is invariably an intimate and continuing association between a research station and the university which is nearest to it.

Few European technologists can understand either how or why we attempt to organise the universities in this country without the help of Extraordinary Professors. Perhaps the colleges of advanced technology will have to show the way to the rest of the university world. How, without such men, can we hope to introduce such novel subjects as the design of machine tools to our undergraduates and graduate students? Both Germany and Russia have large research institutes and university departments devoted to this vital subject. Russia has made extraordinary progress in this field of late. There are a thousand scientists in the main research organisation in Moscow, which in collaboration with the universities, is responsible for the education of machine tool designers throughout the country. The whole of Soviet industry is being revolutionised by new machine tools.

It is curious that continental universities have been much slower than ours to admit chemical engineering as a university discipline despite the fact that the Americans have long known it as 'The Fourth Technology'. Our own universities have been similarly reluctant to accept the study of machine tools which was established in Charlottenburg half a century ago.

Large research programmes have been undertaken by technical universities in Europe; for example the university department of naval architecture in Delft has a big ship tank and is responsible for design studies on new Dutch merchant ships. Dr Larnmeren is Professor of Naval Architecture in charge both of this installation and of the large Dutch testing tank in Wageningen. Most continental technological universities have research or development divisions – some are on the main university campus; some are part of the local university and some are administratively independent. These institutions are staffed by part-time academicians, they are very well equipped and they undertake large research programmes both for the government and for industry. Both in Europe and in America the universities finance a large part of their postgraduate work by 'sponsored' research of infinite variety.

In Russia the association between teaching, research and industry seems to be closer than it is anywhere else in the world. It seems to be achieved by exploiting the best features of both the American and European systems. Such collaboration is, of course, bought at a price. It is sometimes said, for example, that although continental professors may know more about local industry than their English counterparts, they know less about their students. This may be true, but before we begin to congratulate ourselves, let us for one moment try to visualise the English system as it might appear to a visitor.

English universities have never been responsible for much of our national technological research and development. I believe they ought to do much more of it, but for the time being they are not equipped to undertake it. Is it not possible, however, to associate them more closely with the work which is being done in industrial and government laboratories? Many of these great institutions undertake most valuable and interesting fundamental work, much of which is essentially similar to the programmes which play so important a part in the development of foreign institutes of technology. Some of this work is almost indistinguishable in character from that which is already being done in our universities. For example, the physics department in the Radio Research Establishment, Malvern has exploited its magnificent equipment to study the new 'solid state' devices at very low temperatures. Some most beautiful work is being done in the National Physical Laboratory in Teddington and in the National Engineering Laboratory in East Kilbride (which has cost about £6 million so far and is splendidly equipped). All of these great institutions seem to me to suffer because of their present separation from the university world; not only does the research itself suffer, but their discoveries are often inadequately appreciated by those people who could learn most from them. Very few university students go there to work; university regulations make it difficult for the students and our academic traditions are opposed to the development of what might appear to be extra-mural postgraduate schools even in government research stations which are engaged in 'unclassified' pure research. Our students do not exploit as they should the opportunity of seeing and using the best equipment in England. Many students would gain enormously from day-to-day contact with problems of importance which are being faced with a sense of urgency by people whose obvious competence has received the tribute of adequate resources.

The National Engineering Laboratory has recently been reorganised and it is to be controlled by a three-man steering committee, which will help the Director. Why should the administration of this lab. not be intimately associated with the Royal College of Science and Technology in Glasgow, which is only a few miles away? Why should we not try the

American system in this country as an experiment and amalgamate NEL with Glasgow Tech.?

The fundamental research which has been done in our own universities gives them their greatest claim to intellectual eminence; but it is important to realise that to many young men, particularly to young engineers, fundamental research makes relatively little appeal, and many of them (and they are worthy, estimable and intelligent young men) are far more interested in work which is likely to have significant and perhaps fairly immediate application. It is quite wrong for the universities to underestimate the intellectual difficulty of development work and to tell such young men to go away. If adequate opportunities were given to our graduate students to work with the best apparatus available in the country, on problems the significance of which was obvious to them, many of them would give of their best and benefit themselves, the universities and the community as a whole.

I realise only too well the tremendous organisational problems which would arise in any attempt to associate universities with non-academic institutions in a matter of such vital importance. The Americans have the advantage of us because of the very rapid growth of their graduate schools – there are about 250,000 graduate students in America; perhaps 10,000 in this country. (An American is as likely to take a Ph.D. as an Englishman is to take a first degree.) Graduate students in America must undergo tuition and take prescribed courses of lectures, so that opportunities for contacts between the student and his professor are provided automatically wherever he works. Inadequate though our resources may be I do not think they are efficiently deployed. English graduate schools might be far more effective if they provided more formal instruction, and I believe that there should be a continuous and automatic exchange of information, of personnel, of ideas, of machinery and of inspiration between the academic world (in which I include both teaching and research), the industrial world and the government research laboratories.

English universities spend about £12 million a year on research, British industry about £85 million, but the Government spends about £240 million on research for defence. This represents a higher proportion of the total research of the country than any other power has felt obliged to accept. Should our Commission consider why this is necessary, or is this question too difficult for even a Royal Commission to solve?

To recapitulate, our universities appear to be content with the situation in which they find themselves. They seem to believe that their expansion programme is as large as they can handle and many of them have let it be known that they do not think that they could recruit either staff or students more quickly than they are doing. On the other hand, it is quite clear that there is a fundamental difference between the basic principles upon which university education is organised here and those which are accepted in most other civilised countries, almost all of which expect as a matter of course to have a much larger university population than ours. I do not see how this extraordinary difference between British policy and the policy of the rest of the world could be resolved except by enquiries on a scale which could be envisaged only by a Royal Commission.

Secondly, I think that problems of technological education are still underestimated in this country and that we have never faced the problems of technological research in universities. I do not believe that our resources are large enough, nor do I believe that they are deployed as efficiently as they should be. However satisfied we may be with the situation as it appears to us, we should be deluding ourselves if we thought that all foreign observers were as pleased with our system as we seem to be.

It is no longer true as it may have been once that universities have no other function than to provide a gloss on society; they no longer exist, as once they did, so that wealthy young men can pass a few years in acquiring a certain amount of polish and getting to know each other. The industrial revolution owed nothing to the universities. For the first time in recorded history the survival of the country depends upon the universities; their efficiency is of vital concern to the nation and should be studied in the light of contemporary practice both here and abroad. We cannot assert that the rest of the world is out of step. If a Commission decided that we are right after all, then indeed we should have reason for self congratulation.

8. Observations on the American University

Edward Shils

Universities Quarterly Vol. 17 (1962–63), pp. 182–193.

The following remarks, which bear mainly on the ascendancy of research over teaching in the American academic system, have their point of departure in *The American College: A Psychological and Social Interpretation of the Higher Learning*, edited by Nevitt Sanford (John Wiley 1962). This book, which is the work of 30 collaborators and of an editorial committee of eight, is a remarkable achievement. It is remarkable for the indefatigable ramification, sometimes subtle and differentiated and sometimes simply callow, of its analysis of the social processes which go on in classrooms, in the relations of students with each other and with their teachers. It is remarkable also for its summary of past research and its introduction of the results of a certain amount of new research. It is finally remarkable for its 'student-centredness'. The student and his 'needs' seem throughout this book to be the touchstone by which academic things are to be judged. It is not just because so much research and reflection on student motives and responses and on student culture are to be found in the book that one gets this impression. It is rather the constant recurrence of the preoccupation with the full development of the student's personality which underlies this impression. Indeed, the authors seem to regard universities as something like adolescent personality formation institutions and they pay only the most unconvinced and unconvincing lip-service to the obligation of a university to do serious intellectual work.

The British university seems like a determinate, well-defined – perhaps too determinate and too well-defined – institution when it is placed alongside the American university. Whatever the cleavage between the ancient universities and the modern, between the English and the

Scottish, the range of variation of the British universities from the highest to the lowest is very narrow in comparison with the American. New foundations do not change this. The students seem less variegated, the conception, however ambiguous, of the tasks of a university more severe and inflexible, more resistant to criticism and questioning. The students are there. It is their duty to study and to learn. The teachers are there. It is their task to teach and to do research. Increasing numbers do not change this. Here and there, there are criticism and dissatisfaction, occasionally an eagerness for innovation, an eagerness accompanied by awareness of the uncongeniality of the environment to innovation.

How different the present scene in America! It often looks like a vast 'buzzing, booming, confusion'. So many students, so many very different kinds of students, brilliant, imaginative, dull, enthusiastic, routine, distrustful, curious, dutiful, unwilling, positively recalcitrant – covering a variety which seems to be wider and more multifarious than the British student body. So many universities and colleges, small and gigantic, conventional and radical, intellectually backward and intellectually great, colleges which are an evening shambles,[1] and universities as great as any in the history of science and learning, privately endowed and privately conducted institutions, colleges and universities conducted by Roman Catholic religious orders and by Protestant sects and churches, some impoverished, some wealthy, some attended by the *jeunesse dorée*, others attended by those for whom it is just an appropriate stage of life and with little other purpose, and still others by the worn-out and distracted who work most of the day or night in offices, shops and even factories. There is no central authority which grants charters, there is no central body to promulgate standards to which the universities and colleges of the country must conform, no central body provides financially for them. The most diverse 'experiments' are carried on alongside the most reactionary conventionality.

All this heterogeneity and dispersion notwithstanding, the different streams of culture and the different strata of American society which characterise the American academic cosmos are gradually being formed into a new unity. The unity is imposed in part by the fact that the whole affair exists within American society and is accordingly influenced by the common traditions of American culture, of beliefs in the desirability of self-improvement, and, therewith, of a closer approximation to the centre of society. The unity of the university system is coming about also from the unification of the country, arising from the speed and ease of travel and communication, and the enhanced authority of all government, above all, the authority of the central government. The leading universities are becoming the universities of the whole society and not merely a small pluto-aristocracy of the major cities, such as the Ivy League universities and colleges were for a long time, and still are, to some extent. The lowering of the barrier separating Roman Catholics from the rest of American society, and the diminution of Protestant sectarian fervour, at least in the more or less educated sectors of the population, have opened the colleges of church and sect increasingly to the influences of the intellectual community at the centre of the society.

The university system is unified, too, by its own interior development. The advance of research as the major concern of a university and the closely related requirement of the Ph.D. for appointment even to fairly junior teaching posts, have led to the ascendancy of the graduate school within the university. The labour market for scientific and academic personnel has become more national than ever before. Directly as a result of these developments, a relatively small number of universities have become the chief sources of personnel, a standard of assessment and the model of what is academically correct. A hierarchy which was simply a matter of status in earlier years, has now become a hierarchy of intellectual authority and a system of the 'circulation of elites'.

The relatively centralised system of elite (i.e. Ph.D.) production has produced common foci of attention, common heroes and a common body of problems and literature, appreciated and explored with different intensities, but avoided with difficulty. At the peak, a certain competitiveness of individuals for pre-eminence within the same fields, and of institutions for distinction of personnel and activity, heightens mutual awareness; at the less exalted levels of the hierarchy of institutions, there is a correspondingly greater, more acute, awareness of the centre than there used to be when colleges existed to teach a small number of students according to conventional syllabi, and could go their own way without thought or fear of being old fashioned.

The growth of this national system has two faces. The central universities of the country have established their predominance as research universities. Their eminence comes from the quality of the research published by their staff members and by the subsequent achievements of their Ph.D.s in research. The standard for judging the quality of an institution is the research which its members publish. Productivity in research and publication becomes the standard by which university and college teachers judge themselves and are judged by others. Accomplishment as a teacher, unless it is as a teacher of research workers, is likely to be less noticed and, if noticed, less appreciated. Administrators, trustees and teachers who are ambitious to elevate the reputation of their institution do it through devices which shift the emphasis steadily towards research and publication. The teacher of undergraduates is slighted; the value of teaching undergraduates is estimated lightly. The public intellectual functions of the university beyond the conduct of research and the training of future research workers, university teachers who will, in their turn, be primarily research workers, and lawyers, physicians and engineers, are passed over without discussion.[2]

Meanwhile, the number of undergraduates increases. To have a B.A. for all sorts of ill-understood reasons[3] becomes a goal of the multitudes[4] which many attain; and as they do so, those, through whose hands they must pass to reach that goal, care less and less about it. The teaching of undergraduates is coming to be regarded as the activity of juniors, of misfits and of eccentrics who enjoy it. The bachelor's degree is regarded as nothing in itself, as being only the floor from which real life progresses. Undergraduates are thought of increasingly as an affliction or as a reservoir from which promising young men and women can be selected for the career of research.

One of the sources for this disregard for undergraduate teaching is a belief that the undergraduates are too immature for 'serious' work.[5] Many American university teachers think of their students as 'kids' incapable of, or not inclined to do, interesting intellectual work. The poor quality of so much of the American secondary education from which the undergraduates have come sustains the view that the student is not capable of intense or prolonged intellectual exertion and that his absorptive capacities are not great. The result is a syllabus which is adapted to a very slack intellectual life.

The expansion of the general education movement, meritorious though this has been in many respects, has probably accentuated this tendency towards the lightening of the burden which is laid upon the undergraduate. Only exceptional students discover their real interests before their third year, largely, I think, because they have not been pressed or inspired to dig into any subject with an intensity sufficient to arouse their curiosity or to give them a sense of achievement. Consequently, many students who develop an interest in a subject late in their undergraduate years, decide to become graduate students in order to learn more about their subject which has interested them. Many of them do not wish to make their careers in research or even to be trained in research techniques, but since this is the condition of their further penetration into the subject of their belated interest, they are pushed willy-nilly in this direction. The multiplication of research students is thus, in part at least, a complex consequence of the neglect of the intellectual side of undergraduate education, and contributes to its further neglect. Such seems to be the situation in some of the greatest of the private and state universities of the country.

It is not universally the case. There are undergraduate colleges in the country where teachers are not only devoted but demanding and the undergraduates are sufficiently well educated so that when some of them subsequently become post-graduate students in the great universities, they make the dissatisfying discovery that they have already been over the ground. (The impressive density of the American post-graduate syllabus is the counterpendant to the intellectual sparseness of the undergraduate course.)

Are numbers inevitably at the root of this evacuation of the undergraduate syllabus? Are the undergraduates worked so lightly because they are incapable of anything better? Do large classes necessarily attenuate the intellectual intake of the students?[6] As the universities grow in size, the teaching of undergraduates is in danger of becoming more perfunctory and not just because, as is said, 'more means worse'. The increased size of the teaching staff, which must accompany this increase in the number of students, and which is recruited by the newer criterion of a completed Ph.D., will probably be accompanied by a considerable decline in interest in the teaching of undergraduates and a further increase in interest in research. Research, in the mass university, is a sort of island in which intellectual intensity and integrity can be preserved in the midst of a flood of anonymous students whom one cannot come to know because they are seen so transiently and in such large numbers.[7]

The national labour market for university teachers, to which I have referred above, and the competitive search for institutional and departmental distinction – which is perforce a search for distinction in research because there is at present no way for a distinguished teacher to be known except by the legends which are created about him – have parallel effects. They pass over the man who is primarily a teacher. There are brilliant and beloved teachers of undergraduates in the American system. They are not, however, sought out by important universities, when they make new appointments, nor, in fact, do they themselves usually seek to re-enter circulation in the larger world. They are unknown except to former pupils and to friends and immediate colleagues. Outstanding teachers of undergraduates move in a sort of confidential underground; there is no way in which their reputation can be established except through word of mouth. Such teachers are heroes to undergraduates; but they are 'local gods'. They are often unviable outside the environment in which they were formed.

The growth of the national system has another result, beneficial in some respects, injurious in others. Many institutions which were content to perform local services by producing graduates for local employment, and to provide local entertainments in the form of football, track sports and basketball, have since the Second World War raised their sights. They do so partly because the younger generation is now more serious and because *alumni* of the type described by James Thurber in *The Male Animal* are passing from the scene; they also do so because their new staff members have been formed in the national system and have their minds focused on research and high intellectual matters.[8] The senior administrators have decided too that things could not go on as they were. As a result of this, football has been 'de-emphasised' and research has attained a new dignity.

Colleges and universities founded by religious bodies have become more sensitive to their tradition of isolation from the main currents of intellectual life in the country and they have ceased to be content with it. Their own expanding number of students have entailed enlargement of their teaching staffs and this has meant difficulty in recruiting from religious orders or from communicating members of their sponsor-church or sect, sufficient staff members who are proficient in their subjects as well as religiously orthodox.

Agricultural and engineering colleges have been transforming themselves into universities, again partly in response to the growing numbers of students, partly in response to the conviction that a narrowly professional, technical education is inappropriate. This 'metropolitanisation', this effort to enter into the national system has been impelled by and impels the desire to do research on a scale appropriate to gaining national attention and appreciation.

The parochialism of engineering and agricultural colleges, of state universities, and Roman Catholic and Lutheran colleges, was not a good thing from the point of view of the intellectual growth of the country, or the intellectual development of their graduates. The growth of a metropolitan ideal and the culture of the 'centre' has, in general, raised the intellectual level of these institutions. It has given them staff members who feel themselves to be part of a larger intellectual culture which goes beyond their own religious body, their own technical specialty and their own local responsibility.[9]

The growth of the national system has also added to the pressure on outstanding liberal arts colleges to become like universities, to have on their staffs many men and women doing research and training their own students to do research rather than to prepare them with the best possible intellectual foundations for fruitful careers in the professions and in research. The young recruits to the staffs of the best liberal arts colleges have usually taken their advanced degrees at the major centres; they are usually 'research-oriented'. They do not invariably find the vocation of teaching on a high level to undergraduates, which is a very demanding vocation, sufficiently rewarding in the way in which they would like to be rewarded. Opportunities for research in these colleges are bound to be poor because they do not have research libraries and because their laboratories, planned for undergraduate teaching, are not equipped for large-scale research. The sheer fact of availability of funds, and the awareness that colleagues elsewhere receive them are temptations to do research. Quite apart from the intrinsic appeal of the research problems themselves, they are drawn by the prospect of grants from the Atomic Energy Commission, the National Science Foundation, the United States Public Health Service, the Rockefeller Foundation, etc., etc., and they hope ultimately to return to the 'big leagues'. The absence of an imminent prospect of doing so causes them to think of changing their own institution into a microcosm of the metropolis.

Certainly in a system as large as the American system there are bound to be young deviants who, for whatever motives, perhaps not always admirable, wish primarily to be teachers, who do not want to do research or do not wish to do it on the scale and with the intensity and exclusiveness of some of their colleagues. Some of these might be very good teachers. There is a natural harmony of interest between these people and the tasks of undergraduate education. The outstanding liberal arts colleges like Reed, Oberlin and Swarthmore, manage to obtain a sufficient supply. There is no reason why an effective system of allocation, which would discern and direct these people into posts in colleges and universities throughout the country which require primarily the teaching of under-graduates, could not function if the great universities did not permit themselves to be so dominated by the ideal of research that they regard those who seem reluctant to pursue the ideal path as being beyond redemption.[10]

Most university and college teachers in the United States do teach undergraduates and some of them do it very well, but it is a mark of elevation in one's career and a liberation from inferiority to reach the position in which one can, also or exclusively, teach postgraduate students. Unless even the better liberal arts colleges watch themselves carefully in this regard, they will also become the victims of this trend. The teaching of undergraduates in the United States is today a defensive operation in which there are many Trojan horses within the walls. The dignity of an institution is enhanced, in this equine conception, by its provision for the training of postgraduate students, by its 'Ph.D. programme'. The struggle to provide oneself with a postgraduate audience, short of changing one's place of employment, leads directly in the direction of creating postgraduate departments and offering post-graduate degrees.

Observers of this process in the United States – and certain contributors to *The American College* are among the most perceptive – have not failed to see the intellectual evacuation of the undergraduate phase. They avoid a head-on collision with it by stressing the extra-intellectual functions of higher education, the development of the personality, the 'enlightenment of conscience', 'freeing of impulse', 'differentiation and integration of the ego'.[11]

Some simply shrug their shoulders and speak of making up the lost time in graduate school. One of the most recent writers on the subject justified the waste by referring to the lengthened life-span.

The loss of these years is serious, especially in a country which neglects its adolescents intellectually. It is not only a waste of precious years; it is also harmful to the public intellectual tone of the country. For the time being, however, it is hard to see where the impetus for the change will come from in the United States. The amount of work demanded of the student is pathetically small. The student is not forced to extend himself and, not being forced to do so, only those who are driven from within by their curiosity and love of their subject or from the compulsiveness of their characters, drive themselves hard. In consequence of this, the amount that any student knows about any particular subject, even after having specialised in it as an undergraduate, is meagre.

The improvement of the quality of the culture of the undergraduate in the United States is at present taking the form of general education, and more specialised schemes of undergraduate education, which were never as specialised as they are in Great Britain, have been allowed to go by the board. I do not think that the broadening is incompatible with a greater intensity – there is so much slack – but this is not the general view.

These years can be recovered if the postgraduate schools could find an honourable place for prospective teachers as well as for prospective research workers in their outlook. It is not so much that the specific content of postgraduate training should be different as that its cultural penumbra should somehow be modified so that undergraduate teaching would be viewed as an intrinsically worthwhile activity – no less important than research – and not just something that one must do in order to be able to do research in the most congenial atmosphere. Deans and Presidents will not be able to bring about the change, while liberal arts colleges will probably be unable to do more than hold their own. Yet if such a change does take place – and there is no inherent reason to think that the movement of academic opinion is inevitably unilinear – it will find many allies.

The attractive experiments conducted by Wayne State University and Michigan State University in raising the level of undergraduate instruction at the Monteith and Oakland Colleges, as well as the continuing high attainment of the best liberal arts colleges, show that the situation is not hopeless. There are people in the United States who feel that undergraduate years are not to be lightheartedly thrown away.

The renaiscence of a more intense and demanding undergraduate education in the American university system is impeded by some of the same reasons that have helped the research side to gain such ascendancy in recent decades. Research is a public accomplishment, visible nationally and internationally as soon as, or immediately after, it is published. Teaching is one of the few relatively private things left in the world, although it is conducted in public. Colleagues do not go to each other's lectures, except rarely. The testimony of students, either direct or by their examination results, is not very conclusive. The sense of gratitude which students express and their achievements in life come too late and are too difficult to assess to provide the basis for appointment and promotion. Even if appointing bodies had an adequate idea of what is desired of a teacher, and were ready to give it due weight in their decision, it would not be easy to decide about the merits of a particular person as a teacher because of the confidential character of his performance in the past.

Our ignorance of the quality of the past teaching performance of any individual candidate – disregarding extraordinary defects which come to public attention – is matched by our indifference about the possibility of learning how to teach. Although at first glance the very idea of teaching a prospective university teacher how to teach is repugnant, there is really nothing to be said against it in principle. A man learns to do research under supervision, in collaboration with and by the criticism of his supervisor. Is teaching of necessity less routine or less creative than research?

Even though we might accept the principle that the art of university teaching could in some sense be taught, it is something which has not been done in any self-conscious or deliberate way. Certainly there is no systematic body of psychological or sociological knowledge from which we could draw any more certain directives than we can from reflection on individual experience. In principle, however, this does not mean to say that such systematic psychological and sociological knowledge might not be acquired by the systematic study of the process of teaching. The subject could scarcely be said to be in its beginnings at present. The section of *The American College* devoted to teaching and the curriculum show how difficult the matter is, and how much more has yet to be done before it will be possible for these disciplines to contribute significantly to the training and the selection of teachers.[12]

At the same time it would be vain to deny that such research as has been done already has enriched our ideas of the nature of the teaching process and has made us more aware of the obstacles which it confronts within the teacher himself and the student body.

The obstacles to effective teaching arising from the culture of the student body have never been sufficiently well considered by students of university. In this respect the studies of 'Student Society and Student Culture'[13] represent a very considerable advance over the previous discussion and show also the possibilities inherent in further research on this subject. Unlike the activity of teaching in a university, student society and student culture are relatively public matters and amenable to research. The techniques developed by sociologists, social psychologists and anthropologists in recent years are very appropriate to the subject matter and one may legitimately expect considerable progress in the near future, in the study of this aspect of teaching and learning in universities.

The as yet unharvested fruits, even the unsown seeds of sociological and social psychological research into teaching and learning at the university level, can hardly expect it to be a decisive factor in bringing about the needed change in the trend of the relationship between research and teaching in American universities and colleges. A deeper change of opinion will be needed and the emergence of this change is as yet not at all tangible. Still not all the passion for research is a passion for truth. Some of it is just fashionable and fashions, by their very nature, change. It might, therefore, be that within the not too remote future we might witness such a change in fashion. It is also possible that the dissatisfaction with the state of public culture in the United States at a time when particular arts, sciences and humanistic disciplines are flourishing, might cause the leaders of intellectual opinion to see that a richer and more intense undergraduate syllabus could contribute to the diminution of the mixture of vulgarity and philistinism which is so often found in the United States alongside the most brilliantly creative performances. Should such changes occur, then the type of research, only adumbrated, however voluminously, in *The American College* would find its proper calling.

Notes

[1] British analysts of universities would do well to read a story by Herbert Gold, 'A Dog in Brooklyn, A Girl in Detroit', in *Encounter*, 112, January 1963, pp. 20–27. There they will see a facet of American academic life which must remain hidden from them as long as their experience is confined to the great research centres and graduate schools to which British visitors usually attend.

[2] These trends are incisively summarised by Prof. Robert Knapp in 'Changing Functions of the College Professor', *op. cit.*, pp. 290–311.

[3] Drs Elizabeth Douvan and Carol Kaye have attempted to survey these diverse reasons in 'Motivational Factors in College Entrance', *op. cit.*, pp. 193–225. 'Personal metamorphoses, a search for status and a different life style, the wish for unusual and exotic experience', erotic opportunity, freedom from family, training or qualification for an occupation, social mobility and the gratification and elaboration of intellectual interests are among the motives discerned.

[4] Data demonstrating the wide range of intellectual capacities and dispositions of American college and university students are presented by Drs T. R. McConnell and Paul Herst in 'The Diverse College Student Population', pp. 225–50.

[5] Such an opinion is regrettably very noticeable in *The American College*. For example: 'One look at the college curriculum which embodies the history and present state of every imaginable art and science, is enough to convince anyone that it is far beyond the capacity of a four year program addressed to 17- to 21-year-olds, who seem by their very developmental status barred from a proper appreciation of the material. Many serious institutions handle themselves as if attainment of the curricular goal could be actually expected from the students' (Joseph Katz in 'Personality and Interpersonal Relations in the College Classroom', *op. cit.*, p. 380). Thus, even the latter-day allies of the undergraduate in this conflict between postgraduate training and undergraduate teaching seem to favour the further attenuation of the intellectual substance of undergraduate education.

[6] Research on this very important issue is not entirely unequivocal in its answer to the question. Cf. Dr W. J. McKeachie's valiant effort ('Procedures and Techniques of Teaching: A Survey of Experimental Studies') *op. cit.*, pp. 312–63, especially pp. 325–26.

[7] Dr McKeachie has some very thoughtful observations on the significance of the size of a college or university for the intensity of intellectual contact between teacher and student and among students. *Op. cit.*, pp. 354–55.

[8] Younger teachers increasingly try to bring the more interested of their students into contact with a richer intellectual tradition than had been possible as long as the fat textbooks, often of a painful grossness and banality of spirit, held the field. But they too must press on with their research.

[9] The process of transformation of 'provincial' technical, denominational and sectarian colleges into universities with an urge to share in the culture of the 'metropolis' is described with characteristic vividness and subtlety by Professor Riesman and Dr Jenks in 'The Viability of the American College', *op. cit.*, pp. 74–192, especially pp. 118–92.

[10] The odd fact is that, with all the talk about research in the United States, most published research is probably the work of a relatively small proportion of the total practitioners in the field. The atmosphere, however, has become such that everybody must believe that he is doing some research or feel inferior for not doing so.

[11] Cf. Sanford, Nevitt, *op. cit.*, 'Developmental Status of the Entering Freshmen', pp. 253–82, especially pp. 271–82.

[12] All of Part III 'Academic Procedures', pp. 283–462 of *The American College* deals with this subject. As well as documenting the scientifically unformed state of the subject, it contains many suggestive insights and many egregious remarks.

[13] Part IV, *op. cit.*, pp. 463–530.

Part II

Robbins and After

9. First Reactions to the Robbins Report

Charles Morris
Universities Quarterly Vol. 18 (1963–64), pp. 9–16.

After Robbins

At the time these words are being written few people can have had the opportunity for a serious study of the Robbins Report, and indeed may not yet have succeeded in securing a copy. But it seems clear that it has been overwhelmingly well received, and that both the Government and the universities are pretty much committed to implementing it, at any rate in its main policies. If they proceed to do as they now say, this will represent a tremendous step forward.

Everybody who has the ability and qualifications to profit from higher education is to have it if he wishes; and as between subjects and courses of study academic snobbishness is for practical purposes to disappear. Any student who has profited from a certain quantum of higher education of a suitable standard is to have a degree, no matter what his field of study may be. Both these decisions of policy have been overdue for a long time. It is not really clear exactly who has been resolutely opposing them since the Education Act of 1944; though no doubt a great number of people both in the universities and in the Government have, until very recently, felt no great itch actively to promote them. But now the time has come. The walls of the academic Jericho have fallen at the feet of the first really clear and uninhibited blast of the trumpets.

Changes in Universities

But it is a tremendous step forward for all that and it will have tremendous implications. For one thing there will have to be great changes in the universities. No doubt it is not as true as it was 15 years ago that to the university teacher, who, after all, controls the universities, research comes

first and teaching a very poor second. But on the whole it is still true that
university teachers as a clan are not dedicated to teaching in anything like
the degree that schoolmasters and schoolmistresses are. They still do not
think that they ought to be. They still think that their primary vocation is
to maintain themselves as first-class scholars or first-class men of research.
If they make sacrifices for their calling, as many of them do, scholarship
and research are the causes for which they are ready to suffer.
Universities, they still firmly believe, ought to be places where the young
should be given the opportunity for working in contact with lively and
distinguished men and women who are in the front line of scholarship or
research. And it is the esential business of dons to try to be such persons.
Students are no longer children. They must be presumed to know, as
adult people, what they need and what they want, and also to know how, if
given the opportunity, to get it. In their stage of maturity this is their
right. They ought no longer to be conditioned or managed in any way;
they should develop their academic work in accordance with their own
ideas and wishes. But they should be given free access to distinguished
scholars of standing and experience. Only so could the intellectual
freedom of the new generation be secured and its creative imagination be
elaborated. Only so could the young be released from the entrenched half-
truths of the old. Only so could the thought and knowledge of the world
really advance.

A Piece of History

We should remember that such outstanding university teachers as Samuel
Alexander and R. H. Tawney – to mention only two – thought that the
scholars of Balliol were over-taught, and that no great good could come
from that. In the 1930s Abraham Flexner found that Oxford and
Cambridge were primarily finishing schools; and that it was certainly not
through the intention or wishes of the dons that those two institutions
were genuine universities at all. In those days it was probably true that
Oxford and Cambridge were primarily places for the teaching of the
young, and it was against this that such men as Alexander and Tawney,
with their passion for beginning the advancement of truth rather than
finishing the polish of cultures, were protesting. The world, and especially
the modern world, could not afford that the universities should be such
places. The Germans had had a much better idea, and the world must
follow them.

Since then Tawney and Alexander have had their way and the circle that
has been turned has been a full one. University teachers in the next period

conscientiously warned one another against the illusion that teaching was really their vocation, and students were left more and more free to teach themselves. They were exposed, sometimes compulsorily exposed, to exhibitions of the learning of their seniors; but it was left to them to take or leave what was offered them, and inevitably in these circumstances what was offered tended with time to become less and less takeable by a new generation. Dons studied their subjects more and more and their students less and less; and students perhaps inevitably tended in time to become disillusioned and without much scope. Today, as a consequence, the students are demanding more positive and devoted teaching; and the public, supporting the Robbins Committee, is demanding more and better university teaching for more and more of each generation. The world of higher education has indeed turned full circle since the days of Jowett, but with of course a characteristically modern twist. Jowett thought the scholars and commoners of Balliol, including among their number many Alexanders and Tawneys, were the right students for a university to have; or at least he thought that Balliol was happily moving more and more towards getting nothing but the right students. But modern opinion, of course, thinks otherwise. Like the Robbins Committee it has learned a lot from the sociologist, and it thinks that a very substantial proportion of the human race would benefit from a good university education, and that the world would be a better place if they had it.

A Time Lag

As American experience has shown, the new tasks for the universities are going to present much greater difficulties than the old. The colleges of the future are going to have a much more difficult time than the Balliol of Jowett. Yet it is now almost universally believed that they have got, at whatever cost, to succeed. Almost no one accepts that failure would on any terms be tolerable.

Can the universities do it? So far as finance is concerned it is to be presumed that the Government will take immediate steps to put the UGC in funds; and that the Committee will arrange for grants to the universities both for capital and for recurrent expenditure for the next three or four years on a 'crash' basis. I think this may be safely assumed, because both political parties have now accepted immediate and effective action for higher education as good electioneering politics. It will be quite necessary that finance should be *readily* available for new and urgent plans, because the unhappy history of the past years and months have caused most universities to be seriously behindhand with their building programmes for the old plans. The lost ground will have to be made up smartly before, in most cases, the new and accelerated plans, now to be prepared, can begin to take effect.

Economy in Building

It is right and proper, of course, that the Treasury should expect that in so large an operation as the proposed expansion of the universities, good planning, architectural and academic, should make possible the saving of quite a lot of money. The planning of university buildings naturally presents different problems from the planning of school buildings. But even so the broad principles of attack on costs, which achieved so much in regard to schools, must be capable of being applied, on its merits, to universities and of making very considerable savings over a period. This is only common sense. But if an unreasonably rapid application of such economy schemes is given an unreasonable priority in the first year or two of the new expansion, the whole Robbins operation will never get off the ground – or at least it will be several years late. This would show bad judgment by the Treasury and the Government, and it simply ought not to be allowed. There has been too much of it in the recent past of university development in this country.

Recurrent Finances

In considering finance for recurrent expenditure we come up against a problem which is really basic. The authorities in the universities have a clear idea of what they want. They believe only in universities which in addition to teaching are able to be lively in research. On the other side the Treasury and the Government tend to assume that the finding of new places for undergraduates simply must come before the finding of new money for university research. This clash of opinion will almost certainly cause serious cross-purposes and delays in the day to day working out of expansion plans; and it is a really serious clash.

University research used to cost very little but library books, ink and paper; but nowadays, especially in the sciences, it is very expensive indeed. It is well known that scientists in this country, and particularly university scientists, are seriously restive. They believe that in America and in Russia scientists have far more resources at their disposal to buy equipment and materials for research, and far more technical and clerical assistance. All this of course is quite apart from any question of personal salaries. The shortage of support for research the scientists consider to be not just marginal, but very large indeed; they need to look, in their judgment, for an increase not of 20 or 30 per cent, but for a doubling or trebling. All Vice-Chancellors and university administrators know well that these beliefs and judgments have settled into being very much articles of faith with university scientists. So long as this position remains the older men may still stay in their jobs and do the best they can, but the younger men, and especially the very young, will continue in decisive numbers to prefer other employments or to go and settle abroad.

Research

It can be well understood that the Treasury and the Government will press their views that all the new money which the country can find for the universities must be devoted to establish new places for undergraduates, and that the present is no time to attempt to improve the conditions for research by the academic staff. But if they continue to stand very strongly by this principle, they will find that the academic staff of the universities of the country will change its character. In that event the universities will change their characters too; and the students of the future, in their increased numbers, will not have what the students in the past have had. What they receive instead may well have virtues and advantages of its own; but they will not get what the expansion of British universities has so far been intended to provide. The creative scholars, thinkers and researchers of the nation will be outside the universities, and under-graduates will have no more benefit of them than the general public.

Hard as it may seem to the financially-minded, support for university research will simply *have* to be very greatly improved if the universities are to be maintained at their present level, let alone increased in number. The growing demand for research facilities is as hard an economic fact as the growing demand for student places. The second cannot be had without the first.

The Image of the University Teacher

But if this must be accepted by Treasury and Government, as I think it must, there is an element in the total problem which must be accepted within the universities themselves. The good university teacher may need to be research minded; but it is also completely necessary that he should take his teaching duties and opportunities extremely seriously and that he should be *seen* to do so.

It must be accepted, I think, that the weight of opinion outside the universities is less than convinced that, generally speaking, he does so at present. His image in the public mind is predominantly one of a man who likes to devote himself in his own way to his life of personal scholarship or research, and does what undergraduate teaching he must, sometimes, but not always, with a good grace. It is thought that if he has to spend time with students he would prefer to do so with postgraduate students, or with very advanced undergraduates in their last year. Other teaching is, to him, simply and solely part of the price he has to pay if he is to be able to live as a scholar or research scientist.

This picture is certainly not today a true one. But, to say the least of it, it must be supposed that any profession must *in some measure* be responsible for the contrast of its own public image. And this particular image is undoubtedly doing a great deal of harm at the present time. It is very much in the interest of everybody that something should be done, primarily I suppose by university teachers themselves, to change it. If they do nothing, or are unsuccessful in what they do, not only will they suffer themselves, but the universities and the whole cause of university education itself, will suffer with them.

The Public and the Professions

It is not easy in these days for any profession to secure a good public image for itself. The law and the Church, I suppose, have always enjoyed poor images, and on the whole have thrived on them. The doctors have been in great danger several times in recent years, but the accredited saving of a life in the family, from time to time, will always do much to rescue their image on the goal-line, if a rather frivolous metaphor may be used in a matter which so nearly concerns the great emotions common to all mankind at all times. In the past the professions have often overstated their case, sometimes rather pompously or sententiously, and so they are fair game to the modern temper. In these days of the fight to the death for circulation, witty designation and clever criticism are good journalism, and balanced estimates or judgments are not. All this must be recognised. The professions must go with it; and it is not easy for them. They stand upon the impalpables, and on the whole still do very well out of it. But in the spirit of the age they do not enjoy a good press.

Disillusionment among Students

The hard fact – and it seems to be a hard fact if sociological enquiry is to be trusted for anything – is that undergraduates everywhere in this country are disappointed with what they find in universities. Many people had feared that they did not expect very much – merely a bit of training for a job. But evidently this is not so. They expect a great deal – and everybody very much wants them to do so. They feel at the end of their time that they have gained a great deal, and would very much not like to have missed their university lives. But they are disappointed in relation to their hopes and expectations, and they tend – not unnaturally, I suppose – to lay their disappointment at the door of their teachers, who, they rightly think, control the universities so far as students are concerned.

It is clear that university teachers will have to do something about this. There have always been well-known and oft-repeated stories about dons who thought that university life would be perfect if only there were no students; and there may have been periods in all universities when it was the fashion to regard commitments to students as simply nothing but a chore. But contrariwise there have also, without doubt, been periods in all universities when it was *de rigueur* to spend an immense amount of time with students, and indeed to talk in common room about almost nothing else. Curiously enough – in spite of current impressions outside – fashions have been moving towards the taking of greater and greater interest in students in the last few years – steadily perhaps ever since the end of the war. And it may be true, I think, at the present time that the younger generation of university teachers, by and large, are more keenly concerned with the teaching of undergraduates than the older generation. But the profession is undoubtedly not getting the credit for this trend with public opinion. There is a lot of experimenting going on in all universities with methods of teaching for different subjects at different stages. But the press have not been led to be interested in it; and the public – apart in many cases from the parents of the students – know nothing of it. Yet nearly everybody knows that some subjects – for instance geography, physics and probably mathematics – are *very* much better taught today than they used to be, and perhaps better than ever before. Everybody knows that some other subjects – as for instance, classics, philosophy, history and English – are generally no better taught than they used to be, or perhaps not as well. But these facts – and I think they are facts – are never brought out in the press. This may be partly because to the modern temper designation is news, whereas appreciation or approval is bad journalism. But it must also be partly due to the university teachers' unwillingness to take trouble over getting themselves understood. In effect they must be actually misleading people at large about what they are really doing and really thinking.

A Friendly Press?

I believe we are going through a period in which university teaching staffs are increasingly interested in experimenting with new courses, with new syllabuses – and, more radically, with new university subjects and new methods of teaching. If this is true, nothing could be more favourable for the prospects of the Robbins proposals, the experimenters and the young – these are not, of course, quite always the same people – will have more and more to be given their head; and university teachers as a whole will have to take the public more into their confidence about what is being done, and not leave the public relations of the universities entirely to Oxford, Cambridge, Sussex and Essex. Many universities hate publicity and regard it as a black day in their history when they are mentioned in the press; and this may have been a sound instinct in days when it was equally right and proper, and also perhaps possible, for them to live a life apart from the world. But it will not do for today. If all the gifted young people of the nation are going to go to the universities, and a sizeable part of the national income is going to be spent on them, the public are going to want to know all about what goes on inside their walls. What is more the press are increasingly going, at all levels and from all angles, to turn them into news.

This will have to be accepted, and welcomed. If it did not happen, most of the Robbins developments would not happen either.

10. Robbins: A Question of Size and Shape

Martin Trow
Universities Quarterly Vol. 18 (1963–64), pp. 136–152.

The Robbins Report, with its accompanying appendices, is several things in one. It is, first, a superlative collection of social statistics which gives to the scholar as well as to the policy committee for which it was gathered the indispensable facts necessary to grasp the character and direction of British higher education. It is, in addition, the expression of an educational philosophy, a statement of values and preferences regarding higher education. And it is also, perhaps pre-eminently, a political document which makes recommendations regarding the allocation of a nation's energies and resources.

In these comments, and as an outsider, I will try to examine the Report not in terms of my own educational values and preferences, but rather in terms of the Report's principles, aims and assumptions. I will address myself chiefly to two of the central issues of the Report, namely, the size and the shape of British higher education.

With respect to size, Robbins recommends aiming at 558,000 full-time places by 1980–81, of which 350,000 should be university places. It does not say 'This is as many as we think desirable' or 'This is as many as we can afford'. If it did, it would be difficult for an outsider to say very much to the question of size. Robbins doesn't justify its recommendation on those grounds, but rather roots the whole matter on the principle that 'courses of higher education should be available for all those who are qualified by ability and attainment to pursue them and wish to do so' (Report §31). As a corollary, the Report accepts that the numbers who qualify ought not to be governed by manipulating standards of entrance; but rather, that these standards should be somewhat eased and fixed where they were in the mid-1950s. Thereafter, everyone meeting these standards should find a place somewhere.

At this point the Report begins to sound familiar to an American ear. For if this principle is taken seriously, then the Report is not recommending a certain degree of expansion of higher education, but rather is guessing about future demand, and recommending plans to meet that expected demand. And that is what we Americans do all the time.

Now, in so far as Robbins and future governments implement the principle that places should be available to all who qualify and wish to go, then the character of its recommendations becomes very important. As things stand, various public authorities – the Government, the universities, and so on – discuss among themselves how many places in higher education should be provided; these arguments involve political values, estimates of national economic needs and capacities, and other factors. Nevertheless, the decisions are made by people in authority according to their judgment of what is in the nation's interests. The principle Robbins asserts would change that, and would place the decision about the *size* of the system in the hands of the population at large. That, I think, is a fateful step, with many consequences. Among other things, it changes the role that projections of future enrolments will play in planning. Specifically, it will transform growth plans into enrolment estimates, thus reducing the importance to be attached to any given number, while placing the emphasis of planning on the structure and organisation of higher education.

The Report does not do this but places great importance on its recommendations for the future size of British higher education. Discussing it on its own terms for the moment, I believe its estimates of future demand are unrealistically low.

The Committee's recommendations for full-time places in higher education are based on estimates of a number of factors, the chief being:

(a) the size of the age group (the 18- to 21-year-olds);
(b) the proportion of the age group obtaining the relevant qualifications; and
(c) the proportion of those qualified who apply.

The size of the age group is easiest to estimate, since most of its members are already born; an assumption is made of a continuing decline in the death rates of children and young adults. The growth in the age cohorts accounts for 7 per cent of the increased number of places recommended for 1973–74 and 14 per cent of the number of places projected for 1980–81. With respect to the proportions that will obtain the qualifications required for entry to full-time higher education, the Report bases its estimates chiefly on an extrapolation of the growth in the age group gaining these qualifications between 1954 and 1961. That growth rate, which averaged 0·37 per cent per annum over those years, will account for between 55 per cent and 60 per cent of the additional places proposed for 1973–74 and 1980–81.[1] The Report also estimates that the proportion of qualified school-leavers who seek entrance to full-time higher education will grow by about 10 per cent over the next two decades; for various reasons, the Report plans for all of this growth to be achieved (or at least the places provided) between 1968 and 1972.[2] This factor accounts for 18 per cent and 13 per cent of the additional places projected for 1973–74 and 1980–81, respectively. These three factors together account for 83 per cent of the additional places recommended; the remainder of the recommended increases are accounted for by an anticipated growth in the number of foreign students, and by miscellaneous other factors, including changes in the length of courses.

The recommended expansion that results from these projections seems to me almost certainly inadequate to meet the growth in qualified demand over the next two decades. The Report, especially in Appendix 1, IV, §12–27, considers some of the social and psychological forces that might affect the numbers of qualified school leavers in the near future; the same factors would also affect the rate of growth in the numbers of qualified applicants. How complete is this analysis, and to what extent did it influence the Committee's recommendations?

1. The Report expressly makes no provision for the effect on higher education of raising the school-leaving age. The discussion of this in Appendix 1, IV, §25, observes that 'a further raising of the school-leaving age would mean that all pupils stayed at school into the year when GCE "O" level is normally taken. The extra effort required in order to obtain a useful qualification would thus be reduced. It is in any case likely that a raising of the school-leaving age would have a considerable upward effect on the trend to stay on into the sixth form.' Certainly such a step would also accelerate the tendency of secondary modern schools to add on sixth forms or make other provision for transferring students into grammar schools where they can prepare for A levels. As things stand, only a negligible number of students from the secondary modern schools goes on to full-time higher education. If even a fraction of their output begins to go in that direction, it will have very large consequences for higher education.

It is hard for an outsider to believe that a measure that was foreseen 'as soon as . . . it has become practicable' in the 1944 Act and strongly recommended again by Crowther will be postponed for another 10 or 20 years. The pressures for this step will be not only educational and political, but may soon also be economic as changes in the occupational structure associated with automation shrink the job market for 15-year-olds. Despite all this, the Report in its projections 'assumes no raising to 16 of the minimum school-leaving age' (1, IV, §29). (The Committee's own recommendations for the expansion of teacher-training would not provide enough teachers to raise the school-leaving age until 1978/9. 1, IV, §115.)

2. Robbins does not take into account possible improvement in the provision of grammar school places, which varies widely from district to district, and which greatly affects the percentage of 17-year-olds in school. The Report shows (1, II, Table 26) how the percentage of 17-year-olds in school varies from 5·5 to 27·9 in different parts of the country. One would expect that such gross inequities in educational opportunities will decline. If so, this would raise the numbers remaining in school, and thus the number of qualified candidates for higher education. The Report also does not take into account possible growth in the number of comprehensive schools which would make sixth forms available to many for whom they presently are not visible or easily available.

3. Robbins does not take into account possible changes in public sentiments regarding the desirability and the possibility of gaining a higher education. This is already evident in the sixth forms, whose population has been growing by about 0·5 per cent of the age grade per annum (Crowther Report, Vol. I, p. 231, Table 35). And there is a very real likelihood that this rate of growth will not merely persist, but will accelerate, as new segments of the population come to think of their brighter children as potential college or university students.

Ironically enough, the Robbins Report does not take into account its own impact on public sentiments, and that of the attendant publicity and discussion of it in the press and Parliament. All this is likely to affect the educational standard of living of at least parts of the British population, and make higher education seem a reasonable ambition to people who have never previously considered it.

4. Another major fact affecting educational aspirations is the changing occupational structure. If matters proceed in Britain as in America, the automated future holds very marked increases in the demand for educated people, with considerable declines in the demand for unskilled and uneducated people. In America there is a marked inverse relation between education and unemployment, ranging from over 8 per cent among Americans who have not completed high school to 1.4 per cent among

college graduates. Ordinary people know this, and it is a lively spur to educational achievement. I do not know the comparable British figures, but its economy has so far apparently been able to place its 15- and 16-year-olds in jobs. America no longer can. If the job market for adolescents begins to shrink in Britain – as I think it must, sooner or later – one response is likely to be higher rates of retention in school, which will translate themselves, though considerably attenuated, into higher proportions of qualifiers for higher education.

5. Still another important factor affecting school retention is parents' education. Robbins (1, II, §28–33) documents the bearing of this factor in detail. For example, of those children born in 1940–41 having fathers who remained in school till 18, 43 per cent went on to some kind of full-time higher education; of those whose fathers left at 16 or 17, 21 per cent had some higher education; of those whose fathers left before 16, only 5 per cent had any higher education. (These differences would persist even if controlled for social class.) The educational achievement of the British population is continually rising, and this must mean more qualifiers in the future. As the Report notes, 'during the 1970s, those reaching the school-leaving age will include the children of the first generation which received free grammar school education after the 1944 Act. This factor will tend to accentuate the trend [to higher education]' (1, IV, §16). Unlike some of the other factors I have cited, whose effects are very difficult to assess precisely, the bearing of this factor could be measured and taken into account.

I have cited a variety of social and economic forces,[3] all of which would work to increase the demand for higher education *beyond* what would be expected by extrapolating recent trends.[4] It is certainly very difficult to assess the effect of these forces taken together – they are all intertwined, and influence and work through one another. But if we cannot say exactly how much they will increase qualified demand, it is almost certain that they *will* increase it.[5]

Nevertheless, although the Committee considered many of these factors, and others that I have not mentioned, it ignored them in making its recommendations.

Thus, some of the factors suggest that the trend in staying on will increase, others that it may decrease. On balance, an increase seems likely in the long run. But it may be safer to make a neutral assumption, and, with the agreement of the Ministry of Education, it is assumed that, over the next twenty years, the proportions of each age group who are at school will increase at the same rate of simple interest (straight line growth) as over the years 1954–1962. (1, IV, §29)

Now, I accept that the Robbins Committee felt it necessary to work out a projection that was so conservative as to be nearly invulnerable to the criticism of being inflated. This indeed is what they did, and they themselves remind us repeatedly that their projections are conservative. But since they attach such importance to the role of numbers in planning, I think they also should have developed alternative projections which took into account some of these accelerating forces. In such a set of alternative projections, based on differing assumptions, the one they did report would be the most conservative, while some of the others would be a good deal more realistic. The danger of presenting only one projection, and that the most conservative, is the danger of over-selling the country and the Government on an unrealistic estimate, which will make it more difficult to deal with the higher demand when it arrives.

Furthermore, I do not think it either possible or necessary to be able to predict accurately the demand for places in 10 or 20 years. Certainly rough estimates of alternative rates and patterns of growth would be useful as guidelines to expansion. But the very great emphasis the Report places on its projections, and the effort it makes to justify them, reflect a pattern of authoritative planning which the Report itself undermines. For if the principle it enunciates becomes the foundation of national educational policy, then Britain can no longer be in the business of planning places, but should rather be planning a system of higher education which will be responsive to qualified demand while still preserving the educational values it wants to retain. And that is a very different thing from planning for places.

I suspect that an historian of British education will look back on the Robbins Report as a crucial *transitional* document: transitional in the sense that it enunciates a genuinely new principle which rests British higher education on popular demands, but then proceeds to ignore the revolutionary implications of this principle by planning in a more traditional fashion for a specific number of places. Now, if the numbers of qualified candidates will be larger than the Report suggests, but yet indeterminate, that should reduce the importance of their recommendations regarding future size, and greatly increase the importance of their recommendations regarding the future structure of British higher education. The question now is: has Robbins recommended a system of higher education flexible enough to meet a qualified demand that exceeds their projections. I do not think it has.

In brief, their recommendation is for three kinds of 'autonomous' institutions: universities, CATs, and teaching colleges, together with institutions of further education. But the striking thing about the recommendation is that it proposes the greatest expansion in the universities. University places will grow from 130,000 to 346,000 between 1962–1963 and 1980–1981, only 45,000 of which would be in the present CATs (up from 10,300), 146,000 in colleges of education, and 66,000 in full-time study in other institutions of higher education. Thus, of every eight places in full-time higher education in 1980–1981, five will be in universities, two in teacher-training institutions, and one in institutions of further education. If we look only at the increases in places, the prportions are slightly more heavily skewed towards the universities.

The recommended number of university places in 1980–1981 is determined by the Committee's desire that 'the proportion of qualified school leavers entering the universities in 1980–1981 . . . be roughly the same as in the mid-1950s, when the competition for entry had not yet produced its undesirable effects' (Report, p. 152, §465). The result of this is that 'of the proportion entering full-time higher education in 1980–1981, the proportion going to universities will be 60 per cent as against 55 per cent at present'.

Now, is this a sensible way to plan a system of higher education, of high standard but responsive to a large though indeterminate growth in the numbers qualified for entry? I think not.

First, what such a system must have is a set of institutions which are flexible in their size. There is no such cushion in this plan – no set of institutions specifically designed to be responsive, in numbers or size, to unforeseen growth in qualified demand. Realistically, present plans should cover the range of qualified demand that might reasonably be anticipated, with the Robbins projection as the bottom figure. But if I were to predict, on the basis of the American experience, where additional demand above Robbins would be most sharply felt and most appropriately absorbed, it would not be in the universities but in the CATs and the colleges of education. (I consider the colleges of further education below.) I would do so for two sets of reasons. One of these has to do with the nature of the demand – that is, the social characteristics of the push; the other has to do with the nature of the occupational structure – that is to say, the pull.

Let me speak first to the question of demand. The Robbins Report wisely did not try to predict the size of specific occupations (other than teachers) in making its estimate of places needed. No one before World War II could have anticipated the growth of the electronics or computer industries; technological change is very difficult to predict in detail. But if we cannot predict the growth of specific occupations, we can say something about the broad shape of the occupational structure toward which we are moving. I think it very likely that in the next decades increasing numbers of people will be doing technological and scientific work; and increasing numbers will be administering organisations and dealing with people in various kinds of social welfare agencies.

It is unnecssary to say much about scientists and technologists, since I think there is pretty general recognition of needs in that direction, a recognition reflected in the recommended quadrupling of numbers in the CATs (though starting from a low number) and the principle that nearly two-thirds of the added numbers in the universities (including the CATs) will be on the science and technology side (1, IV, Table 54).

But while the Committee comments in several places on the need for scientists and technologists, it hardly recognises the growth of another large class of occupations that appear to be generated by a complex industrial society. These are what might be called the 'applied social sciences', occupations which centre on the social needs of a population; the material they work with are people or organisations. Some of these are old, some are emerging, or changing in character, and thus in the character of their training. Chief among them is education; they also include social welfare, criminology and corrections, city planning and urban development, mental health, youth work, social administration, the merging field of community development and aid to underdeveloped countries, industrial relations, a fair part of business administration, and adult education.

Each of these old or new semi-professions has its own purposes; what they have in common is that much of their training is rooted in the social sciences, and they advance themselves by identical methods of social research. The problems of schools, and of prisons, and of industrial plants are very similar: students in all these fields have to learn such things as the social history of their society, its formal governmental structures and modes of social administration, the conditions and nature of socialisation, the effects of group membership, and so forth. This is not, of course, to say that the professional training of these occupations is the same – each has a core of its own materials and problems. But a part, at least, of the training of each rests on a common basis of the social sciences.

Now, some of these people are currently trained in universities at graduate level, others in CATs. It may be that the purely professional training ought to be at a postgraduate level – the question is, what and where is their proper *undergraduate* training. It seems to me, again drawing on American experience, that it ought to be based on the social sciences, *not* in specialised honours courses in universities but for the most part in colleges of applied social science, where work is done analogous to what is done in the CATs for technologists and applied scientists.

To an outsider it would appear that the obvious nucleus of these colleges of social studies would be the colleges of education, which would remain, certainly, the largest single component within them. But there is little encouragement in the Robbins Report for any notions that the work of the colleges of education could be broadened to contribute to the preparation of these other emerging fields of work. We find that the colleges of education are to cease growing in 1975–1976, at least between 1975–1976 and 1980–1981. (This, incidentally, is a serious consequence of Robbins' conservative estimates of future increases in educational achievement, and presumably would have to be greatly modified if the leaving age is raised to 16.) The Report includes one hopeful sentence, but takes it back to the next:

Some [training] colleges will wish to broaden their scope by providing courses, with a measure of common studies, for entrants to various professions in the social services. We think they should be allowed to do so as soon as practicable, although we believe it would be wrong to suppose that the needs of these professionals are likely to be such as to require large-scale provision in the generality of colleges. (Report, §313)

But the fact is that the social service occupations have been, in Britain as in other advanced industrial societies, among the fastest growing. Between 1931 and 1951, while the whole population was growing by a little over 9 per cent, and the labour force by 14.4 per cent, the number of Civil Service officers (the bulk of them, of course, in the executive category) was growing by 257 per cent; the number of local authority officers by 60.6 per cent; architects and town planners by 70.6 per cent; librarians by 141 per cent; social welfare workers by 206 per cent.[6] And while I do not have the figures from the 1961 census, I would be surprised if those rates of growth were not maintained or accelerated. Robbins recommends that 'plans for colleges of education themselves should also increasingly provide for students who intend to take up careers other than teaching, and after 1980 such numbers should be substantial'. But what if these numbers appear before 1980, as seems likely – will the colleges of education be ready to expand and transform themselves into general purpose undergraduate colleges with special attention to the applied social sciences? And would it be worth anticipating and even encouraging the demand, rather than merely meeting it reluctantly?

Here, Robbins gives us little encouragement. The Report seems to accept at least two limiting conditions on the development of the training colleges. First, it is assumed that these colleges cannot grow very fast or very large; this is asserted but not argued at a number of places in the Report. Second, there is the tradition of residence to be preserved: 70 per cent of full-time students in the training colleges in 1961–1962, 67 per cent after the great expansion in 1980–1981, are or will be in halls of residence. Here we come to an unexamined article of faith. An observer cannot help asking: what is the price paid for this commitment – are you prepared to turn away qualified school-leavers in order to provide residence halls for 70 per cent of those you do admit? What do we know about the educational gains of residence? Is it required for future social workers as well as for future teachers? I merely raise these questions – Robbins doesn't.

I have said I thought it necessary to plan for an expandable segment of British higher education if you are to meet future demands over and above the Robbins projections. These should be the CATs and colleges of social studies, both because of the nature of occupational growth – the pull – and *also* for reasons of public policy regarding the social composition of the increased college population – that is, on the push side.

Robbins shows us first how great are class differentials in educational opportunity in England. The children of higher professionals are 33 times as likely to be enrolled in full-time education at the degree level as the children of semi and unskilled workers (Report, Table 21). These differences exist to some degree in every society, but the question might now be raised: what kinds of educational planning, what kind of system of higher education, would tend to reduce this gap, while maintaining other intellectual and educational values? Of course, the question implies a certain social value, but one that I would have thought would be widely accepted in Britain.

Robbins nowhere asks that question – though his recommendations are in a sense an answer to it. The system of higher education recommended by Robbins will not, I believe, substantially reduce the gross differences in educational opportunity and achievement among the social classes. The evidence suggests that the expansion in university places is much more quickly taken up by children of non-manual than of manual worker origins. For the period 1928–1947 the proportion of boys aged 18 from working class origins who entered university was 1.6; by 1960 it had risen to 2.6 per cent. The corresponding figure for boys from non-manual backgrounds were 8.9 per cent and 16.8 per cent.[7] Thus, the growth of the universities during the post-war years saw the class difference in university entry maintained and even somewhat increased. There are many reasons for this, lying both in the structure of British education and in the values and perspectives of its working class. Together they make it seem very likely that the class distribution of students in universities in 1980 will not be very much different from what it is in 1963.[8]

If the American experience has any relevance, the first experience of *most* working-class youth in institutions of higher education will be not in honours courses in universities, but in the schools and colleges where higher education is more directly linked to the world of work. I see nothing wrong with that, so long as that education is also liberal and humanising. The explanation for this is not very complicated and is well documented – it reflects differences in language, cultural resources, class attitudes towards education. These are simply facts of life.

But in so far as Britain aims to reduce class differences and democratise possession of and participation in the national culture, then it has to provide the kinds of institutions that first generation students will find attractive and rewarding. Some working-class youth can make the jump to the university in one generation. But I suspect that for the bulk of able and talented people from working and lower middle classes, it will not be the university. The Robbins recommendations, in my view, do not confront this problem, and their recommendations do not expand the system sufficiently where it will most need it.

It may be suggested that 'further education', largely in the regional and area colleges, will provide the cushion for presently unanticipated increases in the qualified demand for higher education over and above the Robbins projections. This is already occurring. Between 1954–1955 and 1962–1963, while the numbers of students in universities and CATs grew by nearly half, and the numbers in the training colleges roughly doubled, the numbers of full-time advanced students in further education nearly quadrupled (1, IV, Table 25). This growth was accompanied by an improvement in their qualifications. Between 1955 and 1961 the proportions of school leavers having one or more A levels who went into full-time further education (excluding CATs) more than doubled, rising from 4 to 9 per cent of those with two or more A levels, and from 7 to 14 per cent of those with one A level (1, IV, Table 20). By 1961 over a quarter of the entrants to full-time further education had two or more A levels, while a half had at least one A level (Report, Tables 6 and 7).

What does Robbins have to say about the future of further education? Not counting art schools, the Report recommends that the 31,000 full-time places in further education in 1962–1963 be increased to 51,000 in 1973–1974 and 66,000 in 1980–1981. This would account for about 10 per cent of the total number of full-time places envisioned in higher education for both 1973–1974 and 1980–1981. Looked at somewhat differently, both the universities and the colleges of education are expected to grow by about 165 per cent over their present enrolments by 1980–1981, whereas full-time further education is expected to grow by about 113 per cent

(Report, Table 44), and this despite the fact that the Report anticipates an increase in the proportion of students in these colleges who are engaged in full-time study. Moreover, the number of part-time places in further education is expected to grow even more slowly over the same period (by about 80 per cent). The Report justifies this recommendation in the following terms:

> When we assessed the provision to be made for advanced courses in further education we had, in the nature of things, no guidance on the demand for their products of the kind we have just discussed in connection with the Colleges of Education. We have borne in mind the rapid expansion of student numbers likely to result from the educational developments we recommend . . . But at the same time there are fields of study, such as art, where the number of students is unlikely to show such a rapid increase. We have also taken account of the fact that one in seven of the full-time students in 1961–62 had applied for entry to university and possessed the minimum entrance qualifications. If there is some increase by 1980 in the proportion of places at university level, and particularly if the universities at that time include the Colleges of Advanced Technology and other institutions that gain university status, the demand in colleges of further education will be lessened. (Report, §486)

In other words, while the increases in the places in the universities and colleges of education are based on projections of the immediate past (a procedure which leads to extremely conservative estimates), the future growth in the colleges of further education is assumed to be a good bit slower than it has been in recent years, for the reasons quoted above. (It is suggested (Report, §486) that institutions of further education which advance to university status will have their places made good; but that gain is presumably already taken into account in the projections for the universities, and leaves the places in further education unchanged.)

I have spoken of a need for an institutional cushion to provide for a growth in qualified demand over and above that anticipated by Robbins' projection of recent trends. It is hard to see the colleges of further education providing such a cushion when the Report does not envision them growing even as rapidly as in the past. It may be that the control and financing of regional and area colleges by local authorities will give these institutions greater flexibility and opportunity for growth; certainly their rapid growth in recent years, while the universities have been growing slowly, gives grounds for these hopes. But it is clear from the Report that the Committee has given a good deal more thought to the 'autonomous' institutions of higher education – the universities, CATs and colleges of education – than it has to these institutions of further education, which are moreover explicitly excluded from the responsibility and support of the recommended Grants Commission. Demand for entry to institutions of further education may indeed be discouraged by their lack of status and inadequate financial support. But despite all handicaps, my guess is that the regional and area colleges will grow more rapidly than the Report envisions, especially if the Report's recommendations for a new range of first degrees is implemented (Report, §425–435). And if they become a haven for large numbers of qualified students who do not find places in the 'autonomous' institutions, pressure will develop to equalise the facilities and educational opportunities (and awards) for all qualified students in higher education, wherever they may be enrolled. I suspect that future Committees on Higher Education will be paying far more attention to institutions of further education than the latest one did because of changes in the role of higher education in British society which the Robbins Report will have initiated if not recommended.

The Robbins Report projects into the future not only present rates of growth in student enrolments, but also the present characteristics and balance of British higher education. The pattern it projects is that of an inverted pyramid, with the elite institutions, the universities, maintaining pre-eminence in numbers as well as prestige. As a result, the special conditions attaching to the elite institutions – their common high standards, level of student support, quality of staff and amenities, staff structure and student–faculty ratios, external examinations and the rest – are therefore the characteristics of the bulk of British higher education. All these forms and practices and traditions can be justified in their own terms, and make the British universities distinguished centres of higher learning. But what is the price paid for making the universities, with their high standards and expensive practices, the numerically dominant form of British higher education? One price, certainly, is to slow the rate of growth of higher education, and to reduce its responsiveness to social and economic change. Universities are not the most flexible or responsive institutions, and properly so. To a very large extent, what goes on within them is of intrinsic worth, and not merely a means to some socially defined ends. Their concerns with basic research, first principles, and timeless questions, their very distance from the flux of events, make them a supremely important source of fundamental innovations in thought, as well as increasingly important conservators of social values and standards. But societies have immediate problems as well as long-range interests; and the immediate problems, both social and technological, increasingly call for more trained intelligence. The question might be asked whether Britain in the second half of the 20th century would not be better served by a system of higher education that is shaped like a pyramid rather than an inverted pyramid. Rapid expansion of British higher education gives the country the opportunity to raise this question, and to effect changes in the balance of its component parts, an opportunity that is absent in a static or slowly growing system.

It is perhaps worth emphasising, in conclusion, that my argument is not meant to be a statement of the 'expansionist' position with respect to British higher education. However legitimate such a position may be for a British citizen, it is not, in my view, appropriate for an outsider who will not have to pay the price for expansion, either in his taxes or as a British academic. My aim, as I suggested at the outset, is different: it is to confront two basic educational principles, one explicit in the Report, the other implicit in the society, with an assessment of social trends and forces which will shape future levels of qualified demand for British higher education. The principle explicit in Robbins is that all qualified applicants for places should have them; the implicit principle, on which I have assumed broad consensus in British society, is that, while preserving other educational standards and values, it is desirable to reduce the wide differences in opportunity and achievement among the several social classes. For the reasons I have outlined, I believe that either these principles will have to be sacrificed, or that the recommendations regarding the size and shape of British higher education embodied in Robbins will have to be revised.

I have criticised the Report not so much for its caution as for its unwillingness to accept the full implications of its own revolutionary principles. Yet none of these strictures would have been made had not the Report been written and its factual underpinning presented. The Report's coherent and argued plan for the expansion of British higher education clarifies the issues, allows them to be seen, and gives substance to purpose. For an American, the contrast with the blind evolution of most of his own institutions of higher education could not be greater.

Moreover, an appeal to principle and for an awareness of the full implications of action are the characteristic weapons of the critic against the responsible actor, and, most especially, of social science against social action. The writer is doubly an outsider, as foreign observer and as social scientist; and for the outsider, the references to principle and the consequences of action are as natural as is the actor's appeal to the complexity, the moral ambiguity, and the contingency of events. In that sense, these reflections are part of a very old dialogue.

Notes

[1] From Appendix 1, IV, Table 56. There is an important qualification in the Report to this extrapolation of past trends. The proportion of boys leaving at 17+ who have gained

A-level passes has been roughly constant between 1955 and 1961, while among girls the proportion has been rising. The Report for various reasons assumes that this trend among the girls will cease. This is an important qualification, since 'if . . . the proportion (of the age group achieving the relevant school-leaving qualifications) had been estimated by a straight continuation of the trend from 1954 and 1961, the number of places needed would have been 60,000 higher than has been estimated' (1, IV, §177). For the rationale for this assumption, see *ibid.*, §42–44 and 49.

² The Report sometimes gives the impression, as here, that it is predicting social trends, whereas it is in fact recommending a specific number of places for an increased demand of unknown size and timing flowing from some social trend about which the authors have speculated. The figure of 10 per cent attached to the presumed growth in the proportion of qualifiers who apply for places is almost wholly arbitrary (see the discussion in 1, IV, §85–91); nor is there any good reason for believing that the increased demand resulting from this tendency will be confined to the years when provision is made for it. Yet each one percentage point by which the estimate differs from reality will mean a difference in 5,000 places (equal to one new university) in 1980–1981 (1, IV, §178) – and this is one of the less important factors entering into the estimates and recommendations.

³ Sir Peter Venables in discussion suggested another accelerator which I had not thought of and which is not mentioned in the Report: that is, the rise in the numbers of 'second generation'-educated employers, who will encourage and perhaps even require their employees to continue their higher education. There may well be other accelerating forces at work.

⁴ The Report suggests (1, IV, §29) that there may be other social forces which will tend to reduce the effective demand for places in higher education. One example given is the possibility that increased numbers of graduates in the future would lead to unemployment among them, or to lower salary levels, and thus in turn lead to a reduction in the demand for places, or at least a slowing in the rate of growth of qualified candidates. In principle, of course, such 'decelerating' forces cannot be ruled out. But there is reason to believe that it is extremely unlikely that such negative factors would cancel the forces making for the growth of demand. With respect to the specific 'decelerating' force cited, it is perhaps relevant that, contrary to similar predictions in the United States after World War II, a very large growth in the numbers earning degrees in higher education has been accompanied by an increase in the differential income associated with a college degree, and by a marked inverse relationship between education and unemployment. See Herman P. Miller, 'Annual and Lifetime Income in Relation to Education: 1939–1959', *The American Economic Review*, Vol. 50, No. 5, December 1960, pp. 962–86; and Martin Trow, 'The Collegiate Explosion', *New Society*, 7 November.

⁵ Professor Claus Moser noted that the Robbins enrolment projections are based on recent trends, not all of which are linear, and that some of the forces I have mentioned are at work in these trends, and thus are taken into account. In some measure this is true; these factors are 'not taken into account' only insofar as they will increase more rapidly in the future than in the immediate past, and thus will accelerate the rate of growth in the number of qualified candidates over and above the Robbins projections. For example, the candidates who applied for admission to the universities over the past decade were the sons and daughters of people whose own education had not been affected by the Education Act of 1944. That Act accelerated the gain in the educational achievement of the British population, and those gains will almost certainly be reflected in the numbers of qualified candidates starting in the late 1960s.

It is certainly debatable *how much* this and the other 'accelerators' will increase the qualified demand for higher education over the Robbins projections. It is much more difficult to maintain that they will not have any appreciable effect. Incidentally, if it should be suggested that while these factors may lead students to stay in school longer, they will not affect the numbers of qualifiers, I can only refer to the work of Jean Floud and others, as well as to the relevant section in the Report on the pool of ability. The weight of both English and

American experience is that standards of performance do not decline with rising numbers, but will at least keep step with increasing numbers who want to qualify (see 1, III).

[6] General Register Office, Census, 1951, England and Wales: Occupation Tables (HMSO, 1956), from Table C, pp. 652–65.

[7] 1, II Table 15. See also Jean Floud, 'Social Class Factors in Educational Achievement', in A. H. Halsey, ed., *Ability and Educational Opportunity*, OECD, 1961.

[8] It is likely that students from working-class backgrounds comprise a larger proportion of the student bodies of CATs than of universities. But the Report envisions only 45,000 out of 350,000 university places in 1980 in what are now CATs. Moreover, as the CATs gain in status and enter the circle of elite institutions, they may tend to recruit a smaller proportion of working-class youth. It would be interesting to learn if that has been happening in recent years.

11. The Academic Hierarchy: Robbins, Appendix Three

A. H. Halsey
Universities Quarterly Vol. 18 (1963–64), pp. 129–135.

Appendix Three was sold out in Blackwell's on the first morning. Academic men are unusually self-conscious. They are inclined to accept Oscar Wilde's aphorism that the one thing worse than being talked about is not being talked about. In an age of shifting and uncertain identities they could hardly be expected to resist the chance of eavesdropping on themselves. One in every four of them had already contributed a *curriculum vitae*. Here then was the promise of an orgy of collective self-consciousness.

What have the Hollerith cards foretold? The Appendix runs to more than 250 pages and contains more than 250 statistical tables. It tells us that the 14,849 university teachers in 1961–62 will multiply to 42,433 by 1980 and that in the Robbinsian system of higher education as a whole the present 21,000 teachers will become 59,000. And so it goes on in a welter of impressive numbers to produce an unprecedented assemblage of fact on the guardians of higher learning in Britain. In general its accuracy is beyond doubt, though some aspects of its description of the Oxford don have been challenged in the *Oxford Magazine* (November 1963). I would like to raise the question not of its accuracy but of its completeness as a sociological description of the university teacher and then to discuss one major aspect of its interpretation, namely, the likely effect of expansion on the homogeneity of the higher teaching professions.

Any judgment on Appendix III as an essay in sociological analysis must, in fairness, take into account the context in which it was undertaken. This is a matter of general concern because the 'Royal Commission method' is the most characteristic idiom of social research in Britain. Social analysis and social criticism as well as official attempts to control the direction of social change rely heavily upon it. The aim of official committees is to form policy. Lord Robbins was asked to advise on the future of higher education. Policy formation results from the application of wisdom to relevant fact. Lord Robbins and his colleagues were chosen for their wisdom. The relevance of facts depends on theory – in this case primarily the sociology of a set of professional groups. The collection of the facts depends partly on the amateur methods traditionally used by official committees (i.e. hearings and written evidence from interested parties) and partly on professional survey techniques – in this case a survey of university teachers. Governments can offer all reasonable resources to the process as a whole. Most important perhaps is their backing of enquiry into powerful and sacred institutions which otherwise tend to avoid open discussion behind the principle of 'pas devant les enfants'. In return they expect delivery of the advice within time limits set by political exigencies – and in this case the politics of higher education were becoming increasingly urgent.

Briefly then the Royal Commission method is that of wise men with lavish resources but in a hurry. Unhappily however, the essential theoretical foundation for Appendix III could not be bought quickly: indeed a sociology of the higher teaching professions hardly existed. What little there was in the sociological literature the Committee plainly ignored. The reader will therefore look in vain for an analysis of the role of the academic in a Robbinsian society, for comparative analysis with other nations or earlier periods or other types of profession. He will not even find a description of the self-conceptions and opinions of university and college teachers[1] which would permit assessment of their capacity and willingness to carry through the transformation proposed in the Committee's report.

The Committee's theory was based on commonsense which, together with the reticence one would expect of an official body of public researchers, defined an enquiry confined to the class of facts (age, sex, qualifications, previous posts, hours of work, etc.), which could be left to 'speak for themselves' with the minimum of interpretation either by the researchers or the respondents. In consequence the Appendix is an astringent essay on the commonsensical sociography and social arithmetic of the higher teaching professions. It records the vital statistics of these professions at a critical moment in their history. But, though essential to, it does not constitute, a sociology of the academic occupations.

On the other hand the Committee did not hesitate to turn to modern methods of information-gathering in the social sciences. In this they have been well served. The sample survey is a powerful and economical technique and Professor Moser is a virtuoso of it. The derivation and meaning of his findings are always crystal clear and his tables are, so to say, highly readable. Nevertheless they have suffered a loss of elegance from the fact that the survey of individuals was confined to university teachers in the pre-Robbins sense. Because of reliance on other sources for information on CATs, regional colleges, teacher training colleges, etc., exact comparisons, for example of qualifications and teaching hours, are not possible for the whole population of teachers in the post-Robbins system of higher education.

Professor Moser's examination shows that the condition of the median university teacher is an enviably healthy one. He (only 10 per cent are women) is 38 years old and has a job for life. He is working, according to his own evidence, six hours a week less than the average British workman but for more than twice the pay. He has the status of a lecturer now, but is more likely than not to be promoted in the next five years and has better than one chance in three of being called 'professor' by the time he is 50. He has little to complain of: but then he is a clever chap, not only a graduate but with good class honours and a higher degree.[2] Moreover, if he had wanted more money or more technical or secretarial assistance he might well have been able to find them in business or medicine or the Civil Service or America.

Whether this high scholarly calibre can be maintained into the expanded system recommended in the report (and for reasons argued by Martin Trow the Robbins projections are best regarded as a cautious minimum) is a serious question. At first glance recent trends in the universities at least are alarming. Of honours graduates recruited between 1959 and 1961, 52 per cent had taken first-class degrees compared with 61 per cent of the recruits in earlier years. The authors of the Appendix offer two reassurances on these statistics – that wastage is heavy among young recruits and perhaps the worst are squeezed out, and that degree standards may have risen since before the war. Another way of looking at the problem is to note that this (relatively low calibre) recent intake accounted for 22 per cent of home graduates with firsts or upper seconds. On the Robbins expansion plan this proportion will have to rise to 34 per cent. Looking at teachers in higher education as a whole the comparable slice of high honours graduates was 28 per cent in 1959–61 and would have to rise to 39 per cent for the period 1963–67. Admittedly later in the 1960s the proportionate demand of this 'ploughing back' of high talent into the educational system will slacken and the demands of colleges and universities for a share in their own total output of graduates will not, *in the long run*, rise. Nevertheless, except in the most unlikely event of a reduction in the demand for high scientific and professional manpower from the competing non-academic professions dilution in the shorter run seems to be inevitable. Certainly the expansion of the university umbrella to include CATs and some regional and training colleges *must* reduce the quality of our median university teacher.

In other words there seem to be two concomitants of Robbinsian expansion. The quality of staff will fall temporarily in higher education as a whole and permanently in the re-defined universities. If this is so two questions follow. First, is this an argument against expansion, and second, how will quality be distributed institutionally in the expanded system?

The first question is ultimately one of political and moral judgment. The anti-expansionist argument in the past has rested mainly on a fallacious 'pool of ability' theory in relation to students, and this Robbins has routed. The lesser argument that expanded numbers may *on average and temporarily* be worse taught is unlikely to deter the expansionists. A reduction in the average quality of university teaching is at first glance more serious but here again the proper perspective is surely that lower quality will be added to existing excellence. To argue against expansion of this kind is to prefer that demonstrably capable young people receive no university education rather than something less than the traditional best. And in any case the whole argument contains the two highly dubious assumptions that no improvements are possible in the technology of university teaching and that the existing lavish student/staff ratios are sacred.

The second question is more interesting. Perhaps the most dramatic findings in Appendix III are those relating to the differentiation of staff quality between the institutions of higher education already in existence. Some of them are put together in Table 1. Of course, no one ever imagined that the staffs of non-university institutions were comparable in calibre with the university teachers. But the assembled evidence of a steep descent in average quality within the university system from Oxford down through London and the redbricks to the CATs is more impressive than most readers will have anticipated. It certainly would not have been predicted from the accepted traditions of national salary scales, equal treatment from the UGC and open competition for jobs nationally advertised. Moreover it seems clear that past expansion has already had the effect of lengthening the hierarchy of staff quality. Thus the outstanding exceptions to the evidence that the quality of recent recruits has declined are Oxford and Cambridge where the proportion of newcomers with firsts actually rose from 76 per cent to 78 per cent in 1959–61, while the national proportion fell from 61 per cent to 52 per cent.

Robbins's conception of future development widens the definition of university institutions but continues to acknowledge the distinction between university and other forms of higher education. The plan

TABLE 1
Quality of Teaching Staff at Various Institutions of Higher Education
1961–62

	Oxford and Cambridge %	London %	Redbrick %	CAT %	TTC %
(a) Proportion of all full-time teachers who are graduates	< . . .	100–95	. . . >	81	58
(b) Proportion of (a) with 1st class honours	76	54	52–59	33	17
(c) Proportion of relevant staff who are Fellows of the Royal Society	11.6	3.7	1.8	–	–
(d) Proportion of relevant staff who are Fellows of the British Academy	8.9	3.5	0.2	–	–
(e) Proportion of staff with senior posts★	40+	40	27–23		
(f) Percentage contribution of this group's graduates to teaching staff of other groups	23.7	14.2	10.7		

Source: Appendix III of Robbins Report.
    ★ Senior posts include professorships, readerships and senior lectureships. It seems reasonable to regard Oxford and Cambridge staff with both university posts and college fellowships as at least the equivalent of senior lectureships elsewhere. On this basis the proportion of senior posts is at Cambridge 45 per cent and at Oxford 55 per cent.

envisages a wide field of higher education in which 'there is a need for a variety of institutions whose functions differ'.[3] Institutions with the same functions are to have the same titles, but again even within the same category, differences of eminence are likely to emerge from competition.

Where famous intellectual exploits take place, there should develop some concentration of staff and students especially interested in the subjects concerned. Moreover such concentrations are not only probable but also desirable. What is important is that what differences there are should rest clearly on differences of function on the one hand, and on acknowledged excellence in the discharge of functions on the other. There should be no freezing of institutions into established hierarchies.[4]

All this is most encouraging. It evokes the image of sturdy struggle for places in an informal league table of the kind that has always given life and promise to the American colleges. It resuscitates the hopes for escape from provincial nonentity for which the Victorian foundations temporarily and unsuccessfully fought at the turn of the century.[5] But will it work?

Clearly competitive advantages are most unequally divided between, say, Churchill College and the Birmingham CAT, and something more than the granting of university status to the latter institution will be required to redress the balance. The Committee rightly looks for especially generous capital grants from the state to new and expanding institutions. Nevertheless their advocacy of a competitive system falls far short of American practice. For example, they interpret the evidence of the AUT survey reported in Appendix III to mean that Oxford and Cambridge dons are paid more than people in comparable posts elsewhere which they think is 'unjust', and 'leads to too great a concentration of talent there'.[6]

This must mean that they regard their earlier principle of competition for excellence as subordinate to the principle of equal pay for equal work.[7] But supposing the equality principle is being violated at Oxford (and some would argue that the evidence on staff quality and hours worked invalidates the assumption that the work is 'equal') it must also be noted that the same principle would restrict a new foundation from using financial inducements to build up a strong team in a particular branch of learning by the market methods which are taken for granted between American universities. Indeed it is difficult to see how equality principles in relation to staff salaries can do anything but protect the competitive advantages of the ancient universities. Similarly the widening of contacts between ancient colleges and state schools advocated elsewhere in the report, and especially the entry of the former into the national clearing house scheme will further raise the quality of their undergraduates and hence their attractiveness to the most able university teachers.

The conclusion seems to be inescapable that competition for excellence in the wider system of higher education proposed by the Robbins Committee will take place only within strata of the stable pyramid of institutions which has emerged from the history of the development of higher learning in Britain. The career patterns of university teachers and the distribution of quality may be expected to reflect this hierarchical structure. Some will see this as an amiable result – a spur to individual competition and a recognition of different educational functions within the university system. Others will seek ways to realise the declared aims of the report – equality and fluidity. The hierarchy might be flattened by great generosity in salary scales, senior posts and capital grants to redbrick coupled with drastic meanness to Oxford and Cambridge. The Robbins proposals point very mildly in this direction. Alternatively mobility could be maximised by the development of an academic market-place of the American type. The current search for staff tends to move in this direction within the constraints of the national salary scales and 'UGC rules'. But neither tendency is sufficiently strong to move the system from its half-way house of a stable institutional hierarchy.

Notes

[1] There appear to be three exceptions. University teachers were asked their opinions on the kinds of teaching suitable for undergraduates, the adequacy of technical and secretarial assistance and the usefulness of being taught teaching techniques. But these departures from the stern asceticism of 'hard fact' occupy only five pages (pp. 84–88) of the Appendix.

[2] More exactly, 81 per cent have honours degrees from British universities and of those who took honours 59 per cent took firsts. Of those with first degrees 47 per cent have also obtained doctorates and 13 per cent Master's degrees of the earned variety.

[3] *Report*, p. 8.

[4] *Report*, p. 9.

[5] cf. the discussion of 'The Popularity of Oxford and Cambridge', *Universities Quarterly* Vol. 15, No. 4, September 1961.

[6] *Report*, p. 178.

[7] The principle of equal pay for equal work is, of course, avoided by the medical fraternity. No possible interpretation of the evidence in Appendix III could attribute the medical differentials to merit. Yet oddly enough the Committee appears to let this go unremarked.

12. Review of 'The Uses of the University'

Charles Morris

Universities Quarterly Vol. 18 (1963–64), pp. 419–421.

This important and fascinating book* will strike many readers as very American, but it speaks to our condition in this country much more than may at first appear. Dr Clark Kerr is president of one of the largest and most respected universities in the world, and in these pages he is reflecting from an unrivalled experience on what has been happening to universities in these middle decades of the 20th century. His title, 'The *Uses* of the University', speaks for itself. One could hardly imagine a Vice-Chancellor of Oxford or Cambridge writing about the 'uses' of his university, though his opposite number at one of the provincial universities – and perhaps also at one of the new universities – may have to try and speak to the subject in one context or another every week. But he is rarely or never in as good a position to do so as Dr Kerr.

In the first place, not unnaturally, this is a book for vice-chancellors themselves and the critics of vice-chancellors. The President of the University of California has many brilliant perceptions and judgments about what they can do and what they cannot do and how they will have to set to work to do it. The context in which American university presidents work is not entirely the same as that of English vice-chancellors; but their problems and possibilities are similar enough sometimes to bring a smile to those of us who work on this side of the ocean, and sometimes to touch us on the raw. For this alone Dr Kerr will be read again and again, I am sure, in the coming years in this country.

But the most important part of the book keeps very close to the title. American universities have always been very much aware that they have a place to fill in the American community. The great ones among them play an immensely distinguished part, taken out of their regional or national

---

* Clark Kerr, *The Uses of the University*, Harvard University Press: Oxford University Press, 1963.

context, in the university system of the world. But even they, sensitive as they are to their responsibilities out of time and place, never forget that they have much to do for their own society and for the immediate generation. In the present fast-changing world the reasonable and insistent demands upon universities, Dr Kerr thinks, have changed out of all recognition. His affection for the term 'multi-versity' sufficiently shows the sort of thing which he has in mind.

It is very tempting to give a lot of quotations; but for the present purpose one will have to suffice:

So many of the hopes and fears of the American people are now related to our educational system and particularly to our universities – the hope for longer life, for getting into outer space, for a higher standard of living; our fears of Russian or Chinese supremacy, of the bomb and annihilation, of individual loss of purpose in the changing world. For all these reasons and others, the university has become a prime instrument of national purpose. This is new. This is the essence of the transformation now engulfing our universities. (p. 87)

These are big words, and we in our over-blown revolt from the Victorians are shy of such uninhibited affirmations of prophecy and of faith. But are the American leaders again in the van, and are we trailing behind. If they are right on the general issue – and it *is* a general issue – we are certainly a long way behind and are advancing very painfully and slowly.

But *are* the Americans right? Or is Dr Clark Kerr barking up the wrong tree? One important difference between their situation and ours – and we on our side can see it quite clearly when we co-operate with them in aiding new university projects in the developing countries – is that on the face of it the American university occupies a far more central and commanding position in relation to all post-secondary education than universities do, for better or for worse, in this country. Since the Land-Grant legislation it has been the universities, by and large, which have blazed the new trails and have had the new ideas. They have made mistakes of course and, as they well know, have suffered for them; they have often and again been ridiculed by university men in this country and elsewhere in Western Europe. But they have kept the gift and habit of initiative in higher education; and the initiative remains with them today.

In this country, when anyone begins to think of some advance in this field, the first battle is one of jurisdiction, as for instance between universities and local education authorities. The grave danger is that the first battle goes on and on and becomes the last battle also – so that after an expense of spirit nothing will be done for another 20 years. Many good judges think that this is what is in store for us after the Robbins Report. Robbins has sought to bring the universities much more to the fore in policy-making and much more into the centre in operating. This has been done no doubt largely for the practical reason that there is in fact at the present time a very large popular demand for university places, and therefore quick and effective expansion might prove to be actually practicable even in our conservative society. But it certainly ought to be very seriously and earnestly considered whether it is not the right thing to do anyway on grounds of educational policy and principle. Ought the universities in the circumstances of the modern age to be prime centres of initiative for all higher education?

Local authorities have of course a tremendous reputation in this country, and have a record of many triumphs, not only in the schools but also in the beginnings – after Robbins there can be no doubt that we so far have no more than the beginnings – of the development of an adequate system of higher education. If the universities are to be brought more to the fore, and that is what Robbins is in effect recommending, it will be necessary to give some hard thought to the way in which jurisdictional questions can be prevented from delaying or preventing all advance, taking into account the circumstances of our history and of our present modes of practice. Dr Clark Kerr's book will suggest to many English readers that the main intellectual and social forces which he sees at work, demanding inevitably a quite central and vital place for the university in the advanced society of the 20th century, have validity outside his own country. It could be for us an epoch-making book.

13. Notes on New Universities: British and American

David Riesman

Universities Quarterly Vol. 20 (1965–66), pp. 128–46.

One impression I had had before coming to the United Kingdom was confirmed, namely, that a certain *noblesse oblige* continues to work in the academy as elsewhere in the society. Thus, reading the discussion around the Robbins Report, I was impressed that men of the highest academic attainments who in America would want to get on with their own research have been willing to expend very great energies in academic self-renewal and expansion. Traditionally, the burdens of university administration have in England been borne (notably at Oxbridge) not only by the professors but by a large portion of the teaching staff; for example, the interviewing of applicants for admission by British faculty is almost unheard of in America, where this function is professionalized in an office of admission. I had known before coming of the disdain British academicians often have for all the ancillary non-academic (and sometimes anti-academic) personnel in a large American university, but I had not fully appreciated the price that others than the full professors pay for their share of administration, whether in interviewing or in endless senate and committee meetings of the sort that Cornford satirised.

In planning for university admissions in the United Kingdom, there is great concern not only that every available place be taken up, but that no sudden unanticipated surplus should descend at the opening of term. In the United States, multiple acceptances and, in many parts of the country, a greater casualness about university entrance have the consequence that several hundred more students may turn up than had been counted on. Even a small private college under such circumstances will scrounge for living accommodations and classroom space in order somehow to manage to accommodate the overflow. The British see to it that there is virtually no overflow. The kind of makeshift which Daniel Boorstin finds a virtue in *The Americans* can be found occasionally in the new universities, where a delay in building programmes has sometimes compelled flexible adaptations, but for the British this seems irregular whereas for the Americans it is standard.

For example, the British planners at Sussex, Warwick, East Anglia, and Essex have all been insistent that institutions do not grow too large, not beyond human scale, nor grow too fast to permit the induction of students and faculty into their own collegial and more or less experimental climates. When Oakland University, an offshoot of Michigan State University, opened for its first intake of students on a suburban estate outside Detroit a few years ago, the student union had not yet been completed and for a term students and faculty had to drive off campus to find sustenance. The British could not have improvised in this way because of lack of transport, but also it would not have seemed right. British students and staff alike insist on a standard of amenity somewhat superior to that even in established institutions in the United States. To the American eye, the senior common room often seems extremely spacious and well-appointed, for in America there exist many colleges and universities without a faculty club at all where the professors must go through a cafeteria line along with the students or bring their lunches from home in paper bags. Moreover, students in Britain who are residentially housed are often less crowded than their American counterparts. A good deal of American crowding, as suggested above, has occurred to accommodate unanticipated numbers of students, so that at Harvard College, for example, rooms built for one house two, for two house three, and so on.

There are British makeshifts also as building costs have risen and delays cumulated. However, there are those who have felt that growth of university opportunities has been far too slow and that the amenities of undergraduate life are being purchased at the cost of too few places. It is impossible to visit the older civic universities without hearing bitter, sometimes envious, criticisms of Sussex in terms of its spread-out resort location (as well as its supposedly unsound experiments, its undeniably attractive young women, and its all-too-favourable publicity). In principle, so it would seem, the civic universities could have expanded their enrolments more rapidly than new universities could be built from scratch – although before Robbins, expansionism was not in the air and this course was not undertaken.

More important, in terms of the general scale of the expansion, has been the almost tacit British decision that all students and not only the more well-to-do should have the privilege of leaving home to attend whatever university in the United Kingdom will have them; only in Scotland and of course in London are there substantial proportions of commuters who live at home. We have nothing quite comparable to the system of local authority grants, which means that a young man from Newcastle or Leeds may come to Sussex or the LSE or Bristol and, as the legend would have it, be seduced by the soft and sunny, if also cold and unfriendly, South, never to go home again. Or indeed a young lady from Brighton or Colchester may choose to go to Edinburgh or even St Andrews, if they will have her, and, depending on her father's income, the local authority must contribute to the cost of her upkeep.

To be sure, it cannot ensure that she will live in a residence hall or that the residence hall she may find at Leeds or even Birmingham will be anywhere near the university or have a meandering river at its back. (Yet neither Oxford nor Cambridge has since before the war assured everyone that he will live in college for his three-year term.) What the British have done is to decide that leaving home is everybody's right, even if this means that there is less money for expansion than there would be if commuting from home were encouraged.

It can be argued from an American perspective that some of the British foundations are too small to provide what chemists would call a critical mass in terms of the more specialised human attributes. There may be enough undergraduates to support the department of economic history that almost every new university seems to have established, but not enough to support a wind ensemble or an exciting literary magazine or newspaper. Many of the societies at Sussex and elsewhere seemed to me too small to be venturesome. Paradoxically, some Sussex students complained that their Union was like an air terminal in its anonymity, in contrast with the cosier group in the beginning years. By American standards, the Sussex Union still appeared to be of manageable town-meeting size, given the inevitable apathy that kept many people away. But the ideal of many British students has been set, as the authors of *Camford Observed* remark,[1] by a nostalgic image of the life in college at Oxford or Cambridge – a model that also exists in America in the private liberal arts colleges especially of New England, but which exercises far less hegemony with us. Yet, whatever the ideal, it remains the case that very many British students attend universities that are quite unlike Camford; and many more attend colleges of technology that are not, and do not resemble, universities at all. In fact, if these colleges are taken into account, it may be that the British picture is not quite so different from the American as I may have made it seem.

If the British problem is one of sometimes almost suburban smallness, many of the great American universities seem to me too monstrous to be manageable by staff or comprehensible by students. If students commute from home, as they do in very large numbers, they may in the early months seek the familiar and the comfortable among their former secondary school friends, whether or not the latter are also attending a university. Frequently, on the residential campus, the students huddle for human warmth in fraternities and sororities which are much too small and homogeneous to provide anything but temporary or too confining shelter against the multiversity. The University of Minnesota (which is one of the few great state universities located in a major city) has 40,000 students, two-thirds of whom commute from home. Michigan State University at East Lansing has 35,000 students, most of them residential. On a recent visit, I was told that at least 400 new faculty would have to be brought in for the coming academic year, and the Michigan State official who told me this was aware of the problem as to how one inducts so large a cadre into any kind of sense of the whole complex enterprise. The problem is compounded since the staff will come from a great variety of institutions, having encountered extremely diverse experiences as undergraduates if slightly less diverse in graduate school. Of course, no recruitment of faculty on anything like this scale occurs in Britain even in 'boom' fields such as my own, and the faculty who are recruited are apt to have been exposed to the British collegiate ideal, even if they come from Ontario or Uganda or New Zealand.

The scale on which new universities are being built in the United States can at one extreme be illustrated by the three enormous new universities being planned and now actually under way in the University of California system: San Diego, Irvine, and Santa Cruz. I spent several days at each of these, at Clark Kerr's request, in the fall of 1962. San Diego, building on a research institute in the sciences, had already a nucleus, whereas the other two were still in the planning stage. But all were using as a model the Berkeley and UCLA scale of 27,500 students, of whom an increasing proportion would be postgraduate students. The newly installed librarians were setting out to buy half a million books, as well as to arrange for inter-library loan and for shipping faculty members around if it proved easier to send them to books than vice versa. Some planning had also occurred as to areas of specialisation, so that one of the new universities, for example, would focus on the Far East and another on Africa, but on the whole each would provide the full roster of academic specialisation, community service, and adult education. The newly installed Chancellors or their assistants were building up rosters of potential staff in all these areas. Some they hoped to lure by climate, some by salaries, some by planned faculty housing, and some by the record that the University of California has established in defending its faculty against community political pressure. (Thus, I remember asking one man where he hoped to get faculty, and was told that he could easily raid Ohio State University, which had the advantage for his purpose of having a large and distinguished faculty, but one under right wing pressure from which its timid administration was not then protecting it – and he hoped to lure people and indeed has done so into the no less right wing territory of Southern California: he would provide a better buffer. Fortunately, academic competition on this basis does not seem to occur in England.)

But the most interesting enticement on which the new Chancellors counted in recruiting faculty was the opportunity to help build a new institution both in curricular and extracurricular terms. The charter members would be invited to take part in planning along lines only partially adumbrated; they would have a reasonably free hand and ample resources. A British visitor might have thought of Irvine as a prospective new town, developing an immense estate outside Los Angeles for academic, industrial, residential, and recreational uses. The other two new universities were making comprehensive efforts to cope with giantism in the academic plan itself. At San Diego, colleges were to have approximately 2,500 students in terms of residence, advising, and freshman and sophomore courses. Santa Cruz was to follow a more explicitly British or New England collegiate model, emphasising undergraduate education in colleges of around 600 students, including some residential postgraduates. These innovations have also been a source of faculty recruitment, especially at Santa Cruz. Indeed, the three new universities are an effort not only at regional decentralisation within the state of California, but also at keeping Berkeley and UCLA and the other branches from even more hectic urban sprawl.

I have already referred to Oakland University which was, among other things, an effort by Michigan State University to create a satellite college which might take off some of the pressure of numbers.[2] Oakland began as a commuter college with an intake of 500 students. And whereas prestige in the United States attaches to teaching postgraduate students, it managed to recruit a first-class faculty who were interested in teaching undergraduates, and non-elite undergraduates at that. It provided for these an uncompromising programme in the liberal arts with vocational or pre-professional courses postponed or subsumed. Its programme has allowed the parent university, 80 miles away and willing to provide complete autonomy, to have available a pilot model for its own academic planning.

Michigan State University has also moved on the home campus to experiment with less than mammoth sub-units. Justin S. Morrill College opened there this fall with an intake of 400 students, recruiting a few local faculty who were interested in academic pioneering, and taking over an old dormitory as its locale. The students at Justin Morrill (named after the Congressman who fathered the land-grant college legislation of 1862) can take some of their work in the general undergraduate programme of MSU and of course exploit its libraries and other facilities. The students are not an elite, not an honours college as some institutions have created, but simply a somewhat more experimentally-minded cross-section of the student body.

Wayne State University in Detroit has also initiated a satellite college on its own campus – Monteith College – which is devoted entirely to General Education and which has been in operation for six years. It began with a $750,000 grant from the Fund for the Advancement of Education, a Ford Foundation subsidiary, but has now been adopted by the parent university. With an intake of 300 students, carried through four years, it has helped to provide again a more manageable human scale. Thus the faculty are not seen by the students as a monolithic 'they', a distant power elite, but can be individuated, while the faculty similarly can regard the students as individuals rather than as a mass who help pay the freight for the more valued postgraduate students. The University of Michigan itself is now planning an experimental sub-college as a separate residential unit – again partly an effort to deal with problems of scale as well as curricular experimentation.

The state universities and land-grant (agricultural and technical) colleges of the last century, like many of the state capitals, were typically located in rural areas and away from the supposedly corrupting and politically under-represented cities. Michigan and Michigan State are both examples; so is the University of Illinois in Urbana, the University of Missouri in Columbia, of Kansas in Lawrence, and of Massachusetts in Amherst. Today, to meet the increasing demand for places and to make use of commuter possibilities in the big metropolitan areas, a number of these institutions have been establishing branches in the major cities of their states. The University of Illinois has moved this last fall into a new branch campus in Chicago; the University of Wisconsin is expanding a former branch and teachers college in Milwaukee; the University of Missouri now has branches both in Kansas City and St. Louis. So, too, the opening this last fall of the Boston branch of the University of Massachusetts reflects the new effort on the part of public education to serve the cities as well as the impulse toward decentralisation to prevent cancerous growth on the main provincial campus. With a minimum of resources and lead-time, the Boston branch took over and partially renovated a downtown office building as its sole campus. And with plans made on the run and often desperately, it opened with 1,200 students – 200 more than had been anticipated – and a hurriedly recruited, but on the whole excellent faculty of 70. It did have the backing (and the delay and interference) of the parent University, but on the whole its development, including the adaptations of the old structure, was a patch-work and last-minute affair. Since Massachusetts, like most of the Northeast, is backward in public higher education, most of these students would probably not have found a place in a university at all, for they could not have afforded it, had the branch not been opened. To attend the parent University in Amherst, they would have had to spend upwards of $1,000 a year on room and board, unless they were talented enough to win one of the few scholarships, or they might have found a place at some of the upgraded local teachers colleges which have not yet reached university level.

Yet the efforts just mentioned and others which could be mentioned are minuscule in comparison with the growth by sheer accretion in most public and private universities. St Johns University, a Vincentian institution in the New York metropolitan area which has had a running battle with dissident faculty for over a year, grew from under 1,000 to 13,000 students in about 15 years – and these are students who pay tuition. Fairleigh Dickinson University in New Jersey, which now has a branch near Oxford, is a no less entrepreneurial private post-war bootstrap operation. Likewise, there are state colleges for example in California which, in existence the same length of time as Sussex, already have a faculty of 700 or 800 and a student body of 10,000. It is the automobile that makes this feasible, just as the resort towns of Brighton or Colchester have made Sussex and Essex feasible on their far smaller scales.

Expansion at this rate is supported in the United States because there is only an embryonic national consensus on what a university is, but a very considerable consensus that anyone who wants to go should find a place of some sort to match his aptitude. Despite the virtual lack of local authority grants (the Regents scholarships in New York have some similarity), there is an extensive programme of loans, capped by the federal National Defence Education Act loans, and now there is a new federal programme of scholarships, although just a beginning. Many universities seek to provide jobs by which students can earn part of their keep, and in the summers American students can earn far more than their British counterparts could, even if the latter were not inhibited by local authority hopes that they spend their long vacations reading or otherwise becoming more cultivated. As a result, in California and other Western states, more than half the age-grade is now in post-secondary education. In many communities it becomes easier to attend college than not to. There do remain great regional differences, with both the South and the East backward in providing free and accessible public education for everyone. But, as the new branch in Boston of the University of Massachusetts suggests, these areas are making efforts to catch up, powered by regional pride as well as by federal assistance. To raise and spend money on universities is now popular with voters in all parts of the country; thus, the labour unions have decided that the children of members will only get a chance for social mobility if they can attend college. Overwhelmingly, by more than 90 per cent, Negro parents say that they want their children to attend college. Thus, while mental hospitals and other public services may be starved,[3] universities have some of the qualities of cathedrals, and poor states sometimes spend astonishing proportions of their income on them.

In the selective private colleges and universities, mainly of the East, but also including places like the University of Chicago, Carleton College in Minnesota and Caltech in California, the pressures for entry seem to me quite as severe as in the United Kingdom. For perhaps 50 of these institutions, there is coming to be a national definition of what talent is, through the College Entrance Examination Board and the National Merit Scholarship system. This makes itself felt at the secondary level in pressures to enter our preparatory (in your terms, public) schools or for parents to migrate to the better suburbs where their children can attend what amounts to an elite comprehensive school with a strong college preparatory programme. These secondary schools have been influenced by post-sputnik pressure and by men like Admiral Rickover who have derided the slackness of American schools in comparison with the rigour attributed to European ones. In fact, there is a small minority of American academicians and professional people who avow the dogma 'more means worse' quite as passionately as it is avowed in England, perhaps more so since for them it is a reaction against all that is deemed shoddy and meretricious in American society. Such men are meritocratic rather than aristocratic. They want to make sure that all appropriately talented and motivated young people can get to the university despite financial stringency or despite the disadvantage of coming from homes and secondary schools in the culturally impoverished urban and rural belts of America. But their animus is exclusionary: they are inclined to think that too many people go to college, and that the mass of gum-chewing collegiate young people who do go, get in the way of the potential elite. It is striking that they have not been able to muster support from the taxpayers who are building the large public institutions I have referred to earlier, planning for which is based on the assumption that admission standards will not be raised and that more and more Americans (since in actual fact our secondary schools are getting better) will qualify by prevailing norms.

Yet what has been said so far may understate the extent of ambivalence in some of the major public universities concerning the importance of educating large numbers of only moderately ambitious and talented undergraduates. For many professors at institutions such as Berkeley, Illinois, Michigan or Virginia, the model to be emulated is the selective private university whose increasingly awesome standards of admission are a magnet for many of the most brilliant students who are then in turn funnelled on to postgraduate work. Columbia, Chicago, MIT, Harvard help create an atmosphere of exclusion which the major state universities are already in a position to employ *vis-à-vis* out of state undergraduates, and *vis-à-vis* their graduate programmes in general. Thus, some of the great state universities are already at the point where they are, as it were, subcontracting the education of freshmen and sophomores to junior and community colleges, and concentrating on what in the United States is termed upper-division work and on graduate work. It is the less eminent state colleges and universities which have retained a wholehearted commitment to the idea that university attendance is the right of every young person. But even in these the conflict goes on, showing up in debate as to the appropriate number of failures in a freshman year used as a screening device. In many state institutions and also in some of the private ones, 40 per cent or more may fail the first-year course. (Many of these manage to get a degree eventually, somewhere and somehow.)

At the same time, there are many private universities, dependent on tuition, or largely so, which keep their doors as open as the less exalted of the state universities. Some of these are denominational colleges which in their publicity advertise character-building rather than intellect-building. Others aim to assist a regional or an ethnic constituency. The partly separate, not entirely equal, far flung and diversified system of Catholic higher education includes several hundred institutions at all levels of quality except the very worst and the most distinguished. Some of these, like Notre Dame, Trinity, and Manhattanville College, are highly selective, while still others share with municipal or Protestant foundations responsibility for the rising strata of the big cities. On the whole, however, the expansion of American higher education has been in the public institutions where tax money has been available and could be harnessed to state and civic prides.

As we approach an epoch in the United States when the majority move on after secondary schooling to something called a college, we increase both the percentage of those equipped to attend postgraduate study and the desire to do so. Indeed, the affluence of America, the chronic underemployment among the young, the often naïve and often admirable faith in education, all conspire to increase postgraduate even more rapidly than undergraduate enrolment rates. The proportion at the elite institutions such as my own going on to graduate and professional training is well above the three-quarter mark. Increasingly, undergraduates at the major universities are overshadowed and will in some instances soon be outnumbered by the postgraduate students. The latter are ordinarily recruited from an even wider orbit, across national boundaries as well as within the United States. This very American propensity to go on for a postgraduate degree has meant that a socially and academically poor first degree can be redeemed, almost completely redeemed, by a doctorate from a major university – and even a poor doctorate can be redeemed by post-doctoral work, although this is still far less common. This is changing. As postgraduate enrolments have risen, meritocratic pressures for entry have intensified, and a good undergraduate record has become more essential, although at the same time new graduate programmes in less elite universities continue to open new options for less well favoured students. In these respects, America remains a second-chance country, while the United Kingdom is still struggling with the problem of giving an increasing number a first chance, and only barely realises that many may also need a second. Hence the growing concern in British universities to keep down the undergraduate failure rate; at Sussex it is now as low as 7–9 per cent and the bulk of this from non-academic causes.

It follows from what I have said that the American 'system' is not a 'system', that the level of first degrees is exceedingly uneven, and of second degrees only somewhat less so, and that the elite 'Eastern' stream and the general stream are moving in somewhat different directions. In contrast, the British do seem to have a system and its clarity and centrality are admired by many of my countrymen. The British system carries with it, right through the sixth form and on to university, a conviction of the rightness of the cultural heritage, so that their schoolteachers are less defensive and less threatened than ours and their academicians, derided, it is true, by Bohemians, but no longer bullied by hearties, complain less than ours do about anti-intellectualism. All this encourages the compression by which a still meaningful first degree is conferred after what, to an American, would seem a mere three years. And the model is a standard academic coinage so that a first at Nottingham equals a first at Southampton equals a first at Manchester and so on – though I do remember one provincial professor of English who was proud that he had never given a first, and he probably punished his students for the fact that he was not a don at Leavis's old college.

In my opinion, the sureness with which the British certify their institutions and their degrees has many merits, but also some hidden costs. For one thing, it imports that clarity of location within a single system of status in which all universities are unidimensionally ranked, as against the greater fog in the United States which enables regionally prominent institutions to maintain high morale because they are good of their kind and in their place, or (like Rice in Texas or the University of Wisconsin or Smith College or the Claremont group of colleges) good absolutely. Furthermore, the British assume that the degree must be won by three years in a single place, without the relative ease of transfer that Americans both use and abuse, and without the privilege of dropping out to drive a truck, or to take some kind of job or to enter the Peace Corps or to do one's military service, that brings back to the universities a more seasoned and interesting group of people who have built their own sandwich programmes.

Indeed, the English students cannot afford to squander their one and only chance by experimentation. Before, during, and after the sixth form, they have to get up their subject, and what that amounts to is not clouded either by interesting or shoddy ambiguities. This makes them precociously proficient in what to an American often appears to be superficial academic gamesmanship; and their sureness about what is worth knowing and what they, themselves, know – qualities of course to be found also among the best-prepared American students – made me sometimes homesick for our students' incoherence.

Paradoxically, in the face of what I have just said, the best students in the United States seem to me more driven than those in Britain. The very freedoms that they possess, the many potential choices, can be paralysing as well as emancipating; American students of comparable quality worry more often than British ones about their identities, about the purpose of their studies, about the timbre of their relations to learning and to each other. And while American examinations do not have the nationally certifying once-for-all quality of the British ones, they occur at far more frequent intervals, and, like the too many courses that students take, make commitment to a serious independent course of study difficult. To the extent that undergraduate education in the United States becomes merely a place of preparation for graduate school, it loses its playfulness, its experimentation, its *joie de vivre* – qualities the most alive students I found at Sussex and elsewhere in Britain have in pleasant abandon. Intense meritocratic competition tends to drive out exactly those qualities most needed for unmortgaged learning and intellectual enjoyment. In the best universities and increasingly outside their less and less charmed circle, the pass or gentlemanly degree virtually disappears, and the undergraduates begin to act like little dons, already cautiously inducted into a subject. They are only marginally defended against this by the kind of amateurism still somewhat entrenched in British academic life, where postgraduate study is still exceptional and where therefore the teaching of undergraduates remains the principal preoccupation of faculty.

In part because only a few make it to the university in Britain, there is much greater ease there than in comparable American institutions. This ease is partly refracted from the faculty which, even in the often disgruntled red-brick universities, gives the appearance of being more relaxed and less bustling and busy than its American counterparts. But the other side of this is that the best American students are stretched further and do more impressive work as undergraduates than one is apt to find in Britain. The theses written by seniors at Princeton, Harvard, Reed and elsewhere are sometimes quite awesome in their polish and even depressing in their professionalism (usually of course this is at the end of a four-year rather than three-year period). Likewise, American undergraduates of top quality work harder not only at their studies, but also at their extracurricular activities. The best American student journalism cannot be matched in the far more desultory work even of a journal like *Isis*, and student musical performance in America can be both spectacularly adventurous and talented – only dramatics may have similar quality in England. Furthermore, the extra-academic (as distinguished from extra-curricular) energies of American undergraduates are growing rapidly, as in the many tutoring programmes for Negro and other slum children in Northern cities run entirely by students, or the ingenuity and dedication thrown into Civil Rights work in the Deep South. Teach-ins on the war in Vietnam were held at some 200 institutions, often sparked by students – a far larger number than would have been aware of the problematical nature of any war, even half a dozen years ago. While the traditional fun and games of the Hollywood-type collegiate are becoming attenuated, these other activities, although the work of a small minority, are intensifying. Through them, the students who are precisely those under the greatest academic pressure are testifying to themselves as well as to others that they remain human in the face of meritocracy.

In contrast, as already stated, the British undergraduates I met rarely exhibited the spontaneity and freshness of perception of the most alive American students. Perhaps their superior secondary education exercised a dehydrating effect. They had learned early to put each other down, as if they had been playing parliamentary games since the age of six, long before eleven-plus. I can hear them now saying '*Surely*, I would have thought . . .'. For worse as well as for better, they appeared to me more bookish than American students, able to discuss social class in terms of Bottomore or Runciman, but less given to ruminating on the world immediately around them – more self-distrustful in this respect if more self-confident in their intellectual poise than most American students. These students saw themselves characteristically as against the Establishment, as against the residual upper class (especially if they came from its ranks), against all that was square and Victorian. But their circles of sympathy were not very wide. Neither the race problem within Britain nor anti-apartheid came home to more than a tiny fraction, and I was sorry to see the desuetude of CND in the universities. The great interest in the Third World that I have found in so many of my own students in the United States was not often matched in a now more insular Britain. Unquestionably, compared to an earlier day, the British students have been becoming more open and less inhibited, less prisoners of an earlier form of grace. Undergraduates of good families sing and play folk music, visit the Continent, and wear their hair long, outdoing the Beatles. Living in digs, neither in dormitories nor at home, they have a certain freedom which our students at Berkeley have – with well-known consequences – but which is far less common with us given the usual American alternatives of residential dormitories or commuting from home. (On the other side, many of my own countrymen are magnetised by a fast vanishing Britain, gone with T. S. Eliot as well as with Churchill: a Britain of well-defined classes, distinguishable manners, a limited and educated elite, and non-coeducation.)

Local education authorities may well ask why they should collect rates and taxes so that the young can consume education now and also find more room at the top when they graduate. One reason is that there *is* more room at the top, and not only in occupational terms, but also in moral and aesthetic and intellectual terms. Hopefully, life can be more interesting for those who have had the opportunity for higher education, whatever they may do afterwards in their occupations. Yet of course education has also to be judged in terms of development of economic, political, and social resources, for without these it cannot even sustain itself, let alone help to promote the common good in those parts of both societies struggling with desperate poverty and (in America) with internal violence. Just as a society may get better public officials than, so to speak, it deserves (as I often think we do in America), so its educational institutions may exert leverage for change or may belong among the backward industries, vested and complacent.

It is in this latter perspective that the British new universities made their deepest impression on me. I hardly heard a good word said for Vice-Chancellor Albert E. Sloman's *A University in the Making* (1966)[4], but I felt the plan outlined in that book for providing non-residential students with a *pied-à-terre* on the site the most important single innovation I encountered, which could be immensely useful in the United States where, as I have already indicated, more and more of the new constituencies coming into higher education will be commuting from their homes. What I found at Sussex was an exceptional energy of faculty members talking with each other about education, visiting each other's lectures, and bringing undergraduates into their discussions. One has to see in daily unfolding the details of the Sussex curriculum to realise the tenacious ingenuity: the framework of contextual course, the grouping of people and topics into Schools, the search for intellectual cement to relate the specialties in new and interpenetrating ways, and hence to alter them. Some of these ventures, like the attempts to bridge the arts–science dichotomies, were more heroic than successful, but there is a sense in the educational process in which all experiments 'work': that of the famous Hawthorne plant experiment in which individuals respond because someone takes an interest, because something new is going on. It goes without saying that all novelty has not been engrossed by the newest universities; thus, Keele often gets left out with its four-year plan and Foundation Year scheme unduly deprecated; and, in the circle around Richard Hoggart and Stuart Hall in Birmingham, I found intense intellectual excitement that belied my usual experience of the slowly unfolding guardedness of students.

Almost everywhere in the 19 universities and colleges of advanced technology I visited, there were individuals who were moving away from inherited definitions of what constitutes a university or a particular subject or field. Nowhere, certainly not at Sussex, were people satisfied with the results of experiment. Whether successful or not, experiment is demanding, even exhausting. Not all lecturers like to learn while they earn, and many – perhaps most – prefer to confront students and colleagues from unassailable heights of congealed erudition. Not all lecturers enjoy the endless committee meetings and introspective sessions demanded by new curricular planning. (However, British academicians appear more willing than their American counterparts to assume the burdens of decentralised administration and to pay for faculty democracy by Senate and committee meetings that last too long, though my experience at Sussex here may be exceptional due both to its newness and its belief in equality.) More important, the very centralisation of academic life in Britain, the insistence on a standard, examinable curricular coinage, enforces limits on innovation in spite of a certain leeway in selecting external examiners. Oxbridge is the social and intellectual pacesetter and thus has a greater leeway, just as Chicago and Harvard are freer to back experiment in the United States than more anxious and imitative institutions, though the experiments often begin outside the major leagues. Thus it appears much more difficult in Britain than in America to create alternative models which are really different and yet are recognised as first-rate. It is common in Britain as in the United States to find political radicals who are educational reactionaries, manifesting in both spheres a sometimes too easy querulousness of being against the time. Students are no less and often more conservative pedagogically. At the University of Sussex, they were as apt as staff to comment that the experimental course, 'Contemporary Britain', jointly taught by faculty from the humanities and from the social sciences and with readings drawn from each area, was 'not a subject', or was inchoate and confused – a criticism often to be heard outside Sussex as well. I found the course illuminating just as I did comparable work in the field of American Studies; in any case, the latent assumption that other subjects really *are* subjects resembles the assumption that national boundaries are given in the nature of geography. But student complaint is everywhere a censor of reform, for the students have the power by non-attendance and resistance to scuttle new enterprises before they are fully launched.

The faculty member who wishes to innovate in curricular planning has internalised in his own education the voices of his critics even before they are heard. He has been taught to be original and creative in research, but not as a lecturer or shaper of programmes.

The British assume that Americans innovate readily, and I was often asked if Sussex wasn't very 'American'. In the United States, on the contrary, the major tide seems to be running heavily against innovation at the undergraduate level, less because of student conservatism, although this is a factor, than because faculty members are in such demand that they can set their own terms. Generally the terms include a reduction of hours spent with undergraduates whether in the classroom or as advisors, and an unremitting effort preferably to teach postgraduate students and, failing that, to teach only advanced undergraduates – and to teach these in turn as if they were being prepared for graduate work. Few want to teach introductory or general courses; they want to teach in the terms of their own instruction as postgraduates. Furthermore, because of the competition for postgraduate places, instructors are under pressure to prepare their undergraduate students to enter this competition on reasonably equal terms. It follows that there is some tendency in the major American universities to move in the British direction, that is, toward further undergraduate specialisation rather than 'general education'. The greater the power of the faculty, the more the interest of the 'customer', the student, can be subordinated; and the faculty has the additional impetus that, like any previously aggrieved minority, it scarcely recognises or admits the extent of its gains.

Yet America is so immensely variegated that almost anything one can find in Britain can be in some form duplicated with us – and this includes curricular experimentation in both old and new universities. The support for experimentation often comes from presidents, deans, and other administrators who seek to speak for students as a whole, or for the whole student, as against more specialised departmental demands. Some of the foundations have also supported experimentation, and there has been a dedicated minority of faculty members reacting against over-professionalisation at the undergraduate level.[5] The student demonstrations at Berkeley, although only minimally touched off by reactions to anonymity and lack of faculty concern, have served to strengthen the movement for reform. Thus, a small group of Berkeley faculty has hived off to start an experimental two-year undergraduate college which bears some resemblance to the short-lived Experimental College of Alexander Meiklejohn at the University of Wisconsin in the 1920s. I have already mentioned Monteith College of Wayne State University which is devoted exclusively to General Education, framed in part on a model developed in the College of the University of Chicago (Shimer College, a small college in Northwestern Illinois, also has been elaborating on the Chicago tradition: there is perhaps irony in speaking of an experiment within a tradition). As Christopher Jencks has observed, faculty democracy handicaps curricular change much more directly than the criticism of one's peers handicaps pioneering in one's research, and he argues accordingly that curricular innovation requires as massive outside support from the Federal Government and the foundations as is now provided for basic research.[6]

These are some of the reasons why, as an American, I feel that the British new universities as well as innovative stirrings in the older ones can be important on a transatlantic basis. I hope the experiments are not abandoned because of the work they entail, the emotional wear and tear. Yet I recognise that an experiment which even in part succeeds runs an inevitable risk: that the new recruits it attracts will come not only on account of its difficulties, challenges and unsolved problems, but because it has become a going concern where one can make or at least begin a conventional academic career. At the new 'with it' universities, the inheritors will tend to be different from the explorers who took a chance in landing on an unknown academic seacoast; and to create new unknowns, in which to immerse both new students and staff, is perhaps the greatest challenge the original explorers face.

Notes

¹ Rose, J. and Ziman, J. (1964), *Camford Observed* (London: Gollancz).

² In California, an elaborate Master Plan channels the great majority of undergraduates away from the state university system into the state colleges and the junior colleges. Michigan also has a system of regional universities, upgraded teachers colleges, to which by less formal devices students are channelled who are thought not to be up to state university standards: Oakland was not to be of this sort, but to have standards at least as high as those of its parent.

³ Cf. Riesman, David and Horton, Donald (1965), 'Notes on the Deprived Institution: Illustrations from a State Mental Hospital', *Sociological Quarterly*, vol. 6, pp. 3–20.

⁴ Sloman, A. E. (1963), *A University in the Making* (London: BBC).

⁵ See Riesman (1958), 'Planning in Higher Education: Some Notes on Patterns and Problems', *Human Organization*, vol. 18, pp. 12–17.

⁶ See Jencks, Christopher (1965), 'A New Breed of B.A.s', *The New Republic*, vol. 153, 23 October.

14. Dualism in Higher Education

Peter Venables

Universities Quarterly Vol. 20 (1965–66), pp. 16–29.

In Britain continued education beyond school has been through two main sectors, 'higher education' in the universities and 'further education' in the technical colleges and teacher training colleges. The relationships between these sectors and particularly the respective roles of the institutions within them, have been far from clear. 'Higher education', defined as work of university standard both in teaching and research, has been a significant and integral part of technical colleges for many years. Indeed the quality and growth of this work in the colleges of advanced technology (CATs), after their designation as such in 1956, led to the recommendation of the Robbins Committee Report that they should in general become technological universities, and this was accepted at once by the Government in October 1963. Their transference to the grant list of the UGC in April 1965 did not, however, denude the technical college sector of advanced courses and research. The overlap continues, and the Council for National Academic Awards (CNAA) is committed to enlarging it.

The teacher training colleges were initially part of 'further education', every bit as vocational in purpose as the technical colleges and with entry standards no higher than for advanced courses in those institutions. However, since the setting up of Institutes of Education in universities as a result of the McNair Report (1944), the teacher training colleges increasingly felt themselves to be part of 'higher education' and not 'further education', and they progressively increased their entry standards and the duration of their courses. The climax of this development was to have been the full acceptance of the Robbins Committee's recommendation that they should become colleges of education as constituent parts of university schools of education. In the event, administratively the answer has proved to be negative although academically the answer appears to be affirmative but on much less encouraging and more confusing terms than was hoped. In short, during the period following the Robbins Report very sharp contrasts developed: for the colleges of education a continuing relationship with the universities but no transference; for the technical colleges, the transference of the CATs to join the universities, but no new relationships with the universities for the remaining colleges.

In these circumstances there was an understandable concern in the technical colleges about their future. The President of the Association of Technical Institutions asserted in June 1965 that apart from the establishment of the CNAA little had occurred over the past year to give confidence to those engaged in the field of education lying between the schools and the universities. Although the CNAA offered regional and other major colleges a share in the expansion of higher education, and this should have assured their future, uncertainty and apprehension prevailed among them (*The Guardian*, 1965). This feeling was partly responsible for, if indeed it was not the main force behind moves to establish links with universities: for incorporation within them, or for affiliation with the neighbouring university for the recognition of degree courses. Indeed, Mr T. R. Weaver, Deputy Under-Secretary at the DES, stated that

some people think that the Robbins Committee cast them [the Further Education Colleges] in too modest a role and failed to give a sufficiently stable and clearly defined place in their plans to those institutions which, if all their recommendations were followed, would not share the position of universities as autonomous institutions. Certain it is that within weeks of the issue of the Report leading technical colleges that could be counted in tens rather than units were urging their claims to be promoted to university status . . . the general anxiety and sense of uncertainty in the FE world of which the race for promotion was a symptom must be included in any statement of the general problems presented. (Weaver 1965)

It is a pertinent criticism of the Robbins Report that it did not envisage the consequences of having 40 or 50 universities distributed throughout the country. Most if not all technical colleges are now within easy reach of a university, and staff engaged on advanced courses could work with university staff on boards of studies, rather than in isolation under the remote CNAA as the accrediting agency. Under the scheme for recognition of courses for internal degrees the 'recognised staff' of polytechnics and technical colleges in the London area have had close relationships with the respective boards of studies in London University, in contrast with the virtually complete isolation of staff teaching in courses for London external degrees in technical colleges throughout the country.

The seven entirely new universities did not at first establish technological courses or faculties. However, in response to the country's needs applied science courses have been added or planned, and various kinds of relationships have been sought with neighbouring colleges of technology. The latter moves have engendered resistances for a variety of reasons. One proposal to incorporate a college revived the widespread feelings of loss felt by LEAs at the transference of CATs, perhaps with some emotional resonance from the notable if not notorious period of 'take-over bids' in industry and commerce.[1] In industrial circles there was a growing apprehension that transference to or alignment with the universities would jeopardise the training of technicians and craftsmen within the regional and other major technical colleges: and this moreover at the very outset of the implementation of the Industrial Training Act.

All in all, then, the vigorous speech by the Secretary of State for Education on the occasion of the 75th anniversary of the Woolwich Polytechnic was an effect rather than a cause, a resultant of many stresses, which at least explains if it does not dispel its highly emotive tone.[2] Such anniversaries are apt to be euphoric, so perhaps such descriptions as 'our snobbish caste-ridden hierarchical obsession with university status' may be excused. However that may be, the speech was subsequently issued, in a reduced form and with a cover note, as an Administrative Memorandum (DES 1965) and became an official statement of government policy. Detailed analysis and assessment of its implications and consequences is therefore essential.

The Administrative Memorandum stated that the Government accepted that 'there must be a system of higher education in the sense defined' by the Robbins Report,

with 'co-ordinating principles and a general conception of objectives'. And in Britain the system must be based on the twin traditions which have created our present higher education institutions. These are broadly of two kinds. On the one hand we have what has come to be called the autonomous sector, represented by the universities, in whose ranks, of course, I now include the Colleges of Advanced Technology. On the other hand we have the public sector, represented by the leading technical colleges and the colleges of education. (DES 1965)

The characterisation which follows in the Memorandum might have been in answer to an old-style examination question – 'compare and contrast the two sectors of higher education'.

The 'public sector' is identified as being 'under social control, directly responsive to social needs' – by implication the universities of the 'autonomous sector' are less or even not at all responsive to social needs. The close identification of the public sector with professional and vocational education carried the implication that professional education is of little or no interest to the universities, and that they are not concerned with professional and technological expertise vital to the well-being of the nation. Furthermore, while the importance of sandwich courses is rightly stressed for the public sector, no comparable statement is made about the professional sandwich courses in engineering and other technologies in the CATs. In fact the CATs played the leading part in the great expansion of these courses, and are continuing them as a prime commitment for the future. In addition they are already establishing sandwich courses in other subjects, especially in the social sciences and management studies, and in various technologies at postgraduate level as well. In particular, the fusing of the traditions of the two sectors in the CATs in their new role as technological universities is ignored, and public understanding and appreciation of their work, which has been growing, may be inhibited. Significant changes within the universities in recent years, in contacts with industry and commerce and in the introduction of new courses, are also ignored. Such implications in an official document are not to be treated lightly, or be explained away by the fact that it arose from a technical college occasion in which extended consideration of the universities was not appropriate. A marked change of policy and of attitude towards the universities, new as well as old, seems evident, with potentially far-reaching effects on their future. In assessing what their effects might be, other events and trends need to be taken into account.

The CNAA was established in 1964 with remarkable speed, being granted a Charter within a very much shorter time than that required for new universities. Its Charter confers the power to grant degrees, and the higher degrees of MA, MSc and Ph.D have already been announced. These powers go far beyond those of its predecessor, the National Council for Technological Awards (NCTA), and it is apparent that it is government policy for the CNAA to exert a central role in the rapid development of a quasi-university system within 'the public sector'. It may at least be surmised that such a role was not envisaged for CNAA by university representatives in the discussion which led to its being proposed and established. The significance of the change must be judged against the background of the need for expansion in higher education.

The Robbins Committee recommended that the number of places in higher education should increase from the then total of 216,000 to 560,000 by 1980–1981, and about 350,000 of them should be in universities. It is clear from the National Plan (1965) that the Robbins intermediate target of 219,000 universities places for 1973–74 has been held by the Government at that figure, despite the fact the figures were known to be a serious underestimate. The following comparisons show the latest estimates in this changing situation:

TABLE 1
Numbers Leaving School with Three or More GCE Advanced
Level Passes

	Robbins*	DES 1963+	% increase
1965	41,300	45,800	8.9%
1966		47,400	
1967		47,100	
1968		47,700	
1969		48,400	
1970	41,000	49,700	21.2%
1973	45,400	55,700	22.6%
1975	51,300	63,400	23.5%
1980	68,100	84,300	23.7%

* *Robbins Committee Report*, Appendix 1 Part IV.
+ *Department of Education and Science Statistics of Education 1963, Part 3.*

TABLE 11
Numbers Leaving School with Two or More GCE Advanced
Level Passes

	Robbins*	DES 1963+	% increase
1965	64,300	68,000	5.8%
1966		72,400	
1967		71,800	
1968		72,800	
1969		74,300	
1970	64,000	76,600	19.7%
1973	70,800	85,000	20.6%
1975	79,600	96,000	21.4%
1980	105,800	128,000	20.9%

TABLE III
Increase in Percentage of the Relevant Age Group (England and Wales)

	Three or more Advanced Levels		Two or more Advanced Levels	
	Robbins*	DES 1963+	Robbins*	DES 1963+
1965	5.2%	5.7%	8.1%	8.7%
1966		6.1%		9.2%
1967		6.5%		9.8%
1968		6.9%		10.6%
1969		7.3%		11.3%
1970	6.3%	7.6%	9.8%	11.7%
1973	6.9%	8.5%	10.8% x	13.0% x
1975	7.3%	9.1%	11.4%	13.8%
1980	8.3%	10.4%	12.9%	15.5%

In reply to a question by Sir Edward Boyle (based on the figures marked x) the Secretary of State indicated that he could not give a firm indication of government policy on the subject at the moment, but that he viewed the problem 'from the standpoint of a committed expansionist' (Crosland 1965). But the question may be pressed: in which sector? Will the Robbins university figure be held unchanged, or increased pro rata? Or will the extra 14,200 students with two or more 'A' levels in 1973 be directed in effect to the public sector, the extra 22,200 similarly in 1980. It is, however, not merely a question of extra GCE 'A' level students qualifying for entrance to a university, it is also the increased proportion who will wish to go there. This will be due to a variety of reasons, some trivial or snobbish perhaps, but far more due to an increased awareness of the value of higher education, both to the individual and to industry, commerce and the community generally. Increased school education has always had the effect of increasing the demand for education with each succeeding generation. In addition, we now have the effect of sustained propaganda from Government, industry and the professions.

Why have the targets for the universities not been proportionately increased over the conservative figures of the Robbins Report? In order to build up the public sector? (And simultaneously convey the impression of unresponsiveness to social needs in the autonomous sector?) The National Plan states, in support of the Robbins Committee, that 'technical colleges and other institutions of further education will continue to make a substantial contribution to higher education' and adds, significantly, 'It is expected that over 70,000 places will be available in 1969–70 as compared with the Robbins Committee's estimate of 50,000 by 1973–74.' In this connection it is pertinent to note that, on the grounds of inadequate resources and so on, the Government decided in February 1965 that, with one possible exception, no further universities would be created within the next ten years (Hansard 1965): stated in present terms this meant no further additions to 'the autonomous sector' for ten years. Meanwhile the public sector could continue to expand rapidly. The Secretary of State has set up a working group to consider the granting of greater responsibilities and autonomy in the leading technical colleges, thus taking up the neglected recommendations in paragraphs 679–682 of the Robbins Report. A serious endeavour is being made to encourage local authorities to grant this increased independence, which goes so much against traditional local authority practice (though there are a few notable exceptions). The Ministry of Education Circular 98 on the 'Status of Technical, Commercial and Art Colleges', published as a result of the Percy Committee Report, recommended most of these changes as far back as 1945 (Ministry of Education 1945).

It is at least reasonable to speculate whether, with a ban on the autonomous sector and with a rapid growth in numbers and with a substantially increased degree of autonomy in the public sector, the Government is not thinking of the eventual emergence of 'state universities' within the public sector. The term 'state universities' is used for the purposes of this article to indicate that they would not be under or related to the UGC, but be institutions receiving direct grant from the DES. In this, their position would be very different from that of the CATs which are maintained almost wholly by government grant but come under the aegis of the UGC. They might be called indirect grant institutions, but the House of Commons Estimates Committee was concerned that 'Whereas newly founded universities have gone ahead with large appeals, the CATs, on the whole, possess no such cushion against financial rigours', and they accordingly wished 'to encourage the CATs to start their own private appeal funds' (Estimates Committee 1965). If this is essential for the CATs, what of 'state universities' under direct control of the govenment? It may be doubted if the direct relationship of such 'state universities' would be regarded by Government as being an insuperable barrier to the granting of a Charter. If this were done it would provide an alternative university system, with profound effects on the autonomous sector and the UGC. Would not the political temptation be very strong to use control of the public sector as a lever to produce far-reaching changes in the other?

The Secretary of State did not fail in his speech to refer to the examples of the Grandes Ecoles in France, the Technische Hochschulen in Germany, Zurich, E.T.H. and Leningrad Poly in the Soviet Union, despite the fact that these were the Robbins Committee exemplars for recommending the creation of Special Institutions for Scientific Technological Education and Research (SISTERS), and naming three of them within the traditional university system. Moreover, it should not be overlooked that in paragraph 447 the Robbins Committee recommended that university status should be granted 'either by separate Charter or by combination with an existing institution, to some of the Regional Colleges, Central Institutions and Colleges of Education'; and concluded that 'it is reasonable to hope that some ten of these colleges will have reached university status by the end of the period'.

The role of the CNAA will be crucial in determining whether these ten, or indeed any, institutions may achieve university status after the ten-year period within either sector. Contrast with this prospective ten the recent list published in the *Sunday Times* (12 and 19 June 1965) of some 55 technical colleges offering about 2,250 vacancies to GCE 'A' level candidates in full-time courses for BSc (1,672), BA (308) and other degrees (269 places). It was not stated whether these were for London external degrees, or for CNAA degrees. If the CNAA were to recognise courses in such a wide variety of colleges, it may seriously be doubted whether the courses and the education provided could really be comparable with that provided in the universities. Throughout its period of recognising courses for the Diploma in Technology, the NCTA was strongly insistent on the quality of staff, equipment and amenities, on the development of research, and on the particular college having a substantial proportion of advanced work. This policy was an important factor in the emergence of the CATs to university status, partly because it raised standards of courses, but also because it strengthened them in their task of securing the necessary staff and equipment for their work. In its Statement No. 2 (April 1965) the CNAA sets down similar 'Conditions for the Council's recognition of courses'. For example, 'the College as a whole is expected to provide a substantial programme of advanced studies. In particular, the subjects constituting the course must be conducted in an environment where advanced studies are the main preoccupation of the staff. Library and good social amenities must be available. The staff are expected to be of high quality . . .'. If these conditions are required with the same rigour as exercised by NCTA, it is very doubtful if anything like 55 colleges could be recognised. Such conditions must require concentration of resources. There are similar reasons for accommodating larger numbers by increasing the size of universities rather than creating many more new ones, again especially on the grounds of the efficient use of scarce resources.

It was a great merit of the NCTA and the colleges that they encouraged the entry of students from the technical colleges with Ordinary National Certificate (ONC) of good standard into the courses for the Diploma in Technology. This entry was a quarter of the total entrants, in some colleges as much as a third, and it proved to be a source of highly motivated, able students who had learnt the habit of study and work and had survived the very arduous part-time route. Not surprisingly they have achieved remarkable results and have made a mature contribution to the life of the colleges. A rigid establishment of the dual system would very probably diminish if not entirely prevent this invaluable recruitment, and thus deny to those students the opportunities for study and training in a technological university. This unfortunately might be reinforced by another possibility arising from the Robbins Report and stressed by the Estimates Committee, namely, the need to raise fees for universities to 20 per cent of their expenditure. The proportion has declined steadily in recent years and is likely to be 7 per cent in 1966–67 and the proposal would mean a threefold increase in fees. This would have many repercussions, one of which would be to increase still further the already marked difference between fees paid for similar courses in universities and technical colleges. The present average university fee would become £240 and the technical college fee remain unchanged at about £60. In that event would firms and local authorities not be more inclined to support students at technical colleges rather than at technological universities? A marked reduction in the number of ONC entrants would be held to confirm the present fashionable but quite erroneous attribution to the CATs of a desire slavishly to conform to the traditional university pattern.

The emergence sooner or later of some new institutions of university status can hardly be doubted. If in the Robbins Committee Report (paragraph 477) the suggestion that this should be achieved 'by combination with an existing institution', the word 'combination' means 'incorporation', then this has been decisively rejected by the Government in its decision not to allow the proposal, supported by the Coventry Local Education Authority, to incorporate the Lanchester College of Technology within the University of Warwick. This set the outer limits of permitted change, but the possibility of links between institutions still remains open, for more recently no objection has been raised to the affiliation, proposed by the local authority, of the School of Architecture and of the School of Planning, which are constituent departments of the Birmingham Regional College of Art, to the University of Aston in Birmingham. This decision appears to be in line with that of the Government on the colleges of education, whereby these may be closely linked academically with the universities through schools of education, so that some of their students will be able to take university degrees, but they will remain administratively with the local education authorities. Under the affiliation the students of architecture and planning will take degrees of the University of Aston, but the scheme does not of itself imply approval of the possible future incorporation of the schools within the university.

If 'combination' means 'affiliation' only then, no matter how liberally the scheme may be interpreted and applied, it cannot fully convey university status nor university conditions of work. A question of wider relevance which stems from this is whether the public sector will or can compare with the autonomous sector in academic responsibilities and in working conditions. As the CATs know full well, the challenge of academic and administrative autonomy is most salutary in raising standards, and their experience is not lightly to be set aside. These standards are directly related to staffing ratios, to university salaries instead of the lower and more rigidly applied Burnham scales, to greater opportunities for advanced study and research (at greater cost than undergraduate work) and to a higher standard of amenities and provision for students' activities.

All these stand in the lengthening shadow of the Committee on Estimates and the Public Accounts Committee, with the insistent demand for an appraisal of the work of universities in terms of cost analysis and other accounting procedures. With the great increase in expenditure of public money through the UGC, from £32,284,000 in 1955–56 to £193,074,000 in 1965–66, it is understandable that these procedures should be required as a proper check on the use of public money: but there is a proviso of cardinal importance – that the criteria in these analyses relate accurately to university work, and are not a facile transposition from industry and commerce. The purpose of industry and commerce is the economic production of manufactured goods and provision of services; the prime function of universities is the extension of knowledge and production of graduates with trained minds, of value to the community, but in whose education imponderables and special factors incapable of exact cost analysis play a determining part.

This is the first serious concern, and the second is the use to which the analyses will be put. The first is not allayed by the scheme of cost analysis introduced by the UGC under government pressure for the first time as from 1 August 1965, but there are hopes that by continued consultation with representatives of the universities that the scheme will be improved. The second concern, however, is of a quite different kind, because of the ease with which interpretations can be drawn and misapplied without regard to particular circumstances, or to the traditions of a particular department and so on. Moreover, it is difficult to believe that sooner or later comparisons will not be made between the cost per student place in the autonomous and the public sectors, for students in *comparable* courses – and there's the rub: between incommensurate conditions of staffing ratios, salaries, equipment and amenities as already indicated. Would this be a downgrading effect of 'the healthy rivalry where their work overlaps' of which the Secretary of State spoke, or would the 'mutual understanding' to which he also referred prevail and the standards (and costs) within the public sector be raised accordingly. However that may be, such procedures and analyses will clearly have to be accepted in the universities from now on, and they will need to be expertly devised and properly applied and explained if the universities are to secure the necessary understanding by government and the public at large of the issues involved.

In his paper on 'University-State Relations Re-examined', Robert O. Berdahl (1963) concludes by saying 'Many friends of Britain will be watching with interest and hope as she enters this decisive phase of her adjustment to a mass production civilisation. My own expectation is that she will make the adjustment with the same empirical grace which she has shown when similarly challenged in the past.' Rarely can there have been so generous or so graceful a tribute to the tradition of muddling through. The challenges now are of a quite different order, both educationally and administratively, and time and resources are no longer on our side. There are acute problems of educational policy, of relating the educational opportunity of the individual to the manpower needs of the country, of the administration of certainly large but nevertheless inadequate financial resources among increasing numbers of vigorously demanding institutions of higher education: all this under unfavourable economic conditions in which higher education must be a powerful instrument of change and improvement. Under these combined forces institutions will perforce change; the fundamental question is whether they will change empirically, by reacting to events as they arise, or whether a new hold will be taken on basic principles in order to guide the evolution of these institutions. Not only will universities and colleges change, but the UGC and the CVCP will do so as well, and the same questions apply. The Estimates Committee were clearly of opinion that the roles of these Committees must change radically and urged, for example, that 'with the vast growth in work of the UGC, the burden on its members and staff, and the total increase in Government expenditure on universities . . . it is time for the Vice-Chancellors Committee to become more effectively representative.' The Committee also considered that 'it is the duty of universities to respond to the grant of financial aid by showing themselves willing to take part collectively in negotiation with the UGC and the Government'. Will academic autonomy entail an administrative anarchy for universities at national level or will collective representation on behalf of the universities increase in a way commensurate with the need? The necessary and voluntary limitation of the powers of sovereign political states in the modern world may not be too fanciful an analogy. All of which may be reinforced by consideration of the effects of the binary or dual system in higher education: unless these changes in role take place, the case for the autonomous sector may go by default compared with that of the public sector 'under social control, and directly responsive to social needs'.

Early in their Report, the Estimates Committee state that they 'accept that the principle of academic freedom has been maintained through more than 50 years of Government grants to universities and do not regard it as part of their remit to re-open this controversy.' Nevertheless there are many ways to the other side of the mountain apart from going over the top, and tunnelling to some purpose is currently fashionable. Even if the principle were accepted it could easily happen that some procedures, thoroughly justifiable on certain grounds, might be pressed too far, and the basis of academic autonomy be seriously undermined. Moreover, practice established in another sector might in the long run weaken the grounds for full autonomy. Some there are who hope that such untoward effects of radically changed conditions will not arise, and that 'good sense will prevail' (that traditional guiding light of empiricism). Others perhaps feel that many of the issues touched on in this paper are best dealt with by informal dialogue between the parties concerned, and that to bring to the surface such possibilities as 'state universities', with potentially profound effects on the UGC system, is to increase the likelihood of their coming to pass. There are, however, cogent reasons for ensuring the maximum public discussion of the issues involved in the active preservation of academic autonomy, and in the revaluation of its significance and scope in profoundly changed circumstances.

The administrative means to maintain the academic well-being of both universities and colleges need also to be considered critically and constructively. It will be a far-ranging and searching debate, including many matters scarcely touched upon in the Robbins Report. The Secretary of State set up a committee to consider the governance of colleges of education, but it would appear that representatives of the universities were only reluctantly invited to the conference table despite the long continued membership of the colleges in the university institutes of education. As already noted the Secretary of State has also set up a working group to consider the governance of major technical colleges, but so far as is known, the universities have not been invited to send representatives.[3] Surely the principles of academic autonomy and of the administration of institutions of higher education must apply across the frontier between the two sectors. For the public sector will the consideration of academic autonomy require a revaluation of the effects of the system of joint committees on the work of the colleges, and the requirements of professional institutions? How far will an attempt be made to apply a new Benthamism – the greatest academic autonomy of the greatest number of institutions of higher education: and how far would such a principle receive effective support in the local education authorities?

Whatever reservations there may have been about the Woolwich speech by the Secretary of State, there can be no doubt that it was most timely in focusing attention on issues of far-reaching importance in higher education. It is earnestly to be hoped that the continuing debate on the dual system will not result in doctrinal rigidities. Every endeavour must be made to promote constructive relationships between institutions of the two sectors and to ensure, in due time, that the natural evolution to university status of such institutions as may justify it will not be frustrated.

Notes

[1] This refers to the merger proposed between the University of Warwick and the Lanchester College of Technology supported by the Coventry City Council.

[2] The Woolwich speech announced the Secretary of State's intention to create up to 30 polytechnics.

[3] Both working parties were chaired by T.R. Weaver, the Deputy Secretary, DES.

References

R. O. Berdahl (1963), 'University-State Relations Re-examined' in *Sociological Review: Monograph No. 7: Sociological Studies in British University Education* (University of Keele).

DES (6 May 1965), Administrative Memorandum No. 7/65: The Role in Higher Education of Regional and other Technical Colleges engaged in advanced work.

McNair Committee (1944), Ministry of Education Report: *Teachers and Youth Leaders*. (HMSO).

Ministry of Education (1945) Committee on Higher Technological Education (the Percy Report).

Estimates Committee, Fifth Report, Session 1964–5, *Grants to Universities and Colleges* (HMSO 1965): pp. xxxvi, para. 108.

Hansard, 25 February 1965. Cols. 390–398. Reported *The Times* 25 February 1965.

Guardian, 7 June 1965.

Hansard, House of Commons, 25 March 1965. Cols. 751–841.

The National Plan. Chapter 21: Education, para. 23. HMSO.

Sunday Times 12 and 19 September 1965.

T. R. Weaver (1965), Address to a joint meeting of the Association of Chief Education Officers and the Association of Education Officers, published in *Education* 20 August 1965.

15. The Education of Ministers of State

Alec Merrison

Universities Quarterly Vol. 30 (1975–76), pp. 2–14.

Six years ago Shirley Williams, then Minister of State at the DES, put forward 13 points aimed at making the universities more efficient and cheaper. They were pretty summarily dismissed by the universities, and in particular by the Committee of Vice-Chancellors and Principals, and I think there is little doubt that at least the manner of their dismissal harmed the universities' stock of credit with the politicians and, I would guess, with the civil servants.

When Lord Crowther-Hunt, Mrs Williams's successor at some removes, announced that he wanted to initiate a 'great debate' about the universities, and then went on to do so in a series of speeches, my own reaction – shared, I know, by many – was that whatever they did the universities should not be foolish enough to throw up a wall of the same blankness as that they had presented to Shirley Williams. Sadly I think exactly this has happened. This time at least the Committee of Vice-Chancellors and Principals has maintained a useful silence – useful in the sense that at least the battle lines have not been marked out in the open, so there is still some chance of discussion at that level. Equally the reaction of individual academics has been, to say the least, severe. Of course, the timing of Lord Crowther-Hunt's initiative has been unfortunate. He has insisted on displaying his ideas at a time when the universities, had they not run down their staffs and had not the Government – to its credit – carried out a rescue operation, would certainly have been unable to pay their bills. At the same time the whole academic community has felt a sense of deep injustice about the level of its salaries, and this has by no means been removed. The times are certainly wholly unpropitious for Ministers to initiate cool and constructive debate on how to get more for less money.

But equally the debate must take place. The Minister of State and his advisers carry a very heavy responsibility for defending what we would all regard as an admirable university system, and if he feels it can be improved, economically or otherwise, then his arguments must be listened to and commented on. Dr Dahrendorf has already said firmly that he is worried that the 'great debate' has been formulated in entirely the wrong language – and, to give away the unsurprising dénouement – this would broadly be my own position; and I think it is worth discussing, if that is true, how it has come about. We now have, too, the advantage of Lord Crowther-Hunt's Nottingham speech, which perhaps says many of the things he should have *started* the great debate with and which puts into a different and warmer context his former speeches. But the Nottingham speech does not change the arguments which Lord Crowther-Hunt has used (it is not intended to) so one must still examine those arguments seriously.

It is important, too, to understand that the general tenor of the proposals fits in with a tradition of Government thinking on this subject, so it will be worth starting with Mrs Williams's 13 points.

The Great Debate – Mark I

Since everybody will by now have forgotten what the 13 points were, let me start by listing them in the version given to the CVCP. They were:

(i)   a reduction or removal of student grant-aid, coupled with a system of loans;

(ii)   a similar policy at the postgraduate level only;

(iii)   a more restrictive policy as regards the admission of overseas students;

(iv)   the requirement that grant-aided students should enter specified kinds of employment for a period after graduation, which might have the effect of reducing applications;

(v)   the greater use of part-time and correspondence courses as alternatives to full-time courses;

(vi)   the possibility that the most able should have the opportunity to complete a degree course in two years;

(vii)   the possibility of some students not proceeding to the customary three-year course, but to a different course lasting only two years and leading to a different qualification;

(viii) the possible insertion of a period between school and university, which would give school-leavers a better opportunity to formulate their views as to whether or not they wished to proceed to some form of higher education;

(ix)   the more intensive use of buildings and equipment, including the possibility of reorganisation of the academic year;

(x)   more sharing of facilities between adjacent institutions;

(xi)   more home-based students;

(xii) the development of student housing associations, and other forms of loan-financed provision for student residence;

(xiii) some further increase in student/staff ratios.

I think it is not worth commenting on these in detail, except perhaps to say that some lie extremely oddly in the mouth of a socialist Minister of Education, but it will be interesting to compare some of them at least with proposals which Lord Crowther-Hunt has made. A number, too, have been overtaken by subsequent developments. The welcome success of the Open University, for example, has completely fulfilled any expectation under (v). The comparative failure of the Dip.H.E., introduced by the 1972 White Paper as filling a great and until then unnoticed gap, has shown that not much can be expected from (vii). Loans (point xii)) have become the customary way of financing student residence, but the economics of schemes of this kind are more apparent than real.

In case anyone should imagine that it is only socialist Ministers who have ideas of this kind for economies in universities, then it should be said that Mrs Thatcher put proposals to the CVCP which were very similar to the 13 points, but all that was overtaken by the 1972 White Paper.

The Great Debate – Mark II

I think it would not be unfair to characterise Lord Crowther-Hunt's aim in putting ideas to the universities as 'more graduates in desirable subjects for less money'. There is of course nothing unworthy about that by itself, but it has to be looked at in the wider context of the universities' contribution to society. And it is his apparent ignorance of that context and of the discussions in the last 15 years, say, of the aims of universities that has caused such dismay in the academic world. I think the only way one can display this is to take quotations from his speeches one by one and comment on them, and this I shall do.

Relevance

Though I am and will continue to be an advocate of relevance in higher education, I do not accept the view that we have or are likely to produce too many graduates – at least in the foreseeable future. Now this theme of relevance seems to me to be of particular importance at a time of economic and financial difficulty. We need to be more than ever certain that the money we spend is well spent. Which means that in my view we should do our best to produce the sort of educated people the nation needs. (Crowther Hunt 1975(a))

If this is meant to imply that the universities are failing in this respect then there are three kinds of reply. The first is to examine the range of 'relevant'* courses universities offer. If universities are to be criticised on this score then one has only to ask Lord Crowther-Hunt to look at the list of degree courses offered by universities and set out in detail in *The Compendium of University Entrance Requirements for First Degree Courses in the United Kingdom* (CVCP 1975).

The variety of relevant – even vocational – courses, very much broader than the CNNA range in polytechnics, is quite staggering and it would have to be a pretty mean-spirited and obtuse nation to complain about it and a pretty imaginative one to think up some more – at least at the moment.

The second is to look at the numbers of students in the broad areas into which disciplines fall and ask if they are badly distributed. In my own university we have seven faculties, of which five (Engineering, Medicine, Law, Education, Science) are wholly or broadly vocational, leaving Arts and Social Sciences. Examining Social Sciences in more detail one finds again subjects which have a fairly direct vocational aim – economics and accounting, for example – and some which do not – politics (Lord Crowther-Hunt's own subject) and sociology again are two examples. But 'unvocational' as these last two subjects might be, would he consider them irrelevant? Surely only with a fairly tortured definition of relevance.

Which leaves us with the poor old Arts Faculty (History, Modern Languages, Philosophy, Classics, Music, Drama, Theology). Well, I suppose Classics, Music and Drama had better go (but better keep Theology, just in case!), but I wonder if the others could not be considered quite good general training for at least some professions? All our experience seems to confirm that that is so. And then what about those who take up school-teaching with this sort of university career behind them? Are they bad at their jobs? Completely the contrary has been my experience.

So even in a university like Bristol which hardly sets out to be trendy it doesn't look as if we are completely out of step in producing the graduates which society needs.

---

* I am assuming for the moment that the word relevance has some generally acceptable meaning, though I believe that to be very far from the case. I will discuss this later.

The third argument is suggested by the second. What a totally threadbare method of analysis the second argument is as a description of university education! If I thought that the value of university education in Bristol really could be discussed in such terms then I should be the first to march out. Of course, university education is so much more than this, and because educational planners can only read bare lists of statistics they should not be misled into mistaking this appearance for reality. University education at its best can be described only in the subtle terms of helping the young maturing mind, and no amount of prosing on about percentages of classicists, engineers, scientists and so on is going to be in any way relevant to that. I once heard a previous Prime Minister say that 'it was the job of universities to make good people better', and that I think is not a bad description of at least part of their job.

Now I would like to put in the promised parenthesis about relevance and I will do it in terms of my own subject, physics. Since physics has given us things like radar, electric power and nuclear bombs we don't have to argue about its relevance. A few months ago I wrote a short piece on research for my trade journal on 'Is usefulness a useful concept?', usefulness being a special class of relevance. The argument went like this. There are all sorts of research which we can say are probably useless. For example, I doubt whether it will ever be *useful* to know whether Richard III really did murder the Princes in the Tower. At the other end of the scale there is unquestionably useful research which we should be, and are, doing, like that into the stresses in welded steel joints. But in between there is a vast body of research which it is much more difficult to classify *now* as useful or useless, relevant or irrelevant.

For example, nothing could conceivably have looked more useless in 1932 than Chadwick's discovery of the neutron. Yet here we are, a mere 40 years on, with more than 10 per cent of the country's power depending on Chadwick's discovery and world politics changed as a result. So words like 'useful' or 'relevant' when applied to any kind of human activity have to be applied with a good deal of caution.

And, again, I *want* a few professionals devoting themselves to those Princes in the Tower. Because although such knowledge is, without doubt, useless, I want to feel that I live in a society which sees the establishment of historical truth as of the very greatest importance.

It does seem to me that here the economists, or at least some of them, have done us all a very great disservice. Because by pretending that their subject had anything useful (here we go again!) to say about pain or death or love or hate by means of the total artefacts of 'health economics' or 'education economics' and 'cost-benefit analysis', they have misled the gullible and the busy into the most extraordinary and untenable views and even decisions.

Manpower planning

Here I must quote a fairly extensive passage from Lord Crowther-Hunt's 'Royal Festival Hall' speech:

> Attempts at manpower planning in this country in most fields are of no very great age and have so far not been all that sophisticated. I am not deterred, therefore, from pursuing further a positive approach to higher educated manpower both to look again at what might be the needs of the economic system, and to ask questions not simply about numbers of qualified people but the nature of their qualifications. It simply will not do to allow universities and polytechnics to produce whatever people they fancy, or to relate the number and kind of places they provide to the applicants that come forward . . .
> We already plan our educational provision to take account of the number of teachers we think we need – and we plan it, too, to produce the number of doctors we think we shall need.

It really is extraordinarily difficult to know where to start with this: but let me start with the simplest bit. Why on earth did Lord Crowther-Hunt's advisers let him quote with approval the Government's attempts at planning the supply of doctors and teachers? Did they positively wish him harm? They must have known that both these are at the moment utter disaster areas. Yet these two examples hold very great lessons for us in that they are about the simplest employment areas to apply manpower planning to. Both professions and their employers can be identified easily and the State has had essentially complete control over the supply. Yet here we are with less than two-thirds of the doctors we need and closing down between one-third and a half of the places in colleges of education.

It is simply not that easy to plan the demand and supply of educated manpower and the difficulty is not at all to do with our methods not being 'all that sophisticated'. It is simply that one is trying to make projections into the future on a time-scale which is very long compared with the rate at which society changes. And we should not let the word 'rate' deceive us into thinking these changes occur at a constant rate or even smoothly. There are many things whose future predictability, even with more and more sophisticated forecasting techniques, I would rate on the same rather low par; and among these I would include manpower planning, weather forecasting and picking future Derby winners. I have no doubt that we should, and indeed shall, try to do these things better, but equally I have no doubt that our success will be limited.

To say too that 'the universities and polytechnics produce whatever people they fancy' or that they simply 'relate the number and kind of places they provide to the applicants that come forward' are both complete travesties of the truth. Again, one has only to look at the enormous range of courses 'relevant to society's needs (without enquiring too closely into the meaning of the phrase) to see that the first charge is wholly unfounded. The second point is more subtle. *Of course*, the universities and polytechnics should not simply respond to a demand from school-leavers; but one has to recognise that this is a social demand made upon them to which in some degree they should respond. How much they should respond and in what way is a much more difficult question. There is of course the simple Robbins answer that you provide higher education for all those qualified to receive it, but even Robbins did not suggest that we matched courses and demand in a one-to-one kind of way. There is no answer to this other than that lying in a set of compromises that Government and the universities and society (both as a whole and that part seeking education) have a hand in settling. This may seem awfully weak and feeble but there really is no magic solution.

Priorities

Lord Crowther-Hunt devoted part of his speech to the AUT to the matter of priorities in higher and further education and posed a number of questions. They are important questions and I believe that academics should give the best answers they can – and hope that the examiner will treat them generously.

Universities and polytechnics and further education colleges

Are we satisfied that we have got the right balance between, on the one hand, advanced level work in our Universities and Polytechnics and, on the other, non-advanced level work in our Further Education Colleges? (Crowther Hunt 1975(b))

My personal answer to this, having worked with graduate and non-graduate engineers, both in the UK and on the Continent, is that we certainly have not got the balance right but that what we need is more (and, for that matter, much broader) training for our engineers and not less. I would be quite sure that, as an example, the kind of graduate and postgraduate training of engineers envisaged by the Chilver Report on the Education and Training of Civil Engineers is the way that the training of our technologists of the future must go. We really must get away from the idea that the 19th-century 'trade school' will serve the needs of society today.

We were . . . envisaging that these [640,000 places in higher education by 1981] would be split very roughly half and half between the universities and the rest. But is that likely to be the most economical way of providing for this expansion?

I haven't the least idea: until I know what the relative cost of graduates is in the two kinds of institution, which presumably the DES can answer, and what the nature of the polytechnics will be in 1981. Why the DES is shy about publishing the polytechnic statistics I cannot imagine. The Secretary of State has been asked for such figures and has refused an answer. When he answers that we can attempt some sort of answer to his Minister of State's question.

One plea I would make, however: and that is that when we know all these figures we should stop imagining that by dividing the total expenditure of a university (or any educational institution, for that matter) by the number of its students we get the 'cost per student'. The 'output' of universities, and polytechnics, is very much more than the student heads that roll out of the door.

And I am not at all clear what sort of places the polytechnics will be. Spokesmen for the polytechnics keep assuring us that they will be 'different' but I don't at all understand in what way they will be different and whether that way will be cheaper. There is of course the much deeper question as well of whether that way will be something the nation needs and desires.

But if I had to give a snap answer to the cheapness question I would at the moment put my money on the universities. This is based partly on the little we know of the staff–student ratios in the two kinds of institution (now very much in the polytechnics' favour, according to DES figures) and partly on the curious silence of the DES about all this.

Staff–student ratios

. . . if we now had a student/teacher ratio of 9:1 in the universities instead of 8.4:1, we should be saving some £12–13 million on staffing costs.

Leaving aside the trivial point that the Minister of State had already been told by the UGC that the figure was already 8.9:1 (a figure he uses in the THES of 24 October), one has to admit that there is no canonical way of arriving at the ideal student–staff ratio: none at all. All one can say is that if any sizeable changes are made in it then this will make sizeable changes in the nature of universities. At the moment we are committed to short, intensively taught first degree courses in universities which are committed equally to research. It is certainly fair to say – and Lord Crowther-Hunt has said it – that this system bears comparison with any in the world. Before tinkering with it the Government really must have a very clear idea of what they believe to be wrong and the consequences of any attempt on their part to put it right. The universities have suffered a great deal, in the last two years – my private guess would be that leaving aside the 'expensive' subjects of medicine, dentistry and veterinary science the student–staff ratio must be near 10:1 – and it is my belief they simply cannot take any more.

Undergraduates and postgraduates

We all know of postgraduates in our universities who are neither contributing to the advance of worthwhile knowledge nor even adding in any worthwhile way to their own qualifications. Does too much of our effort go into postgraduate work?

The question is simply not to be answered in this sort of way. We all know of *under*graduates in similar case, and perhaps we know more of them, but that is not an argument for most *post*graduate work. The amount of postgraduate work to be done – and resist the temptation of rising to that 'worthwhile' – depends almost entirely on what kind of institution you want a university to be.

Conclusions

All in all, the points I have quoted from the Minister of State's speeches are pretty thin stuff (and there is, I am afraid, quite a lot more of it) and I believe that all thinking academics were surprised by it all. The surprise was on two grounds. The first is that he seems quite unaware that many of the questions he raises are part of a continual debate in the universities and he seems to imply that they are capable of easy answer. The second is the number of quite straightforward misconceptions of our higher education system and, in particular, of what universities are like and what they do.

There is not a single new thought in Lord Crowther-Hunt's speeches or perhaps, in the spirit of the Ph.D. examiner's comment,* I should say that there is not a single new good thought, and this in itself is illuminating. I started by quoting Mrs Williams's '13 points' and many of the matters she

---

* 'This thesis contains much that is good and original. The trouble is that the original contributions are not good, and those that are good are not original.'

raised reappear in Lord Crowther-Hunt's speeches. I think one must conclude from this that they represent the 'departmental view' in which ministers are bathed and which has been commented on by many ministers and ex-ministers, Anthony Crosland and R. H. S. Crossman among them. If I am right in thinking this, then it seems to me it would be a simple matter for the DES officials and the UGC to get together to sort out an agreed policy on many of these matters. It is after all the UGC's responsibility to advise Government on matters concerning university policy and it hardly seems necessary or productive to use ministers as stalking-horses in this kind of mock battle. But perhaps I am wrong about all this, and all these ideas do indeed spring from the heads of ministers.

The new point which Lord Crowther-Hunt makes much of is his emphasis on manpower planning. I hope I have said enough to show that I believe he is right to insist that such calculations should be done, but that he is wholly wrong to think that they are not done already and to think that any remarkable illuminations are waiting to be discovered here. A careful study – and I recommend this to some budding social scientist – of the planning of medical manpower in the last 20 years would be of the greatest help and education to us all. Quite why was it that the Willink Committee in 1957 recommended that the output of medical schools should be cut by 10 per cent? Why did it take until 1966, when it was all too late, to see that this was a disastrous mistake? Why were their numerical predictions of everything so wildly wrong? The Office of Health Economics made a small but excellent study of this in 1964 but we desperately need a complete and up-to-date analysis.

And how was it that all our planning of the numbers of teachers we needed went so badly wrong? I suppose that this must have been a sum of simple errors by civil servants and ministers, but I really do not know. Again, a serious study of this field would be invaluable and there is no reason at all why the DES should not undertake it – except, of course, it might be objected that they would be acting as prosecuting counsel *and* defendant.

The three most serious matters which Lord Crowther-Hunt has discussed in his speeches, if only by implication, are: what sort of places do we want our universities to be; what sort of system of higher education do we want; and what is to be the role of universities within that system?

Let me make some personal declarations on these matters lest the whole of this article appears completely negative in tone. In the first place, one must see that the debate is conducted in real terms and not only in the style of what A. H. Halsey has so rightly called the 'fish-and-chip shop' approach to higher education. To do so is of course extremely difficult, just as it is difficult to conduct the debate about the Health Service in terms of the real values of pain and death and quality of life, as well as in terms of wage-rates or hours of work or even pay-beds.

And the first thing to take on board is that in using such language one must see the universities as centres of scholarship – not merely as places which absorb public money and which produce graduates. They are so very much more than this and contribute so very much more to our national life and to the world. We have the necessary forums, like for example the UGC, where a proper discussion of matters of this kind can take place.

The second point to make about universities is that they have so far in this country maintained an independence of the state which has been of critical value not only to themselves but to the nation. In the debate which must now take place, particularly in relation to the financial support of the universities, it will be necessary to see that this independence is not weakened. This is not at all an unthinking plea of 'Hands Off the Universities'. The universities' record in being sensitive to the declared aims of Government is good, and, despite the uncomfortable feeling some politicians and civil servants have that the universities are uncontrollable, untidy places, they should be thoughtful from the outset of what a great national benefit this independence really confers.

As one who feels that Anthony Crosland's Woolwich speech was an appalling blunder – and his account of how he was pushed into it by his civil servants is both engaging and alarming[7] – I see the major problem in the higher education field as what is to be done with what has become, through the sheer crassness of politicians and their officials, the other side of the binary line. I think one can see this best by taking a single subject; for the sake of argument, let us pick on civil engineering. Civil engineering, like any other subject, can be taught in a variety of ways; but there remains a core to the subject which will be a necessary part of the training of any graduate civil engineer, and that core will form a substantial part of the three years to graduation. So the number of tunes one can play with this theme is limited and they certainly cannot be separated in a way that one can declare there is a 'polytechnic civil engineering' and a 'university civil engineering', in the way that one can declare there is Vivaldi on the one hand and Stockhausen on the other. Similarly with research, assuming that the Government line on polytechnic research cannot be held – as indeed I am sure it cannot.

A major problem (one of many) I see within the universities lies in their nature as homes of teaching in the atmosphere of research, to use Lord Boyle's expressive phrase. So far we have allowed the funding of research to expand at about the same rate as undergraduate numbers, but there is no obvious logic linking the two. The nation clearly should have, and be able to discuss and express, the level of research it would want to see funded in various broad areas. Equally clearly it should have, and be able to discuss and express, the numbers of graduates it wants in various broad areas. They are not for the nation necessarily linked, but for the universities the relation between the two is vital.

Much as I admire our present system of higher education in this country, I hope I have made it clear that I see no particular perfection in the *status quo*. On the contrary, our higher education system contains within itself problems which, if they are not solved, will be destructive. But the debate which will be necessary to solve those problems cannot be conducted in the crude and misleading language used by Lord Crowther-Hunt. We must all be grateful to him for making the discussion of these questions a matter of public concern, but now the debate must be conducted with thoughtfulness and a good deal of circumspection. It takes a long time to build up first-class educational institutions and the nation is fortunate to possess so many. It takes almost no time at all to weaken them fatally.

References

Edward Boyle and Anthony Crosland (1971), *The Politics of Education* (London: Penguin Books.

Crowther Hunt (1975(a)) Minister of State's Speech at the Conference organised by the North East London Polytechnic in conjunction with the THES at the Royal Festival Hall on 13 May 1975.

Crowther Hunt (1975(b)) Minister of State's Speech to AUT. 16 May 1975.

CVCP (1975), *The Compendium of University Entrance Requirements for First Degree Courses in the United Kingdom* (London: CVCP).

PART III

The Assertion of State Control

16. University Financing 1979–86

Peter G. Moore

Higher Education Quarterly Vol. 41.1 (January 1987), pp. 25–42.

The 15 years 1964–1979

Difficulties began to emerge after the euphoria of the Robbins Report and its acceptance. New buildings, and the associated staff to man them, arose on many campuses, particularly for science and technology. However, as early as January 1965, shortages of good applicants started to become apparent. In schools the rise in the number of science students was well below the proportionate rises in other subjects. A study undertaken by Sir Frederick (later Lord) Dainton highlighted this problem (Council for Scientific Policy 1966), and the UGC policy on subject numbers was substantially revised in 1966, with an appropriate (downward) adjustment being made to the capital programme. A further enquiry was also set up to study the mismatch between the aspirations of the Robbins Report and the potentialities of a largely unreformed system in the schools and their curriculum.

Other problems now started to intrude; the Crosland differential fees policy for overseas students (a small differential by later standards) was announced in December 1967, and the end of the decade was dominated by years of student unrest. A few years later, however, in December 1972 a White Paper was published which raised the sights for university numbers for 1981 even beyond Robbins (375,000 in place of Robbins's 346,000) (DES 1972). The public sector, incidentally, was at the same time asked to achieve unprecedented levels of expansion in a nine-year period. The White Paper simultaneously sought to arrest unit costs, mainly through a stiffer student/staff ratio.

After some half century, the quinquennium of 1972–77 was the last such period for this much vaunted method of university financing, and even that quinquennium was illusory. Financial cutbacks of some severity occurred in 1973–74, and the aspirations for 1981 in numbers terms were curtailed by UGC edict. Staff vacancies were frozen in many universities and maintenance on many buildings postponed. The Houghton Report of

December 1974 awarded large rises to teachers in the public sector, which then led to increased unrest in the university sector which had been treated less generously (DES 1974). The so-called salary 'anomaly' took years to settle and greatly soured relationships between universities and government. The devolution issue arose in 1965 and, for a time, it seemed possible that the UGC framework would be split with separate arrangements for each part of the United Kingdom. However, after much anguished debate, the concept receded and the status quo remained. At the same time the capital spending tap was turned off viciously and 1974–75 turned out to be the final year in which substantial capital funds were available to universities. Many projects had to go by the board (and some worthy items are still today only on the drawing board).

The turning off of the capital tap removed one of the UGC's most powerful weapons. It became clear that henceforth the UGC's power to influence rested primarily with its handling of the recurrent grant. This change had, and continues to have, a powerful effect on the manner in which the UGC operates. The unexpected squeezes that occurred in recurrent grant during the 1972–77 quinquennium, which had in retrospect been a start year plus four annual grants, followed by the increased frequency of grant distributions, allied to further regular squeezes, has unconsciously led to the more dirigiste approach being adopted by the UGC over the allocation of recurrent grant and planning numbers in more recent years.

The Watershed of 1981

During the late 1970s modest expansion was still in the air. The author, joining the UGC at the end of 1978, recalls learning then of the government university planning figure of 312,500 for 1983. That figure was never mentioned again and actual numbers peaked at 300,000 in 1980–81, and fell back to 292,000 by 1983–84. A general election in the summer of 1979 witnessed a change of government and a marked change of approach. In July 1979 the UGC was asked by the DES for their views on the effects that various alternative resourcing scenarios, both upwards and downwards, would have on university numbers. A request was accordingly made in October 1979 by the UGC to all universities for their plans under a number of funding assumptions. An immediate response in terms of student numbers and financial viability was sought within a month, plus a more considered and detailed reply within six months. Well remembered by those who took part in the exercise – because of what happened later – was the argument carefully developed in the subsequent

UGC paper sent to the DES to the effect that reductions of 2½ per cent or more per annum in real resources in university income would lead to chaos and inefficiencies in the system.

The first demonstrable casualty in the new milieu was the recurrent grant funding enjoyed by overseas students (subsequently modified to non-EEC students only). From 1980 new overseas entrants to universities were to receive no subsidy, and the recurrent grant was pro-rated as the existing levels of overseas students ran off the books, broadly in three cumulative annual tranches of 40 per cent, 40 per cent and then 20 per cent. This removed about 10 per cent of university income over the three-year period 1980–83. Overseas fees were already higher than those for home students but, to replace the lost income, fees now had to be raised to more realistic levels in relation to true cost and, at the same time, similar numbers as before had to be attracted if total income was not to decline. In the event, universities charged overseas students fee levels that were somewhere between marginal and true average costs. The consequence was that the overseas numbers fell for about five years but are now (1986) picking up again and are more or less back to 1980 levels, although the distribution between institutions has changed.

At its inception the new policy faced universities where the percentage of overseas students was high with an extremely difficult problem and, in some institutions, income fell substantially. (The average percentage of overseas students was 11 per cent, but some individual institutions had over 20 per cent; such institutions were clearly likely to lose in the short term and fall below the 2½ per cent per annum cut level that had been judged harmful by the UGC.)

This change had no sooner started to be implemented when, at the end of 1980, the Secretary of State announced a cut in the universities' real recurrent grant for home students of 3½ per cent for the year 1981–82. This meant that, taken in conjunction with the overseas students adjustment, the potential average reduction for the year was likely to be of the order of 5 to 6 per cent. The UGC meeting in January 1981 was gloomy, but more so in February when it became clear that further cuts were about to be announced for the two years 1982–83 and 1983–84. It subsequently emerged that the planned total real cuts (beyond the overseas cuts) over the three-year period 1981–84 totalled 8½ per cent. The UGC protested in strong terms at the consequences, reminding the DES of their response to the July 1979 exercise, but were rebuffed. By early March unpalatable decisions had to be made.

In looking at the options open to the UGC, the initial choice was between 'equal misery' and 'selectivity'. Both courses of action had their adherents; the equal misery school being favoured by the Association of University Teachers and many academics. Selectivity was favoured, at any rate in private, by a substantial group of Vice-Chancellors and also by much of the press. The UGC came down in favour of selectivity for two reasons. The first was really a negative consideration. For the UGC to go for equal misery would be the death knell of the UGC or of any alternative intermediary body on the argument that it implied the UGC was unnecessary even when a very substantial change in the system was involved. This was really negative reasoning, however, since the principal reason for selectivity was that the UGC wanted, above all else, to preserve what they felt was good in the system as far as it was humanly practicable, in terms both of quantity and quality, measured in terms of the unit of resource. It should be remembered that the system had broadly been designed for an ultimate capacity of 350,000 students. It had never got beyond the 300,000 mark. One consequence of this gap was that a number of institutions were still effectively unbalanced, their funding over the previous 15 years of expansion having been built up in a series of blocks. The choice was therefore seen as being between rationalisation by the Minister and his supporting civil servants on the one hand, and selectivity by the UGC with its sources of formal and informal knowledge of individual universities and departments on the other. Not surprisingly, with its history and traditions, it chose the latter route and then found itself with about 3½ months to implement the exercise.

The first step in implementing the selectivity route taken by the UGC was to decide as between numbers and resources. Total resources were to fall by between 13 and 15 per cent over the three-year period (dependent partially on the level of success in generating fresh overseas fee income). It was the Committee's view that, coming on top of the small but cumulative cuts that had been made in the unit of resource over the past decade, an extra cut in the unit of resource of around 14 per cent was unacceptable. This could only be ameliorated by a cutback in student numbers and it was decided to cut student numbers by 5 per cent, leaving the balance of the costs of around 9 per cent to fall on the unit of resource.

The next step was to look at the subject balance and to determine priorities. The UGC was working on a three-year timetable and the scope for massive changes, even if desirable, was limited. It was decided, nevertheless, to make some modest shifts towards science, engineering, technology, computer science, etc. with corresponding resource cutbacks in the arts and social studies areas. The relatively heavier student costs of the favoured areas was an important factor that could not be ignored. The changes, it must be emphasised, were committee decisions taken after consulting the principal professional bodies in the country and other interest groups, particularly employers. Although government views were known, they were not foisted upon the UGC as a directive.

The next step was to marry up the totals delineated for the 17 major subject areas commonly used by the UGC with the availability of places and assessed quality of the various individual institutions. The UGC subject sub-committees were asked to provide assessments on quality and viability on all departments in their domain; an exercise that was easier to carry out for large departments than for some of the smaller departments, particularly those in the arts field. An iterative process was adopted to try and ensure that highly graded departments were maintained more or less intact, with any necessary cutbacks being made in those less highly assessed. Finally each institution was looked at as a whole to judge the viability of the subject balance now envisaged.

During the exercise, one substantial difficulty emerged, namely the roll-on effect, that was much misunderstood by later commentators. Since most institutions had been expanding their entries in the years leading up to 1980, the retention of the latest entry numbers would imply an increase in total numbers over the next few years; conversely a cut back of total numbers in stock to a figure lower than the current level would mean in some instances a dramatic fall in the annual entry numbers, with a see-saw effect on entries in later years. The UGC fixed the total planned numbers of home and EEC students for 1983–84 at 249,000 – a figure that was some 6.7 per cent below the 1980–81 actual figures of 267,000 for 1980–81 (the latter figure was not known accurately by the UGC until the exercise had been completed!). If entries had been maintained at the 1980 levels the roll-on would have raised total numbers to about 275,000 by 1983–84. Hence the implicit immediate cut in entry levels was nearer to 10 per cent in contrast to the 5 per cent reduction in the 1980 stock figure. It is interesting that, whereas Government always talks of entry numbers per annum for medicine and dentistry, it is commonly in terms of total student stock for all other subjects.

Because of the process used, the cuts in grant over the three-year period varied widely from university to university. The exercise was condemned in many quarters in particular for the cuts made to technological universities such as Aston, Salford and Bradford which, to the outsider, seemed clear examples of institutions that should have been kept intact. However, a substantial part of the cuts in a number of cases were due to large numbers of overseas students, or to the numbers in the arts and social studies areas, rather than to technology places for home students *per se*.

The 1981 cuts exercise undoubtedly was a landmark both in the history of the UGC, and of the universities themselves. As indicated earlier, the seeds of the cuts themselves were sown a long way back, and can be traced to the Government's fundamental omission of a schools policy to back the Robbins Committee proposals. Whilst the UGC had been dirigiste upwards before, e.g. over the capital grants in expansionist days, it now had to become dirigiste downwards, giving guidance on student numbers in much narrower subject groupings than hitherto. There was a great deal of soul searching and problems over the ensuing three years, and the Government, on UGC urgings, was forced to offer both a premature retirement scheme for staff and a new blood scheme for young lecturers in selected areas, in order to repair some of the damage to the position as regards staff. The UGC prognostication, concerning the maximum rate of decline that could be tolerated without dis-economies, was borne out. So great was the need to save immediate cash that many staff were 'paid off' only to find in a few years that their universities had to recruit in precisely the same subject areas. By 1984, however, it had been hoped that the worst was over and that, at a minimum, level funding would be restored as a basic principle with universities planning accordingly.

An Interlude

Whilst the cutbacks following the 1981 watershed were taking their course, the Secretary of State instituted a further exercise to look at the issues facing higher education over the next ten years. The UGC was asked for its advice and wrote to all universities in November 1983 under the heading 'Development of a Strategy for Higher Education into the 1990s'. The lengthy letter posed 28 questions (quaintly numbered 1 to 29 with 26 omitted) under a number of sub-headings: resources and student numbers, capital, balance of subjects, research, dependence on public funds, nature of universities, validation, tenure and premature retirement, Leverhulme proposals (Morris and Sizer 1982), the role of the UGC. All universities and institutions were required to reply officially to the first two questions on resources and student numbers; responses to the other questions could be made by institutions, groups or individuals. A closing date of 31 March 1984 was set for replies, and 658 responses were received.

Simultaneously the UGC and its sub-committees were set to work on the various issues posed and, over the period April to July 1984, the greater part of the UGC's effort was devoted to the preparation of the UGC submission to the DES. This substantive submission was published in

September 1984 under the title *A Strategy for Higher Education into the 1990s*. The UGC argued that, notwithstanding the drop in size of 18-year-old cohorts, the opportunity should be seized to improve the age participation rate; failure to do so, it argued, would lead to longer-term shortages in many specialist skills. It was therefore proposed that there should be true level funding in real terms at least until the end of the decade, with a longer planning horizon than in recent years; that more explicit guidelines should be drawn up to encourage a greater degree of self-funding, or joint funding and other forms of financial support; and that steps be taken to redress the imbalances in the current structure of academic staff.

It was a bold report and made a case for a strong, substantive and effective university sector within the UK. Its publication was a ten-day wonder and a long wait ensued for the DES response to the submission (and a parallel submission from the NAB). The response finally came, after many leaks, in a Green Paper of May 1985 and was a grave disappointment to all working in the higher education sector (DES 1985). Overall it seemed to hark back to an approach that many believed had been buried, namely that higher education was a consumption good like smoked salmon or video recorders, something that was inessential from an economic point of view, and should be linked with quantity to the rise and fall of the economy. To quote the Green Paper: 'Its [the Government's] provision for the universities will be determined in the light of what the country can afford in all the circumstances of the time and taking account of all other claims on resources.' No real lead was given as to what the country needed and how it might be provided, or how a fruitful marriage of public and private funds could best be achieved. Indeed the paper seemed to confuse money earned by universities against services rendered and the funds required to support the day to day education of students. Ironically, the paper noted the higher levels of qualified manpower (or womanpower) produced in competitor nations, but then had its thinking dominated by the fall in the 18-year-old cohorts which in turn would worsen our comparative position without some positive actions being taken.

The Green Paper also ducked once again the student grants issue. International financial comparisons concerning higher education are bedevilled by the fact that the UK devotes about a quarter of its higher education spend to student grants, whereas other countries do not do so. The consequence is that we appear expensive, whereas the truth is that on an *educational* cost per graduate produced, we are extremely cost-effective. Student awards are, whilst steadily losing their rationale as a full support scheme, far from a negligible cost scheme, and it would seem desirable to review the whole process rather more objectively than has been done in the recent past to decide where financial priorities lie.

During the 1984–85 period while the Green Paper was in preparation, the CVCP and UGC jointly commissioned an enquiry, with Sir Alex Jarratt as chairman, and 11 other members drawn from universities and industry, to promote and co-ordinate a series of efficiency studies into the management of universities, and to report and make recommendations. Their report, in March 1985, made some 26 recommendations, about half relevant to the universities themselves and the remainder relevant to Government, the UGC and the CVCP. Perhaps the most important in the context of this paper was the perceived need for Government to give a clear lead as to what was required of universities over a longer period than hitherto, with appropriate funding indications in order to allow for meaningful strategic planning to take place at the institutional level. The report was published two months before the Government's Green Paper referred to above, but Government made no comment on this recommendation.

The 1985–86 Exercise

Notwithstanding the absence of much key data, the UGC sent out in May 1985 its own planning letter asking each university to provide a strategic plan for the period 1986 to 1990. The Government's financial resource plans, as known at that time, postulated a fall of 1.5 per cent (cumulative) in real resources in each of the three years 1985–86, 1986–87 and 1987–88; no figures were available for the succeeding two years. Universities were asked to provide by 30 November:

(a) a statement of overall objectives for the planning period;
(b) a research statement of achievements and plans;
(c) forecasts of student numbers in various subject groups; and
(d) financial forecasts up to July 1990.

A crucial paragraph in the letter indicated that the UGC was developing a new approach for grant distribution with a model based principally on four components:

(a) a teaching resource per full-time equivalent home and EEC student which would vary according to departmental cost centre, but not according to institution; changes that had occurred over time in the distribution by subjects of student load within an institution would be brought into account;

(b) a research resource which was based partly on the Committee's judgment of research quality, and partly on the quantum of research grants received from Research Councils and elsewhere;

(c) provision for central costs (this item, although mentioned in the May 1985 planning letter, is absent from the grant distribution letter of May 1986); and

(d) special factors (e.g. London allowance, or the possession of a national museum).

The submissions made were voluminous and posed considerable problems for the Committee members to assimilate them all.

The 1986–87 academic year grant letter was finally issued on 20 May, with a follow up letter a week later. It gave planning numbers for 1989–90, but no institutional financial figures beyond 1986–87, indicating however that globally a total cut in real terms of about 7 per cent was expected over the three years 1986–89. The planning numbers for 1988–89 overall went up extremely marginally by about 700 student places, over 1984–85, with the arts/science/medicine mix virtually unchanged, even though some changes were envisaged within these three groups. The May 1985 letter had postulated complete virement between full-time and part-time students. However, in the grant letter of May 1986 all part-time students, whatever the nature of their course, counted as 0.5 of a full-time student thus causing difficulties to a number of institutions, for example at Birkbeck College in London University which consists virtually entirely of part-time students.

The key paragraphs in the (long) letter regarding resources are worth paraphrasing:

(i) The major part of the allocation was based on a common level of resourcing for funded student load in a given (subject) cost centre. (This was the most important cause of changes in grant between institutions.)

(ii) The allocations reflected the distribution of student load. This was affected by the funding numbers which, both in total and in subject mix, might differ from universities' current (i.e. pre-1986) targets. These changes related not only to full-time, but also to part-time students who were thus affected by the Committee's new resourcing policy. (The changes in full-time student load were much smaller than in 1981, and had less effect than the policy of common level of resourcing.)

(iii) Institutions differed significantly in the resources they attracted as a result (a) of the Committee's judgments of their research quality; and (b) of their grants from Research Councils and certain charities, and of their income from contract research.

(iv) The Committee was sparing in making provision for special factors; in general these were only taken into account if they reflected exceptional and inescapable resource commitments, or related to an activity which might be at risk because its costs were above average but which the Committee wished to see retained in the national interest.

The grant allocation was a redistribution at a time of a cut (as was the case in 1981). The then Secretary of State stated in the House of Commons in June 1986 that the changes made to the grants of individual universities reflected in their relativities the rating of universities for teaching and research; this was subsequently denied by the UGC since it was only item (iii) above that attracted major differential support between institutions. The UGC gave no indication as to how they split the total resources between their various categories, nor did they indicate how the research grant element was calculated in relation to the question of research council grants on the one hand, and private money raised for research on the other. Combined, furthermore, with a lack of information as to the relative weightings given to the 37 subject cost centres (over double the number used by the UGC in its 1981 exercise) as regards teaching, the process is shrouded in mystery at a micro-level, although the nature of the changes can be discerned at the macro-level.

Universities which were poorly funded in the past on a student basis, have clearly gained at the expense of those who were previously relatively better funded. However, when combined with the research resource changes, which seem to have operated conversely to the common basis now used for teaching resources, it happens that broadly the same winners emerged as in 1981, only this time the impoverished were not so much the colleges of advanced technology as the institutions in Wales and Scotland. Moreover, as in 1981, the cuts were not due to any deliberate cutting along these lines – the criteria that were judged appropriate for the period ahead produced the patterns.

The consequences in terms of press reactions were strangely muted – as compared with 1981 – even though the cuts were yet again of a significant size at virtually all universities. Most of the criticism that arose was directed, not unexpectedly, towards the viability or otherwise of the research assessments made by the UGC. The other major criticism was that Wales and Scotland have apparently been treated more harshly than England but, as already mentioned, this was a function of the general criteria themselves.

This lack of outburst may have occurred because the variations in the cuts made as between institutions were lower than in 1981, and hence the same sense of outrage then felt by a small number of universities did not exist in 1986. Nevertheless, the sheer viability of institutions has become a greater issue than ever before and is accepted as a real problem on all sides – but with a degree of resignation that suggests the continual non-stop cuts since 1979 may have dulled the senses of many of those concerned. In 1981 'wolf' was cried loudly and was virtually ignored; the universities survived and, even though damage was clearly done, e.g. to the staff balance between subjects, the system did not – as commonly forecast – collapse nor were there massive compulsory redundancies. In 1986 the ongoing debate as to what needs to be done is being conducted in a rather different and semi-secret fashion. This is designed, presumably, to minimise aggravation and maximise persuasion on the many outstanding issues that currently need to be resolved at a governmental level.

Some Comparisons

It is tempting to compare the 1981 and 1986 exercises as one might compare two theses on the same subject. After all, only three members of the UGC were involved in both exercises which suggests that with different people, different arguments and approaches would emerge. However, the changed background circumstances would almost inevitably have induced different approaches. In 1981 the UGC undoubtedly saw its primary role as the safeguarding, as far as was practicable, of its then key indicator, namely the unit of resource. It believed that abandoning the unit of resource concept would be a hostage to fortune even though the 18-year-old cohorts were reaching a peak level. It had a serious 'roll-on' problem from the rapid expansion of previous years to contend with, and also had to contain the overseas subsidy issue which hit institutions differentially. The allocation it made produced a viable and meaningful subject pattern, but did so at the risk of considerable damage to institutional stability. It was a unique exercise at the time for the degree of dirigism that was employed in relation to recurrent grant. In demonstrating that the UGC could handle retraction as well as expansion, around which its whole history had previously rested, it extended the implicit scope of the UGC. However, in having to implement a financial policy with which few of the members were in sympathy, it subtly became to some degree an arm of Government, although members felt that it was better to be in a position from which considered arguments could be made to Government than, through resignation, to be totally excluded from the debate.

The 1986 UGC exercise took the 1981 model and developed it in a number of respects. It asked universities for their own subject area plans, albeit on resource assumptions that turned out to be somewhat below the actual resource levels subsequently found likely to be available. It accepted some of the proposed adjustments to the existing subject balance, for example business studies went up, as did engineering marginally. Most other subjects remained relatively static in numbers for the four-year planning period. However, it introduced a markedly greater degree of formula funding than before (in place of what had been earlier described by some commentators as informed prejudice). This was in many respects a bow to pressure from a number of sources – government, universities and the public generally – to be more explicit in the means by which levels of grant were determined. In particular, teaching costs per institution have been equalised (or are in the process of equalisation) and a formula approach to the allocation of research funds has been adopted, albeit with peer group judgment for the inputs into the formula. Although the split of the resource shares has not been made public, it seems likely that it will inevitably be in the public domain bfore long and, once that is so, universities will treat the process as a game to be played according to a set of rules.

Once this stage has been reached a number of possible consequences arise. The first is that good quality, expensive teaching, will be seen as a hazard to universities in the sense that it brings no direct extra financial reward. Reward would come more directly through starving the resources allocated to the teaching activity, using the funds thus saved to boost research activity output, which in turn could lead to a higher total grant. Research seems to be the one area where performance can lead to extra grant. Secondly, it is inevitable that income garnered per student place on different subjects will reveal opportunities for institutions to optimise income and return by switching between subjects. Thirdly, the approach could lead to a freezing of institutional patterns unless some universities deliberately lower teaching quality to put funds into research in a bid to get themselves back into the more favourably funded group. This could lead, incidentally, the UGC to conclude on the next round of investigation that teaching costs are on average lower than hitherto and hence cut everybody back! Such a vicious circle could only be broken if the UGC formulates a policy of what teaching is, in its eyes, expected to cost, rather than to examine what is being spent. Fourthly, the move opens up the possibility of having universities that are not research-based, but are teaching-dominated, with a lower staff ratio than conventional universities.

Ironically and coincidentally, the move towards formula financing has come at a time when the Government has as a political aim greater freedom for universities, with less bureaucracy and lowered dependence on public funds. Yet the means of achieving these governmental aims are not being articulated in a very meaningful form. Universities are encouraged to seek funds for research grants and contracts, and assured that these will not affect grants. Continuing education, on a full-cost to user basis, is likewise encouraged. But all these methods of fund raising are in general linking funds with new obligations. Whilst they employ staff to give the services expected, they do not fundamentally assist in the teaching of under-graduates and postgraduates for which the great bulk of university income is required and is the criteria by which the general public primarily judge universities. Indeed there is some danger that teaching standards could slide. Government needs to be more explicit as to whether it really believes that top class teaching is expected of institutions from the grants made available, or whether it is reasonable to ask individuals in some instances to pay more for their university education than is currently the case. Sooner or later that bridge has to be crossed and, unless it is done relatively quickly, standards may erode to a point where reversal is difficult.

The role of the UGC has evolved into a more pro-active form over the past ten years. This has raised queries about its composition and its responsibilities. The Jarratt Report recommended that the structure and operation of the UGC be examined. The Government accepted this recommendation and set up a committee to conduct this study under Lord Croham, whose report is expected in early 1987. Calls have been made on the one hand for the UGC to have stronger representation of outside interests in the business and commercial field, and on the other hand for the academic members to be more openly representative, e.g. appointed by regions or by subject areas through some procedure involving university institutions or their staffs. There have also been calls for members to be able to devote more time to the task, and for the secretariat to be strengthened. It is noteworthy that, whereas it was once extremely common for members to undertake two five-year terms on the committee, few nowadays go beyond a single five-year term and some not even that. (Some leave because of appointment to Vice-Chancellorships or similar positions.) Pre-war it was estimated that membership took about 30 working days per annum; in recent years the figure has at least doubled and probably trebled at peak periods.

Opinions will differ on the precise composition of the UGC but, if its role continues to centre around the delineation of the balance of subjects within the university system, it could be argued that the external non-education representation should be increased from three to five, and the university representation reduced from 14 to 12. This would still leave the university appointees with a dominant voice but could assist the promotion of a more meaningful dialogue between the universities and the world without. With the academic members, the aim must be to obtain these from amongst those who are respected in their own fields and, if practicable, in the university system at large. To attract and retain the individuals the work-load must be kept in proportion and adequate backup facilities offered. For the non-education members there are greater difficulties as the time required to participate fully is immense – particularly bearing in mind that these individuals concerned start from a less detailed knowledge of the system. It is therefore unreasonable to expect them to be able to contribute fully to matters appertaining to individual institutions, but nevertheless high class individuals are required if they are to contribute to the Committee's global strategy. This argues for the strengthening of the secretariat, and the formation of an executive committee to relieve the pressure on the main committee itself and so allow it to concentrate its energies primarily on the more strategic areas of concern.

It is clear that there will over time be increased pressure from many quarters for greater co-ordination in higher education across the binary line, particularly as both sides are now operating on a national rather than local basis. Higher education is too important to risk any loss of effectiveness through divided management and thought needs to be given now to alternative scenarios. Whilst it seems desirable to maintain the notion of a plurality of institutions within the total system, ways must be found to ensure appropriate total coverage of subjects, without wasteful duplication, and the nurturing of adequate but not excessive research activity within the total system. One possible solution that needs further exploration is to form a single over-arching body for all forms of higher education, with a series of smaller groupings than now, each dealing with a particular group of institutions. This grouping could either be on a geographic basis, which allows flexibility and changes in institutional objectives, or on the basis of types of institution which would provide greater homogenity within groups. Such an approach could combine the notion of a national system, planned on a global strategic basis, with an ability to handle institutions on a direct and individual basis. This could provide a blueprint for the system as it moves toward the 21st century.

References

Council for Social Policy (1966), *Enquiry into the Flow of Candidates in Science and Technology into Higher Education* Interim Report (London, HMSO, Cmnd 2893).

CVCP (1985), *Report of the Steering Committee for Efficiency Studies in Universities* (The Jarratt Report) (London, CVCP).

DES (1972), *Education: A Framework for Expansion*, Cmnd 5174, (London, HMSO).

DES (1974), *Committee of Enquiry into the Pay of Non-University Teachers* (The Houghton Report) (London, HMSO, Cmnd 5848).

DES (1985), *The Development of Higher Education into the 1990s*, Cmnd 9524 (London, HMSO).

Morris, Alfred and Sizer, John (eds) (1982), *Resources and Higher Education*, Leverhulme Programme of Study into the Future of Higher Education (Guildford, SRHE).

UGC (1984), *A Strategy for Higher Education into the 1990s* (London, UGC).

Access has been had to the various UGC circular letters sent to universities over the period 1979–86, particularly those dealing with forward planning and grant allocations, as well as to the UGC Annual Surveys published by HMSO.

17. Academic Standards and Mass Higher Education

Martin Trow
Higher Education Quarterly Vol. 41.3 (Summer 1987), pp. 268–92

In this essay I want to reflect on standards in academic life, and the somewhat different question of the maintenance of high and roughly uniform academic standards across the whole range of degree-granting institutions in Britain. The first question – the issue of academic standards in a particular college or university – is one of the most important issues that an institution has to confront. Every college or university has to concern itself continually to maintain the highest levels of teaching, and in some, of research, that it can achieve. But the second issue – of the maintenance of those standards across a whole range or category of institutions – is a quite different question, as much an issue of public policy as of academic vigilance, and like most issues of public policy, any 'solution' has its costs as well as its benefits. A central problem for modern societies is how to reconcile the survival and provision of elite education, at high levels both of cost and excellence, with the emergence of mass education, the provision of post-secondary education to large sections of the whole population.

I use the term 'elite higher education' neutrally, not as a term of abuse, as is common these days, nor in reference to the social origins of students, but as a way of pointing to a form of higher education marked by high selectivity, and staff–student ratios which allow close student–teacher relations centering around studies at high levels of intensity and complexity, leading to degrees of high and recognised standard. In English and Welsh universities (and to a lesser extent in Scotland) elite higher education, at least for the past two centuries, has been associated with the idea of 'liberal' studies, sharply distinguished from 'vocational' studies (Rothblatt 1976). And to the extent that the polytechnics provide education keyed to preparation for specific jobs and careers, they are not considered part of elite higher education in Britain. But this conception would also include MIT and Imperial College. Moreover, the distinction between 'liberal' and 'vocational' studies is increasingly difficult to make as undergraduate education, even in 'liberal' fields, becomes increasingly specialised and professionalised. It is, therefore, more useful to distinguish elite from mass higher education not by reference to the content of the curriculum but to the character of the students and the nature of instruction. Thus, mass, by contrast to elite, higher education is marked by its relatively open access to a more heterogeneous student body, many of whom are older, work part-time, are less well prepared, less highly motivated, with higher rates of attrition (wastage), taught less intensively, and to lower standards of achievement (Trow 1974).

To British academics, that may seem to describe the polytechnics. And from a certain perspective, the creation of the polytechnics, across the binary line, was a move towards mass higher education. But, as Guy Neave has observed,

The British move toward mass higher education extended elite criteria to the non-elite sector of polytechnics and colleges of education, thus giving rise to a far greater degree of homogeneity in patterns of access between the different sectors – university and non-university – than had ever existed. In short, mass higher education in Britain was elite higher education written a little larger. (Neave 1985)

From American perspectives, British universities and polys are more alike than either will admit. In respect to access, cost, staff–student ratios, forms of instruction, wastage, the education of teaching staff, above all in their approach to knowledge, universities and polys are *both* part of a common system of elite higher education. Of course the old status distinctions between 'noble' and 'less noble', 'liberal' and 'vocational' studies, survive and continue to affect the recruitment, both of staff and of students, to universities and polys, and to some extent their governance and funding as well. But those differences, which seem so large in England, seem much smaller from a transatlantic perspective, and from American universities which embody both 'liberal' and 'vocational' (or 'professional') studies. From that perspective, the unity of British higher education is a result of the transformation of both 'liberal' and 'vocational' education over the past century.

[While] the trend towards greater specialisation in university education remains basically uncontested, and liberal education continues to narrow in subject concentration, there has been an opposite trend in vocational education. There the instruction has broadened. . . . The result has been that what were once regarded as servile occupations have been elevated into the ranks of professions, where they have then been brought into the world of university education. Because of this reformation in the teaching of vocational subjects, it has become nearly impossible today to distinguish between various kinds of institutions offering advanced instruction, whether or not they are actually called universities. All of them, whether Oxford and Cambridge, London, Redbrick, Plateglass, and Scottish and Welsh universities, and the colleges of advanced technology, incorporate similar ranges of educational methods and ideals, and offer similar mixtures of liberal and professional forms of education. It can be said that the balance of subjects varies from institution to institution, as does the technical or liberal emphasis, and certainly the quality and appeal of institutions differ enormously. But this does not alter the conclusion that all institutions of advanced education share more educational values than at first they might be inclined to believe. (Rothblatt 1976)

In some societies the two forms of education – elite and mass – can be found within the same university, as in France and Germany, and in the big American state universities. In other societies, notably the UK, the division of labour is between sectors, between 'higher' and 'further' education, and only the sector that maintains high academic standards is given the status of 'higher education' and permitted to award the degree. In this paper, and taking advantage of perspectives that come from outside the shared values and assumptions of British academics, I would like to reflect on some implications of that separation, and on the costs and consequences of system-wide academic standards, the standards that characterise the British system of elite higher education.

When I speak of a high and uniform standard of quality in British higher education, I am, of course, referring to the standard for the honours degree. British academics and their supporting institutions make a determined effort to maintain that standard of the honours degree, as high and as uniform as possible throughout the system of higher education. While it is understood that some subjects are more difficult than others, or attract students of higher academic ability, nevertheless within subjects there is an effort to maintain a roughly equally high standard for the degree among the several universities. Indeed, it is also recognised that since some universities tend to attract more able students than others, on average, they will award more first and upper second-class degrees. That in itself is taken as evidence for the uniformity of standards throughout the university system.

But there are a variety of other institutional arrangements that work to maintain this parity of standards. Perhaps the most powerful is the institution of the external examiner, a mechanism recently reaffirmed and reinforced by the Reynolds Report (Reynolds 1986). The external examiner – which British academics all take as a matter of course – appears to Americans to be an admirable device for maintaining standards of performance, effectively preventing what we would call 'grade inflation', that tendency for teachers to give higher marks to students than they deserve because they are diligent, or amiable, or perhaps because a better mark will get them a better job or a place in graduate or professional school at no (apparent) cost to anyone. External examiners do indeed keep internal examiners honest, in this regard at least. The external examiner, of course, is an instrument of quality control. But even more important, the external examiner is there to maintain comparability. As Reynolds puts it: 'It is of first importance . . . that degree classifications from different institutions approach as nearly as possible to common standards within the limits on comparability' (Reynolds 1986). In the United States we do not, with one or two exceptions, employ external examiners for the first degree. In our universities, (and here we betray where it is that we take the maintenance of standards of performance to be most important, that is, in our graduate and professional schools), the examining committees for advancement to candidacy for the doctorate, and for the oral examination on presentation of the dissertation itself almost always include members from outside the awarding department and discipline. But this latter arrangement, in the United States, is for the most part internal to a given university and is very often *pro forma*; we have no arrangements comparable to Britain's for maintaining a standard of degree among colleges and universities, broadly recognised as representing a common standard of excellence or achievement wherever earned.

In support of the external examiner, the British have a number of other arrangements to help guarantee the common high standard of degree. One is the protection of a common unit of resource across universities. Some British universities, in response to cuts and threats of cuts in their annual support grants, have offered, indeed petitioned, to be allowed to enrol more students, even with fewer staff and less funds. The UGC until now at least has adamantly refused such permission. The defence of the unit of resource – that is, essentially, the staff–student ratio – has been in its eyes and in the eyes of many British academics the first defence of academic standards which even the individual universities, under stress and pain, would not be allowed to endanger. While student–staff ratios have drifted upwards in the British universities over the past few decades, it has not been offered as an option to an individual university to dilute its own unit of resource in the service of some other ideas about access, or the survival of a threatened small department, or whatever. Indeed, in relation to the idea of a common high standard, the emphasis has been equally on the words 'common' and 'high'.

A variety of structural features of the British system ensure that the standard is common to all degree-granting institutions, as well as high.

There is, for example, the common level of minimum achievement, two 'A' level passes, required for admission to universities and polytechnics, though here there is considerable variation in the requirement beyond this minimum among different subjects and universities. Nevertheless the requirement of two 'A' level passes itself is a very considerable barrier to entry to higher education. Fewer than a quarter (22 per cent) of the age grade currently take these examinations, and only 15 per cent pass in the two or more subjects that is the minimum qualification for entry to a degree course. If this is not selective enough, those who pass with 'D's or 'E's on these tests are commonly regarded by the universities as 'poor calibre', with three passes and higher grades increasingly necessary for entry to the more popular universities and subjects.

There is, in addition, the roughly common salary schedule for academic staff, and the common formulae for the proportion of staff in different ranks, both of which reduce the incentives available to any particular university which might want to concentrate abler or more productive scholars in some particularly favoured department. That happens of course – there are other incentives besides salary and rank to attract staff to more prestigious departments, and we hardly need the latest UGC league table to tell us that. But the national pay scales, common appointment procedures, external referees, and fixed ratios among the several ranks and grades all tend to damp down the differences between universities in respect to the quality of their staffs.

At the other end, the absence of tuition costs to the students, and the provision of grants to most students, coupled with the similarity of costs and amenities among universities – Oxbridge aside – is another set of forces for the levelling of average student abilities across institutions. What the students get is much the same everywhere, and they might as well go anywhere. Perhaps the most powerful levelling force of all is the formula by which the UGC distributes the Treasury grant to universities. A great deal of attention has naturally been directed to the recent (1986) exercise by the UGC in ranking university departments, and for the role of those rankings in the allocation of the annual grants to the universities. Since that exercise, most of the discussion has been directed to the fraction of the grant which is intended to be distributed unequally, by reference to the supposed research quality of departments in universities. But little attention is paid to the fact that the bulk of the UGC's grant is still distributed as a grant in support of teaching, and very much on the basis of a standard *per capita* formula. It may be that the UGC will discover ways of measuring the quality of instruction, and introduce inequalities in its rewards and incentives in that portion of the university grants as well. But up till now the UGC has tried through its grants to universities to maintain the unit of resource for instructional purposes roughly constant over time, and remarkably equal across institutions. British academics, I suspect, are sensitive to the variations in those allocations; to an outsider, it is the similarity of those allocations that is most impressive. All of these mechanisms and arrangements that I have been describing, taken together, allow us to think of the British universities as the separate campuses of 'the University of the United Kingdom' (Caston 1979).

I have been speaking chiefly of the universities, but what I have said applies for the most part to the polytechnics and other degree-granting institutions. The concern for the maintenance of the standard of the degree in British higher education – that is, the university standard – could nowhere be more strongly symbolised than in the institution of the CNAA under whose tutelage and supervision, through committees staffed largely by university academics, the standard of degree offered by the polytechnics was initially ensured. In recent years the responsibility for the maintenance of the degree standard has been increasingly shifted over to the polytechnics themselves, as particular departments and institutions have emerged from their trial period and demonstrated their capacity to maintain their standards without close external supervision. There is here a direct parallel to the great tradition of the London external degree, and its tutelary relationship to the then university colleges, from Owens to Leicester. For many years, beginning with the etablishment of Owens College in Manchester, as new university colleges were created they were not permitted to award their own degrees, but were allowed to prepare students to take the London examinations. It was only as they emerged from their period of trial and tutelage, and gained the strength, size, and staff necessary to be granted a university charter, that they were authorised to award their own degrees. The polytechnics are currently undergoing the same transition.

I have described, or at least pointed to, a network of institutions and arrangements which together helps sustain the value attached to the first or bachelor's degree, as awarded chiefly by the universities and poly-technics, but also by such other institutions as the Open University and the colleges of higher education. Underlying all these are norms, beliefs and sentiments, broadly held among British academics but also by civil servants and politicians, to the effect that this degree, wherever offered and awarded, should be of high and roughly common value. In this respect the British first degree is, so to speak, still on the gold standard. This is something in which most educated Britons take pride; and indeed, there is, it seems, a constant anxiety that perhaps the value of the degree is not what it was or what it should be, and that the quality of teaching, or the nature of the curriculum, or the abilities of students or of staff, or of the resources available to the universities, have changed in ways that threaten the quality and value of that degree.

This fear, that standards are slipping, that 'more means worse', or will mean worse, has been a strong element in British higher education at least since World War II, and has been a major constraint on growth, even during periods of expansion. After World War II, British university enrolments grew to some 80,000, up from 50,000 just before the war, in response to an imaginative 'Further Education and Training Scheme' (FETS), embodying grants to all ex-servicemen and women. But post-war enrolments probably would have grown even further if the universities had not used this opportunity to raise their marginal entry qualifications so as to eliminate 'a large number of the extremely weak students who used to gain entry before the war' (H. and H. M. Peston 1974). But *despite* this rise in entry qualifications, 'the UGC was also worried that the number of very bright students was not rising at the same rate as the total student body' (*ibid.*). This fear grew stronger in the early 1950s when the FETS was coming to an end, and when it was felt that maintaining universities at their new scale, let alone moving to a larger one, would mean a decline in the relative numbers of those getting first or second class honours degrees. The Ministry of Education itself was worried about all this. 'It remains also to be seen how large a number of students can attend universities and other higher institutions without depressing the general intellectual standard' (*ibid.*).

I happen not to share that anxiety, not only because I am not British, but because I believe that, within broad limits, 'more' does not mean 'worse', and also because I believe that British universities and leading polytechnics are still among the finest in the world, making important contributions to knowledge in every subject and discipline out of proportion to their size and the number of their scholars and scientists, with patterns of teaching and learning, teacher–student relationships, and levels of efficiency that are models for the world.

I find it perfectly reasonable that those in Britain should continue to look seriously and critically at how the high standards of teaching and research in their universities can be maintained. But the question that I want to address is not the one that has been raised so imperiously by Sir Keith Joseph and the Chairman of the UGC: are standards falling, and how can they be sustained and raised? In the remainder of this paper I want to raise the quite different question: what price is paid by British higher education, by its members both junior and senior, and by the society at large, for the effort to sustain this high standard of degree throughout the system, by the effort, that is, to maintain the British first degree on an academic gold standard? I do this not to try to suggest that Britain should go off that gold standard – indeed I think the forces in support of that principle are too strong for any such suggestion. I hope rather to shed light on the system from another quarter, and to point to some consequences of those arrangements that may not be noticed otherwise, since they largely take the form of things that do not happen rather than things that occur. Such negative consequences are surely as real as things that do occur, but obviously a good deal less visible, or maybe only visible in comparative perspective. Moreover, being non-events, it is harder to make the causal connections strongly and persuasively between the forms of higher education and what does not happen in the surrounding society as a result.

The question might be posed in this way: what developments in higher education or elsewhere are precluded, or at least inhibited, by the British commitment to an elite higher education system, marked by high and uniform standards throughout its member institutions, at levels of cost that press against current and prospective resource constraints?

One thing that such a commitment precludes is wide diversity in the system, diversity within and among institutions in their function, level of standards, and *per capita* cost. This is almost inherent in a commitment to high national standards, which as I have said is at the heart both of the academic excellence of the British university, and of its lack of flexibility in the face of new challenges. It is, for example, hard to add new schools or departments of business administration, or electrical engineering, or social welfare, or policy analysis, to existing institutions, not only because their budgets are already fully committed, but also because creating new subjects and departments cannot be accomplished unless the UGC and the institution itself can be sure that the provision of instruction in that subject will almost from the very beginning be of a high enough quality to qualify as of genuine university standard.

New subjects typically find their way into the curriculum under the wing of old ones, as sub-disciplines, so to speak. Thus did molecular biology creep into established departments of biology or botany; thus did psychology and politics and a host of other subjects come into the university under the wing of philosophy, gradually gaining a foothold, creating their own bodies of literature and special ways of looking at the world and studying it, and training increasing numbers of scholars and scientists to look at the world or study it in that way. That is the way in which a subject gives solid evidence of its academic credentials, of being worthy of being accepted as an equal, worthy indeed of being taught and examined as an independent subject in its own right, with people appointed to teach it as their major responsibility and not their private hobby or special interest. That is, of course, a slow process but when the protection of a national degree standard is the first and highest value in a system, diversity of curriculum and function are among the costs.

Perhaps the greatest constraint imposed by a national standard is on expansion. No country in the world could operate a system of mass higher education at the *per capita* cost levels of the British universities and polytechnics. These cost levels are not inappropriate for elite higher education – the higher education of full-time, highly selected and able students, taught at the most demanding levels of intellectual intensity and complexity. That is what British universities and colleges do, for the most part, extremely efficiently and extremely well. But genuine diversity would mean institutions operating at different levels of cost as well as of standard, and the possibility of lower cost higher education would allow academics and officials to at least think about the expansion of higher education. But there is, I believe, a positive horror among the British, academics and politicians alike, at the very thought of the provision of 'education on the cheap'; the chief objection, of course, is that such education would threaten standards. Yes it would, but that, of course, is just my point: the absolute unyielding commitment to high academic standards throughout the system is also a defence of the relatively high costs associated with elite forms of higher education, and that in turn puts an effective brake on expansion.

This horror of 'education on the cheap' helps explain why the polytechnics need to operate at cost levels very close to those of the universities. If we make the adjustments for the most expensive research carried on in universities, and for the peculiarly expensive subjects, especially medicine, taught only in universities, the unit of resource in the polys was close to that in the universities. Only in recent years as polytechnic enrolments increased by some 25 per cent, partly in response to UGC cutbacks, has a gap appeared, and of course the evidence of this gap has resulted in concerns being expressed about the effect on the 'quality' of polytechnic higher education. I do not know if equality of *per capita* cost was in Anthony Crosland's mind when he called for the creation of a binary system marked by 'equality of esteem', to accompany a modest differentiation of function between the two sectors. But the stress on equality of esteem, and the firm determination that the polytechnics would maintain standards equal to or only slightly different from those of the universities, ensure that their costs must be similar – if they were not, what better evidence that they were designed to provide education 'on the cheap'? And the careful monitoring by the CNAA subject committees, largely staffed at least initially by university academics, has ensured that degrees from the polys would be roughly at university standard – and cost.

And, of course, as the polys were drawn into the university orbit they sloughed off much of their non-degree work, which fell from 70 per cent to 30 per cent of their enrolments between 1969 and 1982, along with most of their part-time students, from 60 per cent of the total in 1969 to under a third in 1981 (Cantor and Roberts 1983). At the same time, and for the same reasons, they have increased their research activities, and will continue to do so 'if only for reasons of prestige' (*ibid.*). This development, which some have called 'drift' as function follows cost, quality and esteem, also was encouraged, I believe, by the bad conscience among British middle class and professional people toward the British working class. Where Americans feel guilt toward our racial minorities for past ill-treatment, Britain shows a parallel guilt-ridden policy towards its working class. Or at least they have done so until recently. As a result many Britons of all political persuasions are sensitive to the fact that new, low cost and low status segments of a system of higher education are commonly first associated with and used by students from working and lower-middle class origins: status differentiation in higher education is closely linked to the social origins of students. So many who make this connection are hostile to the whole idea of a binary system, with its non-U sector especially oriented towards technical and practical subjects, which in the English context have lower status in themselves (Weiner 1981; Rothblatt 1968). These 'unitarians' as we may call them, are committed to the slogan 'nothing if not the best' in higher education, and especially so for youngsters from those strata of society which have historically got less, or second best (Trow 1974). But even those academics who support the binary system are not inclined to want *per capita* costs in the polys to be markedly lower than they are in the universities – both for the political reasons that I mentioned (i.e., the ideological egalitarianism of a class-haunted society), as well as for the role of common costs in maintaining common standards for the degree. If the polytechnics are allowed to offer a degree, so this argument goes, then they must be supported as if they were universities or something very near to them, and their students likewise.

If diversity of function is constrained by a national standard of degree, and the size of the system is constrained by its costs, so are the size and diversity of the student body. The requirement that entrants to degree courses have two 'A' level passes immediately disqualifies over 80 per cent of its youth from entering English universities and polys. There are now some experiments, especially in the public sector (Fulton 1986), to admit students without these qualifications, but the numbers of these 'non standard' entrants are not very large, and probably are not intended to rise very high. Indeed, even in the Open University, widely advertised as an 'open access' institution, over 60 per cent of the entrants are people who already have earned two 'A' level passes or their equivalent, and that proportion has been constant almost since its creation (Cerych and Sabatier 1986; Williams 1985). Those 'A' level examinations may or may not screen effectively for future academic achievement, but they are certainly intended to do so.

So the 'A' level as the requirement for entry to higher education effectively constrains demand, whatever the capacity of the system of higher education, whatever its budgets. More resources from central government – much to be desired by all – would, I think, not mean more students: it would mean better student support grants, better pay for staff, improved staff/student ratios, better instruments and equipment for research, more secretaries and support staff – all good and desirable, even necessary things, but not more students, or at least not many more.

And yet there is every reason to believe that modern societies, as they develop into societies that depend on the creation and distribution of information – what have been called 'information societies' – need more and more highly trained and educated people. In the United States, with over 12 million students enrolled in post-secondary education of one kind or another, 'graduate unemployment is less than half that of the general labour force, less than one-third that of all 24-year-olds' (Williams 1985). And, as Shirley Williams observes, 'The ability of the education system to match the needs of the information society for highly educated people has now become the main determinant of a country's employment prospects' (*ibid.*).

I am not here talking about the production of electrical engineers, or experts in the design and maintenance of computer systems, though current shortages in those categories are not unimportant for Britain's future. I am talking about people who have had some experience of education beyond secondary school – almost regardless of its content, and not necessarily to the completion of the first degree. In Britain those who leave college or university before taking their degree are commonly referred to as 'wastage'; no value is assigned to a year or two of experience in higher education beyond secondary school if it does not lead to a degree.

That makes sense when the highest value in a system is the academic integrity of the first degree; it makes less sense if we ask what effect, what influence that experience may have on the students and on their subsequent lives and careers. I do not know of any research in the UK which follows the 'drop-outs' to see what happens to them – their rates of employment or unemployment, of occupational or professional success, however measured. In the United States, there is a clear inverse relationship between the number of years that people have had of post-secondary education and their rates of unemployment, and a positive relationship to their income.

I stress the importance of some experience of higher education, even short of the degree, because I suggest that the latent functions, the by-products so to speak, of post-secondary education are for many people more important in the long run than the technical skills or knowledge that they may acquire there. The Victorians and their successors in this country knew that when they spoke of the cultivation of character, of sensibility, of the qualities of mind and spirit that the university was primarily aimed at creating or enhancing. I am suggesting that that transformation can happen even outside of Oxbridge, even in the absence of the individual tutor, even in non-residential institutions, and for older part-time students who have not earned two 'A' level passes. Of course, the positive effects of exposure to higher education, short of the degree, can be effectively precluded by labelling people who drop out as 'failures'. But in a world of life-long learning, every drop-out is merely a 'stop-out'.

The central difference between schooling and higher education, as we all know, is that, on the whole, schools teach the conventional wisdom – the skills and knowledge that are broadly thought necessary if one is to hold most of the middle-range occupations of life, and for a special few, as a necessary foundation for a higher education. But with some exceptions, schools are places where students learn to show a decent deference to their teachers and their texts, and to the knowledge and wisdom that they can impart. But in higher education, by contrast, students are encouraged, indeed even required to question the conventional wisdom, and are rewarded for it. Of course, in colleges and universities there continues to be a large and continuing emphasis on higher skills and more complex knowledge. But in a genuine college or university even this advanced level of skill transmission is carried on in an educational environment quite different from that of secondary schools: 'facts' are more likely to be presented as elements of problems to be solved or interpreted, and indeed the 'facts' themselves are sometimes subject to question. At its best, students in higher education learn, often in a sudden flash, that they can have ideas of their own, even ideas at variance with the conventional wisdom, at variance with those of their teachers, even, possibly, ideas that no one else has had before.

Of course this is not a description of every college or university either in the US or the UK. But there is a *tendency* for higher education to broaden students' horizons, strengthen their confidence in their ability to have ideas and to act on them, and not merely follow work routines. Nor is this as romantic or idealised a view as it may appear. Students can be *tested* on their knowledge of the standard views (or arguments) of a field, and yet judged informally by their ability to develop critical and original views of the material. And I submit that higher education in most Western societies is indeed a critical education, marked by the steady undermining of deference for the conventional wisdom, and the encouragement of the belief that one can actually have ideas of one's own. That perspective, I believe, is going to be increasingly important, both for individuals and for the society, as the effects of the new technological revolutions of information systems and bio-engineering transform our economies over the next decades, as they have already begun to do. I believe that higher education of *some kind*, not necessarily in elite institutions, and not necessarily to the honours degree, will determine for individuals whether they are to be beneficiaries or victims of the rapid social and economic changes already underway. And for modern societies, the number and proportion of people who feel at home in society, who are not captive to a skill or perspective that is obsolescent almost before it is acquired, will be the main determinant of a country's employment prospects, and more generally, of its economic health and social stability. I do not believe that 14 per cent of the age grade in higher education is adequate to this challenge.

Higher education, I am suggesting, is for society a functional substitute for deference. As deference to traditional political authority erodes or collapses, we had better substitute a great deal of education. Your Victorian ancestors knew it, and we all need to be reminded of it. Social deference in the UK is based on traditional claims to authority of the upper classes; the authority of the modern workplace is increasingly based on claims to technical competence, linked to education. So education is also a substitute for deference in the workplace, and for the customary routines of production and distribution of goods and services. Those routines are being challenged by new ideas, by new technologies, by other societies. We need many people, not just at the top of enterprises but all through them, who are not captive to those routines, who do not defend them as the only (even if illusory) points of security in a rapidly changing world. The mass production of people who have been to college or university – whether at age 19 or 29 or 39 – places people in the middle levels of enterprise who can adapt to change, and even sometimes initiate it, who can accept and use the larger amounts of discretion and initiative that modern industrial enterprises find so important for success in rapidly changing markets. And these same people are more likely to take the risks of entrepreneurship, to start the small enterprises (beyond the family owned shops) where, as we know, the majority of new jobs are being created.

Alongside the cultivation of critical capacities and personal initiative, higher education teaches people to learn how to learn. All the evidence, from Sweden to California to Britain's Open University, shows that the people who continue their education as adults are, on the whole, people who have had a good deal of it when they were young (OECD 1977a, 1977b). This tendency of education to generate a thirst for more of it is hardly even taken into account in estimates of the cost–benefit ratios of higher education, in the UK or anywhere else. But in the contemporary world, hardly any characteristic of a working population is more valuable than its propensity and capacity for continuing education throughout life.

Some may protest that all that is precisely the mission of the Open University, the function for which it was created. I yield to no one in my admiration for the Open University, which I have watched closely and with the deepest respect and appreciation since its earliest days. But in a sense, it is the enemy of a genuine system of mass higher education in Britain, because it contains those qualities, or some of them, in one institution, with one budget, and its own boundaries and limits. The Open University, I suggest, is a kind of safety valve, a token institution by which a highly selective elite system defends itself by accepting in principle the existence of a difference kind of university, not quite elite but not a mass university either, which reconciles 'open access' with a commitment to the university standard for the first degree. While the Open University is nominally open, we know that well over half of its entrants could qualify for entry to the universities or polytechnics. And what makes the Open University acceptable finally is that its degree is a genuine degree, up to national standard, attested so by the external examiners from other universities.

The extraordinary consensus around that gold standard is illustrated by a remark of Shirley Williams. In the course of praising the role of the Open University in British life, she too notes with pride that 'the standards of its degrees have been vigorously maintained, examination papers and course work being regularly assessed by examiners from outside universities' (Williams 1985). But what might the Open University be like if it were not so constrained? Perhaps it had to be if it were to have been permitted to exist at all, and been allowed to survive its early and vulnerable years (Cerych and Sabatier 1986). But that cultural-political requirement has surely limited its impact on British society, and has given the UK another kind of elite university, and not the alternative network of institutions for mass higher education that arguably it needs. Indeed it can be argued that the existence of the Open University has helped to justify the lack of expansion of the university system itself – one can always point to the Open University as the safety valve which would take increased demand for university entrance by those who did not have the full qualification for entry. It is the kind of institutional gesture that accommodates strains and pressures for broader access without endangering the elite institutions themselves, and without threatening a radical change in the system as a whole. It is not irrelevant that the budget of the Open University is less than 5 per cent of the total recurrent expenditure of British universities – and in this respect remains quite marginal (Cerych and Sabatier 1986). Moreover, the Open University is not competitive with the traditional universities – it does not accept university-age students. And it is not competitive for UGC grants, but gets its money directly from the DES. The Open University has many virtues – and the pioneering role it has played in distance learning, and as a model for similar institutions all over the world, not least in the United States, can hardly be praised too highly. But that is very different from seeing it as an institution that might provide broader access of much larger numbers to a system of mass higher education, unconstrained by the standards of the elite universities and polytechnics.

The provision of mass higher education that I have been pointing to is incompatible with the defence of elite standards for the whole of higher education, and of course, with the national standard for the first degree. Mass higher education would involve enrolling, somewhere in a system of post-secondary education, people who do not have the academic credentials that are now required, people who are older, or working, people with families, people who cannot fit into the framework of the British university or even the degree work of most polys. I am not suggesting that British universities and polytechnics transform themselves into American state universities. That is not possible or desirable for a host of reasons, some of which Britons may be too polite to mention. But the greatest price that the UK pays for its elite system of higher education, for its jealously guarded standards of academic achievement and performance, may be that it does not address one of the most important requirements of this age, the creation of a broadly educated society that continues to learn. A 'learning society', I believe, is central to – indeed implicit in – the great social and economic transformation that Britain, along with all the other advanced industrial societies, is currently undergoing.

One cannot stress too often that a criticism of a system of elite higher education need not be directed at the high standards of that system itself, but rather at the way in which that elite system inhibits the emergence of other systems of higher education with lesser, more modest standards. And comments on the costs of elite higher education are not meant to imply that the universities and polys can be maintained on less money, but rather to point out what their costs do to the possibilities of the emergence of a more diverse system of mass higher education. I have said that no country in the world is rich enough to support a system of mass higher education at the *per capita* costs of elite higher education, either as Britain provides it, or as we do in the United States. As rich as it is, comparatively, the United States could never make provision for colleges and universities for 12.5 million students at the *per capita* costs of students in Yale or Stanford or Swathmore or MIT.

And, of course, the costs of Britain's elite system are not only those represented by the unit of resource. We must also add the student grants for all but the children of the affluent, stipends which are intended to make it possible for students to study continuously and intensively for the relatively short period of three years within which they earn the degree. And that grant is supported by very strong sentiments among its recipients. In the winter of 1984–85 Sir Keith Joseph's effort to introduce student loans, thereby shifting some funds away from student support grants into the research budgets, was defeated by a coalition of backbench Tories, representing the parents of children in the universities and polys, and a delegation from the National Union of Students, representing those parents' left-wing children. The student grant system in Britain almost certainly involves a significant transfer of money from the poor to the middle class. But another way of looking at its defenders is as a coalition of the 'ins' against the 'outs'. And indeed that is one way to look at the defence of an elite system based on high and uniform standards throughout. Student grants are a part of the elite system, part of that network of costs and sentiments which constrain the expansion of higher education. Student loans would have a very different significance if they were a means of expanding access, rather than merely of cutting costs. It will be interesting to see what political coalitions develop to oppose or support loans if and when they are proposed on these grounds.

Many British academics are bitterly hostile to the Thatcher Government for its policy towards higher education, a policy which combined savage cuts with a steady pattern of increased intervention into the autonomy of the institutions and a growing institutional structure of direct management from the centre. The irony, of course, is that the Government has gone only a little further than most academics in its passionate defence of high academic standards. The Government simply sees too many students and teachers, where most academics would like to see a few more. But the appeal of higher standards to the Government is that it can be achieved, in their view, by weeding out some dim students and staff, and the creation of a smaller, leaner, and still more efficient system, which happily will cost somewhat less money.

The postwar democratisation of society in all our countries has not taken the form of an extension of the franchise – that went as far as it could many years earlier. Rather it has taken the form of a growing tendency to call on the intelligence and initiative of larger and larger proportions of the society in the direction and management of more and more complex and rapidly changing social, political and economic organisations. The demands for intelligence and initiative from technology and the economy we know. What is less visible is the need for more highly educated people to manage the transition to a multi-racial society; to assess competing political conceptions of the right balance of freedom and authority, of public and private initiative, of foreign relations and military commitments. The erosion of traditional class and party loyalties in Britain and the transformation of the two-party into a three and perhaps four-party system, all make greater demands on the citizens of a democracy of a kind that your Victorian ancestors understood and responded to appropriately for their time. What is the appropriate response of British society to these new forms of democratisation, and what contribution can the members of an elite system of higher education make to that response?

The answer to that question neither can nor should be the transformation of British universities into institutions of mass higher education, comprehensive universities where 'any student can study any subject' (Ashby 1971). There cannot be American solutions to British problems. And the powerful structural and normative forces that I have been sketching – not least the institutional commitment to high academic standards in all degree-granting institutions – surely preclude that. But there is another set of institutions in this society, very little spoken of by educators and almost never by academics, which might be the instrument for the provision of post-secondary education to really large proportions of the adult population. I refer, of course, to the colleges of further education, or regional colleges, under whatever name they may bear. They are, one may hastily point out, not part of higher education: of course not, since they do not award the degree, and do not come under the various rules and mechanisms designed to defend the standard of that degree. I know, of course, that a part of their work is at what in Britain is called 'secondary level', and much else is 'narrowly vocational', keyed to particular skills, trades and occupations that do not require a 'higher education'. They are, one might say, institutions for the non-commissioned officers of the society, the technicians and the foremen who manage the small units of economic life under the broad direction of their better educated superiors.

Whatever they do, whatever services they perform, it must be admitted that the colleges of further education do serve substantial parts of the total society, and not just its leadership. In 1980 approximately 500 colleges of further education under various names, and some 5,300 evening institutes, enrolled some 3.5 million 'non-advanced' students, the great majority part-time (Cantor and Roberts 1983). In 1978 over a million students were taking non-advanced courses leading to specified qualifications in further education establishments (DES 1979). What strikes an outsider – perhaps an American especially – is the enormous gulf that exists between further and higher education in Britain. Further and higher education are simply not part of a common system of post-secondary education, marked by diversity and a broad division of labour. My impression is that a university or poly teacher in the United Kingdom does not feel himself to be engaged in a common enterprise with teachers in colleges of further education, any more than he might with a secondary school teacher or a master chef who teaches the culinary arts.

And yet, to American eyes, your colleges of non-advanced further education are remarkably like our community colleges in many ways –they are relatively inexpensive, open access, full of mostly part-time, older students who have full or part-time jobs; they are heavily vocational, and yet offer academic courses at both the advanced secondary and post-secondary levels. Neither system offers the bachelor's degree. And yet, in the United States community colleges are very much part of higher education: they are included in its statistics of enrolment, and in its calculations of cost and expenditure. And they are linked in everyone's mind as part of a common if differentiated enterprise, and most importantly are so linked in the minds of politicians, civil servants and laymen when broad plans for the reform or expansion of higher education are being discussed. They are linked with the degree-granting institutions in most states through co-ordinating councils, and thus naturally become part of national and state-wide planning for higher education. But they are linked with the degree-granting institutions in at least two other ways: first, their teaching staffs all have earned degrees in four-year colleges and universities, and for the most part have higher degrees, and they have that experience on which to model their own teaching. Second, there are regular paths by which students can transfer from community colleges to four-year institutions, and be accorded credit for at least part of the work that they did in the community college, if that work was of high enough quality and in courses roughly comparable to those offered in the four-year colleges.

Now it cannot be said that many community college students in America do transfer to elite colleges and universities, such as, say Amherst or Princeton or Stanford. But many transfer to big comprehensive state universities, a movement that is warmly encouraged on both sides. And many more transfer to less distinguished four-year state colleges and universities all over the country.

My point is that the connection does in fact bring that whole very large sector of post-secondary education into the realm of higher education, and infuses its forms of instruction, its curriculum, its teaching staffs with the kind of critical independence that I spoke of earlier as a distinguishing mark of higher education. Community colleges thus are genuinely part of higher education, with all its subtle effects on their students' level of ambition, initiative, self-confidence and the like, without their being especially distinguished academically, as given their open access and their almost total absence of research they could not be. Moreover, in many places the teachers in community colleges have a remarkably high level of morale and sense of mission – many of them take pride in being part of genuinely open access institutions, and of reaching students who would otherwise never have gone beyond high school. Above all, community colleges do not see themselves as failed degree-granting institutions.

One aspect of the apotheosis of academic excellence in higher education in Britain is that institutions which cannot claim academic distinction are often thought to have failed in some sense. That message came through very clearly in the UGC allocation of the deep cuts of 1981 and in its 1986 exercise in department rankings. But just as a regional college of technology (or Salford) is not a failed Imperial College or MIT, but a different kind of institution, so an American community college is not a failed Yale or Swarthmore.

One can understand why university and poly academics would not want to bring further education into the charmed circle of British higher education: in their conception, these colleges are simply not institutions of higher education, by definition. But rather than absorb further education into higher education, it might be easier for university and polytechnic people to conceive of themselves as parts of a large and diverse system of British post-secondary education. This does not mean a false claim to equality of further education and higher education – a claim that would be patently false in the circumstances. But to make that connection, for universities and polys to accept a role as the elite sectors of a broad and differentiated system of post-secondary education, might have very large consequences, and I think good ones, for higher education, for further education, and for the society at large. Without in any way surrendering their own jealously defended standards of excellence, institutions of higher education might well find themselves able to redefine the political and financial issues that have recently been formulated by British Governments so much to their disadvantage. To become part of a system of post-secondary education, with broad service functions among the several parts and to the larger society, is a way of reformulating a public policy issue which currently focuses on whether the universities and polytechnics are performing well enough, or efficiently enough, or at high enough standards. I cannot help but think that the problems of higher education as they are currently defined by government and its agencies must continually generate answers to the disadvantage of the universities and polytechnics. In 1986 the party political debate in England over higher education centres on whether to discard the binary line, and bring the polys and universities into a single system (*THES* 1986). However important that question may be to the polys and universities, I cannot believe it has great significance for Britain, except by making further structural differentiation more difficult.

Let me put the matter more sharply. I submit that pressures for the expansion of post-secondary education are inherent in the development of modern societies. But the more this expansion is taken by the elite selective system, the more it tends to become a system of mass higher education, with less money per capita, less autonomy, more central intervention and control, and lower standards. The only way a system of higher education marked by very high academic standards throughout can survive is if there stands alongside it – and related to it – a truly mass system of institutions marked by lower per capita costs and lower standards – one that accepts those democratising pressures, demands and functions, willingly. In this country that system, I suspect, will emerge, if at all, from further education. For universities and polys to welcome that development would be an act not of benevolence or sacrifice, but of survival.

The alternative, which one can see already on the horizon, is the abolition of the binary division, and the welding of the 45 universities to the roughly 30 polytechnics, making some 75 degree-granting institutions, with perhaps another 20 or 30 institutions added to this expanded sector out of the existing colleges and institutions of higher education. Both Labour and the Alliance have called for something like that – (although the Social Democratic Party (SDP) does not want to 'abolish' the binary line but 'believe it may well wither away over the next decade' (*THES* 3 October 1986; SDP 1986)). But this large new system of degree-granting higher education would also expand student numbers, especially of part-timers. It will, in other words, begin to resemble a system of mass higher education. I cannot help but believe that this system will over time become increasingly differentiated in character, function, and in cost and standard. Is that not what the UGC's current efforts are aimed at? I think we will see a genuine stratification of institutions emerge, though with unclear boundaries and disputed functions – and as a result, the emergence of a reluctant and resentful sector of mass higher education. One might ask whether it might not be preferable to upgrade further education to the status of mass higher education than to downgrade some universities and polys to perform the same functions for part-time, older students, for less money and at lower standards. One can see the problems in the latter scenario, which I myself believe to be the more probable one.

It may be that the manifest inequalities in the relationship of higher and further education in this country doom any closer links between them to envy and resentment on one side, guilty defensiveness and snobberies on the other. Those feelings have not been unknown in the relationship of the universities and the polytechnics, and that has been a factor in the pressure for the equalisation of their standards and costs. That equalisation would not be possible in the case of further education, but that very fact might ease the relationship. Where there is no possibility of competition, there may be greater possibilies for co-operation.

As I have said, I am not particularly optimistic about this particular scenario coming to pass in the United Kingdom. Yet, faced with what I take to be a manifest need for a substantial expansion of higher education in Britain, and the deep impediments to that expansion built into the costs, structures and values of elite higher education in this country, an outside observer must look elsewhere. And there, not very far away, is an educational system that might serve such purposes well. A closer association of further and higher education in the British context is fraught with problems and difficulties. There is no way in which those problems and difficulties can be resolved until the possibility of such an association is put on the agenda for discussion. But who is to do that, in the absence of strong popular demand? Not, I think, the institutions of higher education, or the political parties, or industry, for different reasons. And that is why I do not think it will happen.

I do appreciate that some steps have been taken to forge these links between further and higher education: the Education Counselling and Credit Transfer System, developed by the Open University; the Credit Accumulation Transfer Scheme created by the CNAA; the moves to organise higher education into modules; connections such as those made by Warwick University and many polytechnics with their nearby further education colleges, are all examples of a growing flexibility in this area. But these are all small-scale, rather experimental steps, many under attack and on the defensive. What is lacking still is the broad recognition that all degree-granting higher education is only a part – of course a central part – of a system of post-secondary and continuing education, marked by a diversity of standard, mission, and cost, which has as its mission the advanced education of a whole society, and not just of its leadership. British universities and polytechnics can help create that new relationship between learning and society, or they can resist it. History will be making its own judgement of the part that the institutions of higher education will play in the post-secondary education of British society, and it will be an unforgiving one.

References

Ashby, Eric (1971), *Any Person, Any Study: An Essay on Higher Education in the United States* (New York, McGraw-Hill).

Cantor, Leonard M. and Roberts, I. F. (1983), *Further Education Today: A Critical Review* (2nd ed.), (London, Routledge & Kegan Paul).

Caston, Geoffrey (1979), 'Planning, Governments, and Administration in Two University Systems: California and the United Kingdom' *Oxford Review of Education*, 5 (2).

Cerych, Ladislav and Sabatier, Paul (1986), *Great Expectations and Mixed Performance: The Implementation of Higher Education Reforms in Europe* (Stoke-on-Trent, Trentham Books).

DES (1979), *Education Statistics for the United Kingdom* (London, HMSO).

Fulton, Oliver (1986), 'Entry Standards' (Paper prepared for a SRHE conference, London, December 1986).

Neave, Guy (1985), 'Elite and Mass Higher Education in Britain: A Regressive Model?' *Comparative Education Review*, 29 (3).

OECD (1977a), *Learning Opportunities for Adults*, Vol. 1, *General Report*, (Paris, OECD).

OECD (1977b), *Learning Opportunities for Adults*, Vol. 4, *Participation in Adult Education*, (Paris, OECD).

Peston, H. and Peston, H. M. (1974), 'The Further Education and Training Scheme', in Mushken, Selma J. (ed.), *Recurrent Education* (Washington DC, National Institute of Education, US Department of Health, Education and Welfare).

Reynolds, P. A. (1986), *Academic Standards in Universities* (London, CVCP).

Rothblatt, Sheldon (1968), *The Revolution of the Dons: Cambridge and Society in Victorian England* (Cambridge, Cambridge University Press).

Rothblatt, Sheldon (1976), *Tradition and Change in English Liberal Education* (London, Faber and Faber).

SDP (1986) *More Means Better* (London SDP).

THES (1986), 'Defiant Labour to Erase Binary Line', 3 October.

Trow, Martin (1974), 'Problems in the Transition from Elite to Mass Higher Education', OECD, *Policies for Higher Education*, from the General Report on the Conference on Further Structures of Post-Secondary Education (Paris, OCED).

Weiner, Martin J. (1981), *English Culture and the Decline of the Industrial Spirit, 1850–1980* (Cambridge, Cambridge University Press).

Williams, Shirley (1985), *A Job To Live* (Harmondsworth, Penguin).

18. Policy on Higher Education and Research

Peter Swinnerton-Dyer
Higher Education Quarterly Vol. 45.3 (Summer 1991), pp. 204–218.

Even today, British universities are more independent of Government than those of any other Western European country. But that depends on the restraint of Government, whether voluntary or imposed by legislation; and Government is increasingly using its position as our paymaster to impose its will. Government has now assumed a general right to meddle in university management – a position easier to justify because of some notorious examples of management disasters. That battle is lost, and the ground lost with it cannot soon be recovered. But in spite of a few attempts by Sir Keith Joseph, Government has not tried to influence our teaching and research except by constraining the resources available; and I think that line can be held unless we are very foolish.

My starting point must be the replacement of the UGC by the UFC. The UGC had served the country and the universities well for 70 years; throughout that time it had conscientiously obeyed the shifts in Government policy and implemented them with reasonable fairness. During the 1980s, it had pressed the universities for greater economy and greater selectivity, while avoiding any major disaster. Why then was it necessary to replace it?

The only reason Mr Baker gave, while he was steering the Education Reform Bill through Parliament, was that because the UFC was established by statute it would have much more independence than the UGC, which only existed at the Secretary of State's pleasure. That sounded unconvincing at the time; and in fact the UFC has suffered far more nitpicking interference from DES civil servants in the last two years than the UGC did in the previous five. Moreover, the Financial Memorandum which regulates relations between the DES and the UFC manifests in every line that the DES is not prepared to rely on the UFC's competence and good sense. At least the latest version no longer claims for the DES, as earlier versions did, powers of interference with the affairs of universities that were plainly contrary to law; but that is a matter on which universities need to remain vigilant.

It is tempting to seek an explanation in the Preface to the Book of Common Prayer: 'There was never anything by the wit of man so well devised, or so sure established, which in continuance of time hath not been corrupted.' The UGC had always been non-political, and over the years it had become a body of experts and addicted to planning. The present Government has become increasingly suspicious of non-political bodies, on the ground that anyone who was not an overt supporter was liable to be a secret enemy. Ministers and civil servants alike distrust experts: Ministers because experts too often tell them what they want to do will not work, and civil servants because experience has shown that it is much easier to give clear and unambiguous advice if you don't understand the problem. And though early Thatcherism had been prepared to accept planning if it led to greater efficiency, later Thatcherism became much more ideological; planning was seen as a Socialist heresy, and only by giving market forces free play could the gates of the New Jerusalem be opened. The UGC therefore had to go because it was out of keeping with the spirit of the age. But it was an unnecessary piece of symbolism to abolish it on 14 July 1989, the 200th anniversary of the fall of the Bastille.

On this interpretation, the UFC was established in order to expose the universities to market forces – though that was certainly not made clear to most Council members at the time. It therefore did not need the same expertise as the UGC, because it was not going to concern itself with details in the way that the UGC had. In respect of research, it rapidly became clear that reliance on market forces was impracticable, and there was no alternative to the UGC policy of selective funding based on research assessment. In respect of teaching, the first attempt to bring in market forces was the 1991–95 Planning Exercise; that was Lord Chilver's brainchild (though probably with ministerial guidance) and the rest of the Council had very little say. As you all know, the failure of that was acknowledged last November, and it took desperate improvisation on the part of the office to announce the 1991–92 grants at the usual time.* Lord

---

* The universities were invited to submit bids for additions to student numbers at competitive prices but chose not to do so and put in their bids on a broadly common financial basis.

Chilver blames the failure on lack of co-operation from the universities in not tendering at cut-throat prices; but I do not myself see how the exercise could ever have been made to work. It is not just that the universities were asked to cost services to be provided in 1994–95 in terms of 1989–90 pounds, which would then be adjusted for inflation in a way that was never revealed. In addition, the UFC committed itself to announcing the 1994–95 grant to each university in the spring of 1991, at a time when it did not even know how much money it would have for 1993–94.

In its March letter, the UFC announced its second scheme for harnessing market forces. That scheme is certainly better thought out than its predecessor, and I see no reason why it should not work in the way intended. Whether the consequences will be good or bad is less clear. For although it is described as the implementation of market forces, this is not a description which Adam Smith would have accepted. There are two essential ways in which what is proposed falls short of a proper market, and these seem to me enough to prevent the beneficient operation of his 'hidden hand'.

First, in a true market unsuccessful competitors go under; indeed, it is precisely through this process that market forces promote efficiency. But it is hard to believe that the Government would allow a university to close, however grave its financial problems; nor do recent examples suggest that those responsible for the problems will suffer too badly. In fact it would be improvident of the Government to allow a university to close, in view of the amount of public money which had been invested in it, and which would presumably be irrecoverable if it had to be wound up.

Second, there is the issue of quality. Better quality will always cost more, but a market contains a range of customers, from those who can only afford the cheapest to those who are willing to pay for the best. It therefore sustains a range of prices and a range of quality. But this only works if those who decide whether to pay the higher price are those who would benefit from the better quality. As things stand, that is not what will happen in higher education. The consumers – those who benefit from better quality – are the students. But they do not pay the cost of the education, except in the very nominal sense that fees are transmitted through them. The Treasury pays the bills, and it gains no benefit if some institutions provide better teaching at higher prices. This could of course be rectified if the extra cost of better teaching was paid for by top-up fees out of the students' own pockets; but although that is the conclusion which should follow from the Government's own ideology, it seems at the moment politically out of the question. Failing that, one must ask whether there is anything in the UFC's latest funding process that will prevent the steady erosion of quality – and indeed whether the UFC has the means to take account of quality even if it wishes to.

The National Health Service too is in future to be driven by market forces; and that too will not be a true market for the reasons I have just given. The consequences are important to the university system, because of the symbiosis between medical schools and teaching hospitals. Teaching hospitals are recompensed, through SIFT (Service Increment for Teaching) for that part of the cost of teaching which falls on the Health Authority rather than on the medical school. But teaching hospitals also need to maintain higher standards than ordinary hospitals, and higher standards also cost money. Even before the new funding regime for the Health Service became operational, experts doubted whether teaching hospitals would be able to compete successfully with ordinary hospitals; and they were particularly worried about those teaching hospitals whose own districts do not provide enough patients and which must therefore attract patients from elsewhere. But it is still a surprise that, within the first month of the new arrangements, three major London teaching hospitals should have announced substantial job cuts.

Two considerations make this situation even more alarming. The finances of a medical school and of its associated teaching hospital are so intertwined that if financial problems become evident, each of the two funding bodies will attribute them to the parsimony of the other. Even when it is accepted that a rescue operation is needed, it will take a long time to reach agreement on how the responsibility is shared, and during that time the crisis will become more serious. I do not expect a university to need a major rescue operation within the next five years, but I would not be nearly so confident about teaching hospitals. And the most serious aspect would be if the associated university (or multi-faculty London School) damaged its overall finances in the attempt to keep its medical school afloat.

People like Sir John Kingman* point out that if the Government were consistent, the subjection of the universities to market forces ought to bring with it a major reduction in the detailed monitoring of the way in which universities operate. After all, the UFC does not give grants to universities in the way that the UGC once did; instead it buys from them certain services (principally teaching and research) at competitive prices. How they organise these services should be their concern. Unfortunately the recent examples of Bristol, Edinburgh, and Queen Mary College (to quote only those that have hit the headlines) make it clear that there are

---

* Vice-Chancellor of Bristol University.

still things seriously wrong with the management structure of some universities; and bodies like the Public Accounts Committee will hold the UFC responsible for diagnosing the faults and putting them right – however inadequate its powers may be for the purpose. One aspect of this is the continued emphasis on accountability and performance indicators.

It is a pity that the university system has not played a more constructive role in this debate, and that the initiative has largely been left to civil servants. This has had two unfortunate consequences. First, there has been a concentration on whether money has been properly spent, in a sense that could be understood by the National Audit Office, rather than whether it has provided good value. One tiresome aspect of this is the continuing attempt by the DES to distinguish money for research from money for teaching, and to keep these two streams as far as possible separate all the way from receipt to expenditure. I have consistently argued that such a distinction, even if not totally impracticable, will produce serious diseconomies; but that battle is largely still to be fought and it will not be easy to win.

The second unfortunate consequence is the emphasis on performance indicators in their most naive form. A performance indicator is a number which can be calculated by a good statistician without any exercise of judgment and which is seen as a surrogate for a measurement of what one is actually interested in. There are plenty of them, and used intelligently and with judgment, they can be very useful. Unfortunately, outsiders are apt to believe that they provide an adequate means of assessing a system without the labour of understanding it. The traditional stance of the university system has been that universities are so complicated that no outsider can understand them, and that in any case they can be trusted to operate efficiently and keep their standards high. They were thus trusted until about 20 years ago, but that will not happen again in our lifetimes. The only way to avoid assessments based on the naive use of performance indicators is to provide our own assessments, and to do so in a way that makes it clear that they are not simply whitewash – for example, by their not being always favourable.

In this, there is a fundamental difference between research and teaching, both in how the assessment is made and in what use is made of it. Research can largely be assessed on published output, and even within a single subject there will always be some departments which are far better at research than others. It is not easy to assess teaching except by seeing it happen, and there can be no excuse for a low standard of teaching.

There will never again be enough money to support all the research that academics would like to do. To get the best value from the money available for the support of research, the right strategy must be to channel most of it to the departments with the best track record – the more so since those are the ones which attract the most promising young researchers. That was the idea behind the UGC's Research Assessment Exercise and its repetition by the UFC in 1989; they provide essential data for determining the distribution of block grant, and they will have to be repeated at intervals for as long as block grant continues to be provided for the support of research as well as of teaching. I would not claim that the process works perfectly; indeed, there seems to me to be a systematic bias against departments that do very applied work, which I do not know how to cure. But it seems generally accepted that it works much better than any performance indicator which has yet been devised. Most of the latter are based on some form of bibliometric analysis, and these are the subject of a devastating review by the Royal Society's Science Policy Unit; but other countries are using them for policy-making because they have nothing else available.

In teaching, performance indicators have a better reputation, though the messages they convey are sometimes confusing. For example, number of applications per place and average A-level score on entry should both indicate the attractiveness of a university to school-leavers; yet Cambridge comes bottom of the entire system on the first measure, and top on the second. Nor, with the second measure, is it clear which end of the list it is more virtuous to be at. For what an institution should seek to achieve is to maximise 'value added'; and this would have to be calculated by measuring the quality of students on graduation and subtracting a measure of their quality on entry. Fortunately perhaps, the problems of credibly implementing this arithmetic seem insuperable.

In considering other ways of assessing teaching, it is important to remember that the primary purpose is not to compare one institution with another, but to make sure that every institution is maintaining a high standard. It is helpful to consider separately the syllabus, the examination process, and teaching in the narrow sense.

It is generally accepted that external examiners do ensure sufficient consistency in examination standards between one university and another. In some universities, external examiners are also expected to comment on the syllabus – and that is a development to be encouraged. Moreover, courses which constitute professional training are almost always validated by an appropriate professional body; that keeps the syllabus under review, though it is also a serious brake on change. The real problem is with teaching. Most academics are capable and conscientious teachers, but there are too many exceptions to be ignored. It is largely because of this that successive Secretaries of State have pressed the universities to introduce a system of staff appraisal. They are now doing so, but at the point of a gun and with no more apparent enthusiasm than is usual in such circumstances. They have also set up the Academic Audit Unit, but in such a way that even the most nervous university cannot see the Unit as a threat to its autonomy. All this may be seriously intended, but I do not believe that is how DES sees it. Mr Clarke may not yet have decided to give the inspectorate power to report on university teaching, as they already do on polytechnic teaching; but unless universities can convince him that they are putting their own house in order, that day cannot be far off.

There is one other current issue I should like to comment on: that is the indirect costs of research. The UGC and UFC have given advice on this matter, which is designed to help universities recover more of their costs than they now do, but that advice is severely oversimplified. My own attitude is as follows.

Any department knows roughly how much resources it can devote to research, and it has a portfolio of possible research projects. These can range from ones so central to its interests that it would if necessary pursue them even without outside support to ones so intellectually unrewarding that the department would only pursue one of them if it were well paid to do so. There are many possible sources of outside support – charities, research councils, the European Community, industry, and government departments, for example. Some have fixed rules about what costs they will pay. Others, such as ICI, fund projects ranging from the strategies to the immediately and profitably exploitable; and they are naturally willing to pay a higher share of the costs of the latter than of the former. How much outside support a department needs to attract for a particular research project in order to embark on it should not depend at all on the source of the support. The question is simply whether the value of that project to the department justifies the resources which the department itself will have to provide – and remembering that to support one research project means having that much less resource to support others. Sometimes the answer should be 'no'; indeed a Vice-Chancellor should view with considerable suspicion a laboratory-based department which never turns down outside money.

Linked to this is the vexed question of who should own intellectual property rights: the outside sponsor, the university, or the individual teacher? Most such rights have no commercial value, and then it doesn't matter who owns them. Those rights which do turn out to be valuable will need to be defended by legal action, probably in a number of countries. No British university, and certainly no individual researcher, has the resources and skills to mount such a campaign; so it makes no sense for either of them to hold on to the intellectual property rights. That is not to say that they should not seek a share of the profits from the results of research contracts; a company will be much less unwilling to hand over a share of its profits than to part with control of an element of its industrial strategy.

So much for the current scene. What major changes can we already forsee, and what are the implications? There seem to me to be two: the impending merger of the UFC and the PCFC, and the advent of mass post-18 education.

It appears that whichever party wins the next General Election will have the merger of the UFC and the PCFC high on its agenda. The legislation needed will be straightforward, unless it is also used to undermine the safeguards which the House of Lords inserted into the Education Reform Bill. But there are a number of consequential problems which will need to be addressed.

The most obvious of these is what should happen in Scotland. Though the UFC covers the whole of Great Britain, and advises on the universities in Northern Ireland, the writ of the PCFC runs only in England. The Scottish Central Institutions, which correspond to English polytechnics, come directly under the Scottish Office. If it is accepted that all higher education in England should come under a single body, the same logic must apply in Scotland. But it would be politically impossible to hand the Central Institutions over to a body based in Bristol, and any attempt to put Scottish universities directly under the Scottish Office would be bitterly opposed; so a separate Scottish Higher Education Funding Council seems the only feasible solution. Though there is traffic across the border in both directions, the differences between Scottish and English sixth-form education mean that Scottish higher education predominantly meets the needs of Scotland; so to isolate it organisationally would not be unreasonable.

None of these arguments apply to Wales. Only one-third of Welsh university students attend the University of Wales, and only one-third of the students in that university are domiciled in Wales. Nevertheless, the Welsh expect that whatever is done for Scotland should also be done for them; and there will be considerable pressure to set up a separate Higher Education Funding Council for Wales. That should be resisted. The Polytechnic of Wales has already suffered severely from not being treated in the same way as English polytechnics, and I would expect the establishment of a separate Welsh Council to have equally disastrous results for the University of Wales.

A matter of far wider concern is the effect that merger will have on the funding of research. Even in a laboratory-based subject, a department which is seriously engaged in research needs to have at least one-third of its research money under its own control, rather than tied to particular research projects; it is only in this way that it can provide even moderately well-founded laboratories, an adequate research library, and so on – as well as funding the research of those of its members who have not yet established a sufficient track record to attract outside funds. In non-laboratory subjects the proportion needs to be much larger, though of course the total cost of research is less. Some front-rank institutions are already finding that the research support they get from the UFC is not enough to underpin their earmarked research income, and the fact that UFC grant is growing more slowly than other sources of research support can only make matters worse.

Even the least distinguished university gets a substantial amount for research within its block grant. Polytechnics, on the other hand, get next to nothing for research; and the main reason why polytechnics have campaigned for the abolition of the binary line is that they wish to be funded for research on the same basis as universities. (In my view, there are not major systematic differences in the funding of teaching between the two sectors.) However, the Government will certainly not regard the abolition of the binary line as a reason to provide more research support for higher education as a whole. If the polytechnics are to gain, who should be the losers?

The most damaging option would be an across-the-board cut in the research component of the grant, because that would primarily hit the front-rank universities. Nevertheless this will be advocated, both on egalitarian grounds and because the front-rank universities are the ones best able to attract non-governmental money. At the other extreme, it will be argued that polytechnics were established to be essentially teaching institutions and that anyway their research is not on a par with that of universities. I cannot see that argument succeeding. Over the last decade polytechnics have built up far more credit than universities with political leaders in all parties; and though there has been no systematic comparison of research in polytechnics with research in the less distinguished universities, such evidence as there is does not suggest a big difference.

Realistically, therefore, one is forced to advocate extending the research component of block grant to the polytechnics, together with a major increase in the degree of selectivity. The latter might be more easily achieved if the new Higher Education Funding Council only retained responsibility for the teaching component of block grant, and if the research component was handed over to a Research Funding Council; the latter could also replace the Advisory Board for the Research Councils, which has never had the muscle it needed to do its job properly. But with such an arrangement, it would be important that there should be no shift of research support from block grant to earmarked grant.

Such a change would be rough on the less distinguished institutions, because most of the research money that polytechnics gain will come from them. However, it seems that this will happen at a time when student demand for places is increasing, and those universities could be given most of the extra funded student numbers to compensate for the reduction in research support.

There are those who advocate a more radical solution than the merger of the two Funding Councils: that is, to fund teaching entirely through fees and to abolish the Funding Councils altogether. The proponents of this tend to overlook research, but presumably it would be handled through a Research Funding Council in the way that I have just outlined.

There seems to me one insuperable difficulty about fee-based funding of teaching: how is it determined which potential students receive vouchers for fees? At present, with minor exceptions, all full-time undergraduates admitted by a higher education institution have their fees paid by the state. Because there is no cap on their numbers, this breaches the general Treasury principle that all expenditure should be cash-limited. In the early 1980s the Government halved the undergraduate fee in order to make over-recruitment less attractive and so limit the size of the breach; and there can be little doubt that that was done at the Treasury's behest. More recently, undergraduate fees have been greatly increased – though not to the full-cost level. Ministers have made it clear that this was done to encourage the recruitment of fees-only students, and the *quid pro quo* for the Treasury was the more rapid driving down of the unit of teaching cost. But it remains possible for Ministers to say that the reduction of unit cost has been brought about by the voluntary action of universities, and not by governmental or UFC compulsion; the official UFC units of teaching resource, which ignore the existence of fees-only students, will only fall by 1.5 per cent in real terms next year.

There were therefore good political and economic reasons for the Treasury to acquiesce in the recent fee increases without capping the number of students whose fees they paid. But those arguments would not extend to rendering acceptable a full-cost-fee regime with no cap on student numbers. Such a regime would have great attractions for universities, which is why people like Sir Graham Hills* advocate it; indeed, it would give back to universities most of the financial freedom which they have lost over the last 20 years. But I cannot believe that it will happen.

Full-cost-fees therefore involve capping the number of students whose fees are paid from public funds. How is this to be done? There are only two possible ways: by limiting the number of places in higher education for such students, or by handing out only a limited number of vouchers. The first of these would really be no change at all. For it would require a central body which would allocate to each institution its ration of full-cost-fee students, and this would be the old Funding Council reborn. The second would involve giving vouchers competitively to those who wished to enter higher education. This could be represented as merely a reversion to County Scholarships as they were before the Anderson Report.** But that system was only acceptable because entry to higher education was seen as an exceptional privilege, and because mature students could be ignored. Only a government with an electoral death-wish could revert to it now.

The other major change on the horizon is the advent of mass post-18 full-time education and training. This is bound to happen, though it will not necessarily be mass higher education in the sense in which we currently use the phrase. We do not know when it will happen, not least because it will depend on radical reform of our school system.

Within the last few weeks the English school system has been denounced by Prince Charles, ACOST, Sir Douglas Hague, and Jack Straw among others – a formidable consensus, especially as there is little else on which they would all agree. What none of them have identified is what is simultaneously its main strength and its main shortcoming. Each stage of English education is designed for the benefit of those who will go on to the next stage, however unsuitable it may be for the rest. Consequently it does provide a superb education for the top 5–10 per cent of the age group; but at every age from 16 on, we have a smaller proportion of the age-group in full-time education than any of our major competitors. Even more serious, most of those who have left full-time education emerge with a sense of failure and a deep antipathy towards education. In a world in which lifelong education is increasingly important, such an outcome for the bulk of the population is intolerable. Even if reform means lowering the quality of education for the top 5 per

* Principal and Vice-Chancellor of Strathclyde University and a leading proponent of the argument for full cost home fees.

** The Anderson Report (1960) on *Grants to Students* which recommended that all full time undergraduate students in higher education should receive a means-tested maintenance grant.

cent (and it is highly debatable whether it will), that price has to be paid. To those who say that A-levels are the gold standard and must not be tampered with, one must reply with the century-old quotation: 'You shall not crucify mankind upon this cross of gold'.

By the end of the decade English sixth-form education will be broader and less specialised, though it is too soon to predict what its shape will be. The level of knowledge in their chosen subject which one can assume students will have when they begin a single-subject honours course will be lower, and this will lead to pressure for longer first-degree courses. The rationale of this is that if students start further away from the frontiers of knowledge, they will take longer to reach them. There is an unspoken assumption here, that a first-degree course must take students to the frontiers of knowledge; except in professional subjects, it will be hard to persuade any government of this – and especially so if we reject a longer teaching year as the means of achieving it. Apart from clinical subjects, in which the courses are longer anyway (and a year longer in Cambridge than elsewhere), there are only two subjects which provide professional training for large numbers of students – law and engineering. Law lies outside the debate, because courses in law assume no prior knowledge. I have no doubt that those engineering courses which are designed to produce the future leaders of the profession will need to be extended to four years; indeed, that should probably be done now. But that illustrates another disadvantage of our commitment to uniform high standards. A front-rank engineer needs a solid foundation of mathematics; a run-of-the-mill engineer does not. Virtually all engineering courses in higher education are designed to be capable of producing front-rank engineers, so they demand qualifications in mathematics which are a formidable obstacle to entry. In this they are encouraged – even coerced – by the engineering institutions. This is a major reason for the notorious national shortage of engineers. There is a great deal of scope (though not in Cambridge) for courses which will turn practically-minded students with limited mathematical aptitude into useful engineers.

What the lower level of knowledge required for a BA in most subjects will imply is that a Ph.D. will need a further four years' work rather than three. In many subjects the best use of the first of these four years will be both a necessary precursor for those who want to do research and a course for those who wish to acquire more specialised knowledge of their chosen subject before going into the world of employment. Despite the merits of the Scottish system, in which students at the end of their second year decide whether to spend two more years for an honours degree or one for an ordinary degree, we would be unwise to copy that model. The reason is that it offends against the cardinal principle, that students must be able to leave the education system at any stage with honour, rather than feeling they have been thrown out as failures. There was a time in Scotland when the honours stream and the ordinary stream were seen as equally respectable; but that attitude has largely gone, and if we introduced the Scottish scheme into England the ordinary degree stream (however imaginatively renamed) would certainly be seen as inferior.

When the universities expanded in the 1960s and 1970s, they saw no reason to give up the pattern of single-subject honours courses. Insofar as there was a change, it was the introduction of new and trendy subjects – and I need not remind you of the public relations price which the university system has paid for that decision. The courses offered were not a response to student demand; they were those which academics wanted to teach. More recently, there has been a growth in joint-honours courses – and that growth is a response to student demand. But when the big increase in post-18 education comes, educators will have to ask themselves what kind of courses will best meet the needs of the new students. Institutions have a duty to teach courses appropriate to the students whom they actually have, rather than to those whom they wish they had.

This is not a problem for Cambridge, the nature and quality of whose students will hardly change at all; the central problem for Cambridge will be how to remain a world-class research university in a country that is steadily slipping down the economic league. It is a problem which universities like Salford have recognised, and they are already modifying their courses in the light of the changes which they forsee. But there are too many institutions, both universities and polytechnics, which hope that the niche labelled 'elite' will be big enough to accommodate them; and those which are squeezed out will have little time to revise their aspirations. There is a lesson to learn from what happens in the sixth form even now. Nearly all those whose needs are best met by A-levels are already studying them, and the rate of failure and near-failure shows that many of those who are now studying A-levels would be better served by courses of a different kind. More post-16 students will mean a greater diversity of post-16 courses; and that must be true post-18 as well.

Almost every advanced country, and many that are less advanced than Britain, already claim to have mass higher education. We are the laggards, but at least that means that we can learn from the experience of others. Unfortunately, almost all they show us is how not to do it. With two arguable exceptions, mass higher education is everywhere a shambles. That is because it has sought to provide the old recipe in greater volume, though the fact that in most places it is trying to do so with inadequate resources has not helped. The two arguable exceptions are California and Japan. We can certainly learn from California – above all, the importance of a wide range of tertiary institutions, with easy transfer from one to another, and the relatively minor role played by specialised courses. But the Californian system is far more expensive than our paymasters will allow us to be; indeed, it is beginning to look more expensive than even the Californian taxpayer is willing to afford.

I am far more doubtful whether we can learn from Japan. The parts of their educational system that certainly produce enviable results are their schools and their training in skills; in contrast, university courses seem to be the one period of relative relaxation that a clever Japanese will have between the ages of six and 60. A more fundamental obstacle is that the success of Japanese education is rooted in the Japanese culture and way of life. We cannot successfully transplant one aspect of Japan into the British way of life; human societies have mechanisms for rejecting alien organs at least as powerful as those of the human body.

One thing which the Government believes it knows about other countries is that their costs per student-year are lower than ours. This is a very dubious statistic, because it ignores the difference between a registered student and a person actually studying – and one must set against it our exceptionally low cost per graduate. But when the Government is always seeking further economies, this is enough to ensure that higher education will not be exempt.

For most of the last 20 years, there has been in real terms a small year-on-year cut in the unit of teaching resource. It has never been big enough to force radical rethinking of the processes of teaching and learning; instead we have spread resources thinner and forced pay in universities downwards in comparison with most other occupations. That cannot go on for another decade. So we need to consider very seriously whether we can harness modern technology to provide economies in the processes of teaching and learning. In the subjects I know best – mathematics, the physical sciences, and technology – I have no doubt that we can. These are all subjects which, at least at the more elementary levels, deal in certainties; and they are also cumulative subjects. This means that they include courses which must be given in much the same way in every university. Nothing would be lost if the first courses in abstract algebra or thermodynamics were everywhere identical. Once that point is admitted, it would be worthwhile to produce in such subjects a computer-based interactive learning programme. But this will only produce economies if the programme is used right across the system; for the cost of writing the programme initially is high, but the cost of producing an extra copy is small.

In this country, no commercial firm would risk such an investment, for sales resistance will be high and potential profit limited. It would make sense for the UFC to commission such programmes and distribute them to universities without charge – though there would be a corresponding reduction in the money available for block grant. But that would be flatly against the UFC's present ideology. Eventually, no doubt, such programmes will be developed in the United States, where the market is so much larger; and we may find ourselves forced to conform to what they produce, however little we may like it.

I do not suppose that such a recipe can be used unmodified in other subjects. But in every subject – in the humanities as much as in the sciences – there are enthusiasts exploiting information technology to help their teaching. It is at the moment a cottage industry, with all the diseconomies of scale which that implies; but it is the shape of things to come.

I am conscious that I have been able to say little that is cheerful. Universities are indeed on the defensive; and one of the tasks of their leaders is to decide what positions must be defended and what cannot be. But though the university system may be worse off than it was one generation ago, it is certainly far better off than it was two generations ago. Universities are not really in peril, because it is accepted that they are essential to economic success even if they do not guarantee it. Universities are in a time of great challenges, but it is also a time of great opportunities.

19. Elegant and Democratic Values: How Will the New English Universities Gel?

Christopher Price

Higher Education Quarterly Vol. 46.3 (Summer 1992), pp. 243–51

The announcement last year that the English polytechnics may, if they so wish, assume a 'university' title, passed with surprisingly little comment. The decision had clearly been the subject of intense debate between ministers and officials within the DES and only emerged as firm Government policy because of strong support from John Major, the Prime Minister. In past years, such a proposal would have provoked a major debate about the essence of higher education in the serious papers. Had it been proposed by a left-wing administration, the accusations of lowering standards would have been the more vitriolic. It is a measure both of the polytechnics' growing maturity throughout the 1980s and of the radical nature of even the post-Thatcher Conservative administration that the English establishment seemed ready to accept the change and that the issue, when it came before the House of Lords in early 1992, was not in any way, in public at any rate, contentious.

When it was first announced, the *Times* accepted the proposition, publishing an article by Jonathan Clark, the *enfant terrible* Oxford historian, which placed it firmly within the Adam Smith tradition. He reminded us of Smith's acute analysis of historic academic abuse. How the word 'university' had never been an academic monopoly and had originally been equally used by tailors, smiths and other tradesmen; how the English ancient universities were cushioned, like the monastic abbots before them, by endowments that made them lazy and indolent; how the French authoritarian model of central control of universities simply encouraged governments to meddle with academic freedom; and how therefore, in the academic sphere, the 'market' was the best bastion against both 'corporate sloth and administrative tyranny'. In reminding us of the ineffectiveness of attempts at English university reform over the past century and a half, he ended by asking: 'Will polytechnic competition force the universities to reform or will the universities sustain the cultural hegemony of their more elegant values?'

The *Daily Telegraph* responded with a sour leader and a splendidly elegant letter, also from Oxford, in which the nonagenarian Indian author, Nirad Chandra Chaudhuri was aghast at John Major's wish to 'break down the artificial barrier which has for too long divided an academic education from a vocational one'. He had been taught in Bengal in the early years of the century that academics and smiths (or as he put it *homo sapiens* and *homo faber*) were wholly different creatures and concluded that the proposal only confirmed the Conservative Party's slide into the lower middle-class vice of greed. Oxford thus produced an elderly Indian arguing for the continuation of traditional university privileges in order to preserve true Conservatism; and a (comparatively) young Conservative historian welcoming their demise while remaining sceptical, as any Fellow of All Souls might, that it would make much difference in the end. Both correctly identified the issue to be about the sorts of values which might pervade higher education in the future.

The same argument had been rehearsed with the creation of the polytechnics in the 1960s. In 1963, Labour had attempted to over trump the Robbins Report (which recommended a unitary system of universities, technical universities and colleges of education) with an even more ambitious proposal for 80 universities – a proposition surprisingly close to the 1991 White Paper. Two years later, Anthony Crosland, the Labour Secretary of State, overturned this policy by creating a separate 'public' polytechnic sector; he was a passionate egalitarian and was persuaded by his advisers that 'academic drift' would otherwise suck the local authority colleges into what Crosland would have agreed with Jonathan Clark as the existing universities' 'elegant' values. Because at first he was uncertain about the idea, Crosland overcompensated its launch at Woolwich Polytechnic with rhetoric worthy of Adam Smith: 'Let us now move away from our snobbish, caste-ridden obsession with university status' (Crosland 1982).

The result was two decades of argument about the organisation of higher education. A 'binary' system was a radical new idea. Crosland's political opponent at the time, Sir Edward Boyle, was against it, again in language prescient of the 1991 White Paper:

Any attempt at a precise articulation of the difference between what a university is for and what a polytechnic is for doesn't stand up. There's a considerable overlap and there's a ridiculous idea, which I fear is rather prevalent in the DES at the moment, that no universities are interested in teaching. Of course much the most important single difference between the universities, on the one hand, and the polytechnics and the colleges of education, on the other, is that the 'non-autonomous' institutions have so much less money for research. Perhaps the essence of the work of a university could be summed up as 'teaching in an atmosphere of research'. (Kogan 1971)

The binary system was 'inherently unstable'. He predicted close relationships between university and polytechnic departments which he had made some attempt to foster in Leeds when he became Vice-Chancellor of its University in 1970. Noel Annan, Provost of University College, London, resigned from Labour's Education Advisory Committee on the issue. Robbins, Boyle and Annan represented the majority university attitude of keeping the culture of English higher education within the traditional university value system.

A decade later, in 1980, Lord Robbins had undergone something of a conversion. In his evidence to the House of Commons Select Committee, he too alluded to Adam Smith ('In the University of Oxford, the greater part of the professors have long ago given up even the pretence of teaching') and contrasted English universities unfavourably with Scottish ones. He felt the only defence of 'binary' was 'that the universities were so set in their ways south of the Border that the only resort was for [Crosland] to create a new section of the public sector in the conduct of which he would have more control' (Hansard 1980). This was a fair description of Crosland's strategy.

Crosland and his political binary supporters (Tyrrell Burgess, Eric Robinson) saw the English elite higher education system as a barrier to democratic participation. But the genesis of the idea came from a DES civil servant, Sir Toby Weaver, the son-in-law of Sir Charles Trevelyan, Labour's Education Minister in the 1920s. Toby Weaver was the visionary who persuaded Crosland to go ahead; his colleagues, especially those in the Teachers' Branch of the Department, had more mundane motives; they were simply preserving their 'teacher supply' civil service empire, just as the local authorities wanted to preserve their local 'higher education' empire with its big budget and valuable real estate. So political vision and bureaucratic self-interest combined to produce an alternative sector of higher education.

Twenty years later, the binary policy had served its primary purpose. In 1970, Jonathan Clark's question about values would not have been worth asking. Local technical colleges would have been absorbed, like the colleges of advanced technology, into elegant university values. Now it is at least possible to ask questions about the sort of culture which will win higher education hegemony.

Jonathan Clark's hegemony clearly refers to the 'Oxbridge' values with which he is familiar. These are probably less resilient today than they have been for some time. The two universities have been forced into touting for big money in the US; 'Rupert Murdoch' professorships hardly enhance their image; their public (i.e. *private*) school ratio is creeping up again and increasing their yuppie reputation; their Vice-Chancellors are not given any sense of precedence in the Committee of Vice-Chancellors and Principals; nor is the quality of their student intake guaranteed – some colleges now hardly manage two applications for each place awarded.

The two universities certainly remain in a world league academically and well founded financially and their leaders can turn on the elegance when they want to. But their cultural grip on higher education has gone already. Brideshead values are not in fashion. They were all right in the Thatcher era, in spite of the denial of an honorary degree by Oxford to their most famous Somerville graduate; but the replacement of Thatcher by the lower middle-class Major, deep down, is calculated to marginalise both Oxbridge and the traditional university lobby.

The other English universities are also experiencing uncertainty. Many are beset by financial and constitutional problems. The larger, Victorian foundations are highly departmentalised and locked into unresponsive collegiate bureaucracies. Over the past 20 years, they have had physical space into which to expand but their instincts have been against doing so. Some of the 1960s 'cathedral' foundations have been more successful at managing themselves. The ex-CATs have developed manifestly less successfully than the polytechnics they left behind a quarter of a century ago. The sense of a cohesive 'sector' no longer exists.

The collective self-confidence of all the universities has been further dented by the tangled web of inadequate pay for academics. In retrospect, it was a disastrous decision in the 1960s to opt for collective bargaining rather than parity with a civil service pay review body. As a result universities have fallen badly behind the civil service in remuneration; this, together with their reluctance to expand, has produced a decade of quarrels with government.

In spite of these setbacks, however, universities maintain a certain style which can be used towards their own hegemonic ends. Their Vice-Chancellors, being by and large Oxbridge-educated, deal with Government and Parliament with much more confidence and panache than polytechnic directors. In both 1988 and 1992 they forced upon Ministers humiliating U-turns on academic freedom in the House of Lords.

This style is helped by a genuine academic detachment. Their accountability has never been to the local community or even to

Parliament but rather to international scholarship. Endowed as they are with Royal Charters, they have a genuine, robust independence in the face of government directives.

But the Vice-Chancellors' case for hegemony in the newly enlarged higher education sector rests on more than self-confidence and independence of spirit. In Edward Boyle's words, universities (though not polytechnics) teach in an atmosphere of research. They are as much in the business of enlarging knowledge as they are of transmitting it; and however much this idea is debunked as hopelessly out of kilter with the way knowledge actually expands in the 21st century by a range of modern pundits, their access to the vast bulk of the £0.75 billion currently allocated by the UFC to 'research' gives their institutions both higher budgets and greater international prestige than the polytechnics.

Thus to some in the universities, their virtual monopoly of government research resources is a metaphor for Jonathan Clark's 'elegant' values. Research connotes, to many of them, the highest form of academic quality. University values ought to dominate the sector, they believe, because their teachers are cleverer, they recruit brighter students, they can handle more sophisticated concepts and they encapsulate the true 'idea' of the university. The fact that polytechnics have been allowed, for 'trade' reasons, to share their title should imply, some of them confidently assert in the privacy of their common rooms, neither access to their research resources nor equality of esteem in mission.

Polytechnics come to the new sector with a range of immediate handicaps. Most do not *look* like universities; environmentally many remain a quantum leap away from a university campus culture. Their students are taught, *pro rata*, on half the budget accorded to their next door neighbour university. But this very leanness has been turned to their advantage. It remains a matter of some irritation to the universities that, in a decade when 'value for money' became a catchword, the polytechnics have gained (almost certainly ephemeral) popularity with Conservative Governments because they have been a convenient foil to squeeze university costs in the drive towards mass higher education.

Polytechnics also come to a unified higher education system with different and equally authentic notions of quality. They have proved it is possible to achieve a quantum leap in value for money without any measurable diminution in the quality of the learning process. Having worked under a succession of financial regimes which encouraged expansion, they have found it possible, by co-ordinating the management of the four elements of their business, finance, academic programmes, human resources and the buildings at their disposal, to enable far more students than ever before to graduate. It has given Britain an extremely important supply of skilled manpower.

But the *managerial* task could not have succeeded without the *democratic* mission behind it. It is important to try to elicit what 'democratic' values mean for polytechnics. It does not imply the collegial 'democratic' values of the Oxford Senior Common Room or the University Senate. Polytechnics come from a more autocratic, further education, tradition; there is no question of their directors or principals being, like Vice-Chancellors, merely *primus inter pares*. They, and other managers, are in a position to maintain the momentum of change and mirror modern forms of management in private industry.

Nor are 'democratic values' synonymous with local democracy. Until 1989, polytechnics were under the control, to a greater or lesser extent, of democratically elected local councils. As they became larger and larger cuckoos in the council nest, any affection they may once have had for control by locally elected democrats deteriorated. Money became tighter and tighter and they were accorded a lower and lower priority. The relationship in some big cities became positively poisonous. All polytechnics were relieved when they were given the freedom to manage their own affairs.

They do, however, have a certain democratic accountability in their bones. The colleges of technology, commerce, art and design and home economics of which they were made up to 1970 were almost all municipal creations and the threads of these communal origins survive. This sense of accountability to the community, if no longer to the local council, is reinforced by the much higher proportion of *local* students. Just as universities look up to international scholarship, polytechnics look down to local and regional roots. It is an important strength.

So if polytechnics have a common set of values, it is probably best expressed in the awkward and often misused word 'access'; they have never been as fussy as universities either about the shape of courses they put on (some polys have 50 per cent of students on part-time courses) or about the exact qualifications of students who come to them. As a result they have come to take an optimistic view of the educability of human nature. It is in this sense also that their values are 'democratic'. They are involved with local economic needs, rather like the former US 'cow' colleges; as such, they feel they have a general responsibility to make provision for the greater possible number of aspirant students.

So it is unlikely that either of these twin traditions will achieve cultural hegemony over the other in English higher education. The new situation of over 80 universities will destroy popular myths, of the kind Nirad

Chaudhuri was taught in his Bengali childhood, especially that of 'vocationalism'. Higher education has always consisted of vocational schools – universities for the higher professions, polytechnics for the less elevated ones. Oxford was always, at root, a clerical training establishment, before it switched its emphasis to imperial proconsulships, the home civil service and the multinationals companies' milk round. Easy and facile binary distinctions between 'education' and 'training' no longer fit. As a result of the end of binary, all universities, new and old, are having to redefine their missions more carefully. As we move from elite to mass higher education, it will become more and more difficult to discern a single thread in the system. A plurality of missions and cultures will emerge; leagues and superleagues will develop.

There may also be unifying factors. In the face of government attempts to control costs and curriculum content, universities will rediscover a certain solidarity; a single teachers' union will come together to do much the same task, as will Vice-Chancellors in conclave. In these circumstances some gradual convergence of democratic and elegant values could emerge as both old and new universities learn new habits.

The 'old' universities should begin to learn that there is no merit in research for its own sake. Some mechanisms for distributing research cash are necessary. Peer review will continue to play a part. But government-funded research is now only a small sub-set of what universities and other institutes do to expand knowledge; clean distinctions between pure and applied research are less and less easy to define. The reputation of Oxford as a university was never built on research so much as its unique teaching environment. Britain needs to keep some world-class research universities – six or even 12 perhaps. But not all 'old' universities can possibly aspire to this status; nor should they be seen as a model for all universities to copy.

Similarly, the former polytechnics should realise that there is no point in expansion for its own sake. It is true that in the US enrolment levels of 40,000 to 60,000 are not uncommon; but hypermarket higher education is not necessarily a sensible path for England. If Britain's university leaders are to convey to its people the essence of the university, neither size nor research superleagues should be on the list of essentials.

The essence of the values of both new and old universities should concern quality – in particularly the quality of the learning and nurturing environment that can be offered to the student. Students need both the curriculum and the physical surroundings to help them learn and grow simultaneously. The idea of the school as nurturing 'mother', *alma mater*, has been around as long as education. The attack on US universities, prestigious and more lowly, over the past few years, has centred round the loss of this idea – that young Americans are now fed with an empty, fragmented curriculum. It has been most eloquently articulated in *The Closing of the American Mind* by Allan Bloom (1987) – probably the only serious book about higher education in the US to have become a best seller. Bloom is a traditionalist, who would have young Americans learn more Plato. But his real message is that Government is not the only, or necessarily the most dangerous, enemy of higher learning. University teachers themselves, when they are obsessed either with their own narrow research or by some political ideology, all too often abandon their sacred trust to help their students learn by using them as cheap labour or as comrades in some new ideology. The new Higher Education Funding Council is due to seek measures of 'quality'. A substantial debate must emerge before they are allowed to impose some simplistic, crass set of 'quality' performance indicators of their own. Any new definition must address some of the wider issues about the integrity of the curriculum and the learning and growth that it actually fosters.

High quality does not of course mean *identical* quality. Different students will opt for, and sometimes be able to pay for, different environments. But the *values* acquired during higher education should not solely rely on the virtues of the teachers but rather on that of the whole institution, including the students; and these should encompass both the traditional university virtues of confidence and robust independence in the face of *diktat* from above; and the polytechnics' tradition of customer care towards all students, both the intellectually sharp and academically less confident. The higher education mission of the new universities should centre round a robust defence of a set of well-managed institutions which, however different their missions, are all committed to offering students a quality learning experience.

References

Bloom, A. (1987), *The Closing of the American Mind* (New York, Simon and Schuster).
Crosland, S. (1982), *Tony Crosland* (London, Cape), p. 59.
Hansard (1980), *5th Report from the Education, Science and Arts Committee*, HC 787, HC 63–i–xiv, para. 1040.
Kogan, M. (1971), *The Politics of Education*, (London, Penguin) p. 28.

20. Reflections on the British Government and Higher Education in the 1980s

Richard Bird
Higher Education Quarterly Vol. 48.2 (April 1994), pp. 73–85.

The whole history of the British Government's relations with British higher education is found curious by many foreign observers. Not actually that one may easily speak of British higher education, for the background and situation in each of England, Scotland, Wales and Northern Ireland is different. Moreover, the English situation is anything but straightforward and symmetrical: the long seniority of Oxford and Cambridge, the notably tardy achievement of a reasonable regional spread of fully-fledged universities, and historically the local authority stake in a particular part of higher education: all combine to ensure otherwise. And it is interesting to recall that, up to the mid-1980s, it was forcefully and frequently asserted by many senior university figures that general legislation touching the universites would be 'out of order'.

At the entry point of the 1980s the higher education landscape seen from DES was, at the least, untidy. Also, there was an awareness that the 'Thirteen points', which had been addressed by a former Minister in 1969 to the universities as 'autonomous institutions in receipt of public funds', had produced little reaction beyond dismissal (see pages 174 and 175 above). How much all this mattered would naturally be viewed differently by various groups and individuals. But there were certainly topics which, from 1979–80, seemed to most of those involved in Government to need attention. Some of these, naturally, faded with the years, whether because apparently solved or because other concerns displaced them. And again, new issues came forward as the years went by. Amongst those with a long run were:

- Should policy be directed to raising the numbers of higher education students?
- Should resourcing be tightened?
- Could better value for money be achieved?

- Is research funding sufficiently disciplined?
- Are students making enough contribution to the costs of their education?
- Should institutions become more accountable for the service they give and for quality within that service?

I intend to traverse at least this ground, however superficially, dividing my material into three main chunks. To these I give the one-word labels: resourcing, quality, structure. Within each I shall direct my attention to whether, and to what extent, there was any sort of an agenda, or strategy even, through the period, and how far aims related to such an agenda were translated into reality. On this, interpretation and opinion must play a large part: my view, from part-way up one of the relevant trees, is merely one of those possible.

Resourcing

Resourcing is self-evidently a major function of Government in relation to higher education. No one could sensibly claim that more than a small fraction of higher education institutions (HEIs) could be self-supporting from fees and endowments, or that most HEIs could earn more than a part of the income they need. The original establishment of the UGC reflected this realisation and, as the years passed and the numbers of students rose, so self-sufficiency receded further.

Thus the state must produce money; and the former constitutional responsibility of local authorities for many institutions introduced merely a difference of detail, given the central government component of their revenues. And it then follows inexorably that the Government will be concerned both about total outlays from public funds and about the return to the nation from the outlays. The latter aspect has increasingly travelled under the value-for-money banner.

But what competence, many have insistently asked, does the Government have in such a matter; or perhaps even its agencies, such as the UGC, the UFC, the Polytechnic and Colleges Funding Council (PCFC), and now the Higher Education Funding Councils (HEFCs)? Indeed, but the questions about scale and value-for-money will not cease to be asked, and the Government might take the position that only by progressive involvement could it ever come to decide and act more soundly. And of course, the more those involved in the actual delivery of teaching and in the conduct of scholarship and research within higher education helped those concerned within Government, the better progress might be made.

Action by the Government in the early 1980s on resourcing levels was certainly in no way sophisticated. For a start there was lacking, even in the most general terms, any policy on student numbers – apart from the Robbins declaration that those 'willing and qualified'* should be admitted, a statement accorded much reverence even while its precise interpretation might be disputed. However, some in Government had sympathies with those arguing that 'more might mean worse' and that some higher education was relatively useless or even damaging (echoed in the opening chapter of the much disliked 1985 White Paper which has something to say about the alleged negative link between much of higher education and the spirit of enterprise). With a demography-driven surge looming, with public expenditure under attack, with the academic community vocal about the unit of resource: there was no great surprise at the time, if certainly much criticism, that the Government was distinctly passive on expansion.

On this front the mood began to change in the middle of the decade. Looking back, I am not sure I can identify all the influences, let alone rate their relative importance. International comparisons of the state of education of the British workforce and its apparent consequences played a part (albeit these suggested, then as now, that the most serious inadequacies lay at lower levels of qualification). Then, attitudes amongst those most influential in the business community seemed to shift in favour of more graduate output, even if more must be spent to get it. With this might be coupled a general retreat by the 'more might mean worse' campaigners. Crucially too, Treasury reluctance was lessened by the experience that more could be had with an apparently steady squeeze on the unit of resource; by the changed demographic outlook; and by recognition that frustrated students frequently swelled the ranks of the unemployed.

In this setting all the political arguments might seem to point towards giving positive messages on student numbers. These began, then, in 1986–87, and received formal expression in a speech given by the then Secretary of State to an audience at Lancaster University in January 1989. The precise words used on that occasion to welcome a transition to 'mass higher education' deserve historians' attention. No proclamation was in fact made of a government policy towards achieving this aim, which might have stoked demand for some corresponding level of additional resourcing. But of course the message was favourably received, not least by the higher

---

* Later, following National Advisory Body (NAB) initiative, modified to 'willing and able to benefit'.

education community. Moreover institutions responded to the incentive to enrol more students which came from the move around this time from grant-funding into fees. (This action reversed a contrary move some five years earlier; and it is interesting of course to observe that in 1993 the engine was reversed yet again.*) However, what was done in the second half of the decade was directed solely to full-time undergraduate students. Part-timers, and institutions with a large commitment to such students, were effectively unhelped. Nor was any serious consideration given to postgraduate provision in its own right or in relation to research.

If one goes back to 1979, what first happened was adoption of the assumption that institutions would in future charge foreign students full-cost fees, with funding abated correspondingly. (This was intended to hold for those from European Union (EU) countries as much as from the Commonwealth and elsewhere, until later it was ruled inadmissible under EU law.) Then in 1980, as from 1981–82, the universities were visited with substantial cuts in recurrent expenditure, beyond what the UGC or academia believed manageable or supportable. Having received its marching orders and resolved to carry on with its task of distributing the funds available, the UGC implemented the cuts with positive differentiation, with some universities losing much more than the average (see Table 1 in Chapter 1 and pages 188 to 192). Overall, given the nature of the enterprise, the dispensation was harsh. For many universities, finding a way to live within expected future income was difficult. Staff reductions, where desired, were often hard to achieve. The view grew that something must be done about 'tenure', though legislation appeared only in 1987–88. What was provided in 1982–83 was rather more scope for early retirement, and then the so-called 'new-blood' scheme aimed at ensuring a sufficient inflow of high calibre young people into research in universities. With this it turned out that 'the system' could cope; and apparently without modifying established features such as the pattern of the academic year, or giving any widespread consideration to possible new approaches to the learning process. As to value-for-money, the quality effects remained elusive. Even on the research front it was hard to know what part of the change in the fortunes of British science should be attributed to what the Government did to university funding.

For the 'public sector' (a term thankfully kicked into touch with the 1988 Act) in England, funding followed a different path. Local authority

---

* When the level of fees was once again reduced and a period of consolidation in student numbers was introduced.

influence and the functioning of the National Advisory Body (NAB) had the effect that there student numbers rose rapidly – and the 'willing and qualified' on the whole did find a place somewhere in higher education. Previously often lax staff–student ratios were tightened, with the certain appearance that value-for-money was advancing. But, despite proclamations about maximum tolerable ratios, neither in principle nor in practice did any clear stopping point emerge. All this helped place the spotlight more on quality. It also saw the growth of intersectoral tension, with the DES invited to take sides. The polytechnics, for their part, by-and-large complained that the universities were better set up to do the same job. All the universities (and this included the Open University) asserted the research mission of the sector to which they belonged.

This, in turn, brought into sharper focus issues concerning research funding. Besides the monies coming from the research councils and other external sources, it was clear – and the calculations got refined during the period – that more than half a billion pounds a year was reaching the universities via the UGC to support research endeavour. This provision became known, derogatorily, as the Black Hole, and Treasury pressure meant that preserving this flow of money depended on improved analyses and procedures. Some of the groundwork for the redispositions announced in the 1993 Science White paper was done in the late 1980s. Perhaps implementation of what this White Paper promises will sort matters out, and at a resourcing level which commands reasonable acceptance. But it would be hard to claim for the 1980s that policy-making spanning 'science' and the world of higher education was pursued with notable competence. And questions may, I feel, still be outstanding about the relative roles of Government, different types of central agency, individual institutions and research groups – and how each of these interacts more widely, with industry and with actual and potential students.

Another issue which received intermittent treatment (not for the first time in history) was how far, and how, the central authorities could usefully intervene to achieve an increase in the output of graduates with science and engineering qualifications. Even if the roots of any problem lay in attitudes developed in students' earlier years, in the structure of the country's 16–18 education and in the lack of motivation given the careers on offer and their entry requirements: nevertheless, perhaps enhanced opportunity to study could make a difference. Various programmes were in fact stimulated with specific funding in both sectors, until it came to be held unfashionable for central agencies to 'plan' at the expense of institutional freedom to determine expenditure. Of these possibly the Masters programme in Information Technology did most, by arousing interest and enabling students to acquire new relevant skills quickly, to benefit individuals and the economy.

Student resourcing also came up for scrutiny in the 1980s. Introduction of a loan scheme related to student living expenses was eventually achieved, albeit the scheme put in place commands scant agreement. The expensive British study-away-from-home culture has hardly been dented. Serious consideration of tuition fees, abolished in 1977, has been slow to start. The 1980s were perhaps only marginally productive in this area: but then, closely coupled with 'student' is 'middle-class parent', and it was not as though even the Government and the leading lights in the universities and polytechnics were united on policy.

Finally, I do not feel I can conclude this section without mention of management. Here there was much clamour against Government involvement: what business was it of Government how any university was run, and how could its intervention help? Well, the Jarratt Committee deliberated and reached conclusions which, with interpretation, may have led to improved practice. And certainly not at any point did anyone in Government circles, I would confidently assert, even toy with seeking to introduce Government involvement in the making of senior appointments (despite the many foreign examples). As for the polytechnics and higher education colleges, they were perceived to have more of the managerialism which the Government viewed with favour, hence no Jarratt-equivalent; while the NAB-sponsored 'Good Management' investigation reported, within the local authority context, just as the 1987 White Paper was published.

If one looks across the principal identified funding topics, it is striking how far each has run on its own track with its own timing. So, in effect, a fairly disorderly process, with some risk of disasters. Yet the upshot, on the whole, has been less bad than might have seemed likely. This may be due to the resilience of those working in higher education, and no thanks to the Government and small thanks to its agencies. But then again, if any credit is due, there may be a case for sharing it a little more evenly.

Quality

On the quality front, the Government began to move the business up the agenda only from the mid-1980s. One need not go back far to re-enter an era where the universities looked after their own performance and reputation; and where, to the extent that the UGC did appraise them relatively and absolutely, Whitehall Department assessors, and thereby

DES Ministers too, were rigorously denied its findings. University departments of education were an exception to the general exclusion, on the grounds of the Secretary of State's special responsibilities for the supply and training of schoolteachers: there HMI did have access, if nominally by gracious permission only. It was also the case that, in areas where professional accreditation operated, assessments of quality filtered into Whitehall. But overall the position in the then university sector was very different from that in the rest of higher education. As regards non-university institutions, the CNAA and HMI between them were seen as ensuring that things went on as they should. Moreover, to the findings of these organisations Government did have access.

But these certainties began to become precarious. For one thing, there was no common code of practice in the university sector and mostly, other than through external examiner activity, no provision for any outside look at how a university operated quality controls, curriculum development, appeals procedures and much else. The doubts about the CNAA were rather different, centring on its apparent concentration on programme approvals and limited monitoring of practice.

No less in this area than elsewhere, the constitutional position in each sector was quite different from that in the other. After all, the Secretary of State had powers of appointment to the CNAA and his assessors were much involved; he could expect answers to questions he might put to its leading figures. If change was already afoot in the way CNAA conducted its business, the DES could speed that up and probably influence direction and detail.

The university sector was potentially much less amenable. The universities might be reluctant to act collectively at all; and then, even where a collective label might seem to be attached, some universities might be unpersuaded and act otherwise. Besides there are always not a few in the universities who strongly query the Government's competence in regard to anything to do with the universities (beyond supplying funding, preferably on demand). But a pragmatic way forward was found, the CVCP establishing a group chaired by a Vice-Chancellor and the Government having opportunity to comment on the content and scope of the codes of conduct which the group produced.

A longer-term objective always was a much closer identity of regime across the whole of higher education. Whatever the legitimate differences within higher education, it was hard to see why concern with the quality of teaching, and with its preservation and enhancement, should manifest itself differently between one institution and another. But the route could not be mapped in advance. In the late 1980s things simmered forward, with increased devolution within the CNAA Charter and the establishment by the CVCP of the universities' Academic Audit Unit.

As late as 1990 several outcomes seemed possible, and it was in the White Paper of 1991 that the Government announced the structures and patterns of answerability which it intended to ensure by persuasion or legislation. What has been put in place by and in accordance with the 1992 Act, is now itself of course attracting some criticism. However, this Act could sensibly address these issues precisely because it constructed for the first time in Great Britain a single higher education sector for each of England, Scotland and Wales. It is not evident, to me at any rate, that this business could have been moved ahead faster or more harmoniously than in fact happened.

Structure

And so to structure, which second only to public resourcing is the most obvious territory for government action. Within 'structure' I embrace the pattern of institutions, their constitutional position, the machinery for channelling public money, oversight mechanisms. The last 12 years have seen a good deal of activity here. In contrast the 15 years before that were relatively quiet: once the CATs had become universities and the polytechnic sector had been established, only the teacher training reorganisation in the late 1970s much disturbed the tranquility – and this was driven by assessment of the scale of need for trained teachers.

What was already in play in the later years of the late-1970s Labour Administration, and still very much alive for their Conservative successors, was concern at the lack of control over current expenditure on what was then called advanced further education (AFE). While the apparent extravagance of AFE institutions in terms of their staff–student ratios also registered, it was much more the inherited inability to limit overall outlay which led to 'capping the Pool'. That action left outstanding the issue of how to handle whatever sums the Pool was allowed to contain.

Early 1981 saw the first flurry of movement touching actual ownership of the polytechnics and other AFE. Removing such institutions from the local authorities and delivering their core funding through a Government-appointed agency would have dealt with the 'capped Pool' problem, and could have additionally brought capital and recurrent expenditure into the same hands. Some – Ministers and officials – saw a case also in the behaviour of some local education authorities (LEAs), which could be censured as too uninterested or too intrusive (or even both). But thinking was far from monolithic, and this plot foundered not only on the skill and determination with which the LEAs moved to defend their patch, but in addition because Ministers collectively were less than fully convinced in favour of the change.

Soon afterwards the NAB was born and developed, and it is fair to say that for the early years of its life all the parties involved strove by-and-large to make a success of it, in hopes of seeing it yield what each most wanted from it. Perhaps, despite its curious birth and legislative backing, the NAB would fulfil the adage about the provisional alone enduring. Just as, after all, the UGC had survived remarkably for a body with no legislated presence and appeared able, as it handled 'the cuts', to do a hard job really rather well.

Policy evolved as the NAB and the sector for which it had major responsibilities went about their business. Striking linked features of the mid-1980s were the growth in student numbers in the polytechnics (especially) and the functioning of the NAB set-up to provide funding which matched, if only in part, the scale of this growth. Local authority higher education, as AFE (other than in the voluntary colleges) had now generally been renamed, was found virtuous in the Government's eyes partly for its 'efficiency gains'; and the sector was gaining standing year on year as it successfully educated a growing proportion of the nation's undergraduates.

It is almost imaginable that this arrangement might have gone on for ever. But the local authorities and the Government fell out over how the sector should be run. At the same time, other forces were at work. First, the Government's much-commented-on anti-local-government crusade had gained strength since 1981. Second, many of the polytechnic directors were successfully campaigning on the iniquities of some LEAs. Third, the various incursions into parts of the universities' 'secret garden' (a more apt image here than ever in reference to the school curriculum) suggested that the university sector's position could not, perhaps should not, be left untouched. Fourth, 'Cardiff happened', which led to the view that existing moves for sounder audit regimes needed reinforcing and that, in the matter of financial accountability at any rate, the UGC was 'bust, and needed fixing'. The Croham Committee then went on to recommend a different-style UGC successor.

Thus was the stage set for the relevant parts of the 1987 White Paper on Higher Education and of the 1988 Act. By the time of these events, there was almost consensus that, in broad outline, the changes made sense. Those who would then have gone further, to the immediate creation of a single sector of higher education, could see that this was impracticable, even had it been politically reachable. The polytechnics and an appropriate additional group of colleges (their identification for legislative purposes being itself a matter of some complexity) had first to be incorporated. Besides, there was a disposition for the successor-body to the UGC to continue to span the universities in Scotland and Wales, where prospects in the 'other' sector were different. Those, whether in the universities or local government, who wanted less change or none, found themselves with few allies on the main outlines – although some government ambitions to take more control were, as again in 1992, rolled back.

However, to most of those with a stake in all this, it did seem that the 1988 set-up must be unstable. Although the details of governance and internal structure were (and are) substantially different as between the then universities and what was inelegantly called in the Act 'the PCFC sector', there was inevitability about the evolution of a single higher education sector(s). The surprise for many was that this point was reached in 1993 rather than perhaps 1997.

So what we have historically is many years of uncertainty over the binary line and its future; policy towards its disappearance formed as opportunity drove; a clear view of the finishing line (if not of when it might be reached) only quite late on. 'Finishing line' is of course too simple, there are things yet to be done; but each country of the United Kingdom does now have a 'higher education sector'.

Some Concluding Observations

This completes my account of events. It has been necessarily selective and abbreviated. (I would have liked to include the 'freedom of speech' saga, but would most likely have said too much or too little!) The general message I offer is that most of the significant developments of the decade happened in piecemeal and pragmatic fashion. There were certainly some overall trends of policy, though these could by no means be assembled into any kind of grand strategy. Indeed, in my judgment, the creation of an embracing strategy was always beyond reach because of the Government's refusal to appoint royal commissions (to which the Leverhulme/Society for Research into Higher Education studies of the early 1980s* were seen as no substitute) and the usual insistences that certain actions could 'brook no delay'.

If any full strategy was impossible across higher education, an even less

---

* The Leverhulme Study on the Future of Higher Education, 1980 to 1983, was conducted by the SRHE and resulted in a series of volumes culminating in a report *Excellence in Diversity* (SRHE 1983).

realistic target was a cohesive policy, or set of policies, across the whole of education and training. Some links were operational: notably perhaps, the role of higher education in the education of schoolteachers, and the performance of the schools as affecting the supply of potential higher education entrants. But the distance between most of higher education and the further education system, for instance, was barely acknowledged: neither element seemed to feel in any sense positive about how university research competence might help the development and performance of FE; and it was well on in the decade before FE's potential contribution as a feeder to higher education began to be taken seriously, especially by the 'old' universities. Well outside my period the National Commission on Education has at last made an attempt at a comprehensive appraisal and set of recommendations. Note the inclusion amongst these of a proposal that the split of central responsibility for education and training across two government departments be scrapped.

However, perhaps there was a guiding philosophy, which ministers brought to the feast and to which they and civil servants together gave effect. By guiding philosophy I think one must in fact mean more than the pursuit of 'more for less' or attacks on alleged entrenched privileges. The obvious candidate for consideration is promotion of some sort of 'market' whose functioning compels greater attention to the customer. For my own part, I have always found it hard to discern any clarity of theme or practice which would justify an assertion that a 'market approach' (never mind just who are the customers!) was being pursued. In detail, there was not always consistency. For example, the possibility of universities disappearing following insolvency was not denied in the middle years of the decade, and the idea of endowing some into independence from future public funding was positively studied. Concurrently, however, the UGC and the NAB were operating substantially 'in planning mode'. Then followed a period of rather greater reassurance, this only to be followed again by the shift to more funding through fees with all that this unleashed. Alongside that, thoughts about vouchers had an airing, with the Government taking a cautious line, however, on whether it might favour something of this character and/or moves by universities to charge real fees to full-time home undergraduates. The rhetoric varied also, although there was some consistency of theme that institutions should consider themselves in competition and, without detriment to standards, earn what they could. But did *this* in fact go much beyond what was already the situation and practice? – after all, universities had always sought to earn money on the right terms and had competed for students. Regretfully, I must class the necessary analysis as 'too difficult' and leave it to someone else.

Another belief which some may hold, even assert, is that officialdom maintained some kind of pervasive intention which was and is progressively being realised. But the truths about power and influence within the workings of Government deny this possibility. First, while officials will aim collectively to establish facts and appraise consequences, their views on important issues will seldom be monolithic. This is the more true because more than one department is likely to be involved. Ministers will normally have alternatives put before them, even where one line of decision is clearly recommended. Second, Ministers have other sources of advice also and are themselves capable of questioning what they are told. And by ministers I do not just mean the Secretary of State: over the last 25 or so years, the role of the junior minister has much increased. Third, large decisions just have to be taken by the Secretary of State, with at least acquiescence by the Prime Minister and other important colleagues: on no other footing could the Government's position be promoted and defended. Fourth, although one Administration may be in power for many years, as was the case in the 1980s, senior ministers change, and each of a succession of Secretaries of State for Education may have different priorities and in part a different agenda.

Alongside whatever may be the internal processes of Government, and in many ways more important, lies of course the relationship, the co-operation or lack of it, between Government and those in positions of leadership within the actual world of higher education. The word which springs to my mind here is 'patchy'. Personal relations can often be splendid. But to my observation there is also much mutual suspicion and untoward adversarialism. Senior people in higher education often feel, and indeed say, that Ministers and civil servants are underinformed and incompetent, but seem hardly keen to help correct what they perceive as their inadequacies. Even routine information can be routinely withheld. Government, for its part, invests reluctantly in dialogue which might build consensus. These brief statements oversimplify of course: there are many different circumstances and patterns of behaviour. But in some other places in the world these things do seem generally to be better handled – though whether the upshot is better in consequence would be hard to establish.

21. Editorial: The White Paper – Higher Education: A New Framework

Michael Shattock
Higher Education Quarterly Vol. 45.3 (Summer 1991), pp. 201–203

The publication of the White Paper, *Higher Education: A New Framework*, marks another stage in the disintegration of the higher education structure which has been in place since the creation of the polytechnics a quarter of a century ago or, as far as the centralised management of the university system, since the establishment of the UGC over 70 years ago. The White Paper is, however, anything but a clear statement of policy and raises more questions than it answers. The recent announcement that the PCFC Chairman, Sir Ron Dearing, is to take over the Chairmanship of the UFC – an appointment much to be welcomed – and the steps which the Secretary of State has required the two Councils to take to align their policies mark a distinct departure from the 'free market' approach espoused by Lord Chilver which are given short shrift by Peter Swinnerton-Dyer (see pages 225 to 228).

But the Government has saddled itself with a commitment to a unified system of higher education with effectively four funding bodies, if Northern Ireland is taken into account. The bureaucracy of co-ordinating this unlikely quartet will quickly stifle the freedom which the new system ought to offer institutions. Swinnerton-Dyer's complaint that the DES interfered much more in a UFC whose independence was protected by statute than a UGC that was not, must be a warning that civil service interventions can only increase with such a structure. To add to the confusion, the layers of decision-making to be erected in Wales seem to be in inverse proportion to the size of the system they will control. Moreover the failure to articulate a policy for research seems to contradict reports that the Prime Minister is to give civil research high priority. The assumption must be that policy on research will emerge by fudge and formula through bureaucratic moves like the transfer of DR⋆ funding from the UFC to the Research Councils and the substitution of JR⋆⋆ for SR⋆⋆⋆ research funding. But this juggling of the figures is no substitute for policy particularly for the creation of a more coherent strategy for research which takes in both the research councils and the funding councils.

The failure to announce a re-look at the Morris Committee's recommendations for a unified Research Council structure (presumably because it might add to the legislative burden in an election year) reflects the fact that in the DES at least, the issues about student numbers take precedence over research. In effect, the constant reiteration by higher education critics of the Government that Britain compares badly with its continental European partners, let alone the USA and Japan, in the proportion of the relevant age group entering higher education has backfired in the subordination of policy on research to a policy on numbers. Nor is there any evidence in the White Paper that the long-term implications of the imbalance of numbers coming forward for science and technology programmes, as against arts and social studies, have any priority for solution, and yet so much of the evidence provided by the EC and the OECD about global competition in technologically-based products, points to an acute need for a reiteration of the policies of the early 1980s, which emphasised the need to improve the output of qualified scientists and technologists.

Swinnerton-Dyer's contribution was delivered as the Rede Lecture before the publication of the White Paper, but he focuses on the question of cost. No-one can expect governments to make promises about funding higher education many years in advance, especially in the difficult financial conditions of the early 1990s, but we must wonder whether the commitment on numbers has been given any comparable commitment by the Treasury. A better balance of science to arts teaching in schools and higher education is inevitably costly. After a while, reducing unit costs in science teaching simply eliminates consumables, equipment, computer maintenance and technician support. In the end it can make science teaching non-viable. The DES forecasts suggest a 50 per cent increase in

---

⋆ DR: The element of UFC research funding which is intended to match research grant and contracts awarded by the research councils.

⋆⋆ JR: The element of UFC funding which is awarded on a judgmental basis against the results of the research selectivity exercise.

⋆⋆⋆ SR: The element of UFC research funding which is related to the student number target for which the UFC is providing recurrent grant.

student numbers in higher education, but unless there is also to be a commitment to transfer significant additional funding into the DES from other departments, the dilemma that the Government will face will be a choice between cutting back on expansion or reducing the lower end of the higher education system to the kind of conditions which operate in similar institutions in many continental European countries and increasingly in the United States. The ability of institutions to withstand such a depreciation in quality by generating new incomes is related not just to their own management skills, but to their location and the buoyancy of the economy. No one should argue that lowering unit costs in higher education is an impossible task, nor in the face of other legitimate financial demands, an intrinsically irresponsible expectation by Government, but there must be serious doubts whether the expansion proposed is affordable.

Let us, however, warmly welcome the demise, long anticipated, of the binary line. The higher education community should recognise this development as providing an immense opportunity to debate and ultimately re-shape the institutional structures which have for so long constrained attitudes in British higher education. A reflection of these defensive attitudes can be seen in the CVCP's reiteration of its concern about the names to be adopted by the polytechnics in its published comments on the White Paper. One would have thought the topic to have been given such an airing that the CVCP did not need to labour the point. On the contrary, the debate needs to be vigorous, well-informed and open-minded or we shall find that we have perpetuated the inhibitions of the past and nullified the benefits that change can bring.

Contributors

RICHARD BIRD, Deputy Secretary for Higher and Further Education at DES until retirement in 1990. Awarded CB 1983.

VIVIAN BOWDEN (1910–89), a physicist by training, was Principal of the University of Manchester Institute of Science and Technology 1953–76, became a Life Peer in 1963 and was appointed Minister for Education and Science in the first Wilson Government, an appointment he held for only two years. An influential spokesman on technological themes, his greatest achievement was to build up UMIST to become a major institution.

A. H. (CHELLY) HALSEY FBA, Professor of Social and Administrative Studies, Oxford, now Emeritus Professorial Fellow at Nuffield College. Has written extensively in the fields of social class and social policy but his two best known works in the field of higher education are *The British Academics* (with Martin Trow) (1971) and *Decline of Donnish Dominion* (1992) (2nd edition 1995).

PROFESSOR KEITH KELSALL, (1910–96) was Professor of Sociological Studies at Sheffield University (1960–75), author of, *inter alia*, *Higher Civil Servants in Britain* (1955) and *Graduates, the Sociology of an Elite* (1972).

ALEC MERRISON FRS (1924–79), trained in nuclear physics, created the SERC Daresbury Laboratory and became Vice-Chancellor of Bristol 1969–84. He chaired the Royal Commission on the NHS 1976–79, the ABRC 1979–83, the CVCP 1979–81 and the Council of the Association of Commonwealth Universities. Knighted 1976.

PETER MOORE, Professor of Statistics 1965–93, and Principal of the London Business School 1984–89, Director of Elf Aquitaine 1989–95, President of the Royal Statistical Society 1989–91, President of the Institute of Actuaries 1984–86, member Jarrett Committee on University Efficiency 1984–85, member of the UGC (1977–84).

CHARLES MORRIS (1898–1990) trained as a philosopher and was a philosophy tutor at Balliol where he was a close colleague of John Fulton (first Vice-Chancellor, Sussex). He became Vice-Chancellor of Leeds 1948 retiring in 1963, just after the publication of the Robbins Report. Chairman, CVCP 1951–55 and of the Inter University Council. Knighted 1953; made Life Peer 1967.

CHRISTOPHER PRICE has spent the past 30 years in educational journalism, practical politics and higher education management. He writes for a wide range of newspapers and journals; as a city councillor he introduced comprehensive schools to Sheffield in the 1960s and as an MP he chaired the House of Commons Select Committee on Education in the early Thatcher years; he was then Director of Leeds Polytechnic as it altered its title (though not, he says, too much of its culture) to Leeds Metropolitan University.

DAVID RIESMAN, born in 1909, was Henry Ford II Professor of Social Science from 1958 at Harvard and a member of the Carnegie Commission for the Study of Higher Education (chaired by Clark Kerr) 1967–75. His best known books are *The Academic Revolution* (with Christopher Jencks) and *Academic Values and Mass Higher Education: The early years of Oakland and Monteith* (with Seymour Lipset).

MICHAEL SHATTOCK is Registrar of the University of Warwick and was General Editor of the *Higher Education Quarterly* 1986 to 1996. His best-known book is *The UGC and the Management of British Universities* (1994). He has succeeded Edward Shils as Editor of *Minerva*.

EDWARD SHILS (1910–95), Professor of Sociology, Committee on Social Thought, University of Chicago, Editor of *Minerva* 1962–95. A prolific writer and 'sage', his best known books were *The Torment of Secrecy* (1956), in the field of higher education *The Intellectuals and the Powers and other Essays* (1972) and *Universities, Politicians and Bureaucrats* (with Hans Daalder) (1982).

ERNEST SIMON (1879–1960), Chairman of the Simon Engineering Group and of the Council of the University of Manchester, associated with the Webbs in founding the *New Statesman*, member of the Liberal Party and Member of Parliament (1923–24 and 1929–31). He joined the Labour Party in 1946 and became chairman of the BBC 1947–52; his name is perpetuated through the endowed Simon Fellowships at the University of Manchester. Created Lord Simon of Wythenshawe.

PETER SWINNERTON-DYER, KBE, FRS, Professor of Mathematics at Cambridge 1971–88, Master of St. Catharine's College 1973–83, Vice-Chancellor of Cambridge 1979–81, Chairman of the UGC 1983–89, Chief Executive of the UFC 1989–91.

MARTIN TROW is a Professor in the Graduate School of the University of California, Berkeley, having previously served as the Director of the Centre for the Study of Higher Education 1976–88, and as a Professor in the Graduate Schools of Public Policy. He has written very widely about higher education in Britain and elsewhere. His best known book is *The British Academics* (1971) with A. H. Halsey, but his best-known writing is related to the theme which he first identified as 'Problems in the transition from elite to mass higher education' (1974).

PETER VENABLES (1904–89) was Principal of the Birmingham College of Advanced Technology from 1955 for its whole life as a CAT and became first Vice-Chancellor of the new University of Aston in Birmingham. He was also chairman of the planning committee and first Pro-Chancellor of the Open University. He published widely in the field of technical education and in 1978 published *Higher Education: The Technological Universities 1956–76*. He was knighted in 1963.

SOLLY ZUCKERMAN (1904–93) was Sands Cox Professor of Anatomy at Birmingham, but was also chairman of the Committee on Scientific Manpower 1950–64, chairman of the Central Advisory Committee for Science and Technology 1965–70 and Chief Scientific Advisor to the Government 1964–71. Created a Life Peer in 1971.